Scribes, Visionaries, and the Politics of Second Temple Judea

Scribes, Visionaries, and the Politics of Second Temple Judea

Richard A. Horsley

Westminster John Knox Press
LOUISVILLE • LONDON

Book design by Sharon Adams
Cover design by Mark Abrams
Cover art: Model of Temple of Jerusalem © Bojan Brecelj/CORBIS

First edition
Published by Westminster John Knox Press
Louisville, Kentucky

This book is printed on acid-free paper that meets the American National Standards Institute Z39.48 standard. ♾

PRINTED IN THE UNITED STATES OF AMERICA

07 08 09 10 11 12 13 14 15 16 — 10 9 8 7 6 5 4 3 2 1

Library of Congress Cataloging-in-Publication Data

Horsley, Richard A.
 Scribes, visionaries, and the politics of Second Temple Judea / Richard A. Horsley.
— 1st ed.
  p. cm.
 Includes index.
 ISBN 978-0-664-22991-7 (alk. paper)
 1. Judaism—History—Post-exilic period, 586 B.C.–210 A.D. 2. Jews—History—586 B.C.–70 A.D. 3. Bible. O.T.—Criticism, interpretation, etc. 4. Dead Sea scrolls. I. Title.
BM176.H567 2007
296.09'014—dc22

2007007083

Contents

Acknowledgments

In many ways this book has been a collective effort among colleagues and friends. An informal conversation with George Nickelsburg and Patrick Tiller over a decade ago led to the formation of the Wisdom and Apocalypticism in Early Judaism and Early Christianity Group in the Society of Biblical Literature. In the intervening years I have received an invaluable education in the most important texts produced in late second-temple Judea and the assumptions, approaches, and problematic issues involved in their interpretation, mainly from friends on the steering committee of the group. My education had begun years earlier, at the feet of former students of Krister Stendahl and John Strugnell. George Nickelsburg and John Collins laid a solid foundation for all of us with their pathbreaking books on Judean texts. Since then, George, John, and Pat Tiller have been my mentors on apocalyptic texts, particularly the sections of *1 Enoch* and Daniel. Wisdom texts such as Sirach always seemed more opaque to me than the coded revelations of apocalyptic texts. In a graduate seminar on the wisdom of Ben Sira under the tutelage of John Strugnell in the mid-1960s, none of us "had a clue" about what to do with the text before us. In more recent years, Ben Wright and Pat Tiller have led me step by step into what was a forbidding world of instructional wisdom. On closely related materials, Susan Niditch, Robert Doran, and Sarah Tanzer have generously shared their wisdom on visions, Maccabean history, and Qumran texts.

The suggestive initiatives of the Sociology of the Second Temple Group in the SBL, under the leadership of Philip Davies, provided the occasion to rethink the history and texts of this period. I especially appreciate the encouragement of Joseph Blenkinsopp to pursue analysis of the relations between political circumstances and production of texts.

Along with many others, I owe a great deal to the patient innovative work of Werner Kelber in introducing us to the oral as well as scribal media environment of antiquity and how to understand the relationship between oral communication, cultural memory, textual composition, and the continuing development of written texts. Susan Niditch opened up the relation of orality and writing in the production of texts of the Hebrew Bible for me, and introduced me to the theoretical work of John Miles Foley, from whom I have learned so much in recent years. Ellen Aitken has been patiently and suggestively mentoring me on the relation between oral performance and the composition and cultivation of texts.

It will be readily evident that this book is not the work of a specialist on second-temple Judea and its texts. So I am especially grateful to generous colleagues and friends who are specialists in this period for critical reading of earlier drafts of the chapters below and many helpful suggestions, saving me from egregious errors of interpretation. George Nickelsburg read the whole manuscript, raised hard questions, and straightened me out on many matters. Ellen Aitken, David Carr, John Collins, Phil Davies, Robert Doran, Werner Kelber, Susan Niditch, Larry Wills, and Ben Wright all read several chapters and provided sharp criticism and helpful suggestions. These friends and colleagues can take much of the credit for what is well grounded in these chapters, but only I am to blame for the many mistakes, missteps, and misunderstandings that surely clutter the pages below. Ran Huntsberry patiently read through the whole manuscript, asked hard questions about what in the world I was trying to argue, and valiantly attempted to instill some intelligibility here and there. And Jon Berquist, scholar of the second-temple period as well as editor, patiently and knowledgeably read earlier drafts and helped shape the argument and presentation.

Research assistants and friends Stacey Gilchrist, Maja Guduras, and Keith Coon have patiently helped me find and process scholarship in the many areas of research that converge in this project and have taught me many things in the process. The staff of the Library of Episcopal Divinity School/Weston Jesuit School of Theology have patiently and generously facilitated the research process, for which I am continuously grateful.

Abbreviations

(not including Hebrew Bible, Apocrypha, and New Testament)

AB	Anchor Bible
ABD	*Anchor Bible Dictionary.* Edited by D. N. Freedman. 6 vols. New York: Doubleday, 1992.
ABRL	Anchor Bible Reference Library
AEL	*Ancient Egyptian Literature.* Compiled by M. Lichtheim. 3 vols. Berkeley: University of California Press, 1971–80. Reprint, 2006.
ANET	*Ancient Near Eastern Texts Relating to the Old Testament.* Edited by J. B. Pritchard. 3rd ed. Princeton: Princeton University Press, 1969.
Ant.	*Jewish Antiquities,* by Josephus
AOAT	Alter Orient und Altes Testament
BA	*Biblical Archaeologist*
2 Bar.	*2 Baruch*
BASOR	*Bulletin of the American Schools of Oriental Research*
BJS	Brown Judaic Studies
CBQ	*Catholic Biblical Quarterly*
CBQMS	Catholic Biblical Quarterly Monograph Series
CD	*Damascus Document/Rule* (texts A and B, from Cairo Genizah; copies from Qumran Caves 4, 5, and 6, DSS)
CP	*Classical Philology*
CPJ	*Corpus papyrorum judaicarum.* Edited by V. Tcherikover and A. Fuks. 3 vols. Cambridge, MA: Harvard University Press for Magnes Press, Hebrew University, 1957–64.
CRINT	Compendia rerum iudaicarum ad Novum Testamentum
DSS	Dead Sea Scrolls, from Qumran area
1 En.	*1 Enoch*
FAT	Forschungen zum Alten Testament
HDR	Harvard Dissertations in Religion
HSM	Harvard Semitic Monographs
HTR	*Harvard Theological Review*

JAOS	*Journal of the American Oriental Society*
JBL	*Journal of Biblical Literature*
JCS	*Journal of Cuneiform Studies*
JJS	*Journal of Jewish Studies*
JSOT	*Journal for the Study of the Old Testament*
JSOTSup	Journal for the Study of the Old Testament: Supplement Series
JRASup	Journal of Roman Archaeology: Supplementary Series
JSJSup	Journal for the Study of Judaism Supplements
Jub.	*Jubilees*
m. Yad.	*Yadayim* tractate in the Mishnah
OBO	Orbis biblicus et orientalis
OGIS	*Orientis graeci inscriptions selectae.* Edited by W. Dittenberger. 2 vols. Leipzig, 1903–5.
PCZ	*Zenon Papyri.* Edited by C. C. Edgar. 5 vols. Cairo: L'Institut Français d'Archéologie Orientale, 1925–40. Reprinted, Hildesheim and New York: Georg Olms, 1971.
Phil.	*Philopoemen,* by Plutarch
Pss. Sol.	*Psalms of Solomon*
1QM	*War Scroll* (DSS)
1QS	*Community Rule* (DSS)
4Q212	*Aramaic Enoch* (DSS)
4Q158, 364–367	*Reworked Pentateuch* (DSS)
4Q422	*Paraphrase of Genesis-Exodus* (DSS)
4QFlor	*Florilegium = Midrash on Eschatology^a* (DSS)
4QMMT	*Halakhic Letter = 4Q394–399* (DSS)
11QMelch	*Melchizedek* (DSS)
RB	*Revue biblique*
SAOC	Studies in Ancient Oriental Civilizations
SBL	Society of Biblical Literature
SBLDS	Society of Biblical Literature Dissertation Series
SBLEJL	Society of Biblical Literature Early Judaism and Its Literature
SCI	*Scripta classica Israelica*
SCS	Septuagint and Cognate Studies
SEG	*Supplementum epigraphicum graceum.* London, 1923–.
SFSHJ	South Florida Studies in the History of Judaism
T. Naph.	*Testament of Naphtali*
P. Tebt.	*The Tebtunis Papyri.* London. 5 vols. University of California Publications et al. 1902–2005.
UPZ	*Urkunden der Ptolemäerzeit (ältere Funde).* Edited by U. Wilcken. Berlin and Leipzig, 1927. Berlin, 1935–57.
VT	*Vetus Testamentum*
War	*Jewish War,* by Josephus
ZAW	*Zeitschrift für die alttestamentliche Wissenschaft*

Introduction

It was a time in the Near East when indigenous intellectuals and local insurgents were challenging imperial rule. Inspired by the revival of traditional religion, exclusive devotion to the one God, intellectuals and peasants alike became increasingly unhappy with their own rulers, who were being maintained in their positions of power and privilege by the imperial regime. Intellectuals were bothered that the rich and powerful elite were becoming ever more wealthy at the expense of the poor. Some of the more tradition-minded intellectuals continued to support the established order and incumbent rulers. Others struggled to comprehend why the times seemed so out of joint, why their own aristocratic families collaborated with the imperial power and assimilated more and more to the dominant imperial culture, and how the imperial regime was becoming an ever-greater threat to the traditional way of life.

This may read like a description of the Middle East in the early twenty-first century CE. But it also fits the situation in second-temple Judea that gave rise to the most important Judean writings in the last two centuries before Herod, Hillel, and Jesus: Sirach (or Ecclesiasticus), Daniel, and *1 Enoch*. All of these books were responses to the escalating crisis that led directly to the Maccabean Revolt, which led to a period of Judean independence from imperial rule and set the tone

1

for the continuing resistance to Roman imperial rule, the context of Jesus' mission, and the seeds of rabbinic Judaism. This escalating crisis and these books that responded to it were political-economic as well as cultural-religious, and these dimensions were inseparable.

"LIMITED INTELLIGENCE"

Standard interpretation of these books in biblical studies, however, usually focuses on religion, on Judaism. Rooted in the modern Western separation of religion and politics, biblical studies sometimes even seems to ignore the political circumstances in which texts classified as religious were produced. Daniel is somewhat of an exception, since the visions deal explicitly with imperial rule, yet the emphasis is squarely on the religious dimension. Still heavily influenced by Christian theology, moreover, biblical interpreters often focus especially on the theology of such books, Sirach being a principal expression of "wisdom" theology and Daniel and *1 Enoch* of "apocalypticism."

As the earliest and/or some of the most important texts of wisdom and apocalypticism, these texts have played a key role in standard interpretation of the origins of both Judaism and Christianity. In what has been the most prominent view, Judaism of late second-temple times has been seen as dominated by two conflicting theologies or worldviews. In apocalypticism, the historical world is understood as hopelessly under the control of evil forces. Only after destruction of the world in divine judgment at the end time will the true believers be rewarded with eternal life in a heavenly world. Wisdom theology, on the other hand, offered individuals an understanding of the standard patterns in social life, the natural world, and (increasingly) the nature of wisdom as a personified semidivine being, in contemplation of which one could attain immortality of soul.[1]

For much of the twentieth century, many interpreters believed that, as an ideology or even a widespread cultural movement, apocalypticism inspired resistance to foreign rule. Starting with the visions in Daniel 7–12 and the Maccabean Revolt, and continuing in the *War Scroll* found among the Dead Sea Scrolls and the "Zealot" party's agitation against Roman rule, apocalyptic fanaticism finally inspired the great revolts against Rome in 66–70 CE. Meanwhile, on the other hand, more sober and realistic people, such as scribes and sages, focused on how they could attain wisdom by reflecting on common patterns of social and natural life and the recognition that the beginning of wisdom was the fear of the Lord, which meant basically adherence to the Torah. The latter were presumably the intellectual-religious ancestors of both the mystical devotion to heavenly wisdom found in the Wisdom of Solomon and the Alexandrian Jewish philosopher Philo in the Greek-speaking Jewish Diaspora. Although apocalypticism was helpful in interpreting the disastrous Roman defeat of the first great revolt (e.g., the books of *4 Ezra* and *2 Baruch*), the rabbinic movement, heirs of the scribes who had combined wisdom and study of the Torah, suppressed apocalypticism after a second disastrous revolt against Roman rule in 132–35.

Christianity as well was the product of wisdom and apocalypticism in various combinations, according to standard twentieth-century interpretation. In his now famous *Quest of the Historical Jesus* at the beginning of that century, Albert Schweitzer concluded that Jesus was an apocalyptic prophet who believed that the end of the world was at hand. Rudolf Bultmann, the most influential New Testament scholar of the twentieth century, similarly insisted that Jesus delivered his teachings under the threat of an imminent "cosmic catastrophe." This continues to be one of the most prominent views of what was driving Jesus' ministry.[2] In the late twentieth century, however, liberal interpreters came to have serious doubts that Jesus was caught up in an apocalyptic worldview. But since wisdom was supposedly the only other prominent worldview in Judaism at the time, the alternative to viewing Jesus as an apocalyptic preacher was to reconstruct him as a sage teaching mainly individual wisdom sayings to individual believers.[3] Only later did Jesus' Jewish followers revert to apocalyptic theology, with its belief in judgment and the end of the world, to interpret his significance, evident for example in the Gospels of Mark and Matthew. The assumption that individual sayings and even particular images can be sorted out according to a dichotomy between wisdom and apocalypticism thus became the basis on which critical liberal scholars determined that the historical Jesus was a sage.

Twentieth-century interpreters have also understood the apostle Paul as an apocalyptic thinker convinced that the crucifixion, resurrection, and Parousia of Christ were the final events of the end time. He also supposedly incorporated some of the more speculative or mystical elements of wisdom into his theology, as seen particularly in 1 Corinthians, where he identifies Christ with Wisdom. The prologue to John's Gospel is rooted in the same speculation on Wisdom (= Logos). The more sober, ethical aspect of wisdom teaching persists elsewhere in early Christianity, as seen especially in the Letter of James, while apocalyptic theology persisted into the third generation, as evident in the book of Revelation. Much of the current theologically oriented interpretation of New Testament texts continues to be framed in terms of the dichotomy of wisdom and apocalypticism, the two worldviews that are assumed to have dominated both early Judaism and early Christianity.

The prevailing theological interpretation of Sirach and of Daniel and *1 Enoch* as the prime examples of wisdom and apocalypticism, respectively, has thus had a determinative effect on the standard twentieth-century interpretation of the origins of Judaism and Christianity. Although it dates from two centuries before Jesus, Sirach is virtually the only (extant) book of wisdom from late second-temple Judaism that gives access to wisdom teaching and reflection on transcendent personified Wisdom. Ecclesiastes is a separate branch of skeptical wisdom. Daniel was long thought to be the prototypical apocalyptic book, on which later revelations were patterned. Images and motifs from Daniel were traced in New Testament literature. When copies of sections of *1 Enoch* were found among the Dead Sea Scrolls at Qumran, Enoch literature also seemed to offer strong evidence of the apocalyptic ideology in Judaism.

Many interpreters who focus on texts such as Sirach, Daniel, and *1 Enoch,* however, no longer accept major aspects of this standard picture of Judaism. Although most still think and write in terms of a synthetic construct of Judaism, they are fully aware of the complexity and pluralism in second-temple Judean society. It now seems unclear that wisdom and apocalypticism were prominent ideologies (worldviews) in Jewish society, much less that they were the dominant ones. The dichotomy between wisdom and apocalypticism is particularly questionable. Texts classified as "apocalyptic" contain elements of wisdom. Scrolls containing wisdom teaching were found at Qumran, which had been presumed to be an apocalyptic community. Scholars working intensively on particular texts such as *1 Enoch,* which was known mainly in an Ethiopic translation, began to question interpretation that had been standard since the late nineteenth century, when some of those texts were discovered and first studied.[4] A number of scholars who sensed that the standard dichotomy of wisdom and apocalypticism did not fit the texts they were studying formed a working group in the Society of Biblical Literature.[5] Their critical analyses suggest that there were no defined boundaries between texts and other cultural expressions previously categorized as either apocalyptic or sapiential.

Even this elementary questioning of older assumptions and generalizations throws into question the way that much twentieth-century discussion of early Judaism and early Christianity was framed. What if wisdom and apocalypticism were not opposing and alternative worldviews? What if texts such as Daniel and *1 Enoch* are not evidence of a widespread apocalyptic ideology or movement, and peasants did not share the ideas of these texts? Then popular movements such as the so-called Zealots and the widespread revolt against the Romans in 66–70 cannot be attributed to the inspiration of apocalyptic ideology, contrary to much twentieth-century interpretation. What if the very texts—such as Sirach, Daniel, and *1 Enoch*—that have been used as the basis for wisdom and apocalypticism as dominant theologies in Judaism turn out not to attest such worldviews, thus in turn undermining the basis on which the individual sayings attributed to Jesus are classified as one or the other? Then the whole discussion of whether Jesus was an apocalyptic prophet or a sage turns out to be a debate couched in modern theological terms, a debate that has little to do with leaders and followers in first-century Galilee and Judea. It is thus important for the broader interpretation of Jewish and Christian origins to explore the implications of recent critical reexamination of Sirach, Daniel, and *1 Enoch.*

The process of critical reexamination of these texts, however, has barely begun. Once the discrepancy between critical rereadings of the texts and the previously standard interpretation has been noticed, it is difficult to avoid further questioning of standard assumptions and interpretive concepts. The problems with the way in which we have been dealing with "wisdom" and "apocalyptic" texts, however, runs much deeper than abstraction and dichotomization. This can be seen in several connections; we focus on two in particular.

First, perhaps largely because it originated in a field deeply embedded in theology, the concept of "apocalyptic" is a synthetic construct of features drawn from a variety of texts whose origins range over four or five centuries.[6] The synthetic construct is then routinely applied to particular texts that may or may not exhibit those features. The same is true of the concept of "wisdom," which is so vague that it varies according to the context and connections in which it is being used. In contrast to treating texts as instances of a synthetic modern construct, it is appropriate rather to appreciate the texts in their own literary integrity and historical contexts. Since those texts constitute some of the principal sources for Judean life in late second-temple times, moreover, this is important for understanding Judean history and society in that period as well. Since, by widespread consensus, "apocalyptic" texts were a new development in late second-temple Judea, an obvious procedure in dealing with the earliest examples, such as Daniel and *1 Enoch,* would be to compare their features with those of earlier texts that may have influenced their form and production. Also, since there were different kinds of wisdom, it only makes sense to be as specific as possible.

Second, again partly because of the theological orientation of biblical studies, interpreters often apply theological categories to texts and read selectively for theologically useful statements and themes. Almost certainly, however, the production and use of these texts in antiquity did not proceed according to modern theological categories. The contents of texts that have been classified according to different types of theology, apocalyptic or wisdom, have concerns much wider and often more "down to earth" than religious ideas. Indeed they are concerned also with political-economic issues, and their religious symbols and ideas are usually related to those political-economic issues.

This is abundantly evident in the three texts on which we are focusing. In Sirach, Jesus ben Sira boasts about the wise scribe serving in the assemblies of the priestly aristocracy of the Temple, yet also expresses a considerable degree of personal distrust in those same aristocrats, at least some of whom he declares are exploiting the poor. The Epistle of Enoch (the last section of *1 Enoch*) pronounces woes against the wealthy and powerful for their extreme exploitation of the poor and the righteous, while the very *maskilim* (scribes) who produce the visions and interpretations in Daniel 7–12 are being killed, evidently by those who have broken the covenant with God, for teaching the many to remain faithful to the covenant. Both Daniel and sections of *1 Enoch,* moreover, state clearly that the principal problem with which they are struggling is oppressive violence by foreign imperial rulers.

There is thus another analogy related to the current crisis in the Middle East, only an inverse analogy. Western governments have sent military forces into areas of the Middle East on the basis of limited or even faulty "intelligence": focusing on politics and economics, they underestimated or simply ignored the importance and inseparability of the cultural-religious dimensions of societal life. Biblical studies has studied life and literature of the ancient Middle East on the basis of equally limited intelligence: focusing on the cultural-religious, while underestimating the importance and inseparability of political-economic dynamics. We can seek more comprehensive "intelligence."

BROADER STRATEGY OF INVESTIGATION AND INTERPRETATION

That these texts address issues such as distrust of superiors, their exploitation of the poor, political repression, and imperial domination suggests that we broaden the scope of investigation and interpretation to match the concerns of the texts. It is not simply an optional matter of enriching our appreciation of the "apocalyptic" or "sapiential" worldview by attending to the social location of the producers of the literature. We cannot begin to interpret the very content of instructional wisdom (in Sirach) or judgmental pronouncements on the wealthy (in 1 Enoch) or visionary accounts of political history (in both Daniel and 1 Enoch) without understanding both the social location and the fundamental dynamics of political-economic power relations and the contingencies of imperial politics. Sirach, Daniel, and Enoch texts deal with certain political-economic-religious circumstances that are having an adverse effect on themselves and other Judeans, and they articulate responses to those circumstances that have further political implications. To deal more comprehensively with these ancient texts, however, a many-faceted multidisciplinary approach must become even more complicated. Recent research on orality and literacy in ancient societies and on the manuscripts of ancient biblical and other texts found among the Dead Sea Scrolls is challenging some of the basic assumptions of biblical studies about ancient texts.

In the last several decades, intense and probing study of "apocalyptic" literature such as 1 Enoch and Daniel has brought *literary analysis* to far greater sophistication than achieved by earlier work on such texts, many of them only recently discovered. New translations and careful critical exegesis on the basis of comparative materials far superior to those generated a century earlier have made a dramatic difference in how these texts are read.[7] Taking a cue from modern literary criticism, specialists defined a *genre* of "apocalypse."[8] Close attention to the literary form of different sections of 1 Enoch and Daniel, however, suggested that they did not fit the recent definition of "apocalypse." Rather, they resembled other forms evident in Judean and ancient Near Eastern texts, such as "testament" or "court tales."[9] Actually, 1 Enoch and Daniel are composite and mixed in form, and closer determination of the framing *genre* may not be all that significant for understanding these texts.[10] There has been far less critical discussion about literary forms and patterns in literature classified as sapiential,[11] although significant studies have clarified the text of Sirach,[12] explored its relation to Egyptian wisdom and Greek philosophy,[13] and further illuminated the hymnic material in the book.[14] These probing literary studies have laid a solid foundation for more multifaceted exploration of Sirach, Daniel, and *1 Enoch* and the context in which they were produced.

A major obstacle to greater knowledge of the *historical situation* in which Sirach, Daniel, and the Enoch literature originated has been the continuing use of the synthetic essentialist construct of "Judaism" in reference to life and literature in second-temple Judea. Another has been the lack of evidence, particularly for the first century or so of Hellenistic rule, the period immediately before the Maccabean Revolt in the 160s BCE. Yet another obstacle has been the tendency to take the literary evidence that does exist at face value, as if the praise of the ancestors in Sirach 44–49, for example, did not have its own agenda or political-religious purpose. Recognition that texts were composed to persuade people and/or to authorize certain institutions or circumstances and the revival of rhetorical criticism should encourage more critical use of sources as historical evidence.

For the period of Persian rule, on the other hand, the wealth of evidence from surrounding areas and sobering evidence from recent archaeological surveys has made possible a vigorous debate about the origins of the second Temple.[15] Two of the most significant features of recent scholarly debate are the recognition that, far from being a unified and monolithic community focused around the rebuilt Temple, Judean society was divided by several overlapping conflicts and subject to Persian imperial control throughout the period. Recognition that some of those conflicts will have continued makes a difference in how we read and use the minimal sources for the early Hellenistic period.

Interest in the *social origins* and *social context* of apocalyptic literature has grown considerably in the last two decades.[16] Perhaps the most influential attempt to discern the *social origins* of apocalypticism, for a time, was the hypothesis that the *Asidaeans/Hasidim* mentioned briefly in 1 and 2 Maccabees produced both the book of Daniel and *1 Enoch*, which in turn inspired subsequent apocalyptic ideology and groups.[17] Organized supposedly as small "conventicles," the *Hasidim* had long cultivated a continuing prophetic eschatology (Isa. 24–27; Zech. 12–14; Joel) over against the established theocracy of "Judaism" (a religious community) in control of the Temple.[18] The problems with this thesis, of course, are that it stretches the brief passing references to the *Hasidim* far beyond anything indicated in the text. These "mighty warriors" (1 Macc. 2:42) are unlikely candidates to have produced the book of Daniel, which takes a quietist position prior to or on the sideline during the Maccabean revolt.[19]

This hypothesis is typical of the idealist approach in biblical studies, which posits a group as supposedly implied by a text or, in this case, a particular ideology. No attempt is made to discern the social structure and to consider how particular ideas might correspond to particular social locations. Both the *maskilim* in Daniel and those who produced the sections of *1 Enoch* appear to belong to a cultural elite, with sophisticated knowledge of dream interpretation and astronomy,[20] yet they are engaged in sharp conflict with the political elite. Yet no attempt is made to examine how their relationship may be determined by the structure of society and/or change in historical circumstances. The social basis of wisdom does not even appear to be an issue. Wisdom is cultivated by wisdom teachers, sages. It seems to be more or less assumed that such sages teach anyone and everyone, with no attention to the social location and social function of wisdom teaching.[21]

Various suggestions have also been made about the *social context* in which "apocalyptic" emerged. The most common and persistent explanation has been the cultural conflict between "Judaism" and "Hellenism" (which eventually escalated into "religious persecution" by Antiochus Epiphanes).[22] The impact of Hellenistic culture on Judaism supposedly worked in two opposite ways. Wisdom teachers such as Ben Sira calmly assimilated certain influences from Hellenistic philosophy into traditional Jewish wisdom teaching. Others, sensing Hellenistic culture as a threat to their traditional loyalty to the Torah, sought to find an alternative to assimilation in apocalyptic visions.

Also influential has been the argument that under the influence of traders and merchants in the Hellenistic period, Judea suddenly became commercialized.[23] Both Ben Sira's conservative wisdom teaching and the particularist reaction of apocalyptic literature such as Daniel were supposedly reactions to the entrepreneurial individualism and the cosmopolitan spirit of Hellenism. This picture of rapid commercialization appears to be a projection of developments in early modern Europe onto the ancient world. Such projections of conditions from modern experience that scholars are familiar with from their schooling is typical of a biblical studies that has yet to consider that ancient political-economic structure and historical developments may have been different from those of modern Europe.[24] In the last decade or so, a number of scholars involved in the Sociology of the Second Temple Group in the Society of Biblical Literature have examined several social facets of key texts from the second-temple period.[25] Yet little attention has been given to bringing those facets together systematically into a broader picture of the overall structure of second-temple Judea.[26]

Recent research on orality and literacy in ancient societies is undermining some of the basic assumptions of biblical studies and bringing into play factors that we have not previously considered in dealing with ancient texts. Biblical studies, including the dominant "historical-critical" method, are based largely on the assumptions of modern print culture. Books are assumed to have been "written" by "authors" and then to have been widely available for "reading." Recent research is demonstrating, however, that in ancient societies such as Judea literacy was rare, confined to specialists in writing and reading.[27] This simplifies the quest for who produced wisdom and apocalyptic literature or for that matter any books: those who were literate, professional scribes. As important to recognize as the limits of literacy are the kinds and uses of writing.[28] In ancient Near Eastern societies writing was often understood as sacred or numinous, and some texts were written more as sacred monuments than as means to communicate messages, and would not have been regularly read or consulted even by scribes. Writing, moreover, was embedded in a predominantly oral communication environment, even in scribal circles. The very books produced by scribes offer indications that they cultivated the various texts they composed by oral recitation as much as by the reading of written scrolls.[29] These factors will clearly complicate the way we understand the social role of scribes and their production of texts.

Finally, the results of careful, detailed *study of the scrolls of biblical books found among the Dead Sea Scrolls* are also challenging basic assumptions of biblical studies rooted in print culture. Biblical books had supposedly reached stable textual form by at least late second-temple times. Careful examination of the manuscripts of "biblical books" found among the Dead Sea Scrolls, however, indicates that there were multiple versions of many books, and that they were still undergoing development, apparently through the end of the second-temple period.[30] Texts other than those later included in the Hebrew Bible, moreover, commanded as much authority as the "biblical" books. Critical examination of such previously unavailable evidence is thus suggesting a much wider range of Judean culture than known from previously known "books," and a more fluid scribal cultivation and continuing composition in the Judean cultural repertoire than biblical studies has allowed.

STEPS IN THE ARGUMENT

This investigation aims to understand the three key texts, Sirach, *1 Enoch,* and Daniel, in the context of second-temple Judea under Hellenistic imperial rule in a wide-ranging approach that considers the interrelationship of the political-economic structure, the historical background and crisis, and the cultural resources and circumstances. The question now is how to organize consideration of those interrelated factors into an intelligible sequence of analysis. Insofar as the analysis will be complex, it may help to have an overview of the procedure and argument at the outset.

Chapters 1 and 2 sketch the history of Judea that led up to the escalating series of crises in which Enoch literature, Daniel literature, and Sirach were produced. Second-temple Judea was not an independent society (contrary to what Haggai and Zechariah may suggest), and far more complex than suggested by the concept "Judaism." In the centuries after Babylonian armies destroyed Jerusalem, the Davidic monarchy, and its temple and deported the ruling elite, the Persian imperial regime presided over developments in Judea, through governors and other envoys, as the memoirs of Nehemiah and Ezra indicate. From its origins the Jerusalem "temple-state" was an instrument of Persian imperial rule. Nor was Judea an irenic monolithic society. In placing the previously deported elite families of Jerusalem in control, the Persians in effect subordinated most of the Judean people and other priestly groups. Rival families or factions among the powerful in Judea competed for power and exploited the desperate condition of the peasantry, leading to repeated Persian intervention to stabilize the temple-state they depended on for imperial revenues and localized control of Judea.

A hereditary high priesthood may have consolidated power in the Jerusalem temple-state by the time Alexander the Great and his "Successors" replaced the

Persians as imperial rulers of the Near East. But the Ptolemaic regime in Egypt only exacerbated the local struggle for power in Jerusalem by contracting collection of tax revenues to a local military strongman instead of the high priest. The struggle for control of Palestine between the rival empires of the Ptolemies in Egypt and the Seleucids in Syria opened further opportunity for local rivalry between aristocratic factions in Jerusalem. A series of crises in the continuing factional conflict in the aristocracy escalated to the point where the dominant faction negotiated with the Seleucid emperor for the high priestly office and permission to carry out a Hellenizing reform, making Jerusalem into a Hellenistic city.

This was almost certainly a key historical factor in why different circles of scribes came to articulate different stances toward the Jerusalem high priesthood and its incumbents. Yet we would not discern this without a sense of the social relationship and relative roles between the Jerusalem scribes and the priestly aristocrats in control of the temple-state, the agenda of chapters 3 and 4.

The book of Sirach yields just enough information to give us a picture of the basic political-economic-religious structure of Judean society. This information is comparable to that in studies of "tributary" societies that comparative sociologist Gerhard Lenski drew upon but somewhat obscured in his synthetic model of agrarian societies. Ben Sira also offers plenty of clues to the ambiguities and dynamics of power relations between the rich rulers and the poor peasants, and especially between the wise scribes and the high priestly rulers whom they served as intellectual "retainers" (chap. 3). A wide range of earlier evidence for scribes in ancient Mesopotamia, Egypt, and Judea confirms this picture of the wise scribes' role as officials who assist the rulers in governing society. A central part of their training for and duties in their service as intellectual retainers of the rulers was cultivation of elite culture in its various "literary" forms, ranging from instructional wisdom and historical legends to collections of legal rulings and omens to royal hymns and astronomical knowledge. The wise scribes of Judea were thus not simply experts in "wisdom-teaching" but also cultivated all segments of the Judean cultural repertoire (chap. 4).

Given their economic dependence on their aristocratic patrons, scribes would have been unavoidably involved in some of the factional struggles among the high priestly rulers. As professional scribes devoted to the cultivation of traditional Judean culture, however, they had developed their own sense of authority, independent of their priestly patrons' authority. And they had their own sense of the Temple and priesthood as the representative of the people to God and of God to the people, all according to the sacred authority of the covenant and commandment of the Most High. Aristocratic factions' close collaboration with imperial rulers and their assimilation of the dominant imperial culture in ways that compromised the traditional covenantal Judean way of life would have been threatening to the position of many scribes who were firmly committed to their role as the guardians of Judean cultural tradition (chap. 3).

Just as the juxtaposition of the escalating historical crisis in Judean society under the Seleucid Empire with the ambiguity of their political-economic position helps us understand the conflicted situation of scribes such as Ben Sira, so recent research on orality-literacy and the textual fluidity of "biblical" and other books may lead to fuller appreciation of the scribal cultivation and composition of texts, as explored in chapters 5 and 6.

We have it in writing, but Ben Sira represents his own teaching as oral and his listeners' learning as aural. Contrary to the previous assumptions of biblical studies so deeply rooted in modern print culture, not only was writing limited mainly to scribes in a society otherwise dominated by oral communication, but also scribal culture itself was strongly oral. Writing in ancient societies such as Judea, Mesopotamia, and Egypt, moreover, had numinous or sacred qualities, different from what we assume in print culture. Sacred "monumental" documents deposited in temples, such as "the book of the covenant/teaching of Moses," served a constitutional function as an authorizing document for a royal regime or temple-state. Such sacred monumental documents may not have been consulted or read, even by scribes whose professional colleagues had inscribed them. In the oral-written culture of the scribes, texts were inscribed on the heart (memory) as much as on clay tablets and parchment scrolls. Scribes cultivated texts of the Judean cultural repertoire orally: they learned them by recitation and recited them orally. Correspondingly, composition would have been embedded in such cultivation of traditional material in the cultural repertoire, and would not have resembled modern individual authors writing completely new, "original" texts (chap. 5).

Careful analysis of scrolls of books, including "biblical" books of the "Law and Prophets," has demonstrated that they existed in multiple versions, which were still developing and not yet standardized in late second-temple times. Judging from the numbers of scrolls of particular books found among the Dead Sea Scrolls, moreover, books such as *Jubilees* and sections of *1 Enoch* and alternative books of Torah were authoritative. The books that later became biblical apparently commanded only a relative authority among many other texts. The phrase-by-phrase "interpretations" of prophetic books apparently produced in the Qumran community itself in the late second century BCE stand out as unique. Otherwise, in the book of Sirach or in texts produced at Qumran, quotations of authoritative books are rare, and authoritative texts do not appear to have been studied and particular passages explicitly interpreted. Rather, texts of Torah and others were recited ritually and learned by recitation. It appears that in second-temple times scribes were engaged in oral cultivation, along with written copying, of a wide range of texts and other cultural materials. The cultural repertoire they cultivated included texts of Mosaic Torah, prophetic texts, and historical-legendary texts. It also included a segment of at least four different kinds of wisdom, including mantic and cosmological wisdom as well as the more familiar instructional and reflective wisdom (chap. 6).

Finally, in chapters 7–9 we explore how different circles of learned scribes, who were "caught in the middle" in the political-economic structure of Judea during the escalating crises of conflicting aristocratic factions in Jerusalem under imperial rule, produced the texts of Sirach, *1 Enoch*, and Daniel out of the rich Judean cultural repertoire that they cultivated.

In the collection of instructional wisdom and hymnic cosmological and reflective wisdom in Sirach, Yeshua Ben Sira presents himself proudly as a learned scribe who cultivates the full repertoire of Judean culture, especially proverbial wisdom, as preparation for his primary calling, which is serving among the aristocracy of the temple-state. In connection with this primary role, however, he is also a teacher, and most of his book consists of his instructional speeches on various topics important in the training of scribes. Studies of oral communication help us discern that in composing these speeches he is drawing on traditional sets of particular language dedicated to each particular topic of teaching, such as friendship or caution in relations with powerful patrons. While he is suspicious of mantic wisdom, Ben Sira also composes new hymns of cosmological wisdom and reflection on wisdom, again from traditional registers of speech devoted to those subjects. Once we are aware, from other sources, of potential threats from rival aristocratic factions keen on Hellenistic political culture, we recognize more clearly how Ben Sira draws on particular segments of his cultural repertoire to enhance the authority of the incumbent high priest. In a typical hymnic praise of Wisdom (Sir. 24), he pointedly has her establish her domain in the Temple. And in the lengthy hymnic praise of the ancestors, he draws on legendary, historical, and prophetic tradition to laud the great officeholders of Israel, all of which leads to the glorious present occupant of the high priestly office (Sir. 44–50).

Some scribes would likely have been struggling to understand the escalating conflict between rival aristocratic factions at the head of the temple-state they served and the increasingly obvious imperial influence in Jerusalem. They would have been ever more intensely aware of how these conflicts were threatening the traditional Judean way of life, of which they were the guardians as cultivators of Judean cultural traditions. Those who produced the texts of revealed wisdom ostensibly from the hoary antediluvian figure of Enoch were a circle of such increasingly dissident scribes (chap. 8). In the Book of Watchers they drew on a combination of traditional astronomical and mantic wisdom and adapted prophetic forms to understand violent imperial domination, which was clearly contrary to the previously revealed will of God. From heavenly wisdom they discerned that imperial violence fit into a larger cosmological-historical context in which divine forces had rebelled against the divine emperor of history, yet that God was still ultimately in control. The Enoch scribes also combined historical traditions with visionary speculation about the future in visionary "histories," both to articulate grand overviews of universal history in which the second Temple itself was implicated in the illegitimacy of the incumbent high priesthood and to reassure themselves that history would be resolved in a restoration of God's direct rule. In the Epistle of Enoch they drew on prophetic tradition and forms in pronouncing God's condemnation on the exploitative wealthy rulers in Jerusalem.

The book of Daniel is also a composite of materials produced by yet another circle of wise scribes, the *maskilim*. Like the Enoch scribes they drew upon traditional mantic wisdom and prophetic lore and forms. The collection and further development of tales of scribes in the service of imperial courts, who in their God-given wisdom interpreted dreams to declare the ultimate judgment of God on the arrogance of imperial rule (Dan. 1–6), reinforced Jerusalem scribes' persistence in their traditional loyalty. As the crisis escalated into the Hellenizing reform and violent repression by Antiochus Epiphanes, the *maskilim,* well-versed in the tradition of dream interpretation, produced new visions and their interpretations, which placed the violent imperial invasion of Judean life in the broad perspective of the succession of Near Eastern imperial rulers. The current crisis of extreme violence and martyrdom could thus be seen as the last and worst episode prior to divine intervention that would restore the people to sovereignty and/or vindicate the *maskilim* who had suffered martyr deaths (Dan. 7–12).

Chapter 1

Origins of the Judean Temple-State under the Persian Empire

I returned to (these) cities on the other side of the Tigris, the sanctuaries of which have been ruins for a long time, the images which (used) to live therein and established for them permanent sanctuaries. I (also) gathered all their (former) inhabitants and returned (to them) their habitations.

Edict of Cyrus (*ANET,* 316)

Here we are, slaves to this day—slaves in the land that you gave to our ancestors to enjoy its fruit and its good gifts. Its rich yield goes to the kings whom you have set over us because of our sins; they have power also over our bodies and over our livestock at their pleasure, and we are in great distress.

Ezra, in Nehemiah 9:36–37

The Babylonian conquest of Judah in 587/6 BCE destroyed the Davidic monarchy, its Temple, the royal palace, and the mansions of the wealthy in the city of Jerusalem, according to the account in 2 Kings 25:8–11. The Babylonian armies had already deported most of the officers of the monarchy, its military forces, and the artisans who served its needs after the first conquest of Jerusalem ten years earlier; now they took away many of the remaining Jerusalemites, including the priests of the Temple and the scribes. Their experience became the basis on which Israel was understood to have been taken into exile, which underlies the traditional periodization of Israel's history into the formative stages of the exile and the postexilic age.

The majority of the people in Judah, however, were not taken into exile. The land was not "empty." The Babylonian army left "the poorest people of the land to be vinedressers and tillers of the soil" (2 Kings 25:12; 24:14). Like other agrarian empires, the Babylonian regime depended on the peasantry as its labor force, from whom it could extract tribute and taxes. The Babylonians appointed

Gedaliah, descendant of a line of royal officers, "as governor over the people who remained in the land of Judah" (2 Kings 25:22; "governor of the towns of Judah," Jer. 40:5–6). Although we know little of life in Judah in this period, it is possible that one of the traditional sacred centers for service of Yahweh, the God of Israel, such as Mizpah or Bethel, may have become the center of administration after the destruction of Jerusalem.[1] Thus, in the aftermath of the massive turmoil of the Babylonian conquests, many villages under the Babylonian governors of Judah were still populated by peasants who continued to "gather wine and summer fruits and oil, and [to] store them in [their] vessels" (Jer. 40:10). Some of these peasants, moreover, having been previously displaced from the land, must have taken over new fields on which they could struggle for a livelihood (40:10).[2]

Once Persian imperial rule replaced the Babylonians, however, the previously deported Judean elite were restored to prominence and power in Jerusalem and the Temple was rebuilt—the beginnings of the second-temple era in the history of Judah-Judea.

It is impossible to reconstruct the development of the temple-state with any degree of precision and certainty, given the uncertain dating and reliability of our sources for Judah in the Persian period. A clearer sense of how developments in Judah itself depended on the contingencies and policies of the Persian regime stems from closer attention to the richer supply of sources for the empire more generally.[3] Judean sources, however, do give many indications of the political-religious struggles that were involved.[4] While the books of the prophets Haggai, Zechariah, and Malachi surely reached their present form much later, they provide a (highly supportive) picture of the initial foundation of the Temple in the late sixth century. The books of Ezra and Nehemiah are more problematic as sources. The respective missions of Nehemiah and Ezra are now dated to the middle and end of the fifth century BCE, respectively, and the books based partly on their "memoirs" come from later in the second-temple period. Yet they present a telling picture of the rival forces engaged in the struggle to consolidate, subvert, or reform the nascent temple-state in Jerusalem—a struggle that seems to have continued through much of the Persian period.

THE JUDEAN TEMPLE-STATE
AND PERSIAN IMPERIAL RULE

Until recently life in Judah from the mid-sixth to the late fourth centuries has been represented as relatively independent of Persian imperial rule. Discussion tended to focus on ancient "Judaism," as if the cultural-religious life of a people could be abstracted from the contingencies of imperial history and local political-economic conflicts. Even in recent decades when the presence of the Persian Empire has been acknowledged, Judah has been presented as, for all practical purposes, self-governing. Although the Persians may have fostered rebuilding the Temple in Jerusalem for their own imperial purposes, they allowed and even commanded the Jewish leaders whom they placed in charge to guide the temple-state according to indigenous Judean/Israelite traditions and institutions. Indeed, it is even claimed that indigenous legal traditions established by local Judean authorities were "authorized" as the local manifestation of imperial law.[5]

Only in recent years has fuller attention been given to the ways in which imperial rule impinged on life in second-temple *Yehud,* because of Persian military contingencies and strategies, imperial policies of taxation, or imperial concern to control local populations and local conflicts. The result is greater awareness of how Persian imperial rule was far more intrusive than previously imagined. In some cases literature and inscriptions previously read as evidence for Persian imperial grants of local autonomy and affirmation of local tradition turned out rather to indicate Persian steps to control local affairs.

Temple-states, with their surrounding peasant villages, were one of the standard forms in which civilization developed in the ancient Near East. Rooted in the traditional religious culture focused on divine forces that determined their lives, peasants rendered up percentages of their produce and labor to a central managerial priesthood as the service they owed to the god(s). The ruling classes that emerged in Mesopotamia and Egypt built up empires by combining under their rule many cities centered around one or more temples. The fundamental political-economic-religious structure remained the same as one ruling elite succeeded another in a succession of ever-larger empires, from the Akkadians and Assyrians to the Persians and, eventually, the Greeks and Romans.

As a basic component of the Persian Empire and its successors, the temple-state fulfilled three closely interrelated functions. A temple-state staffed by a central (usually indigenous) priesthood allowed and required an indigenous people to serve their own ancestral gods (or those of the local elite) with tithes and offerings. The latter provided revenues to support the managerial priesthood. In turn the local priesthood maintained order and appropriated revenues for the imperial regime to which they owed their position of power and privilege.

The Persian imperial regime apparently sent a colony of immigrants from Babylon to Jerusalem and sponsored the rebuilding of the temple there as part of the consolidation of its power in the west. The project, possibly inaugurated by Cyrus himself, at the very beginning of Persian rule, was carried further under Darius I (522–486).[6] Establishing a temple-state in Jerusalem was a means of generating increased production as an expanded base for taxes as well as a way of securing imperial control with the presence of a Persian governor and military detachment.[7] Rebuilding temples such as the one in Jerusalem gave credence to the Persian imperial propaganda that the great emperor was the liberator who restored gods, temples, and peoples, after the terrible destruction and deportations of the Babylonians.[8]

The initiative came from the Persian imperial regime, according to the books of Ezra and Nehemiah. In this respect the (re)building of the Temple in Jerusalem fits the standard ancient Near Eastern pattern. According to the ubiquitous imperial ideology, temples were built by kings. Under the Davidic monarchy the divinely anointed king of Jerusalem/Judah/Israel had built the Temple. Much of the narrative of Solomon's kingship is devoted to his building of the original Temple in the Jebusite city of Jerusalem, which King David had conquered with the aid of his mercenary troops (1 Kings 5–8; 2 Sam. 5:6–10). Now, however, the Persian emperor was the divinely directed builder (Ezra 1:2). And although Judeans provided the labor, it is the Persian satrap of the province Beyond the River and the governors of Yehud appointed by the emperor, Sheshbazzar and Zerubbabel, who were designated as the builders (Ezra 1:8, 3:8–13).

Far from attempting to hide this, literature produced by the restored Jerusalem elite appealed to imperial initiative for its own legitimation as well as the Temple's authorization. The book of Ezra appealed to an imperial edict as the divine authorization for the project: "Thus says King Cyrus of Persia: The LORD, the God of heaven, has given me all the kingdoms of the earth, and he has charged me to build him a house at Jerusalem in Judah" (Ezra 1:2). It also claimed that by decree of the emperor Darius I, based on the earlier decree of Cyrus found in the Persian archives, the cost of building the "house" of "the God who is in Jerusalem" was "paid from the imperial treasury" (Ezra 1:3; 6:1–12). In the quid pro quo that restored them to power in Jerusalem, the exiled elite seemed only too eager to acclaim Cyrus with the title of the Davidic king, "YHWH's Messiah," along with the traditional Davidic imperial ideology of the nations falling under his feet. The priests of Marduk acclaimed their conqueror Cyrus as "King of Babylon," and the priests of certain Egyptian temples honored Darius with the title of Pharaoh.[9] Similarly, the long prophetic poem in Isaiah 40–55 proclaimed that YHWH had commissioned the first Persian emperor as his *messiah*: "I have aroused Cyrus in righteousness, . . . he shall build my city and set my exiles free" (Isa. 45:1, 13).

Control and supervision of Yehud, moreover, was maintained by governors sent by the imperial regime. This was not simply a temporary device at the outset (Sheshbazzar, Zerubbabel, Elnathan, at the end of the sixth century) and revived at times of disorder (Nehemiah, mid-fifth century), but then discontinued once a high-priestly regime consolidated its authority in Jerusalem. The personal names of governors stamped on the handles of storage jars along with papyri and literary sources now enable us to construct a list of ten or more governors sent by the imperial regime through the whole period of Persian rule.[10] That is, Yehud was a subdivision of the Persian Empire and not an autonomous temple-state.

Zerubbabel, Ezra, and Nehemiah have all been traditionally understood as heroes of the restoration of Judah. Yet these figures known from later biblical books, two of them governors and the other an imperial envoy, all had either Babylonian names (Zerubbabel) or roots in the imperial court (Nehemiah and Ezra).[11] Although all three apparently had ties with the deported Jerusalemite elite living in Babylon, they were all clearly appointed by and were taking orders from the Persian imperial regime. Zerubbabel, whose role appears to have been primarily rebuilding the Temple in Jerusalem, has previously been interpreted as a descendant of the Davidic monarchy, even as a "messianic" pretender. He apparently did have ethnic ties to the deported Jerusalemite elite, but he had become a Persian courtier.[12] The prophet Haggai, however, never identifies him as a Davidide. It is possible that the notion of a diarchy (rule by a high priest and a prince) was influenced by later views of early second-temple times. The "memoirs" of Nehemiah make it clear that he was sent by the Persian court as governor (Neh 2:9–10, 19–20). Similarly, Ezra was also commissioned by the Persian imperial regime to impose order on the situation in Judah, one that repeatedly became contentious.

As indicated in Nehemiah's "memoirs" as well as in other sources for Persian imperial rule, the Persian governors of Yehud operated as representatives of the empire, to impose order on the province, even to forcibly require the restored but recalcitrant elite to implement imperial instructions. The emperor sent him and equipped him appropriately to oversee the (re)building of the Temple citadel's gates and the wall of the city (Neh. 2:8). As indicated by the Aramaic term that corresponds to the Akkadian *birtu,* the "citadel" was a fortress staffed by a garrison of soldiers. Accordingly, the emperor had also sent with Nehemiah "officers of the army and cavalry," that is, imperial military forces known as the "King's men."[13] It is clear that the labor on the (re)building was to be done by details of corvée, "forced labor," from all of the Yehudim, including even the high priest as well as "the priests, nobles, and officials" (2:16; 3:1–33). But Nehemiah, aware that the project was controversial and would meet with resistance, maintained command of the project in his own hands (2:16–20). Once the city wall had been (re)built, Nehemiah arranged the appointment of Judean gatekeepers, singers, and Levites in the Temple, and then deployed his brother Hanani as the garrison commander in charge of the city, under Nehemiah's own overall command of the province (Neh. 7:1–2). All of these measures—the deployment of Persian imperial troops, the fortification of cities, and use of forced labor among subject peoples—were standard Persian imperial practices.[14] Their purpose was clear: control of local populations.

Ezra, subsequently remembered primarily as the great (re)giver of the Torah/ Law, was commissioned by the emperor Artaxerxes to

> appoint magistrates and judges who may judge all the people in [the satrapy] Beyond the River. . . . Anyone who would not execute the law [*dātā'*] of your god and the law [*dātā'*] of the king zealously, let a judicial verdict be executed on him: either for death, or flogging, confiscation of property, or imprisonment. (Ezra 7:25–26, au. trans.)

By comparison with sources for other areas of the empire, it is clear now that this is not a reference to Ezra's role in bringing the Mosaic Torah to the restored Judeans in Jerusalem. It is rather a matter of judging cases according to a culturally derived sense of justice identical with the rule of the Persian deity Ahura Mazda and the decrees of the Persian emperor—backed by rather stern sanctions for violation.[15]

While the authorization for rebuilding the Temple and controlling the population came from the Persian imperial regime, the building and maintenance of the Temple was the responsibility of the previously exiled Judean elite, which the Persians restored to power in Jerusalem. The prophets associated with the restoration hail Zerubbabel, the Judean governor, and/or Joshua the high priest, as leaders of "the remnant of the people" called to build the Temple (Hag. 1:12–2:9; Zech. 4:8–10; 6:9–14). Thus in the same collection of prophetic materials are varying representations of the respective roles and responsibilities of these two figures. This may reflect the fluidity of relative power and prominence among figures in the restored elite in Jerusalem. In any case, Zerubbabel, the governor sent by the Persian regime, was also the chosen agent of the God of Israel. Hence, the establishment of the Temple was both an instrument of imperial rule and a project of the returned Judeans.

The prophets of the restoration also touted the building and maintenance of the Temple, its sacrifices, and officiating priesthood as the responsibility of the people to serve their God with their agricultural produce and labor. They called upon "the remnant of the people" and "the people of the land" to labor on "the house of the LORD of hosts" (Hag. 1:14; 2:2, 4; Zech. 1–7 by implication). Malachi exhorted the people, "Bring the full tithe into the storehouse, so that there may be food in my house" (3:10). These prophets emphasized that the fertility of the soil and productivity of the people's fields, thus their own survival, depended on rendering up a percentage of their produce to the Temple (Hag. 1:2–11; 2:15–19; Zech. 8:9–13; Mal. 3:8–12).

The people, moreover, were expected to render the finest and unblemished of their crops and animals to the Temple and its priesthood. Malachi includes a telling rhetorical comparison with reference to blemished beasts offered up for the LORD's table: "Try presenting that to your governor!" (Mal. 1:6–8). This comparison has two clear implications with regard to the temple-state in Yehud. One is that the products of the finest quality that the people were obligated to offer up for service at "YHWH's table" were also support for the priests. This is explicitly laid out in extended passages of Leviticus and Numbers, which were probably produced in the Persian period to lay out the priestly prerogatives. "[YHWH] spoke to Aaron: I have given you charge of the offerings made to me. . . . Every offering of theirs that they render to me as a most holy thing, whether grain offering, sin offering, or guilt offering, shall belong to you and your sons" (Num. 18:8–13, 21–23; Lev. 7:28–36). Material evidence from the Persian period, such as inscriptions on jar handles, storage pits, and archaeological surveys, now supplements information from Judean texts for how the temple-state worked as a religiously based political-economic system.

The other implication of Malachi's sarcastic comment is that the people were expected to render quality produce to the governor and his staff as well as to supply economic support to the Temple and priesthood.[16] The Persian regime apparently delegated certain administrative functions such as collection of the tribute to the priestly officials heading the Temple.[17] They were expected to collect the tribute, a poll tax, and a land tax for the emperor (Ezra 4:13, 20; 6:8; 7:24; Neh. 5:4), as well as to collect the firstfruits, tithes, and other contributions into the Temple storehouses (Neh. 10:36–40 [35–39E]).[18] As indicated in the books of

Ezra and Nehemiah, taxes and tribute as well as tithes and offerings were collected in kind, not coinage.[19]

Insofar as the imperial revenues were integrally related to support of the Temple and priesthood, the Persian regime had a vested interest in the viability of the peasant families whose produce supplied both. The economy of the province must have been coextensive with that of the temple economy.[20] Since the distant imperial court suspected that local elites might well overexploit their common economic base, collection of both local and imperial revenues, along with attention to local exploitation, proceeded under the watchful eye of a Persian imperial governor.[21]

The book of Nehemiah, which reflects a situation no earlier than mid-fifth century and perhaps at a later time, presents a Persian governor in command of internal affairs in Yehud as well as the imperial revenues. In addition to his commission to rebuild the walls of Jerusalem, he was clearly also responsible for regularizing the revenues of both the imperial regime and the Temple. Thus not only did Nehemiah expropriate payments in kind (allotments of grain, wine, and silver) from the populace (Neh. 5:14–15), but he also saw that "the king's tax" on cultivated land was collected (5:4). He also regularized the contributions of goods and funds to the central storage area of the Temple for the support of the priestly families (10:36–40 [35–39E]).[22] It is also clear that Pethahiah the overseer was an imperial appointee (11:24).[23]

Under Persian rule the province of Judea was in any case both small and poor. Close analysis of the archaeological evidence that has recently become more available provides a sobering control on speculative claims about second-temple "Judaism." The economic base on which the second Temple was built in the Persian period consisted mainly of small and very small settlements.[24] In contrast to grandiose earlier projections of the population of Persian Yehud, recent surveys of settlements suggest that, limited to the traditional territories of Judah and Benjamin, it had been reduced to 30,000 or even less, partly from the Babylonian destruction.[25] The population of Jerusalem itself would have been no more than 3,000, which accords with usual percentage of the 10 percent or less that can be supported by the productive agricultural base in such traditional agrarian economies.[26]

The small populace was also poor. The peasantry of Yehud worked under a double demand for "surplus" produce, supposedly above and beyond what was needed for subsistence, but actually threatening it. The extra demand on producers to support the Temple and priesthood, touted by its prophetic advocates as promising economic prosperity, contributed to the people's economic difficulty for much of the Persian period.[27] Restoration prophetic voices attest a struggling economy and considerable poverty. Haggai mentions famine, blight, and drought, complaining that the people were preoccupied with their own affairs rather than contributing to the elite's project of building the Temple (Hag. 1:3–11; 2:15–19; Zech. 8:9–13). Several generations after the temple-state had been established in Yehud, Nehemiah supposedly found the walls of Jerusalem in disrepair (Neh. 1–2) and the Levitical priesthood dispersed because of insufficient revenues to support them (13:10–13). Inevitably in such a tributary system, moreover, the wealthy and powerful took advantage of their power in ways that ultimately weakened the whole system. Nehemiah found the peasantry seriously in debt from heavy taxation and exploitation by the wealthy, with the corresponding disintegration of family structure and village community (5:1–19).[28] He took measures supposedly to alleviate their desperate situation by pressuring their wealthy creditors to ease their demands. But his memoirs mention nothing about alleviating the demand for either imperial revenues or tithes and offerings for the Temple.

MULTIPLE CONFLICTS IN YEHUD UNDER PERSIAN RULE

Despite, or perhaps rather because of, the arrangements imposed by the imperial regime, it is difficult to imagine that Yehud ever became a unified society under the Persians. Our sources for the period indicate several interrelated conflicts. The most fundamental, because rooted in the very structure of imperial Yehud, were two conflicts that persisted throughout second-temple history: (1) the division between those who had remained on the land after the Babylonian conquest, and the restored elite who controlled the temple-state, initially as a virtual colony of immigrants in and around Jerusalem; and (2) the division between the peasants living in village communities and the Jerusalem aristocracy centered in the high priesthood. Compounding those overlapping structural conflicts were (3) divisions between various priestly factions, which overlapped the conflict between immigrants and indigenous, and (4) struggles and maneuvering for power both between local magnates and between local magnates and the Persian governors. These multiple conflicts were evident from the very foundation of the Jerusalem temple-state, as attested in Haggai, Malachi, and Isaiah 56–66. They became sufficiently severe in the second half of the fifth century BCE that the Persian regime was apparently forced to intervene in the successive missions of the imperial governors, Nehemiah and Ezra.

The Immigrant Elite versus the People
of (Who Had Remained on) the Land

The Yehudim who returned from exile in Babylon to establish the temple-state in Jerusalem owed their new positions of power and privilege to their Persian overlords. They were also people who, from several generations' residence in Babylon, had been influenced by Babylonian and perhaps Persian culture and who, regardless of their sense of identity and political sympathies, understood the realities of empire. Ideologically, to judge from literature such as the books of Haggai and Ezra, the newly installed immigrant elite of Yehud identified their

God's purposes with Persian imperial purposes.[29] By entrusting the imperial order and revenues in Yehud to these immigrants, however, the Persians were imposing a privileged group of semiforeigners, who were strongly identified with the imperial overlords, on the indigenous people in Judea.[30]

It seems highly unlikely that the immigrants sent by the imperial regime would have been able to assert their dominance unchallenged by the people who had remained on the land. The latter had developed their own functioning village communities and indigenous (Israelite/Judahite) traditions. Local leadership would have emerged during the generations since the former Jerusalem elite had been deported. The vigorous exhortations by prophetic advocates of temple building indicate that the indigenous people put up stiff resistance to the project of the immigrants: "The time has not yet come" (Hag. 1:2). They did not have to be reminded that the recently restored Jerusalem elite, who would benefit from the construction, viewed them ("this people") as inferior, "unclean" (2:14).[31] Once the Temple was built, moreover, the "cursed" people apparently resisted bringing "the full tithe into the storehouse" (Mal. 3:10).

The response of the restored elite, however, was to assert their exclusive claims to the land, as well as to its fruits that were produced by the "cursed" people who labored on it. Some of the prophecies in the book of Ezekiel attempt to bolster the exiles' claim to the land as opposed to those of the people still living there (e.g., Ezek. 11:14–18; 33:23–27). Concern about the immigrants' claim to the land is also evident in the books of Ezra and Nehemiah (however late they may be dated). In Ezra the people of the returned (gōlâ) community, "the assembly of the exiles" (Ezra 10:8 NIV) or "the assembly of those who had returned from the captivity" (Neh. 8:17), were defined as the only true Yehudim. But this either excluded the indigenous "people of the land" or subordinated them to the higher caste of immigrants in control of temple-state as lesser-status people.[32]

The immigrants also justified their claim to the land with a self-serving construction of the Babylonian conquest: representing the land as destroyed and emptied of people. The only survivors, the only significant people, had been taken into exile (2 Chron. 36:17–21; Lev. 26:27–39). Hence the land was vacant, just waiting for their return. Significant sections of much Judean literature that later became part of the Hebrew Bible reflect their ideology and articulate their claim to the land.[33] Similarly the obsessive emphasis on genealogy, as in the book of Ezra, serves to justify the returnees' claim to the land. And the heavy emphasis on the imperial initiative in Ezra, with extensive citation of emperors' edicts and other official documents, indicates a need by the immigrants, who claimed the land and ruling power over "the people of the land," to legitimate themselves. But that also reveals the real source of their authorization and basis of their somewhat shaky position in Yehud.

To reinforce the severe exclusivity of the immigrants who claimed to be the only true Yehudim, intermarriage was strictly forbidden. Those already married to nonreturnees were forced to put away their "foreign" wives. All this was done with Ezra and the officials and elders of the community enforcing the ban of intermarriage under threat of exclusion from the community and forfeiture of property (Ezra 10:1–17). Clearly at least one motive for the prohibition of inter-marriage was to keep the landed property in the control of the "assembly of the [returned] exiles." That Ezra and Nehemiah, who insisted on this ban, were act-ing as agents of the Persian imperial regime, suggests an imperial agenda in this mechanism to maintain the land in the control of the "exile" assembly.[34] From the imperial viewpoint, conquered land belonged to the emperor/empire, and the imperial regime had sent the returnees to settle and hold it as a means of both security and revenues. And since marriage has implications for the transfer of property, it was important to maintain control through the returned community by banning marriage outside of the community of returnees.

This exclusive definition of who belonged to Yehud, while presumably strengthening the dominant group, however, would more likely have alienated the people of the land than to have reconciled them to the immigrants placed in charge of the temple-state in Jerusalem.[35] Indeed, the very establishment of a Temple and privileged hereditary priesthood would have had effects divisive as much as integrative in Yehud. Ideologically the Temple established sacred space and activity that separated the priesthood from the populace, those set apart for service at the altar from those who were rural, "unclean," and inferior.[36] As a religious-economic system, moreover, the Temple set up an inherent conflict of interest between those who were to bring the tithes and those who received and consumed the tithes. It seems inappropriate to refer to Yehud as "united" or as a "nation" since it was so fundamentally divided by the foundation of a temple-state.[37]

The Wealthy and Powerful versus the Peasantry

The other structural conflict, which probably overlapped with the previous con-flict to a considerable degree, was between the wealthy and powerful elite in Jerusalem and the subsistence peasantry living in village communities. The obli-gation of Judean villagers to pay both imperial taxes and tithes and offerings to priesthood and temple left them vulnerable to heavy indebtedness, perhaps even loss of children as debt-slaves and control of their lands to their wealthy credi-tors. Such exploitation of the peasants is a perennial problem in agrarian soci-eties, and Yehud was no exception.

> Now there was a great outcry of the people and of their wives against their fellow Yehudim: "We must get grain, so that we may eat and stay alive." . . . "We are having to pledge our fields, our vineyards, and our houses in order to get grain during the famine." "We are having to borrow goods on our fields and vineyards to pay the king's tribute. Now our flesh is the same as that of our kindred; our children are the same as their children; and yet we are forcing our sons and daughters to be slaves, and some of our daughters have been ravished; we are powerless, and our fields and vineyards now belong to others." (Neh. 5:1–5, alt.)

It would not have been historically unprecedented for a "higher authority," such as a king or an imperial governor, to intervene when exploitation by local nobles and officials threatened the survival of the peasantry, which constituted the productive base of the economy, as Nehemiah reportedly intervened in Yehud.

> I brought charges against the nobles and the officials: . . . "Let us stop this taking of interest [from your own people]. Restore to them, this very day, their fields, their vineyards, their olive orchards, and their houses, and the interest on goods, grain, wine, and oil that you have been exacting from them." . . . And I called the priests, and made them take an oath to do as they had promised. (Neh. 5:7–13)

As formulated, Nehemiah's speech appears to be informed by traditional Israelite (Mosaic) covenantal principles, such as the prohibition of interest (Exod. 22:25), and mechanisms to keep peasant households economically viable on their ancestral land, such as the seventh-year cancellation of debts (Lev. 25). This points to an important aspect of the two interrelated structural conflicts in Persian Yehud. Social-economic interaction among peasants in village communities operated according to a people's customs and cultural traditions, which in Yehud were presumably Israelite. These can perhaps be detected in the traditional materials edited in the Mosaic covenant itself, the "Covenant code" of Exodus 21–23, many Deuteronomic laws, and the various sabbatical provisions in Leviticus 25.

In cross-cultural terms, such Israelite traditions would have constituted the "moral economy" of the Judean peasants. Historical studies of medieval European peasantries and anthropological fieldwork among villagers in southeast Asia, for example, have found that people living in traditional village communities remain committed to a "moral economy" that guides local social-economic interaction. Peasants have certain mechanisms by which the community as a whole manages to keep each component household economically viable.[38] Cancellation of debts and release of debt-slaves every seven years would be obvious examples of this "moral economy" in Israelite tradition. The nobles and Temple officials in a position to make loans to desperate peasants, however, were not members of village communities. Hence they had little incentive from regular social interaction to observe such traditional customs. Indeed, by taking interest on loans they could expand the wealth of their own households.

A key aspect of the structural conflicts, both that between wealthy (priestly and lay) aristocracy and peasants and that between the immigrant in and around Jerusalem and the people who had remained on the land, may thus have been the different set of customs and covenantal/legal traditions they cultivated. In many agrarian societies one of the functions of religious elites is to develop an ideology, to cultivate cultural traditions in certain ways, in order to persuade the peasant producers to generate and part with a "surplus" that will support the wealthy and powerful. The immigrant Yehudim, however, seem to have been preoccupied with legitimating their own tenuous position in the newly established temple-state. The measures that Ezra found necessary to bolster the communal discipline of the immigrant community indicate how slow the more ambitious figures of prominence were to internalize the ideology of the returned exiles. And, as we can see in the memoirs of Nehemiah, it was necessary for the Persian governor to strong-arm the rapacious wealthy families so they would not destroy the viability of the peasantry, who formed the economic base for both temple-state and empire.

Priestly Groups

Another conflict, or perhaps a set of conflicts, was between priestly groups. It is very difficult to correlate the various lists and representations of the priests and Levites in Judean sources. It is even more difficult to make correlations between textual representations of priests and historical situations and political-religious relations. Recent surveys of the sources draw some important distinctions.[39] The only text to identify the priests qualified to serve at the altar as Zadokites is the description of the ideal temple in Ezekiel 40–48; this suggests caution about the standard assumption that the Zadokites were the dominant priesthood in second-temple times. Texts from second-temple times, the Priestly sources in the Pentateuch and Chronicles, represent the priests who serve at the altar as "sons of Aaron," with the Levites in important but subsidiary roles. The Deuteronomic history (Joshua through 2 Kings) and the prophets, however, barely mention Aaron.

At least three particular conflicts between priestly groups are evident in Yehud: (1) between priests who remained in the land and the priests who came to dominant positions under the Persians; (2) between priests and Levites, also involving other groups that served in the Temple; and (3) between the emerging priestly aristocracy and other priestly lineages.

1. While the Babylonians deported the Jerusalem priesthood based in Solomon's Temple (Zadokites? others?), other priestly groups were left on the land (some Aaronides, some Levites, sons of Abiathar). There is evidence that, after Jerusalem was destroyed, other sacred sites and attendant priestly families continued to function. It seems likely that a temple at Bethel or Mizpah even served as a central sanctuary, with an Aaronide priesthood (as mentioned above).[40] These Aaronide and perhaps Levites and priests of the Abiathar lineage (in Anathoth) who had remained in the land would have been displaced by the immigrant priestly families in the Jerusalem Temple. Presumably they offered resistance, criticizing the immigrants as having been defiled. The prophecy in Zech. 3:1–10 is presumably the response, declaring the divine purification and investment of the high priest Joshua and his colleagues as the legitimate priesthood.

2. The conflict best attested in Judean sources was between the Aaronide priests and the Levites. This conflict appears (eventually) to have also involved other groups who served in the Temple apparatus: the singers, the temple servants, and the gatekeepers (Ezra 8:15–36; Neh. 3:26, 31; 7:1, 43–46; 11:19–22). There are a number of indications that the Levites gradually lost status over the course of second-temple history.[41] Especially striking are the indications that the Aaronides and/or Zadokites consolidated their own power by diminishing the

role and status of the Levites. A fragment included in the book of Jeremiah antic-ipates a standard priestly role for them in the aftermath of the Babylonian con-quest: "The levitical priests shall never lack a man in my presence to offer burnt offerings, to make grain offerings, and to make sacrifices for all time" (Jer. 33:18). In Nehemiah the Levites are responsible for collecting the tithes and bringing them up to the storage chambers in the house of God (Neh. 10:35–39). Here the Levites still have greater responsibilities and status than "the gatekeepers and singers" (10:39). The Aaronide priests, however, are to supervise: "The priest, the descendant of Aaron, shall be with the Levites when they receive the tithes" (10:38). The Aaronide priests would appear to be exerting control over the gath-ering and storage of Temple revenues. Perhaps priestly manipulation of distrib-ution stands behind Nehemiah's discovery that the Levites and singers had ceased conducting services in the Temple and gone back to their fields, since "the por-tions of the Levites had not been given to them" (13:10).

Nehemiah's "reform" evidently restored the role and rights of the Levites, although it would not have changed their second-class status. Ezra certainly appears to have cooperated with them, perhaps even favored them. Ezekiel 44, on the other hand, even charges the Levites with apostasy, while the Zadokites faithfully run the sanctuary. As punishment the Levites were supposedly banished from service at the altar and confined to more menial chores such as gatekeeping and custodial care of the Temple premises. Passages in Chronicles suggest that during the Persian period the singers, gatekeepers and other low-ranking temple servants were gradually associated with or even identified as the Levites (1 Chron. 9:26, 33; 23:3–5; 25:1–7; 26:1–11). The book of Malachi may reflect the Levites' attempt to fight back. It appeals to the tradition of God's covenant with Levi, which supposedly antedated God's covenant with Zadok (Mal. 2:4–10). It assures that the Lord will come to his temple and, like a refiner's fire, "purify the sons of Levi . . . until they present offerings to YHWH in righteousness, . . . as in the days of old" (Mal. 3:1–4, au. trans.).

3. From the outset the prophets of the restoration have the high priesthood central to the temple-state. There are several indications that a priestly aristocracy emerged that was closely associated with the presiding high priest. Closer analysis of genealogies in Ezra and 1 Chronicles that were previously taken as legitimating lineages of the high priests of the second Temple suggests that they functioned more generally as the authorizing lineages of priestly families or branches of priestly families of special rank, qualifying them for high office, including the high priesthood.[42] Late in the Persian period a petition of the Judean military colonists at Elephantine in Upper Egypt mentions "our Lord Yehohanan the high priest and his colleagues the priests who are in Jerusalem" (parallel to "Ostanes the brother of 'Anani and to the nobles of the Judeans").[43] The priestly colleagues are pre-sumably a small elite group, not all the altar priests (cf. "the elders of the Judeans and the temple officers," 1 Esd. 7:2, au. trans.; the Judean gerousia in Jdt. 4:8; 11:14; 15:8). Other priestly families accordingly had to settle into less prominent roles, subordinate to the direction of the priestly officials.

Persian policy surely strengthened the position of the priestly aristocracy. But the other priestly factions, although gradually losing ground to the dominant elite, while leaving few traces of their interests and viewpoints, did not disappear from the society. Insofar as priestly groups were the principal cultivators of legal and historical traditions, they would almost certainly have cultivated their own versions of Judahite/Israelite tradition, alternatives to that cultivated by the dominant.[44] The different legal collections that were eventually included in the Pentateuch may well have been associated with the different groups of priests and Levites that struggled for position and influence in the temple-state. The compromise represented by the Pentateuch attests precisely such different priestly groups and their traditions that contested the dominant ideology and legal tradition.

Local Magnates and Persian Officers

Far from Yehud having been stabilized under a strong monarchical high priesthood, there appears to have been repeated struggles and maneuvering for power, position, and wealth between local magnates and representatives of the Persian regime and/or among the local magnates. The book of Nehemiah provides several (retrospective) windows onto such struggles; other sources indicate that such maneuvering must have been endemic in the Persian imperial system and not peculiar to Yehud or to the situation dealt with by Nehemiah.

The priestly families in charge of the temple-state knew well that their positions of power and privilege depended on imperial favor, yet pretended that they were independent. They needed Persian authorization and Persian governors for rebuilding the Temple. Their prophets (Zechariah, Haggai, Malachi), however, claimed that they were commanded directly by their God Yahweh to rebuild the Temple. The visions of Zechariah downplay the role of Zerubbabel while emphasizing that of Joshua the high priest and his colleagues. The Persian governor (and Davidic descendant), to be sure, is the one commissioned to construct the Temple, but he acts only as an administrator (*mšl*) on behalf of the real king (the emperor or YHWH), and not as a king himself (Zech. 4:8; 6:9–13). What might have been thought to be his crown is deposited as a memorial in the temple (6:14). The high priest Joshua, on the other hand, envisioned as standing before the angel of YHWH, is clothed with festal apparel and receives both a turban and a crown and is given charge of the Temple (3:1–10; 6:9–13). At the more mundane level of the construction of the Temple or city walls, however, the high priest and other priestly aristocrats took their place alongside the ordinary Judeans in the labor gangs who did the physical work—as supervised by the Persian governor and his Persian military officers.

As was true in any ancient Near Eastern temple-state, monarchy, or empire, those in positions of power sought to enhance their own income by taking advantage of the perpetual difficulties of a marginal peasantry. The typical device was to make loans to desperate peasants at high rates of interest and, as peasant indebtedness spirals, to take effective control of their (family inheritance) land

and/or of their children as debt-slaves. Kings and emperors, however, have a longer-range interest in the viability of the peasantry as their economic base. This was apparently the situation in fifth-century Judea, as Nehemiah took severe measures against the priestly aristocracy and/or the nobles and officers of the temple-state (Neh. 5:1–13, see just above). Yet in some cases the Persian governor or other imperial officer might also have engaged in such exploitation of the people, something that Nehemiah claims to have scrupulously avoided (5:14–16).

In addition to the Judean priestly aristocracy, powerful figures in adjacent subdivisions of the satrapy Beyond the River had interests and influence in Yehud that did not coincide with Persian imperial interests, at least as represented by Nehemiah and other governors. The book of Nehemiah claims that from the outset his project of (re)building the Temple fortress and the city walls was opposed by three magnates in particular: Sanballat the Horonite, Persian governor in Samaria just to the north; Tobiah the Ammonite, apparently the Persian-appointed official in charge of Ammon to the east; and Geshem the Arab (2:10, 19; 6:1–9; cf. 3:33–4:17 [chap. 4E]).[45] The Persians had appointed powerful local sheikhs or "big men" as imperial officers, whose families had effectively gained hereditary local power. These local power holders had also established a degree of influence in Yehud by various means, such as the Tobiads' and Sanballat's intermarriage with the high-priestly family (Neh. 13:4, 28). The reassertion of more effective Persian control and supervision of Yehud by the new governor Nehemiah, however, effectively placed a check on their influence and maneuvering in Judean affairs. Yet as local appointees of the Persian regime, they could themselves undermine their rival Nehemiah's position (accuse him of "rebelling against the king," Neh. 2:19).

As indicated in the intermarriage between the ruling families, local power holders such as the Judean high priest and Tobiah conspired to advance their mutual interests to the detriment of other officers and beneficiaries or the temple-community, and against the authority of the Persian governor. Apparently while Nehemiah was on an extended journey to the imperial court, Eliashib, the priest in charge of the storage chambers of the Temple, cleared out a large room previously used to store temple vessels and the tithes for support of the Levites, singers, gatekeepers, and priests for the use of his relative Tobiah (Neh. 13:4–6). Eliashib thus set Tobiah up to conduct his enterprises directly out of the precincts of the Temple, which was the controlling center of the Judean economy. When he returned to Jerusalem, however, Nehemiah "threw all the household furniture of Tobiah out of the room" and gave orders to purify the chambers for storage of the temple vessels, incense, and tithed grain and oil (Neh. 13:4–9). This action may have temporarily checked the Judean operations of Tobiah in Jerusalem, but the Tobiads continued to exert considerable influence in Judea by maneuvering between the local and imperial power holders (as discussed in the next chapter).

The cases of the Tobiads and Sanballat also illustrate how elite families among the Yehudim intermarried with prominent families in surrounding areas. Such intermarriages enhanced the political-economic power of these already powerful families and cemented their interrelations at the expense of their individual subordination to Persian control. This intermarriage also undermined cohesion among the Judean aristocracy and led to the diffusion and dilution of the language and culture that might hold them together. In connection with these intermarriages, Nehemiah is portrayed as complaining that half of the children could not speak the language of Yehud (was it a dialect of Hebrew or Aramaic?) "but spoke the language of various peoples" (13:23–24). Even Jerusalemite prophets, who may have been clients of some of the Jerusalem priestly magnates or of Tobiah, attacked Nehemiah and his programs.

This, along with the previous examples, illustrates how the cohesion of the temple-state and the Judean elite that the Persians had placed in charge was a key concern of the Persian regime. It was a principal means of controlling the subject population of Yehud, perhaps especially the very families that the Persians placed in charge, who often sought their own interests to the detriment of both the temple-community and Persian imperial interests. In a seeming irony, it was the representatives of the Persian Empire, Nehemiah and Ezra, who pressed the prohibition of intermarriage with other nearby peoples, an action against the leading families of the priestly aristocracy.

A combination of evidence, finally, points to a case (was it unique?) of a governor and a leading priestly figure engaged in mutual machinations against other powerful priestly figures. This case, moreover, is interconnected with a conflict within the Persian imperial regime over a related conflict in a district of Egypt. The first-century CE Judean historian Josephus writes of a power struggle between a high priest named Joannes (Yohanan, son of Jodas/Yehoida, son of Eliashib) and Bagoses, the general of Artaxerxes.

> Joannes had a brother named Jesus (Yehosua), and Bagoses, whose friend he was, promised to obtain the high priesthood for him. With this assurance, therefore, Jesus quarreled with Joannes in the temple and provoked his brother so far that in his anger he killed him. . . . When Bagoses attempted to enter the Temple, they sought to prevent him. [But] he went into the Temple, and on this pretext . . . made the Judeans suffer seven years for the death of Jesus. (*Ant.* 11.297–301).

Not only does this appear to be the same high priest as "Yohahan the Priest" in the Paleo-Hebrew legend on a silver coin minted around the 380s BCE. This also is apparently the same "Yohahan the high priest" with his priestly colleagues to whom the Jews in Elephantine had written three years earlier, appealing for aid "to our lord Bagavahya, governor of Yehud," who along with Delaiah, son of Sanballat, governor of Samaria, responded to their appeal after Yohahan had not.[46] It is difficult to tell whether Jesus/Yehosua was the ranking priest who married the daughter of Sanballat (mentioned in Neh. 13:4). It is at least clear that Bagavahya, the governor of Yehud, together with Delaiah, the governor of Samaria, came down on the opposite side of a conflict in Elephantine from

Yohanan the high priest, and that Bagavahya also conspired with Yehosua/Jesus against Yohahan (had the latter sided with the central Persian authorities?). And when Yohanan foiled the conspiracy, Badavahya asserted his power forcibly against Yohahan and other priests in the temple.

THE TEMPLE-STATE AND THE PEOPLE OF YEHUD TOWARD THE END OF PERSIAN RULE

Given the multiple conflicts, it seems inappropriate to refer to the Judeans as a "unified people." To imagine Yehud as a "nation" developing a "national" heritage is simply anachronistic.[47] To say that the Judeans were "governing themselves" more or less "according to their own laws" may have been partly true of the immigrant minority in Yehud. The majority, however, the descendants of those who had remained on the land after the Babylonian conquest, were in various ways subjected to the laws and religious-economic demands of those in charge of the newly established temple-state. It seems unlikely that "the people of the land" would have become reconciled with the immigrants backed by the Persians, particularly when the latter, at the insistence of representatives of the imperial regime such as Ezra and Nehemiah, withdrew within boundaries of exclusivity guarded by prohibitions of intermarriage. And Yehud was hardly "autonomous," but subject to the governors sent by the Persian imperial regime.

A priestly aristocracy headed by a "high priest" was apparently able to secure at least a tenuous hold on power in the Jerusalem Temple itself, yet checked and limited by several factors. This could hardly be described as a "priestly monarchy," for the high priest shared or competed for authority with other powerful figures.[48] The high priest and the heads of the most prominent priestly families probably operated in ad hoc fashion and should not be misunderstood as a formal council with a set membership (the "Sanhedrin" of later, rabbinic literature).[49] Nonpriestly magnates also played a prominent role in Jerusalem, but Tobiah's intermarriage with the high-priestly family suggests that the high priesthood was the center of power.

This suggests a different way of reading the description of the Judeans in the late fourth century by Hecataeus of Abdera, which has been taken as solid evidence that a priestly monarchy had been firmly established in Jerusalem by the close of the Persian period.[50] Most of the key features of Hecataeus's portrayal— the priests as judges and guardians of the laws as well as temple officiants, headed by a high priest revered as messenger of God's commandments, all authorized by the laws of Moses—resemble, and could have been derived (directly or indirectly) from, the dominant Jerusalem priestly circles, who were earlier authorized by the books of Ezra and Nehemiah and their version of the laws of Moses. That is, Hecataeus's representation apparently derives from the idealized self-image and self-legitimation of the high priesthood and priestly aristocracy struggling to consolidate their power in late Persian times.

Underneath the idealized self-image of the priestly aristocrats, however, was a continuing struggle with rival priestly groups, powerful nonpriestly figures, and the Persian governors. They must have subordinated other priestly factions, but the latter apparently persisted as factions struggling for influence in the Temple and wider society. Governors such as Nehemiah may have temporarily checked the maneuvering of magnates such as Tobiah and the nobles' and officials' exploitation of the people. Yet high priests, other powerful Judean figures, and "big men" such as Tobiah continued their maneuvering for power and advantage. That the Persian regime sent Nehemiah and Ezra to carry out "reforms" indicates that the immigrant families backed by the Persians were unable to establish stabilizing control of Judea by the end of the fifth century.[51]

However the high priesthood of the Jerusalem Temple may have thought of itself as authorized by and in service of its God, it continued to be a political-economic as well as religious institution that served as the instrument of imperial rule of Judea. Throughout the local struggle for power in Yehud, the priests in charge were dependent on imperial favor, were expected to meet imperial demands, and at times were subject to direct intervention by the imperial authorities. It appears that the struggle for power at the top in the temple-state persisted through Achaemenid times, and that the local struggles in Yehud were closely related to policies and decisions in the imperial court. This situation continued into the Hellenistic empires, as we shall see.[52]

Chapter 2

The Judean Temple-State
under the Hellenistic Empires

*[Moses] picked out the men of most refinement and with the greatest abil-
ity to head the entire people, and appointed them priests . . . and entrusted
to them the guardianship of the laws and customs.*

Hecataeus

*When the emperor assented and Jason became [high priest], he at once
shifted his compatriots over to the Greek way of life. He set aside the existing royal concessions to the Judeans . . . and dissolved the laws of the constitution and set up new customs contrary to the laws.*

2 Maccabees

After Alexander the Great's whirlwind conquest of the territories of the Persian
Empire in the 330s BCE, his "Successors" established rival empires, the Ptolemies
in Egypt and the Seleucids in Syria, Babylonia, and eastward. At first the patterns
of societal life in Judea continued more or less as they were at the end of Persian
rule. The families backed by the Persians had, to an extent, consolidated their
power over the people of the land, who had remained after the Babylonian conquest. The high priesthood and priestly aristocracy headed the Temple, which
stood at the center of the religiously focused economy of Judea. Powerful families such as the Tobiads in the Transjordan still intermarried with the leading
priestly family and otherwise maneuvered for position and influence.

The primary purpose of the Ptolemaic and Seleucid empires, like that of the
Persians, was the extraction of revenues from the territories they controlled.
When they replaced the Persians, the Hellenistic empires perpetuated the fundamental tributary structures of empire, with minor variations. The multiple
conflicts in Judea that we detected under the Persians, moreover, continued under
the Ptolemies and Seleucids. Because of rivalries and instabilities at the imperial

level, however, the situation in Jerusalem became even more susceptible to maneuvering between rivals for power and position during the Hellenistic period.

CHANGES IN THE IMPERIAL SITUATION
AND ADMINISTRATION

The extreme paucity of reliable sources for the Ptolemaic period in Judea makes it extremely difficult to reconstruct its history. Evidence that is often fragmentary, however, suggests that four interrelated changes in the imperial situation and administration contributed to intensified struggles among the powerful families that controlled affairs in Judea. Competition between the imperial regimes for control of Palestine and shifts within each imperial regime's means of maximizing its revenues opened greater opportunities for rival factions in the Jerusalem aristocracy to maneuver for position and power. Because such maneuvering was related to increasing the imperial revenues, it inevitably meant increased exploitation of the peasants, exacerbating tensions between "the people of the land" and the power holders in Jerusalem. Caught somewhere in the middle would have been the ordinary priests, Levites, and scribes. After sketching the four interrelated changes in imperial structure and administration, we can then focus on three crises in which conflict came to a head in Judea, at first within the ruling aristocracy, but eventually leading into a wider conflict that engulfed the whole society.

1. Power Struggles between and within Imperial Regimes

The "Successors" (*Diadochoi*) of Alexander the Great divided among themselves the territories previously held together by the Persian Empire and engaged in periodic warfare with one another to control disputed areas. Judea, located in the crucial buffer area between the Ptolemies in Egypt and the Seleucids in Syria, was caught in a century-long series of wars and other disputes for control of Syria-Palestine.[1]

Thirty years after Alexander's conquests a treaty among some of his Successors warring over the imperial territories assigned Syria to Seleucus. But Ptolemy had seized control of southern Syria and Palestine. The Seleucids spent the next century periodically trying to regain what they viewed as their territory, with only temporary successes until 200 BCE. Through the first four of a series of prolonged "Syrian wars," the Ptolemies managed to hold on to the area. For the third of those wars (246–241), however, there is evidence that Judeans cultivated memories of considerable uncertainty about which regime would prevail (Dan. 11:5–9). In the fourth Syrian war (221–219) Antiochus III did manage to take considerable territory in western Syria before being driven back in 217, a war whose implications for Judea were still on the minds of Judean scribes two generations later (Dan. 11:10–12). In the fifth war (201–200) Antiochus III finally took control of Syria and Phoenicia, bringing Judea under Seleucid rule.

Compounding the rivalry between the two empires for control of Palestine were periodic conflicts between rival claimants to the kingship among both the Ptolemies and the Seleucids, and periodic rebellions, especially in territories subject to the Seleucids. Shortly after the Seleucids took control of Judea and the rest of Syria-Palestine, moreover, the Romans intervened more actively in the eastern Mediterranean, checking their advancement. Payments of reparation as well as military defeats by the Romans left the Seleucid regime weakened and desperate for funds.

These periodic imperial wars and conflicts within imperial regimes set up a periodically uncertain situation for the heads of the temple-state and other powerful figures in Judea. Uncertainties at the imperial level and the imperial regimes' greed and urgent need for revenues opened opportunities for ambitious local figures to maneuver for position and gain.

2. No Governor in Judea

The Ptolemies and later the Seleucids appointed military governors (*stratēgoi*) for the whole area of Syria and Phoenicia. The Greek historian Polybius supplies the names of several of these toward the end of the third century, of whom Thraseas and his son Ptolemy, who defected to the Seleucids, are of particular interest for events in Judea (Polybius 5.65.3–4; 5.87.6).[2] The Ptolemies and the Seleucids, however, did not continue the Persian practice of appointing governors specifically to supervise affairs in Judea, with a military garrison at their disposal.[3] On the one hand, this would seem to have strengthened the position of the high priest(hood) at the head of the temple-state in Jerusalem, who could operate without the immediate oversight of an imperial governor. On the other hand, the absence of an imperial governor left more room for power struggles within the mainly priestly aristocracy in Judea. It opened the way for powerful and ambitious figures in Judea to seek influence in the imperial regime parallel to that of the high priest, as happened in the area of tax collection.

3. Uncertain Imperial Support of the High Priesthood

The temple-state continued into the Hellenistic period. A priestly aristocracy, headed by the high priest, consolidated its control over the Temple, with the Levites and other priests and temple-servants in a subordinate role. While the description of the Judeans by Hecataeus cannot be taken at face value as attesting a priestly monarchy in Judea,[4] this sketch of the Judean "constitution" (*politeia*) probably reflects how the Judean priestly elite viewed their own position as an aristocracy headed by a high priest in charge of Judean society.[5]

> [Having] established the Temple that they hold in chief veneration . . . , [Moses] drew up their laws and ordered their political institutions. . . . He picked out the men of most refinement and with the greatest ability to head the entire people, and appointed them priests. . . . [and] judges in all major disputes, and entrusted to them the guardianship of the laws and customs.

> For this reason the Judeans never have a king, and representation [*prostasia*] of the people is regularly vested in whichever priest is regarded as superior to his colleagues in wisdom and virtue. . . . the high priest, who in their assemblies and other gatherings announces what is ordained.
> (Hecataeus, in Diodorus Siculus, *Biblioteca historica* 40.3.3–6)

As in the Persian period, however, there was plenty of push and pull from other priestly groups and from other power brokers such as the Tobiads.

Under the Ptolemies, however, the relative power of the temple-state was diminished. In contrast to the Persians, who had actively backed the temple-state (while periodically trying to reform its operation), the Ptolemaic regime appears to have simply let it remain in place to run affairs in Judea so long as expected revenues were forthcoming. That may have meant, on the one hand, that they did not intervene in the priestly aristocracy's internal administration of the temple-state. On the other hand, we have no evidence that the Ptolemies appointed or formally approved the high priesthood to head the temple-state and to rule Judea. This meant that, without the strong backing of the imperial regime, the Jerusalem high priesthood was vulnerable to the machinations of rival local figures. The imperial regime, moreover, not having committed to maintain the high priesthood in power, could easily undermine its position in Jerusalem, for example, by alternative arrangements for collection of tribute. The Seleucid regime, apparently following more the Persian practice than the Ptolemaic, used the priestly aristocracy and high priesthood as its instrument for control and taxation of Judea. In its desperate need for revenue, however, it opened the way for one aristocratic faction to outbid another for control of the temple-state.

4. Shifting Patterns of Financial Administration

Some recent treatments of Ptolemaic administration of Judea make what appear to be mutually contradictory statements.[6] On the one hand, relying on older reconstructions of Ptolemaic political economy as a rigidly centralized system closely managed down to the village level, they state that the regime treated Judea as just one more subdivision of Egypt. They do not explain how a supposedly "expanding trade" was possible outside of such a centrally administered state-economy. On the other hand, when they deal with the limited evidence available for Judea and western Syria, they note that the Ptolemaic regime was often de facto dealing with and through local magnates. Other studies of Ptolemaic Egypt have recognized that centralized control of the economy was an idea never realized in Egypt itself, much less in other subjected areas.[7] It is beginning to appear that although the Ptolemies set up an elaborate system of military and economic administration in Egypt, they adapted it to local circumstances. For example, they worked through many of the age-old temples in parts of Egypt, which were thus allowed a degree of self-administration, rather than replacing them with other bureaucratic structures.[8]

Certainly the Ptolemies adapted to local circumstances in Syria-Palestine. The well-known Zenon papyri give clear evidence of large estates managed, with considerable attention to local details, by officers of the king. But generalizations cannot be drawn from the management of these estates to the administration of Palestine generally. Some of the Zenon papyri themselves indicate that the Ptolemies depended on local sheikhs and their armed men, such as the Tobiads in the Transjordan, to maintain the imperial order, at least along the frontier.[9] The Ptolemies would likely have appointed a financial officer generally responsible for oversight of the state-managed "trade" of goods taken from Palestine to Egypt. That may have included tax collection as well. But they also clearly generated revenues from the area by means of "farming" the taxes: taking bids from local power brokers who guaranteed a certain level of taxes from a given area, and then extracted more that they kept as their "profit." This tax-farming arrangement set up potential rivalry between the tax-farmers and (other) local rulers, aristocrats, city elites, and sheikhs. It also created opportunities for ambitious figures to exploit the tax-farming system to augment their own wealth and regional power. The Seleucid regime reverted to the Persian practice of working through the high priestly administration of the Jerusalem temple-state. But they also took opportunities to augment the imperial revenues by taking higher bids for the high priesthood from rival factions of the Jerusalem priestly aristocracy. This invited destabilizing power struggles between the aristocratic factions in Jerusalem.

These interrelated changes in the relation between the imperial regime and the temple-state exacerbated conflicts within the Judean aristocracy. We can see how this complex interrelationship between the conflicts at the imperial level and the struggles for power and position in Jerusalem worked in a succession of three ever more intense crises in the temple-state in the late third and early second centuries BCE—the time during which early Enoch texts, Sirach, and Daniel were produced.

FIRST CRISIS: ARISTOCRATIC FACTIONS UNDER THE PTOLEMAIC EMPIRE

Our principal (but by no means only) source for the first and second of these crises is "the Tobiad romance" that Josephus follows at some length in the *Antiquities* (12.156–222, 228–236). It reads like a historical novel, rich with fictional embellishments. The romance presents both of its heroes, Joseph son of Tobias and Hyrcanus son of Joseph, in ways reminiscent of the portrayal of the patriarch Joseph, son of Jacob, in the Genesis narrative.[10] Even though its legendary features have been acknowledged, too much credence has been placed in its value as a reliable source.[11] Yet it cannot be dismissed as "a completely fictitious story."[12] Some of its claims about Hyrcanus seem to contradict reasonable inferences from other sources. Yet its main characters are known from other sources, its geographical information is confirmed by both literary and archaeological evidence, and many of its details about tax-farming as practiced by the Ptolemaic regime are corroborated by papyri and inscriptions.[13] Analyzed critically in connection with these other, corroborating sources, the Tobiah romance can be used, along with supplementary sources, as a source for these crises among factions of the Judean ruling elite that are interrelated with the rivalries and fissures of imperial control.

The first major crisis that emerged between factions in the aristocracy that ruled Judea revolved around Joseph son of Tobias, the first hero of the Tobiad romance. The best procedure may be to summarize the story and then analyze it from the perspective of the major features of the imperial situation sketched just above. The following summary of the first part of the "romance" (*Ant.* 12.156–191)[14] purposely omits most of what are clearly entertaining embellishments and allusions to the Joseph story in Genesis. Included are details that, while probably fictional, have figured importantly in scholarly reconstructions.

After Onias, son of Simon, had taken over the high priesthood, he did not render the tribute that his ancestors had paid to the kings out of their revenues, thus rousing the anger of Ptolemy. The king accordingly sent an envoy to threaten that Jerusalem would be made into a military colony. In response the young man Joseph, son of Tobias by a sister of the high priest Onias, argued that his uncle was placing the people [*ethnos*] in danger by not paying the tribute on account of which he had received the *prostasia* of the people and the high priestly office, and he managed to get himself appointed emissary to the Ptolemaic court. When the Ptolemaic envoy arrived in Jerusalem, Joseph presented him with valuable gifts and entertained him lavishly for many days, thus winning his admiration and favor. In turn, the imperial envoy greatly assisted Joseph in gaining high favor at the imperial court, which he funded from what he had borrowed from friends in Samaria. Enamored by his charm, Ptolemy invited him to take up residence in the palace.

Thus when the time came for "all the chief men and magistrates of the cities of Syria and Phoenicia to bid for the tax-farming rights which the king used to sell every year to the wealthy men in each city," Joseph was in an advantageous position to outbid them all, collectively. Having offered to double the king's revenues, he was rewarded with the tax-farming rights to all of Syria, without the usual guarantors, and given imperial cavalry with which to enforce his demands for higher taxes. When Ascalon and Scythopolis proved recalcitrant, he simply executed "the principal men" and expropriated their property for the king. Having made great profits for himself as well, he used his wealth to consolidate his power, with lavish gifts to king and queen and high ranking officers at the imperial court, in a career that lasted twenty-two years. "This good fortune he enjoyed for twenty-two years, becoming the father of seven sons by one wife, and also begetting a son, named Hyrcanus, by the daughter of his brother Solymius. . . . He sent his sons one after another to those who were then famed as teachers (*paideuein*)" (summary paraphrase of Josephus, *Ant.* 12.156–191).

Evident underneath all the fictional embellishment in this part of the Tobiad romance are some key interrelated patterns in which the relations of power between the Ptolemaic regime and the principal wielders of power in Judea were structured. Those key patterns can be discerned by comparison with corroborating sources. The overall course of the story, moreover, indicates how the overall pattern of those power relations was shifting.

There is general consensus that the figures and events portrayed in the story belong at the time of Ptolemy III Euergetes (246–221 BCE) rather than under Ptolemy V Epiphanes (204–180 BCE), where Josephus has placed the story in his history (when the Ptolemaic regime no longer controlled Syria). This dating meshes well with evidence for the Tobiads in the Zenon papyri, our other major source for affairs in Judea and Syria in mid-third century. Zenon, the agent of Apollonius, finance minister (*dioikētēs*) of Ptolemy II Philadelphus (282–246), traveled extensively in Palestine and southern Syria in 259 BCE to tend to various matters of administration, including the large estate at Bet-Anat (along the Huleh valley in the north of Galilee) assigned to Apollonius. Some of his correspondence from this journey provides evidence of affairs in Judea and immediately surrounding areas. Most significant here are his exchanges with Tobiah, who must be the father of Joseph.

As indicated in these papyri, the Ptolemies established cleruchies (*klērouchia*), military colonies as local garrisons to control various areas in Syria-Palestine as well as in Egypt. In Egypt itself, the commanders of these garrisons were always Greeks. In Ammon, across the Jordan from Jerusalem, however, they placed a unit of cavalry under Tobiah (*CPJ* 1). This must have been the latest head of the same Tobiad family that had controlled the area under Persian rule, and had long since been intermarrying with the high priestly family in Jerusalem and playing a prominent role in the temple-state. In other papyri this same Tobiah writes to Ptolemy Philadelphus himself as well as to the *dioikētēs* Apollonius and sends them gifts, rare animals, and four young slaves accompanied by a eunuch (*CPJ* 4–5). Another papyrus refers to "Tobiah's land," suggesting that he was "a wealthy 'sheikh' known throughout the region."[15] Tobiah's cavalrymen were of mixed background, Macedonian, Greek, Persian, and Judean (*CPJ* 1). And his own household or staff seem to have been multiethnic as well. The formula of greeting that began his letters to Apollonius has the Greek expression "many thanks to the gods," which must have been written by his scribe, who was probably a Greek (*CPJ* 4). But it also suggests that Tobiah understood that knowledge of Greek was necessary for a family operating as a local agent and military officer of the imperial administration. Tobiah's son Joseph, after his wider experience in the cosmopolitan world of Hellenistic imperial administration, knew even more the importance of exposure to high culture for his sons, as suggested in his having them tutored in Greek *paideia* by the best-known teachers.

As the son of the high priest Onias's sister, Joseph would have had considerable influence in Jerusalem as well as a military fortress and forces across the Jordan. On the basis of his father's role as a local representative of Ptolemaic imperial rule in Ammon, he already had the basis from which he could seek fuller influence in the imperial regime and a wider role in Syria and Phoenicia.

In the Tobiad romance Joseph's rise to power entailed a change in the arrangement by which the Ptolemies received tribute from Judea. The occasion for Joseph's skillful maneuvering for position in the Ptolemaic regime was the refusal by the high priest Onias to pay the tribute as his ancestors had. In Egypt the Ptolemies used the long-standing temples as instruments of imperial control and revenues, and it makes considerable sense that they did the same in Judea. The statement (by Josephus) that payment of the tribute was the basis on which he held the high priesthood—along with the angry king's threat of imposing a military cleruchy upon Jerusalem—points to the regime's (at least passive) acceptance of the high priest(hood) as the head of the Jerusalem temple-state so long as their revenue was forthcoming.

However, there is no reason to take *prostasia/prostatēs* as a technical term for a formal office (chief magistracy) or even as some sort of "authority over" the people of Judea conferred by the Ptolemaic regime.[16] *Prostasia* may indicate rather that the Ptolemaic regime had recognized Onias or the high priest as the representative head of the Judeans in relation to the regime, at least for purposes of the tribute. This accords with the use of the same term in Hecataeus's account of the Judeans, where "high priest" indicates the religious-political office or role within the priestly aristocracy that headed up the temple-state, and *prostasia* indicated a representative headship of (not necessarily "authority over") the people vis-à-vis the imperial regime.

To replace the ridiculous reasons offered in the Tobiad romance for why the high priest Onias withheld tribute from the Ptolemies (he was mean and greedy), historians have suggested that Onias was pro-Seleucid.[17] It was simple political-economic realism for local rulers and other magnates to gauge the winds of imperial political fortune, and to be prepared to shift loyalties with changes in imperial regimes. The most likely time at which the Jerusalem aristocracy would have been prepared to shift allegiance, as well as the most likely for Tobiad chronology, was in the late 220s, in connection with the Seleucid Antiochus III's advances into Syria-Palestine.[18]

The most historically credible part of the whole Tobiad narrative is the description of how the tax-farming was set up (Josephus, *Ant.* 12.168–169, 177–178, 181–183). Taxes were auctioned every year, in Alexandria[19] and by the emperor himself.[20] Those who bought the tax contracts were indeed required to supply guarantors.[21] And the property of those who failed to render the taxes was indeed confiscated, although the tax-farmers themselves did not have the power to execute such confiscations.[22] As noted above, recent studies of Ptolemaic administration recognize that the regime relied on local power holders to control the populace and especially to gather revenues in Syria much more than in Egypt itself.[23]

The whole Tobiad romance depends on Joseph having attained a position of considerable power with regard to taxation in Syria-Palestine. Even if his authority and influence had focused as much or more on Palestine outside of Judea as in Judea itself, it would have made him a powerful figure in the affairs of Judea.

If the Ptolemaic regime did indeed make a change in the way they obtained trib-ute from Judea, then it may well be that the regime worked through Joseph as the "representative" (*prostasia*) of/for Judea. The Ptolemaic regime, whose main interest in any case was to maximize its revenues, could have simply bypassed the high priesthood and contracted with a local power holder in a family whose loy-alty it trusted to supply the tribute from Judea.

The expanding role of the Tobiad Joseph would have correspondingly weak-ened the power of the high priesthood. Joseph himself would have become a prominent player in Judean affairs, rivaling the power of the high priest, both because of his expanding wealth and because of his favor and influence in the Ptolemaic regime. This rivalry for power in Judea was new only in its degree, and it was not a "new class" of "country landlords."[24] It was rather a development on the basis of internal conflicts that continued from the Persian period. For gener-ations the Tobiads had an independent power base in lands across the Jordan, had intermarried with the high-priestly aristocracy, and played an influential role in Judea's affairs. Joseph's expansion of Tobiad power in Judea and beyond, however, relativized that of the high priest and prepared the way for further maneuvering by rival factions within the Jerusalem aristocracy, just at a time when the rivalry between the Ptolemaic and Seleucid imperial regimes was coming to a head.

SECOND CRISIS: ARISTOCRATIC FACTIONS AND THE CHANGE OF IMPERIAL REGIMES

The struggles between factions within the Jerusalem aristocracy continued dur-ing the last decades of Ptolemaic rule in the late third century. Much of the schol-arly discussion of these events has been conducted on the belief that long before the "Hellenizing" reform launched in 175 BCE (see below), two opposing par-ties had crystallized among the aristocracy in Jerusalem: a more traditionalist pro-Ptolemaic party and a Hellenizing party that was pro-Seleucid, presumably because of the latter's supposedly more aggressive advocacy of Hellenistic cul-ture.[25] These parties are presumed to have been operative already in the maneu-vering of Onias and Joseph and especially in the more serious conflict connected with the Seleucid takeover of Palestine around 200, well before conflict came to a head in the reform under Antiochus IV Epiphanes.

A closer scrutiny of information in the fragmentary sources finds no evidence of well-defined parties before the events of the Seleucid takeover of Palestine in 200, much less that they were driven by distinctive ideologies. The conflicts within the aristocracy in Jerusalem instead appear to have been shifting local struggles between factions that were closely interrelated to the Ptolemies' and Seleucids' continuing competition for control of Syria-Palestine. Again the Tobiad romance must be read critically, in the context of information from other sources, and used as a window onto power relations in Jerusalem affairs as they were connected with power struggles at the imperial level.

Although the success of Joseph the Tobiad as tax-farmer for the Ptolemaic regime had weakened the power of the high priesthood, there is no evidence to indicate that a simple division had arisen between the Oniads on one side and the Tobiads on the other, much less that one or another had a particular ideology. So long as the Ptolemies were in control, through their agents such as Joseph, members of the aristocracy looking for some leverage could hardly make moves that were clearly anti-Ptolemaic. Yet they could pay attention to imperial affairs, particularly the relative situations of the rival imperial regimes.

After consolidating his hold on his territories to the East, Antiochus III attacked a weakened Ptolemaic regime in 202–201 BCE and quickly took over most of Syria-Palestine. It seems likely that one factor in the relatively easy Seleucid advance was the defection to the Seleucid side of Ptolemy, who had succeeded his father Thraseas as (the last) Ptolemaic military governor of Syria and Phoenicia. He would have had cooperative relations with the governing elite of the cities, and both could see the likely outcome of the strengthened Seleucid regime and the weakened Ptolemaic regime.[26]

A combination of hints in several sources confirms that a faction in the Jerusalem aristocracy, in response to the Seleucid advance into Syria, had indeed taken action to join the Seleucids, and that they continued on this course through the often-devastating course of the imperial war in 201–200 BCE. Accounts in Polybius and in Josephus, who follows Polybius, indicate the sequence of events. When Antiochus attacked the Ptolemaic forces, those in control of Jerusalem were apparently ready to back the Seleucids. This is clear because when the Ptolemaic regime sent an army under Scopas, he had to attack the Judeans who were resisting, subdue them, and install a garrison in the Jerusalem citadel (*Ant.* 12.132–133, 135). After Antiochus decisively defeated the Ptolemaic forces at Panion and came to expel the garrison in Jerusalem, "the Judeans of their own will went over to him and admitted him to their city and made abundant provision for his entire army and his elephants; and they readily joined his forces in besieging the garrison left by Scopas" (*Ant.* 12.133). The only "Judeans" who had access to such an abundance of "provisions" were the Jerusalem aristocracy. That it was the priestly aristocracy in particular who welcomed and provisioned Antiochus is indicated in the latter's decree that rewarded the Temple, the priestly aristocracy, and others who operated it with imperial funding and tax and tribute relief (*Ant.* 138–144, excerpted just below).

Two other fragmentary texts can be understood as references to these same events. The narrative of events in the vision of Daniel 10–12 mentions that "in those times many shall rise against the king of the south [the Ptolemies]. The lawless [or the children of the violent] among your own people shall lift themselves up in order to fulfill the vision, but they shall fail" (11:14). Centuries later Jerome reproduced a memory of the same events in commentary on Daniel. While Antiochus was battling the forces of Ptolemy, Judeans were divided into pro-Antiochus and pro-Ptolemaic camps. Quoting Porphyry of Tyre, he says that after retaking Jerusalem, Scopas took "the heads of the pro-Ptolemy party" back to

Egypt (*optimates Ptolemaei partium*). It certainly makes no sense that Scopas would have taken the leaders of a faction loyal to the Ptolemaic regime out of the city when, backed by the Ptolemaic garrison in the citadel, they were needed in Jerusalem to help maintain control. But "Ptolemy" here can also be a reference to Ptolemy son of Thraseas, the last governor of Syria who defected to the Seleucids. The governor Ptolemy was a likely link by which the pro-Seleucid faction in the Jerusalem aristocracy had come to actively support Antiochus.[27] Finding this pro-Seleucid party in control of Jerusalem and resisting his reconquest, the Ptolemaic general Scopas deported them to Egypt, thus (he thought) decapitating the opposing party in Jerusalem. But the pro-Seleucid forces were larger than he thought and joined with Antiochus's troops to defeat the Ptolemaic garrison.

Information gleaned from the later parts of the Tobiad romance can flesh out this picture of conflicting factions in the Jerusalem elite involved in the events of the Seleucid takeover in Palestine (*Ant.* 12.186–224, 228–236). Joseph's youngest son, Hyrcanus, picked up his father's ambition and his skill at maneuvering in the Ptolemaic regime. By manipulating the "steward" (*oikonomos*) whom Joseph had established in Alexandria to handle the substantial funds that he was remitting to the imperial treasury, Hyrcanus diverted large amounts of those funds for elaborate gifts to the king and his key advisers to gain favor for himself at court. All of this maneuvering and display of wealth, however, angered his father and evoked the active opposition of his brothers. When Hyranus returned to Jerusalem, his brothers engaged him in battle, each side apparently having armed men in their entourage. Hyrcanus had to withdraw from Jerusalem and its politics; he retreated across the Jordan to the traditional power-base of the Tobiads, where he "levied tribute on the barbarians" (as a representative of the Ptolemaic regime?). The continuation of the narrative speaks of "factional strife" between the older Tobiad brothers and Hyrcanus, with the high priest Simon on the side of the brothers.

It is inviting to juxtapose this information gleaned from the Tobiad romance with that gained from other sources, especially because Hyrcanus's maneuvering in the Ptolemaic court and conflict with his brothers appears to have taken place just before Antiochus III's campaign to take control of Syria-Palestine. His brothers, who engaged him in battle when he returned to Jerusalem and made common cause with the Oniad high priest Simon, could hardly have displaced him in Ptolemaic favor. Indeed Hyrcanus's aggressive maneuvering in the Ptolemaic regime may have helped drive the other Tobiads toward the Seleucids even before it was clear that the latter would take over Syria-Palestine.

The factional struggle in Jerusalem was thus clearly not a simple division between Tobiads and Oniads, for the Tobiads themselves were divided. And if anything, judging from Hyrcanus's flair for Hellenistic culture and pleasures that exceeded that of his father, the pro-Ptolemaic faction was as enamored of "Hellenism" as was the pro-Seleucid party. All of the brothers had supposedly been tutored in Greek *paideia* by the most famous tutors that their father's profits from tax-farming could buy. Rather than an ideological struggle, the conflict within the Jerusalem aristocracy was more of a basic struggle for power and position.

The possibilities for maneuvering in Jerusalem depended on the contingencies of the continuing struggles between imperial regimes for control of Syria-Palestine.

Resolution of the crisis, of course, came with the Seleucid victory. And in Judea Antiochus III appears to have reverted to the Persian practice of explicit support for the Jerusalem temple-state as the principal instrument of imperial rule. The key source is the decree of Antiochus to the governor Ptolemy regarding the Judeans and the temple-state cited by Josephus (*Ant.* 12.138–144). Most scholars judge the decree in Josephus as basically authentic, with some "editing" by Judean scribes in its transmission.[28] The stela found near Hefzibah (in Israel) tends to confirm this judgment. It displays several decrees by Antiochus at the time of his takeover of Palestine, protecting local peasants from billeting and other mistreatment by the army. Antiochus's decree regarding the temple-state fits with his practice elsewhere of rewarding those who had helped him and confirming traditional local "constitutions" and customs.

> Inasmuch as the Judeans . . . gave us a splendid reception and met us with their council [*gerousia*] and furnished an abundance of provisions . . . and helped us to expel the Egyptian garrison in the citadel, . . . we require them for these acts and we restore their city which has been destroyed by the ravages of war. . . . We have decided, on account of their piety, to furnish them for their sacrifices an allowance of sacrificial animals, wine, oil, and frankincense to the value of twenty thousand pieces of silver, etc. . . . It is my will that . . . work on the Temple be completed. . . . The timber shall be brought from Lebanon . . . and other materials needed for restoration. . . . And all members of the people [*ethnos*] shall be governed according to their ancestral laws, and the council [*gerousia*], priests, the scribes of the Temple and the temple singers shall be relieved from the poll tax and crown tax and the salt tax which they pay. And . . . the inhabitants of the city . . . we shall also relieve from the third part of their tribute, so that their losses may be made good. (Josephus, *Ant.* 12.138–144)

The decree focuses almost exclusively on the Temple and temple-state and its operation in the economy and governing of Judea. The Temple and temple-state are placed in charge of Judea and the *gerousia* in charge of the temple-state. *Gerousia* was a Hellenistic term for the elders that presided over the affairs of a city and/or people. Insofar as the other groups included—"the priests, the temple scribes, and the temple singers"—were all clearly Temple functionaries, the *gerousia* almost certainly refers to the aristocracy of the temple-state. But we cannot tell whether, functionally speaking, it included heads of wealthy and powerful nonpriestly families, since there was probably no set membership. In a significant shift from the Ptolemies' farming of the tribute to a powerful figure other than the high priest (e.g., Joseph), the whole Jerusalem aristocracy appears to be in charge of collecting the tribute from the Judean villagers, and it was allowed to use a third of the revenue to rebuild the city, at least temporarily. Only the temple functionaries, who must be the bulk of the "inhabitants" of Jerusalem, were given tax relief (to enable the temple-state to recover), with the Judean peasants expected to render up tribute as usual.

Absent from Antiochus's decree is any mention of the "high priest." Should we assume that he is included in "the council" as the primus inter pares? Was the temple-state more or less an aristocracy at this point anyhow?—after the high priestly office had been weakened when Joseph had dominated affairs in Jerusalem in the late third century—only to become raised to prominence by the Seleucids' "deals" made with successive figures who "bought" the office (see just below)?[29] Had the Seleucid takeover simply caught Simon II (son of Onias II) off in exile as a result of the turmoil? Or had he been among "the heads of the pro-Ptolemy party" (i.e., Ptolemy the governor, hence pro-Seleucid) deported to Egypt by Scopas? Josephus mentions him as collaborating with the older Tobiad brothers, who must have been prominent in the pro-Seleucid party in the battles for control of Jerusalem in 201–200. And it appears that he quickly moved into leadership in the Temple aristocracy following Antiochus's takeover. This is surely the implication of Ben Sira's hymnic celebration of Simon for heading the repair of the Temple and fortification of Jerusalem (Sir. 50:1–4)—presumably taking advantage of the funding provided in Antiochus's "charter."

We cannot, on the one hand, explain away the omission of the high priest in Antiochus's decree as merely due to the "outside" view that Judea was an *ethnos* headed by a council. Nor, on the other hand, can we place too much weight on the "inside" view that some see articulated by Ben Sira, that Judea was a hierocratic state headed by a "priestly monarchy," since Sir. 50:1–4 is part of an idealizing hymn of praise from a protégé and advocate of Simon.[30] Even Ben Sira portrays Simon less as a monarch than as the most prominent figure among his brothers, "the sons of Aaron," a picture similar to that presented by Hecataeus. It seems, therefore, that after the Seleucid takeover, Judea was ruled by the Jerusalem aristocracy, mainly priestly, and headed by a chief priest, only now with less rivalry from a powerful tax-farmer in charge of imperial revenues. But within the Jerusalem aristocracy there were still other powerful figures, besides the high priest and competing factions, who understood the contingencies of competing and internally conflicted imperial regimes.

THIRD CRISIS: ARISTOCRATIC FACTIONS UNDER THE SELEUCID REGIME

The third crisis led directly to the widespread revolt against the Hellenizing priestly aristocracy and Seleucid imperial rule. It unfolded over nearly ten years in three steps of escalating conflict between shifting aristocratic factions that exploited the Seleucid imperial politics and need for revenue to further their own agenda.[31]

In a harbinger of future events, after Onias III had succeeded his father Simon II as high priest, and Seleucus IV had succeeded his father, Antiochus III, as emperor, the "temple-captain" (*prostatēs tou hierou*) Simon, of the priestly family of Bilgah (Neh. 12:5, 18),[32] challenged Onias about the administration of public finances (*agoranomia*, 2 Macc. 3:4–8). It is not clear whether the "temple-captain," who apparently had something to do with temple revenues and deposits, was appointed by the aristocracy in Jerusalem or was a representative of the emperor (or both). Unable to prevail against Onias in Jerusalem, Simon reported to the Seleucid governor of western Syria and Phoenicia that "the treasury in Jerusalem was full of untold sums of money . . . , and that they did not belong to the account of the sacrifices, but . . . [could] fall under the control of the king" (3:6). When the king sent his officer Heliodorus to expropriate these funds, Onias explained that the deposits belonging to widows and orphans, along with some money of the prominent Hyrcanus son of Tobias, which did not amount to a large sum, had been entrusted to the inviolable sanctity of the Temple (2 Macc. 3:10–12). The attempt to seize the funds having failed, Simon and his henchmen plotted further against Onias and others, even involving some "murders." Knowing that Simon had gained the confidence of the Seleucid governor, Onias appealed to Seleucus himself (2 Macc. 4:1–7). Just at that time the latter died, and Onias was retained indefinitely at the Seleucid court.

Although Tobiads may have been involved in Simon's plot and subsequent factions' maneuvers with the Seleucid regime, it is overly schematic to see these events as a continuing conflict between Oniads and Tobiads.[33] The only text fragment that mentions the Tobiads' involvement is in Josephus (*Ant.* 12.237–241), an otherwise confused account that fuses the faction of Menelaus, the brother of Simon the temple captain, with the Oniad brothers, Onias III and Jason. Similarly, this conflict cannot be understood as an opposition between a pro-Seleucid party and a revived pro-Ptolemaic faction, presumably led by Onias now somehow allied with Hyrcanus. Although the Ptolemaic struggle against the Seleucids continued, the latter were so clearly in control of Palestine that Onias hardly dared subvert their rule in any serious way. On the other hand, the Seleucids may not have been so thoroughly in control as to have brought Hyrcanus and the frontier territory he dominated under their control. He had come into some sort of symbiotic relationship with those who controlled the Temple, such that Onias mentioning his deposits there would not have been tantamount to a declaration of disloyalty to the Seleucids. Both imperial and Judean affairs were more complex than the simple opposition of two parties.

The occasion for the next major step in escalating crisis was the succession of Antiochus IV Epiphanes in 175 BCE. Onias's brother Jason, at the head of a large faction that included Tobiads, took advantage of the new emperor's desperate need for revenues. He obtained the high priesthood from Antiochus in return for raising the tribute from 300 to 360 talents, plus another 80 talents from another source. In an ominous shift, the high priest thus became a Seleucid imperial official by negotiating the amount of tribute.[34] Much more ominous was the new "constitution" that Jason and his aristocratic faction obtained, for a price.

> In addition to this he promised to pay one hundred fifty more if permission were given to establish by his authority a gymnasium and a body of youth [*ephēbeion*] for it, and to enroll the Jerusalemites as citizens of Antioch. When the emperor assented and Jason came to office, he at once shifted his com-

patriots over to the Greek way of life [*pros ton Hellēnikon charaktēra*]. He set aside the existing royal concessions to the Judeans, . . . and he dissolved the laws of the constitution [*tas nomimous politeias*] and set up new customs contrary to the laws. He took delight in establishing a gymnasium right under the citadel, and he had the noblest of the young men [*tōn ephēbōn*] exercise with the broad-brimmed felt [Greek] hat. (2 Macc. 4:9–12)

The account in 2 Maccabees (4:9–17), like that in 1 Maccabees (1:11–15), expresses horror that Jason and his compatriots would thus "abandon the holy covenant" for alien customs. It mocks the priests for neglecting the sacrifices in order to participate in the athletic exercises of the Greeks. But far more than discus throwing and donning the broad-brimmed felt hat were involved. While it involved culture and had implications for religious ritual, Jason's project was political. The *gymnasion* was the city facility for the (mainly athletic) training that qualified young men for citizenship in a Greek *polis,* and the *ephēbeion* was the body of youth being trained for membership in the citizen corporation.[35] These institutions were integral to a city's "constitution" (*politeia*) or "ancestral laws" (*patrioi nomoi/nomima*), as Greeks noted about their own and other peoples (Herodotus 2.91; Diodorus Siculus 1.81.7; Xenophon, *Cyropaedia* 1.2.2–15). Hence "to change the education system was to change the *politeia*" (Plutarch, *Phil.* 16.5–6), to change a city's distinctive "constitutive" stamp (*charaktēra*).[36]

And that is precisely what Jason and his compatriots were doing, according to 2 Maccabees (4:9–17). The language of the account features the key terms of a city's or people's "ancestral laws," its "constitution." By obtaining the "authority" (*exousia*) of the emperor to establish a *gymnasion* and *ephēbeion* and to enroll citizens, Jason "dissolved the (ancestral) laws of the constitution" (*tas nomimous politeias*) of Jerusalem and introduced a new "Greek way of life, . . . customs contrary to the law" (*Hellēnikon charaktēra . . . paranomous ethismous*).[37] Jason and his compatriots thus established a new political corporation, Antioch, named presumably after its official founder, the emperor Antiochus IV Epiphanes.

Interpretations of what this "reform" meant for life in Judea have varied from a more or less complete substitution of one cultural "way of life" for another, "Hellenism" replacing "Judaism," to recent claims that the changes were superficial, with virtually no change yet in "religion."[38] Recent studies of the extent to which the "Hellenization" of the cities and peoples of the ancient Near East left much of the traditional culture intact underneath an overlay of public institutions provide some comparisons on which to make a more nuanced estimation of the shifts involved.[39] Many of the Hellenistic cities established under the Seleucids involved few Macedonian and Greek immigrants. Native elites took initiatives in establishing new public institutions, such as *gymnasia,* according to the Greek patterns. Indigenous gods and temples were given Greek names, with traditional culture thus continuing, while having been relativized in the broader, more "cosmopolitan" Hellenistic culture.

The new *politeia* for "Antioch" in Jerusalem set up by Jason and his faction seems to fit this general pattern. Their "reform" did not (yet) displace the Temple altar and sacrifices (2 Macc. 4:14–15). No city "council"(*boulē*) replaced the high priesthood and "council" of elders (*gerousia*) as the ruling aristocracy (2 Macc. 4:43–44).[40] And traditional Judean laws and customs were not yet actively rescinded and suppressed. But to claim that establishing the new city of Antioch did not yet mean religious and political changes in Jerusalem is to construe religion in the narrowest cultic sense and politics in a merely formalist sense. In the sense that religion was inseparable from the political economy of the Judean temple-state, the Temple and its rituals had been decisively "demoted" and relativized.

Political power was now monopolized by the elite "enrolled" as the citizen body of Antioch, with those who did not participate in the gymnasion training left as mere "residents" in the new city.[41] The effective relativization of the temple cult would have posed a particular threat to the regular priests, Levites, scribes, and others whose lifework and livelihood were tied up with the Temple. They, like ordinary Jerusalemites and Judean villagers, would appear to have had no political rights in the new arrangement. The economic as well as the cultural gulf between the reforming wealthy aristocracy on the one hand and the regular priests, Levites, other temple staff, and the Judean peasantry, on the other, would have been exacerbated.[42]

The "reform" carried out by Jason and his aristocratic faction was hardly a pervasive transformation in which one culture, "Judaism," was replaced by another, "Hellenism." The latter term is rare, used for the first time in 2 Maccabees, and should not be reified into a wider cultural program, much less a movement. The cultural motives and effects of the reform were more *political*-cultural. The language of the imperial administration was Greek. Local elites such as Tobias, head of a family long since intermarried with the high-priestly family, had "Greeks" on their administrative staffs and tutoring their children. The sons of a provincial sheikh, such as Joseph, could maneuver with considerable facility in the Hellenistic imperial court, with its lavish lifestyle (palatial quarters, slaves), indulgence in sensual pleasures (cuisine, dancing girls), and sophisticated culture (exotic animals). Such provincials who wanted to be players in the dominant imperial culture and politics—and wanted to cultivate influence at the imperial court for leverage in local affairs—knew the importance of training in language, diplomatic protocol, and lifestyle. Joseph's sons, cousins of the leading priestly figures, were surely not the only members of the Jerusalem elite to have been tutored in Greek and the developing amalgam of Hellenistic culture.

As the Jerusalem aristocracy moved from under the Ptolemaic regime to control by the Seleucids, they would surely have recognized that the Seleucid Empire operated basically as an alliance between the imperial court and the elites that controlled the various Hellenistic cities of the empire. It is significant that soon after obtaining imperial authorization to establish Antioch in Jerusalem, with gymnasion, *ephēbeion,* and citizen body, Jason sent envoys to the quadrennial games in Tyre, presided over by the emperor (2 Macc. 4:18–20). Shortly thereafter Jason and "the city" (Antioch) staged a magnificent "welcome" for Antiochus IV Epiphanes, with a torchlight parade and acclamations (4:21–22). Those were the ways, in the dominant Hellenistic political culture, that the Jerusalem aristocracy could themselves finally become more complete players in the empire, by participating in its basic political-cultural forms.

In yet a third major step the crisis deepened into an escalating sequence of sharp conflicts between aristocratic factions that led eventually to armed conflict and intervention by imperial armies. Three years into his high priesthood Jason delegated Menelaus, brother of the temple captain Simon of the priestly Bilgah family (who had challenged the high priest Onias III a few years earlier), to deliver the tribute to the emperor. Menelaus seized the occasion to secure the high priesthood for himself by promising to raise the tribute by yet another three hundred talents (2 Macc. 4:23–24). This move not only split the "reforming" party, but the high priesthood now passed out of the Oniad family and high-priestly lineage in which it had been hereditary for generations. Jason fled to the Transjordan. Presumably in order to raise the exorbitant amount of tribute he had promised Antiochus, Menelaus began plundering the golden vessels of the Temple. When the previously deposed high priest Onias, who had taken refuge at the sanctuary of Daphne near Antioch (in Syria), exposed him publicly, Menelaus bribed an imperial official to assassinate Onias (4:30–34).[43] The Jerusalem *gerousia,* now presumably comprised of those who had gone along with the "reform," sent three delegates to testify against Menelaus, who again bribed his way out of the challenge (4:43–50), while the delegates were executed. This would only have left the Jerusalem aristocracy even more deeply divided.

The sources for the ensuing escalation into armed conflict, imperial intervention, and Antiochus's violent suppression of the traditional Judean laws and rituals, while differing markedly in details, have similarities in overall outline sufficient to reconstruct a basic sequence of events (1 Macc. 1:16–63; 2 Macc. 5–7; Josephus, *Ant.* 12.242–256).[44] It seems clear that Antiochus invaded Egypt twice, the first time successfully, in late 170 (1 Macc. 1:16–24), after which he looted the Jerusalem Temple treasury on his way back (with the acquiescence or cooperation of Menelaus?), but with no fighting (Dan. 11:28). When he again invaded Egypt, in the spring of 168, the Romans intervened, forcing him to withdraw. Perhaps on hearing a rumor that the emperor had been killed, Jason invaded Jerusalem with a large force, and Menelaus took refuge in the citadel (2 Macc. 5:1–7). Hearing of what he would have interpreted as a revolt, Antiochus sent military forces, under Apollonius, to put down the insurrection. His main concern was probably to keep Jerusalem and Judea under the high priesthood of Menelaus, whom he continued to support.

The only way for Antiochus to secure control of Judea was apparently to establish a military colony in Jerusalem. The military settlers, perhaps from Syria or Asia Minor, would have brought their cult of Baal Shamem (Lord of Heaven) with them. If the military colonists shared the Temple and its altar, their sacrifices to "the Lord of Heaven," who was often identified with Zeus and sometimes with Yahweh, would have been what tradition-minded priests and other Judeans considered an abominable pollution. Although it is not clear just what measures were taken, it was apparently at this point also that Antiochus took action to suppress the ancestral laws and sacrifices of the Judeans. In response to these events, the wider insurrection and guerrilla warfare known as the Maccabean Revolt erupted, the revolt that eventually fought the Seleucid armies to a standoff and toppled the reformist priestly aristocracy.

EXACERBATING THE DIVISION BETWEEN TEMPLE-STATE ARISTOCRACY AND JUDEAN PEASANTRY

The interrelated struggles for power between rival empires and conflicts between rival factions in the Jerusalem aristocracy would only have further aggravated the other divisions in Judea that continued from the Persian period.

The Ptolemaic period is often characterized as "a time of peace and economic growth," when "backward Jerusalem gained considerably in political and economic significance," and "young enterprising forces endeavored to break through the constraints of their native land and pave the way for the new spirit."[45] Only if we ignore the way the tributary political economy of the Ptolemies and other ancient Near Eastern empires worked could we believe that Joseph the Tobiad "was able to protect his countrymen from excessive exploitation."[46] "Economic development" Ptolemaic-Tobiad style would only have expanded the wealth of the powerful families while further impoverishing many villagers.

The structural political-economic conflict established in second-temple Judea under the Persians was, if anything, intensified under the Ptolemies and the power holders in Judea who collaborated in the imperial order.[47] If we can believe the memoirs of Nehemiah, the Persians may even have taken measures to protect the economic viability of the Judean peasantry from the predatory exploitation of the wealthy elite. By contrast, the Ptolemies' contracting tax collection to ever-higher bidders in order to enhance the imperial revenues would only have exacerbated the already marginal condition of the Judean peasantry, the economic bases for both local aristocracies and imperial regime. The Tobiad family's expansion of its wealth and political influence, moreover, would only have induced other families of the Jerusalem aristocracy—including the high-priestly family with whom it was intermarried but whose preeminent position it was undercutting—to strive for increased resources in order to compete in the struggle for power, with predictable effects on the peasantry. The moves by leading priestly aristocrats, first Jason and then Menelaus, to obtain appointment to the high priesthood by dramatically increasing the tribute payment from Judea, would have drained temple resources and, in turn, brought increased demands on peasant producers.

Shortly after the Seleucid regime had taken control of Judea, it became obligated to make huge payments of war reparations to the Romans. Precisely in that context the scribal teacher Jesus ben Sira repeatedly characterizes the peasantry as "poor," "hungry," "needy," "desperate" (e.g., Sir. 4:1–9). Just as they were at the time of Nehemiah, there was a sharp conflict between the wealthy elite and the peasants, who were vulnerable to the predatory practices of the powerful.

> What peace is there between a hyena and a dog?
> And what peace between the rich and the poor [*penēs*]?
> Wild asses in the wilderness are the prey of lions;
> likewise the poor [*ptōchoi*] are feeding grounds for the rich.
> (Sir. 13:18–19)

The power struggle between factions of the Jerusalem aristocracy would also have adversely affected the relative position of Levites, ordinary priests, temple singers, "scribes of the Temple," and others involved in and dependent on the operation of the temple-state. If imperial tribute was channeled through tax-farmers such as Joseph Tobiad, then it was not channeled through the high priesthood and temple-state, and indeed competed with Temple and priestly demands for tithes and offerings, thus lessening the resources commanded by the Temple. Jason's and Menelaus's blatant "purchase" of the high priesthood from the Seleucids meant a severe drain on temple resources. The increasing passion for Hellenistic imperial culture among aristocratic families such as the Tobiads led to a widening political-cultural gulf between the priestly elite and the lower-status functionaries of the Temple. Then especially Jason and his faction's formation of the city of Antioch in Jerusalem not only widened that gulf but also left ordinary priests, Levites, and others with relativized traditional roles and, in effect, without rights in the new order.

Chapter 3

Ben Sira and the Sociology of Judea

The one who devotes himself to the study of the law/torah of the Most High;
who seeks out the wisdom of all the ancients, and is concerned with prophe-
cies. . . . He serves among the great and appears before rulers.

Ben Sira

Second-temple Judea was not a monolithic society, unified by Temple and Torah, as often assumed in biblical studies. Multiple fault lines are clearly visible, judging from the principal literary sources for the period, such as Ezra and Nehemiah, Sirach and Josephus. Not only was the society fractured by vertical divisions of rival factions in the ruling aristocracy closely related to parallel conflicts between and among rival imperial regimes (as explored in chaps. 1–2). But horizontal divisions were visible as well, both between the aristocracy and the people, and between the priestly families who controlled the Temple and other priestly groups who also served in the temple-state. Some of the governing concepts of biblical studies, such as "Judaism" and "the Bible/biblical," tend to obscure these divisions by obscuring the diversity of texts and groups. Conflict that is too obvious to ignore is attributed to cultural influence from the outside.

A typical example is the most influential construction of "Judaism" in conflict with "Hellenism" in this last generation, that of Martin Hengel,[1] a further development of the view of Victor Tcherikover. They portrayed second-temple Judea as suddenly abuzz with commercial activity in the Hellenistic period.

Ben Sira frequently mentions merchants and their pursuit of profits, and these passages again reflect the new period which began in Judaea under Greek rule, when the money economy, the opportunity to invest one's means in profitable enterprises, and lively and absorbing commercial traffic had begun to develop.[2]

Adducing a variety of archaeological and textual evidence, Hengel argued that Judea became more prosperous as a host of Greek agents and merchants penetrated even into village life, an increasing circulation of coins monetarized the economy, and foreign trade increased. He explained both Ben Sira's harangues against merchants and the Maccabean Revolt as the conservative reactions of a particularist traditional "Judaism" against the entrepreneurial individualism and cosmopolitan spirit of "Hellenism."

Hengel's explanation of Judea under the impact of "Hellenism" is typical of a field that has not yet incorporated critical sociological analysis.[3] He has projected onto the Hellenistic period the kinds of social-economic relations that are familiar to biblical scholarship from early modern European society, with its rising "middle class" and increasingly commercialized economy.[4] Lacking in studies of second-temple Judean history and literature has been any clear sense of the concrete historical political-economic-religious structure and dynamics of Judean society.[5] The field is thus unprepared to deal critically with the historical conflicts and crises that are reflected in and that gave rise to texts such as Sirach, Enoch, and Daniel, and major upheavals such as the Maccabean Revolt.

In pursuit of just such an overall picture of Judean society, biblical interpreters have borrowed certain sociological approaches. Most influential in studies of Judah under the Davidic monarchy and of Judea under the later Herodian kings has been the model of advanced agrarian society developed from studies of a wide range of societies by Gerhard Lenski.[6] Application of Lenski's model has resulted in important insights, for example, into the social stratification of the monarchy or into the social location and role of the Pharisees as "retainers" in late second-temple Judea.[7] Compared with other structural-functional sociology, which has been developed on the basis of complex modern societies but then applied to New Testament materials,[8] Lenski has carefully articulated a genuinely historical sociology. Recognizing that societies have undergone great changes over long periods of time, he has constructed models of different types of social structure. Most significantly for biblical studies, he fully recognizes that agrarian societies of the past involved a premarket economy.

In several significant respects, however, Lenski's model of agrarian society is not applicable to second-temple Judea. His construction of an elaborate system of social stratification in twelve "classes" tends to obscure the fundamental social conflicts evident in Judean literature. It seems fairly clear from the outset that a separation of a "priestly class" from "the ruler" and "governing class" and "retainer class" does not fit a temple-state such as Judea. Thus, whether or not Lenski's sociology may be applicable to the monarchic period of Judah, it seems best not to proceed by applying his "agrarian society" model to second-temple Judea.

It is not a question of whether we utilize a particular model of society. In recent years even biblical scholars have recognized that, consciously or not, when we (re)construct history, we make use of particular models of social structure and social relations. It is not a question of whether we utilize a particular model of society. The key is whether we do so with some critical awareness and some basis of comparison with studies of similar societies. I am convinced that literary and historical analysis remain primary in our attempt to understand ancient literature and history, with sociological and anthropological analysis playing an ancillary role.[9] Rather than start from a model, therefore, I would like to begin with information derived from Judean sources. And the book of Sirach, one of our principal texts from the Hellenistic period, contains a great deal of information about social structure and social relations in Judea. We can then evaluate this information about Judean society on the basis of comparative historical-sociological studies of traditional agrarian societies in order to gain a better sense of the political-economic-religious structure and power relations in second-temple Judea.[10]

BEN SIRA'S PORTRAYAL OF SOCIAL STRUCTURE AND SOCIAL ROLES IN JUDEA

Ben Sira, who was himself centrally involved in the temple-state in the early second century BCE, turns out to have been an astute "participant observer." He repeats some telling proverbs and offers a number of illuminating comments both about his social-political superiors and about those he views as his social-cultural inferiors. It is not difficult to recognize his perspective and partisan point of view. He is a strong advocate for the incumbent Oniad high priesthood of Simon II and a dedicated servant of the temple-state. Yet he often makes critical comments about abuses of power by the high and mighty. As an intellectual with an apparently comfortable living, he looks down on those who work with their hands. Yet he also sympathizes with the plight of the poor and exploited.[11]

In an adulatory reflection on the important role of the scribe, Ben Sira sketches the principal political-economic roles in the social structure of Judea.

> How can *one who handles the plow* become wise, . . .
>   *who drives oxen* . . . and whose talk is about bulls?
> He sets his heart on plowing furrows,
>   and he is careful about fodder for the heifers.
> So too is every *artisan and master artisan*,
>   those who cut the signets of seals. . . .
> So too is *the smith,* sitting by the anvil; . . .
>   he struggles with the heat of the furnace. . . .
> So too is *the potter,* . . . turning the wheel with his feet. . . .
> He moulds the clay with his arm, . . .
>   and he takes care in firing the kiln.
> All these rely on their hands,. . .

Without them no city can be inhabited,
   and wherever they live, they will not go hungry.
Yet they are not sought out for *the council* of the people,
   nor do any of them attain eminence in the public assembly.
They do not sit on the seat of a court,
   nor do they understand the decisions of courts;
They cannot expound discipline or judgment,
   and they are not found among *the rulers*.[12]
But they maintain the fabric of the world,
   and their concern is for the exercise of their trade.
How different the *one who* devotes himself
   to the study of the law (torah) of the Most High!
He *seeks out the wisdom* of all the ancients. . . .
He serves among *the great ones* [*megistanōn*]
   and appears before the *rulers* [*hēgoumenōn*];
he travels in foreign lands
   and learns what is good and evil in the human heart.
         (Sir. 38:25–35; 39:1, 4, abridged, alt.; italics supplied)

The principal political-economic roles in this portrayal of Judean society (or is it primarily Jerusalem) are neither many nor complex. The city is habitable because agricultural laborers provide food and manual laborers such as artisans and smiths supply the amenities of civilized living. The scribes do the intellectual labor of perpetuating the culture and maintaining the knowledge necessary for the social and political life of the city. And "the great ones" and "rulers" at the top apparently sit in command over the whole. Ben Sira's praise of the ancestors (Sir. 44–50) presents a similarly simple picture of society, a concentric hierarchical political-economic-religious structure in full ritual dress. Temple, state, and society, undifferentiated, are headed the high priest, surrounded by the inner concentric circle of "his brothers," the aristocracy among "the sons of Aaron." The priesthood is, in turn, surrounded and supported (with sacrifices brought to "the Most High") by the outer concentric circle of the people, "the whole assembly of Israel" (50:1, 12–15; 45:14, 16, 20–21). Supplementary references from the rest of Ben Sira's teaching supply further information that fills in this basic picture.

Rulers/the Great/Nobles/Elders

Ben Sira uses a variety of terms for those who rule Judea. The terms clearly overlap, indeed they are virtually interchangeable. The meaning and reference of these terms can be discerned from the "synonymous parallelism" (parallel poetic lines more or less synonymous in meaning) in which Ben Sira often formulates his teaching, as well as from comparisons with usage in other Hebrew and Greek literature.[13] The terms used in those parts of Sirach that are extant in Hebrew were evidently traditional terms that had become standardized in earlier wisdom teaching, and were virtually interchangeable and synonymous. The ancient Greek translation and the modern English translations of these terms (and/or their Greek translations) render them variously with terms that are also virtually interchangeable and synonymous: "the great, rulers, princes, judges, nobles, elders," and others. Most references to these figures are in the plural. Most singular references to a ruling figure are to a typical one among many, for example, "a noble" or "a great one." And Ben Sira refers several times to scribes standing in gatherings or assemblies of the rulers/great ones/princes/elders (6:34; 7:14).[14] All such references suggest that "the great ones of the people/rulers of the assembly/nobles/princes" were the same people, who had collective authority, exercised various functions, and operated collectively in relation to scribes and to the people. They were the ruling aristocracy of the Judean people and/or the city of Jerusalem.

That Ben Sira, even in short poetic lines, often refers to such figures in connection with the "people" or "city" or "assembly" that they rule or judge indicates that the references are not simply to social status, but also to figures with certain powers and functions in the whole society (9:17; 10:1–3; 33:19 [30:27]; 39:4). The sage's frequent warning of his addressees to mind their words and "watch their back" when dealing with such figures indicates that they indeed wielded considerable power over others (8:1). It is simply assumed, moreover, that "the powerful" were also "the rich," as in the parallel lines in 8:1–2.[15] In addition to holding political power and social prestige, the aristocracy was also economically wealthy.

Scribes

The principal role of the scribes or sages, in Ben Sira's instructional wisdom generally as in his reflection on the role of the sage, was "to serve the magnates/rulers" (*megistasin, sārîm,* 8:8). Their particular functions included service as advisers of the collective rulership in Jerusalem (6:34; 7:14; 15:5; 21:17; 38:32–33), members of (or more likely advisers of) courts that heard cases (for they understood the decisions of courts and could expound judgments; 4:9; 11:7–9; 38:33; 42:2), and travel, perhaps on diplomatic missions (39:4). They devoted themselves to the study of the torah and to the wisdom of the ancients precisely for such service among the rulers (39:1–4).[16]

They evidently stood in the middle, between the rulers and the people. Ben Sira indicates that scribes felt ambivalently about both their social-political superiors and their social-cultural inferiors. He looks down on manual laborers such as the plowman, the smith, and the potter, who lack the sage's "leisure" for learning wisdom. Yet Ben Sira also sees the scribe as responsible for protecting those vulnerable to exploitation (4:1–10). He insists that the sage must bow low to the ruler (4:7). Yet he also cautions scribal protégés about the potential dangers involved in dealing with the powerful (13:9).

Artisan, Smith, Potter; Physicians; Merchants

Ben Sira's statement about the artisan, the smith, and the potter, that "without them no city can be inhabited," indicates that they are basically engaged in service of, and are thus economically dependent on, the aristocracy who also reside in the city (38:27–30). By comparison with artisan laborers, physicians clearly enjoy much higher social rank, like the sages themselves working among and being honored by the great ones (38:1–3). Merchants and traders appear explicitly only at three points: passing references to merchants and buying and selling at 37:11 and 42:5, and the brief but sharp criticism in 26:29–27:2 ("A merchant can hardly keep from wrongdoing, nor is a retailer innocent of sin. . . ." [au. trans.]). Contrary to statements commonly made by interpreters, there is no indication that these are the same as the wealthy mentioned in other contexts.[17]

Agricultural Workers, Slaves, and the Poor

In contrast to trade (buying and selling), farmwork is honorable, "created by the Most High" (7:15). Ben Sira's focus on "the plowman's" driving oxen with a goad and feeding the draft animals (38:24–25) suggests that he may be referring to workers on large estates well equipped with draft animals rather than to (semi-)independent peasants, who often had to borrow an animal from a neighbor. His advice on treatment of slaves evidently refers to household slaves, not large gangs involved on agrarian estates, as in Roman Italy (see 6:11; 33:25–33 [30:33–40]; 42:5). The "hired laborer," parallel to the slave in the previous line (7:20), is also evidently a reference to a household servant, not an agricultural laborer. These passages give no indication whether these slaves were primarily in the households of rulers' families or also in those of the scribes.

Although Ben Sira does not refer explicitly to the Judean peasantry, he does indicate their presence and role in two connections. First, tithes and offerings (35:1–12) and firstfruits, guilt offerings, and animal sacrifices as revenues to "honor the priest" (7:29–31; 45:20–22)—these could not have come from the artisans, smiths, and potters, much less from the scribes, whose "produce" was nonagricultural. Such tithes and offerings can have been produced only on "the land of the people" (45:20–22), the Judean peasants who worked the land. Second, the poor appear in several of Ben Sira's teachings (4:1–6, 7–10; 7:32; 13:17–24; 29:1–8, 22; 34:24–27; 35:16–26). These references to the poor imply that they have roofs over their heads, have some agricultural holdings that can be (wrongfully) expropriated (presumably by foreclosure on debts), and make appeals to the courts regarding their oppression by the powerful.

SOCIOLOGIES OF AGRARIAN SOCIETIES

This information gleaned from Ben Sira on social relations and roles in second-temple Judea simply does not fit Gerhard Lenski's model of agrarian societies in several fundamental respects. Although the model itself may not be directly applicable to second-temple Judean society, however, the wealth of comparative material he draws on can help us discern the dynamics of the political-economic-religious structure in Judea. Since Lenski has been used to advantage on monarchic Judah and Herodian Judea, moreover, his sociological analysis may be somewhat familiar to biblical interpreters.

In a moment of self-criticism that is refreshing among scholars, Lenski mentions in a footnote that Robert Bellah, in response to his discussion of agrarian societies, had argued for division of agrarian societies into three subtypes: city-states, bureaucratic empires, and feudal regimes.[18] As one reads through Lenski's discussion, it becomes evident that the differences between these three different kinds of societies keep cropping up when Lenski discusses variations within his broad model of agrarian societies. For example, in European feudalism (or in the ancient Greek and Roman city-states for that matter), the "state" is strikingly diffuse when compared with the far more centralized "state" of ancient Near Eastern, Indian, Aztec, Inca, and certain African societies. Or, in feudal Europe a good deal of mercantile or artisan specialization developed independently of feudal lords, whereas trade and artisans do not appear to have been independent of the "state" in the ancient Near East and other bureaucratic empires. Or again, in feudalism, higher lords granted "fiefs" to lower lords, which included both relatively independent political jurisdiction together with a hereditary claim to the produce of the peasantry and even to the land. By contrast, in the ancient Near East rulers granted their high officials' incomes from large landed estates without hereditary rights and without independent political jurisdiction.

If with Lenski we focus on the different social strata, we end up with a vertical stratification of a populace into many "classes." If we focus instead on the basic political-economic-religious relations between these social strata, on the relations between (higher) ruler and subordinate governing class and the peasant producers, we can better appreciate the dynamics as well as the structure of agrarian societies. The differences between the three subtypes of feudal societies, city-states, and bureaucratic empires constitute a decisive systemic variation in the fundamental political-economic relations between ruler, governing class, and peasantry. In some of the societies among Lenski's comparative materials, the ruler was the sole political authority figure, who then economically supported the governing class with goods appropriated by the state from the peasants. In other agrarian societies members of the governing class enjoyed a combination of political authority over the peasantry and hereditary rights to the land or to the produce of the land. Most of Lenski's materials illustrate the former system. For study of second-temple Judea and other ancient Near Eastern societies and ancient empires, which display such decisive differences from both feudal Europe and the city-states of Greco-Roman antiquity, a far more precise comparative model of agrarian societies could be constructed by focusing on the majority of Lenski's materials. The excluded feudal European materials and city-states of Greco-Roman antiquity could then be used as illustrations of different systems for comparison and contrast.

Some of the remaining problems with Lenski's model when applied to second-temple Judea are rooted in the basic systemic differences just outlined. A key example is his delineation of the "priestly class" as separate and different from 'the ruler," the "governing class," and the "retainer class." Lenski was apparently making the Western differentiation between religious and political roles and institutions normative for his model. In much if not most of his materials, however, these dimensions of life have not been separated, or have been unevenly divided at different levels. The very use of terms such as "king" and/or "priest" may be a projection based on a more differentiated social system. Since in fact the category of "the priestly class" is not central or determinative in the majority of Lenski's comparative materials, making a distinction between priestly and other aristocrats or rulers (Lenski's "governing class") does not seem appropriate for agrarian societies generally. It is certainly not appropriate for ancient Judea.

Perhaps the major problem with Lenski's model is that the elaborate scheme of social stratification (the predilection of much American sociology) tends to obscure how social dynamics and conflict are rooted in the structure of power relations. It makes sense, therefore, to replace Lenski's twelve-class stratification with a focus on the fundamental political-economic-religious relations, using the wealth of comparative materials he has pulled together. By this refocusing of our inquiry, it becomes clear that the fundamental and controlling relationship lies between the rulers and the agricultural producers, the peasantry who comprise the vast majority (usually roughly 90 percent) of the people of such an agrarian society. By virtue of their power, military and other, the rulers are able to demand rent/tithes/tribute from the peasant producers whom they rule (but who are otherwise virtually self-sufficient). Then, as Lenski himself explains variously, the rulers (official ruler and governing class) use part of what they appropriate from the peasantry (1) to support a staff of military and legal-clerical "retainers" through whom the society is "governed," (2) to organize or support traders who obtain the luxury and other goods the rulers desire, (3) to pay or support artisans who make the various products required by the rulers and their retainers and supporters in the cities. The retainers, merchants, and even the artisans are thus all dependent upon, as well as subordinate to, the ruling class. This is a much simpler model than Lenski's ("advanced agrarian societies"), which enables us to better appreciate the fundamental divide in agrarian societies as well as the dynamics between rulers and peasants and between rulers and their retainers.

Lenski is sensitive to the fact that modern Western assumptions about private property tend to obscure our understanding of political-economic-religious relations in traditional agrarian societies (which is not generally noticed by biblical scholars who use his model). This is of inestimable importance in understanding how a ruler or state can lay claim to such a huge share of a society's productivity. "At the head of nearly every advanced agrarian state was a single individual, the king or emperor. Monarchy was the rule." If we approach such societies with the modern capitalist concept of private property in mind, it must appear that the monarch is the "owner" of the land. But then how do we explain that the peasants in such societies are by and large not slaves but free (to a degree), and that they also have certain claims to the land and its produce? The concept of private property or ownership may simply be inapplicable. More appropriate to traditional agrarian societies would be to reconceptualize property *in terms of rights, not things,* with the possibility of overlapping rights to the land, or perhaps better, to the produce of the land and the labor of the peasants.

Accordingly Lenski suggests "a proprietary theory of the state" as a way of understanding what "property" or "ownership" might mean in the concrete relational terms in which such societies apparently operated. The common or corporate "ownership" can be understood as vested in the head of state. "*All agrarian rulers enjoyed significant proprietary rights in virtually all of the land in their domains*" (italics Lenski's).[19] It may thus be possible to understand how agrarian rulers appear to be "owners" or rather "part-owners," not only of their own "royal estates," but also of all other lands that they grant as prebends to their officials and/or from which they extract taxes or tribute.

The "proprietary theory of the state," however, does not yet help us understand second-temple Judea and other temple-states. It is curious that in this connection Lenski does not discuss the mechanism by which such "proprietary rights in virtually all of the land in their domains" is legitimated for the monarchs of traditional agrarian societies. Ironically, Lenski focuses almost exclusively on the material level, though the *dialectical* materialist Karl Marx provides a far less reductionist approach, one that takes the religious dimension more fully into account. Lenski does mention in passing, with regard to the advanced horticultural system of Dahomey (in West Africa), that the rulers were regarded as divine or semidivine and thus the owners of all property in the land.[20] And he notes the ancient Mesopotamian conception of the land as the estate of the society's god(s), the temple as the house of the god(s), and the king or high priest (sometimes the same) as the chief servant of the god(s). But it is Marx who recognizes more generally that in such societies it is by virtue of being the symbol of the society as a whole, the head of the whole body, that the god or the god's regent (priest-king) is the controller (and beneficiary) of the tribute taken from the members of the social body. Biblical interpreters can surely appreciate that the working of such a societal system is dependent on just such an ideology or mythology of god(s) and king and/or high priest as the representative(s) and symbol(s) of the whole.

Perhaps because of its part in his overall evolutionary scheme, Lenski's model does not take into account the fact that most concrete examples of agrarian societies are parts of larger agrarian empires. This is a serious omission, as the previous two chapters above should make clear. As John Kautsky explains,[21] the aristocratic rulers of a large agrarian empire usually comprise a different society from the peoples they dominate, and even the rulers of subordinate states are often of different ethnic and cultural heritage than the people(s) they rule. Since many large aristocratic empires ruled their subject peoples indirectly through the native aristocracies or monarchies, the overall political-economic-religious system was usually more complex than Lenski's model allows. This subordination of one society to another and one ruling class to another should then be juxtaposed with the previous point about how the social system was held together by an ideology of a god and/or king/high priest at its center as a symbol of the whole. This juxtaposition enables us to discern the interrelated issues of (1) the "legitimacy" of the ruler(s), local and/or imperial; and (2) the potential conflict between the levels of rulers with different legitimating ideologies.

Critical review of the majority of Lenski's wide range of agrarian societies, those that come from outside feudal Europe and the ancient Greek and Roman city-states, thus results in a simpler picture of the fundamental political-economic-religious structure of agrarian societies. In the basic power relations of this structure, the rulers are able to demand tribute from subject peoples, which leads to the designation of such systems as "tributary." Both the stability and the potential for conflict in such societies are rooted in these basic power relations. This is the fundamental structure of ancient Near Eastern societies in general and, apparently, of second-temple Judean society, judging from information provided by Sirach.

SOCIAL STRUCTURE, SOCIAL RELATIONS, AND SOCIAL DYNAMICS IN BEN SIRA'S JUDEA

By comparing the information gleaned from the book of Sirach with the cross-cultural studies of agrarian societies consulted by Lenski, we may be able to gain a more precise picture of Judean society under the Hellenistic empires. In his instructional speeches and praise of the ancestors, Ben Sira portrays a simple political-economic-religious structure of a ruling aristocracy in Jerusalem supported by tithes, offerings, and sacrifices from the agricultural produce of ordinary "poor" Judeans. Scribes serve among the great ones, artisans and physicians supply basic services in the city, merchants supply goods from the outside, and slaves provide services in well-off households.

Lenski's elaborate scheme of stratification, in which he assigns people with similar functions in most agrarian societies to multiple "classes," obscures the power relations and the structural conflict between the various "strata." Read with a critical eye, Ben Sira's speeches on topics such as the relations of the rich and the poor and the obligation to pay tithes and offerings (7:29–31; 35:6–12) point fairly clearly to the fundamental division and conflict in second-temple Judea, which corresponds with that in similar "tributary" societies. Ben Sira also offers fairly clear hints of the power relations and potential conflict between aristocracy and the scribes. With Ben Sira's picture of the overall structure of Judean society in mind, we can further explore particular social relations and potential conflicts by focusing on the key roles of the aristocracy, the peasantry, the artisans, and finally the scribes, our special concern in this volume.

Ben Sira, however, utterly ignores the wider political-economic-cultural context in which the Jerusalem temple-state fits as one tiny subordinate unit in the larger Seleucid Empire. From that wider perspective the Jerusalem aristocracy was subordinate to and the representative of Seleucid imperial authority, responsible for maintaining the imperial order and collecting imperial taxes. Throughout our exploration of other social roles and relations, therefore, we must keep in mind the imperial rule on which Ben Sira is silent.

The High Priesthood and Ruling Aristocracy

Many modern interpreters have simply assumed that there were both a priestly aristocracy (headed by the high priest) and a lay aristocracy at the top of second-temple Judean society. Ben Sira would seem susceptible to this reading insofar as he refers to the Aaronide priesthood as having "authority over" and a special "inheritance in" the people, on the one hand, and yet refers to "the great, rulers, nobles," and others periodically gathered in various courts and assemblies, on the other. Several considerations, however, suggest that these terms refer to the same set of aristocratic figures. Most fundamental is that the small size of the territory and populace of Judea placed a limit on the size of aristocracy that could be supported economically. Perhaps the key indication is that with regard to both "the sons of Aaron" and "the great/rulers/princes," Ben Sira's portrayal of economic support is the same: the tithes, offerings, and sacrifices brought to the priests in the Temple. The reason that "priests" is missing from the set of synonymous terms the Ben Sira uses with reference to the aristocracy in the instructional speeches is that in those speeches he was using traditional language derived from the earlier monarchy. Another indication that the Judean aristocracy was (predominantly) priestly is that the ambitious Tobiads repeatedly married into the high-priestly family, presumably in order to enhance their power in Jerusalem and Judea (see chap. 2).

The decree of Antiochus III about the restoration of the temple-state in Jerusalem (quoted in chap. 2) has been taken as a reference to a lay aristocracy alongside the priesthood. It declares tax exemption for "the senate of elders [*gerousia*] and the priests and the scribes of the temple and the sacred singers" (*Ant.* 12.142). Modern interpreters' reading of the *gerousia* as a purely lay body,[22] however, appears to be determined by the modern Western assumption of the separation of religion and politics. In the historical surveys in chapters 1 and 2, it has been evident that the high priesthood and priestly aristocracy wielded political-economic power inseparable from their religiously authorized position at the center of the Judean temple-state.

The *gerousia* in Antiochus's decree more likely refers to a (mainly) priestly aristocracy. The decree as a whole (*Ant.* 12.138–144) focuses on the restoration of the Temple, with provisions of resources for the sacrifices and materials for reconstruction. Then, after granting the whole people permission to conduct their affairs according to their ancestral laws, the decree gives special tax relief to a specific list of "the senate of elders and the priests and the scribes of the temple and the temple singers." "The senate of elders," like the priests, scribes, and singers, would appear to belong with the Temple, the restoration of which is the principal focus of the decree. This is a list of functionaries of the Temple, arranged from highest rank to lowest. *Gerousia* is simply the Hellenistic Greek term for what appears to the imperial regime as the council of elders that heads the temple-state in Jerusalem. This way of understanding the list is confirmed by other formal communications in slightly later texts. The letter of the Hasmonean high priest Jonathan to Sparta a half-century later lists at the head of the Judean people "the high priest, the senate of elders of the people [*gerousia*], and the priests" (1 Macc. 12:6, au. trans.). As in this letter, so in Antiochus's decree, "the priests" refers to the ordinary priests, while the *gerousia* refers to the priestly aristocracy.

Ben Sira's grandson does not use the term *gerousia* in his Greek translation, either with reference to "brothers" of Simon, son of Onias, or with reference to the group of "great ones, nobles, judges," and others. In Ben Sira's teachings, the Hebrew *'ēdāh*, translated by *laos* (people) or *synagōgē* (assembly) and *qahal*, consistently translated by *ekklēsia* (assembly)—both generally refer to the (assembled) people (of Jerusalem or Judea or specifically, "of Israel"). He does, however, refer to a "gathering/council" (*plēthos*) of "nobles/elders" (*sārîm, presbyteroi*), a council in which he and other sages/scribes were (sometimes) present (6:34; 7:14; the same *sārîm* or "nobles" that the sages serve, as in 8:8). It may be significant that *sārîm* can be understood as "elders," which is evidently just how they were understood in the imperial chancery of Antiochus III, where his decree was drafted.

It seems reasonable to conclude, therefore, that Judean society was headed by a mainly priestly aristocracy. Many have assumed that the priestly aristocracy of the second Temple was Zadokite, although Ben Sira does not mention this. Since Ezekiel provides the only attestation of Zadokites as high priests, this may be questionable (see pp. 26–28 above). And perhaps not all members of the aristocracy were priests. The originally nonpriestly family of Tobiads intermarried with the high-priestly family repeatedly, over several generations. Some members of the aristocracy may have held a particular office. But we should not imagine that all members held the "portfolio" of a particular "ministry," as in the cabinets of modern governments.

The central figure and institution in the aristocracy, as well as symbolic head of the society as a whole, was the high priest(hood). In order to understand how the whole political-economic-religious system of second-temple Judea worked, we must devote more attention to the religious dimension focused on the high priesthood, a dimension simply neglected in Lenski's model. The people are to fear and to serve "the Most High," who is explicitly understood as "the king of all." Correspondingly, the whole temple-state apparatus is structured ostensibly toward the service of God. The priesthood headed by the high priest(hood), established by everlasting covenant and given "authority and statutes and judgments" over the people, is the people's representative to God as well as God's representative to the people. Therefore the people (are to) honor the priest with their tithes and offerings as the way of "fearing the Lord" (see esp. 45:15–21; 7:29–31).

Ben Sira thus presents a "proprietary theory of the state," but in a combination of theocratic and hierocratic terms (not taken into account by Lenski). God, as the ostensible "head of state," is the "proprietor" of the land, with the (high) priesthood as regent and actual head of (temple-)state and economy. In that position Aaron was granted a "heritage" but no "inheritance" among the people/land

(45:20–21). The modern Western concept of private property "gets in the way" at this point. The priesthood has no land of its own because as the head of the whole it receives a (special) heritage of "first fruits and sacrifices." Ideologically at least, the high priest(hood) and priests have no individual or personal wealth and power separate from their wealth and power as public figure(s) representative of the whole. The high priest and other members of the priestly aristocracy may well have used their public wealth and power as a means of generating what would appear as private wealth or property, as by charging interest on loans made from the stores/wealth they controlled (as representatives of the whole). But the basis of their wealth, power, and privilege was their position as the representative head of Judean society as a whole.

This particular hierocratic ideology was essential to the working of the Judean temple-state, both in its internal power relations and as a component political-economic unit of the reigning empire. Yet therein lay also the potential for conflict, both within the temple-state and between tradition-minded Judeans and the ruling imperial regime. Insofar as the (high) priesthood was representative of and had authority over the whole, then it both claimed support from the agricultural producers and commanded the loyalty of the governing apparatus it developed in addition to the priesthood itself, such as scribal advisers and administrators. So long as the traditional Judean hierocratic ideology and institutional forms were left intact, the Judean temple-state could operate in a semiautonomous way, with the high priesthood serving its traditional function as representative of the Judean people focused on God, Temple, and high priesthood, while simultaneously serving as representatives of the imperial regime, maintaining the imperial as well as domestic order.

However, to the extent that a leading faction of the ruling aristocracy in Judea appeared to compromise with or sell out to the ideological or institutional forms of the imperial regime, it would presumably have lost "legitimacy" among Judeans. This would have happened especially among those who strongly believed in and/or had a stake in the theocratic-hierocratic ideology. And such a compromise of Judean traditions and compromise with an alien culture would have affected Judeans according to their position and role in the social structure of the temple-state or temple-community. Adherence to the traditional hierocratic ideology could thus become an issue about which rival parties among the aristocracy and/or different circles of scribes might divide, or about which scribal circles might come into conflict with their patrons in the priestly aristocracy.

The Judean Peasantry

There would have been no glory for the high priest and priestly aristocracy—indeed no priesthood at all—without the peasant producers who supported the whole temple-state apparatus with their tithes and offerings. But peasants, like women, have generally been hidden from history. Insofar as the taxation to support the temple-state apparatus took the form of tithes and offerings from agricultural products, the whole system rested on peasant labor. Comparative studies suggest that since the level of agricultural production was traditionally low, the peasants who supported the rest of the society as well as themselves with food usually had to comprise about 90 percent of the population. They generally lived at the subsistence level, constantly threatened with poverty and hunger since their "surplus" produce had been expropriated by their rulers.[23]

This is precisely the picture Ben Sira offers in the few references he makes to the peasants' situation. He leaves us with no illusions about "the life of the poor under their own crude roof" (29:22). "Poor," "hungry," "needy," "desperate," and other such terms in his speeches apparently refer not to exceptional cases, but to a large proportion of the people (e.g., 4:1–10). Being economically marginal like peasants in most societies, the Judean producers were therefore chronically in need of loans and alms (29:1–20). Because they were marginal, however, they were all the more susceptible to the predatory practices of the wealthy and powerful (34:24–27).[24] That "the poor" were the "feeding grounds of the rich" (Sir. 13:18–23) was common in an agrarian society such as Judea.

This fundamental structural opposition in the society had potential for more overt class conflict. Studies of comparable agrarian societies, however, suggest that peasant resistance tends to be covert and to take subtle forms, with widespread popular revolt being rare. This suggests that economic pressure on Judean peasants in the early third century BCE, threatening their tenuous hold on rights to ancestral land and their subsistence living, was a significant factor in one of those rare outbursts, the Maccabean Revolt of the mid-160s BCE.

Artisans and Traders

The artisan, smith, and potter were essential to the operation of Jerusalem, as Ben Sira states (38:27–32). Some of Lenski's principal points about the "artisan class" appear to be based on evidence from medieval European towns and may not apply to most traditional agrarian societies. There is certainly little evidence from the ancient Near East generally indicating either that artisans were "originally recruited from the ranks of the dispossessed peasantry" or that "the majority of artisans were probably employees of the merchant class."[25] Nor is there evidence of artisans rebelling against those in authority over them. In the case of a temple-city such as Jerusalem (or for that matter in any capital or royal city), the artisans would have been economically dependent on the (priestly) rulers in command of the temple, city, and society. In the case of a temple-community, one wonders the extent to which the ordinary priests and/or Levites may have performed some of the supportive services.

Merchants in Jerusalem would also have served the needs of and been dependent on the ruling families. Perhaps it was true in late medieval Europe that "from a very early date merchants managed to free themselves from the direct and immediate authority of the ruler and governing class."[26] But that should not be projected onto ancient Judea. In the Ptolemaic Empire, which dominated Pales-

tine just before the time of Ben Sira, trade was a virtual monopoly of the imperial regime. It seems highly unlikely that things were any different in a far smaller
entity such as the Judean temple-state.[27] There would thus appear to be no more
basis in evidence from comparable agrarian societies than in Ben Sira's teaching
or archaeological findings for extensive commercial activity by merchants in Hellenistic Judea. Far from being a reaction to an upsurge of commerce, Ben Sira's
negative attitude toward traders and merchants was common in ancient litera-
tures and among ancient aristocracies, whose values they articulated.

Scribes/Sages

The scribes and sages, Ben Sira himself and the typical scribe-sage he speaks about,
clearly fit into what Lenski called "retainers," those who assist the rulers in "governing" an agrarian society.[28] In serving among "the great ones," they play a role
in councils of state and judicial courts, as the ones who "understand the decisions
of courts" and "can expound discipline and judgment" (38:33–34). Significantly,
Antiochus's decree also closely associates "scribes of the temple," like "the priests,"
with the *gerousia,* who comprised the rulers of the Jerusalem temple-state.

From Ben Sira's extensive reflections on the activities of his own "profession,"
it is clear that the sages were retainers with scribal-legal-cultural-religious functions, some of which may have overlapped with those of the priests. Wise scribes
performed functions that Lenski ascribes to "the clergy" in societies of limited literacy. They also served as diplomats and especially as educators. According to Ben
Sira's ideology of the priesthood, the function of teaching the law, having originated with Moses (45:5), belonged to the Aaronid priesthood (45:17). In second-
temple Judea the (high) priesthood over a period of generations must have, in
effect, "delegated" that authority and function to the sages, with regard to the
exercise of their own governing authority (38:32–39:4), and perhaps with regard
to the people generally (37:23). The sages are the ones whose distinctive role is
"to study the law [torah] of the Most High" and to serve as guardians of Judean
culture in general (38:34–39:3).

The distinction between the scribal retainers and the rulers in Ben Sira's Judea
was relatively clear, compared with other agrarian societies included in Lenski's
synthetic study, where the boundary was "often fuzzy."[29] In the Judean temple-
state before the Maccabean Revolt, belonging to the aristocracy presumably
depended on having the requisite priestly lineage. Thus scribes from nonpriestly
or ordinary priestly families could not have moved into the sacerdotal "governing class" even if they held considerable de facto power. Ben Sira gives no indication that scribes wielded much power in his own day. The sage "serves among
the great ones and appears before rulers." But, Ben Sira warns his fellow sages,
"Among the great [ones] [*sārîm, megistanōn*] do not act as their equal" (32:9).

Learned scribes appear not only to have served the priestly aristocracy, but also
to have been dependent economically on the rulers as well. The principal clue
is that Ben Sira repeatedly cautions his scribal students about the deference

incumbent on them in their close contact with their powerful patrons. The sage must bow low to the ruler (4:7). When invited to dinner by rulers, they must know how to handle themselves prudently, so as not to give offense (13:8–11; 31:12–24). Their economic dependence on aristocratic patrons also meant that their exhortation about the importance of tithes and offerings involved a certain self-interest.

The scribes' vulnerability in their relations with their aristocratic patrons is reflected in Ben Sira's teaching about women, especially about wives. The fundamental social-economic form in ancient Judea, as in any traditional agrarian society, was the transgenerational patriarchal family headed by the husband-father as a petty monarch. Ben Sira's instruction about women, however, strikes a tone even more negative and controlling than already traditional proverbs and previous wisdom-teaching in Proverbs.[30] Instructional speeches about women lay great stress on the stability and security of marriage and home and the respectability and obedience of wives and daughters (Sir. 25:1, 8, 13–15, 16–26; 26:1–9, 13–18). The husband-father has a special concern about being completely in control and the strict obedience of wives (25:24–26). This need for security and control in the marriage and home is very likely related to scribes' lack of control in their relations with their superiors who exercised control over them.

Despite their dependency on the aristocracy, learned scribes had an authority of their own. At least in their own mind, their own authority stemmed from their knowledge of wisdom and their faithful adherence to the torah of the Most High (which Ben Sira, at least, understood as more or less the same). Just as the high priesthood had its power, privilege, and authority from God through an eternal covenant, so also the sages had their authority as the custodians of divine revelation in the torah of God and prophecies. They themselves were the heirs of earlier generations of sages. Ben Sira even claims that his wisdom has a certain affinity with prophecy as well (24:33).

Viewed in the broader political-cultural context of the Hellenistic imperial situation in which they were operating, this dedication and sense of independent higher authority should alert us to the potential for eventual overt as well as latent social-political conflict. Insofar as the sages' professional role or function was the cultivation of the traditional Judean covenantal laws as (at least in effect) the official state law, their dedication to these laws would have been far more than a matter of individual morality. The sages had their own clear sense, independent of their employers, of how the temple-state should operate: in accordance with (their interpretation of) the covenantal laws. Their high-priestly superiors, however, had regular dealings with Hellenistic imperial officials and were susceptible to influence from the wider Hellenistic culture. As noted in the previous chapter, some and perhaps many in the (priestly) aristocracy were seriously distracted by the "opportunities" of Hellenistic culture and politics. Eventually these aristocrats spearheaded the Hellenizing "reform" in 175 BCE, in which they seriously compromised the traditional Judean way of life. In just such circumstances scribal circles who were rigorously loyal to the tradition of which they were the custodians would have been caught in an acute dilemma, torn between their loyalty to the traditional way of life and their dependence on the aristocracy they served.

The scribes' strong personal and "professional" dedication to the Mosaic covenantal commandments, along with the independent authority they claimed on that basis, may also have contributed to their concern for the poor, judging from Ben Sira's "wisdom." His exhortations include not only admonitions of personal ethics to "stretch out your hand to the poor" (7:32), but also what look like instructions to other sages not to "cheat the poor" or to "reject the suppliant" and even, more actively, to "rescue the oppressed from the oppressor," presumably in their official or professional capacities (4:1–10). Clearly Ben Sira's view of the sage's function in society included more than simply an obligation to his aristocratic patrons. It also included a perceived obligation to God to mitigate the abuses of the poor by the powerful.

In both their potential opposition to certain actions or policies of the high-priestly rulers and their concern for the poor, the sages display similarities to the clergy in medieval Europe described by Lenski. But their social structural position was quite different. The medieval Christian clergy was "a specially protected class," economically and politically separate and independent, whereas the second-temple sages were economically dependent and politically-religiously subordinate. Yet the claim to direct divine authority independent of the rulers was clearly asserted by the scribal class, as evident in Ben Sira, and helped to set a precedent for what the Christian church eventually institutionalized more securely.

Presumably the high-priestly rulers accepted this semi-independent role of the sages because it was part of the foundation of their claim to divine authority and this made the sages able to provide the ideological basis for the priests' rule. Ben Sira's praise of the ancestors provides a prime example of how a staunchly partisan sage could play this role faithfully. It indirectly served the interests of the wealthy as well, insofar as the scribal circles that defended the interests of the poor may have provided a legitimate (but nonthreatening) outlet for the frustration that may have developed among the impoverished peasantry.

Dependency on Superiors and Factional Conflict

The potential for conflict in the political-economic-religious relations between the priestly aristocratic rulers of the Judean temple-state and their scribal retainers came to a head in the late third and early second centuries. The key factors were two: (1) the potential conflict between the legitimating religious ideology of the temple-state and the dominant imperial culture into which the priestly aristocracy was drawn by their dual and potentially conflictual role as heads of the temple-state and agents of the imperial regime; and (2) the conflict between scribes loyal to the ancestral traditions of the Judean temple-state and high-priestly faction(s) prepared to compromise those traditions in their assimilation to the ways of the dominant imperial culture and politics.

Under the Persian Empire, the Jerusalem Temple, dedicated to "the God who is in Jerusalem" (Ezra 1:3), was set up purposely to provide a basis for the temple-state in traditional local Judean culture. The high priesthood stood at the head of Judean society as the mediator with the God of the Judeans, even as they also delivered tribute to the Persian court and shaped the temple-state according to the commands of the Persian governors. In their service among the priests, "the scribes of the temple" took responsibility for shaping and cultivating Judean culture focused on the legitimation of the Temple and priesthood. As noted above, however, Judean scribes had developed a sense of their own authority as devoted to the keeping of the commandments and cultivation of other traditional culture, an authority semi-independent of their aristocratic patrons. Some scribes such as Ben Sira might draw on their higher independent authority to support the incumbents of the high priesthood. But other scribal circles could do so in opposition to the priestly aristocracy, as evident in sections of *1 Enoch* and the visions in Daniel 7–12.

The Ptolemaic and Seleucid imperial regimes left the Jerusalem temple-state intact with its traditional Judean cultural forms of temple, priesthood, and authorizing history and law codes. In the surrounding territories, however, they fostered the formation of cities on the pattern of Greek polity and culture. Inconsistent policy and rival factions within and between the Ptolemaic and Seleucid imperial regimes, moreover, created opportunities that in effect encouraged power struggles within the Jerusalem aristocracy. Some aristocratic families were attracted by the dominant imperial culture as well as opportunities for political-economic prominence. To the degree that leading members of the aristocracy appeared to be compromising the commandments of God and the Temple's and priesthood's devotion to the God of the Judeans, however, scribes strongly devoted to the traditional culture would have been increasingly torn between obedience to the commandments and loyalty to their aristocratic superiors. This set up the possibility that scribal circles might split into different factions, perhaps in correlation with factions among the aristocracy, and might be divided in their loyalty or opposition to particular occupants and policies of the high-priestly office. It is just such conflicts that underlie the various texts combined in *1 Enoch* and the visions now in Daniel 7–12, as we shall explore in chapters 8 and 9, below.

Chapter 4

Scribes and Sages

Administrators and Intellectuals

The scribes were an elite group of learned, literate men, an intellectual aris-
tocracy which played an invaluable role in the administration of their peo-
ple in both religious and political affairs. They were dedicated to a variety
of roles: guardians of their cultural heritage, intellectual innovators, world
travelers . . . , lawyers, doctors, astrologers, diviners, magicians, scientists,
court functionaries, linguists, exegetes, etc. Their greatest love was the story
of themselves and they guarded and transmitted their teaching. . . . They
speculated about hidden heavenly tablets, . . . about the beginning and end
and thereby claimed to possess the secrets of creation. Above all, they talked,
they memorized and remembered, they wrote.

Jonathan Z. Smith[1]

Ben Sira's portrayal of wise scribes as advisers and administrators of the Jerusalem
temple-state might appear to stand at some variance with standard pictures of the
wisdom teachers who authored wisdom literature, such as Proverbs, Job, Ecclesiastes, and Sirach itself. The reflection on the role of the wise scribe in Sirach needs
to be checked against the much briefer references to scribes in earlier Judean texts.
Moreover, since Judea was embedded in and influenced by its ancient Near Eastern context, comparisons with the role of scribes and sages in the great civilizations of Egypt and Mesopotamia may enable us to appreciate how Ben Sira and
his students stand in a venerable tradition of intellectual retainers. The increasing
information now available about scribes in the ancient Near East confirms that
cultivation of wisdom was integrally related with their function as administrators
at various levels in the service of rulers. It also suggests that their range of knowledge was far wider than what has usually been understood as wisdom.

SCRIBES AND SCRIBAL TRAINING
IN MESOPOTAMIA AND EGYPT

Plenty of evidence is available on scribes in Mesopotamia, from the thousands of clay tablets recovered that they produced over many centuries. From well before the time of Hammurabi (ca. 1750 BCE), scribes had assumed important roles in the administration of Mesopotamian cities and empires. They fulfilled a variety of functions in royal and imperial regimes and, especially in later times, in temple administrations. Titles such as "palace scribe" (*dub-sar-e-gal*) and "king's scribe" (*dub-sar-lugal*, literally "scribe of the great one") were standard from earliest records and resurface in the Neo-Assyrian period (Akkadian *tupsar ekalli*). In sources for the period around 2100 BCE (Ur III), the grand vizier had a number of scribes under his command in the royal administration. A list of professions includes eighteen kinds of scribes as officials of the monarchy.[2] While they refer to themselves generally as "scribes" (*tupsarru*), they served in variety of capacities. And although some may have specialized in one or another function, many probably performed more than one, especially since the functions overlapped.[3]

In administrative capacities, many probably served as mere recorders of goods received as payment of tithes and tribute by the temples and/or royal storehouses and the disbursement of goods to workers on state building projects. Their records would have required coordination by supervisors. At the top of the administration, a few sages served as "secretaries" and advisers and high-ranking officers in the imperial court. Some of these "chief scholar-experts" (*rab ummani*) were apparently very powerful figures in the Babylonian and Assyrian regimes they served in the early first millennium.[4]

Scribes also composed, cultivated, and copied a range of official statements, ritual texts, and other texts. They composed the royal pronouncements that justified the rulers' policies, the messages or formulas to be inscribed on monuments, founding inscriptions for the erection of temples and palaces, as well as official correspondence. They provided hymns of praise to the king and royal mythic epics for court entertainment, edification, and self-justification. On behalf of the rulers that came after the Babylonians, scribes preserved the cultural legacy as well as language of the earlier Sumerian and Akkadian rulers.[5] Scribes also cultivated collections of official laws. Previously understood as "law codes," these collections are recently being recognized as more like scholarly jurisprudence, compendia of (royal) decrees and decisions that were not intended for application by courts.[6]

Divination was a particularly important function of Mesopotamian scholar-scribes. It became a highly sophisticated skill based on scholarly compendia of predictions from previous generations and centuries, organized by topic for accessibility. Such collections, in fact, comprise the most voluminous kind of texts recovered from the imperial civilizations of Mesopotamia.[7] Asked for advice about upcoming events or plans, the scribes searched their repertoire for earlier predictions that might bear on the future events. By interpreting ominous signs, wise scribes predicted the future for the king. With kings and military commanders eager for the best "intelligence" about the future, good diviners (*baru*) were in demand at court. A diviner such as Asqudum, known from the Mari texts, could be included in the highest councils of state.[8] Rulers' continuing patronage of divination, given their keen interest in knowledge of the future, was surely what made possible as well as necessary the elaborate scholarly record keeping of previous predictions.

In the first millennium there was a decisive shift in technique of divination from inspection of the entrails of sheep (extispicy) to the observation of celestial signs (i.e., early astronomy, often called "astrology"), atmospheric phenomena, and abnormal animal behavior. This development of celestial observation led to further multiplication of specialized scholarly compendia. The development of greater specialization in divinization led to the emergence of different local "schools" of experts with distinctive codes of interpretation and hermeneutical traditions in many of the major cities. Assyrian rulers could consult different circles of scholarly diviners for signs and predictions bearing on their decisions and ventures. Out of such celestial observation for divination developed the most abstract mathematical astronomy in certain circles of scholarly Babylonian scribes.

The find of hundreds of letters addressed to the Neo-Assyrian kings Esarhaddon and Ashurbanipal by learned scribes provide abundant evidence for the central importance of scribal experts in the imperial courts.[9] Scribes (*tupsarru*), diviners (*baru*), exorcists (*asipu*), physicians (*asu*), and lament-singers (*kalu*) commanded a wide range of knowledge on matters such as celestial phenomena (e.g., eclipses), meteorological portents, ritual affairs, auspicious days for undertaking various activities, and the health of rulers. The vast majority of the scribes who produced these letters were evidently in close relationship with the king and his inner circle.

Gaining the skills and knowledge entailed in all of these specialized functions of professional scribes required years of rigorous training.[10] The modern concept of "school" may be misleading, since the training was more like an apprenticeship conducted on a small scale.[11] A master scribe (*ummia*) presided over an *edubba,* a Sumerian term translated as "tablet-house" (*bit-tuppi[m]*) in Akkadian. Terminology for the training process is all familial: the teacher/trainer was the "father," the student/trainee the "son." The "tablet-house" was probably the master scribe's own house, scribal offices having been largely hereditary. If a nonfamily member were brought into the training, he was in effect adopted as a "son." The "sons" were not only being trained in the technical skills and specialized knowledge required for their professional functions, but were also being socialized into a whole system of values focused on loyalty and obedience to the rulers they were preparing to serve.

Biblical interpreters often think of students of wisdom as having focused primarily on "wisdom literature" under the tutelage of a "wisdom teacher." In Mesopotamia, however, proverbs and reflective wisdom composed only a small part of the scribal trainees' curriculum. They also learned standard hymns, royal prayers, songs of praise to the king, laments over destroyed cities, love poetry, and myths of origin.[12] In some of these materials the apprentice scribes worked with

Akkadian adaptations of older Sumerian works. Although the curriculum of scribal training became remarkably standardized, some significant shifts are evident in the first millennium.[13] Texts connected with Babylon such as the epic of origins, *Enuma Elish,* and letters to Marduk became more prominent and, as divinization became more important in ruling circles, many student-scribes focused on lists of predictions and omens.

The goal or purpose, and presumably to some degree the effect, of this scribal training was the formation of a certain type of person, understood as a higher "humanity." "Master god who [shapes] humanity," says a Sumerian trainee to his teacher, "you are my god. You have opened my eyes as though I were a puppy; you have formed humanity within me."[14] In many of the Sumerian and Akkadian texts that the students learned to copy, it was the king, as the paradigmatic scribal scholar, who embodied the ideal of humanity. He maintained the stability of the universe by embodying *me,* or "order" (cf. the *dātā*, "law" or "order," embodied in the Persian emperor and his word, in chap. 1, above). The result was the formation of a group or "class" with specialized knowledge and functions set apart from the general populace, a group of people loyal and obedient to the rulers they served and economically dependent on those rulers.

The position and functions of scribes in Egypt were similar to those in Mesopotamia, as suggested by the stereotyped phrase that appears repeatedly in Egyptian texts, "the scribes and sages of Pharaoh," or "his scribes and sages."[15] Sources are far fewer for Egypt than for Mesopotamia, but they portray a similar range of capacities in which "the scribes and sages" served, primarily in the administration. In Egypt there appears to have been more of an overlap between scribes and (lector-)priests. Sources represent scribes primarily in service of the royal court and administration in the second millennium, and more and more in association with temples in the first millennium.[16] This shift of their activity from court to temple may be correlated with the temples having become the centers of preservation of traditional culture once the center of imperial rule shifted to foreign courts, and/or foreign rulers became dominant in Egyptian and Mesopotamian cities. While the vast majority of scribes probably served in lower-level administrative capacities, it is the scribes and sages of high position who left inscriptions on statues and gained fame in literature about whom we have information.

On the monument of Amenhotpe son of Hapu, the royal scribe and overseer of royal works under the Pharaoh Amenhotpe III (Dynasty 18)—whose fame lasted into Hellenistic times (as attested by Josephus and Manetho)—the inscription declares:

> I am a great man, greatest of the great, skilled in hieroglyphs and reasoned (?) counsel, adhering to the king's plans, whose position the sovereign advanced [or: who was advanced because of the excellence of his plans, whom the king exalted above his peers]. . . . I was appointed to be the royal scribe at the palace, and moreover was introduced to the god's book(s), saw the powers of Thoth and was equipped with their secrets. I opened up all their mysteries and my advice was sought concerning all their matters.[17]

The inscription on the statue of Nebneteru, royal secretary under Osorkon II (Dynasty 22), represents him as "an official of the outer chamber who guides the land by his counsel" (*AEL* 3.21), with "a mouth effective at privy speech, . . . whose coming is awaited at the palace and whose sagacity has promoted his person" (*AEL* 3.20). That the highest ranking "scribes and sages" operated in the inner councils of the court is illustrated in a (photo of a now-destroyed) relief from a tomb at Saqqarah, from Dynasty 19. In the top row are seated kings; in the second and third rows are "standing mummiform figures . . . , including viziers, high priests of Ptah, lector-priests, and chief embalmers."[18]

As in Mesopotamia, the range of scribes' functions was wide. The "scribes and sages of Pharaoh" (or "learned scribes"), some of whom were also lector-priests, were called upon to compose diplomatic correspondence, on the one hand, and to find the source of a strange perfume in the royal laundry (*AEL* 2.203–211), on the other. A story from the Persian period tells of the "Council of the Court," senior palace officials, charged with selecting from their number a sage with competence as a physician to examine the sister of the queen, who had been stricken with a mysterious malady (*AEL* 3.90–94).[19] In another story, the "Council of the Court," asked to recommended a sage who could entertain the Pharaoh with his eloquence, put forward the soothsayer Neferty, "that sage of the east, . . . a great lector priest of Bastet . . . , a scribe with excellent fingers" (*AEL* 1.140).[20]

As illustrated by Neferty's reputation as a soothsayer, prediction of the future and interpretation of dreams was an important function of scribes. "Learned scribes" were also "those who predicted what was to come." Thuty, the royal butler and herald of Queen Hatshepsut (Dynasty 18), had on his monument: "I investigated a time and predicted what was to come, (being) one who was skilled in looking at the future, aware of yesterday and thoughtful concerning tomorrow, ingenious regarding what would happen."[21] Linked with their soothsaying and prediction, as they served the rulers, was the learned scribes' skill in the magical arts.[22] As portrayed in Genesis, the Pharaoh "summoned all the magicians [*hartummîm*] of Egypt and all the sages [*ḥăkāmîm*]" to interpret his dream (Gen. 41:8). Again in the confrontation with Moses and Aaron, Pharaoh summoned "the sages and sorcerers" and "the magicians" of Egypt to transform their rods into serpents with appropriate incantations (Exod. 7:11; 8:7). The pejorative modern English terms "sorcerers" and "magic/ians" are misleading. Significantly the later Egyptian demotic term for "sorcerer" is an abbreviation of the earlier title "chief lector-priest," and that same demotic term is the likely source of the Hebrew term *hartummîm,* which is translated with "magicians." In Egypt a "magician" was also a "learned scribe," a sage, magical arts being one of the many functions of capacities in which "scribes and sages" served the rulers.

Scribes, finally, as the name indicates, were also responsible for the composition, cultivation, and copying of texts. In this connection Egyptian civilization had a distinctive institution called "the House of Life," which became more prominent in later periods of Egyptian civilization. The "houses of life" were usually, but not always, located near temples and had some connection with them. Although they seem to have been more than libraries or scriptoria, they were centers for the preservation, copying, and perhaps composition of texts, including books of magic, medicine, dreams, and religious texts.[23] Some scribes are referred to as "a scribe of the House of Life," or "a scribe of the god's book(s) in the House of Life."[24]

All of these capacities in which scribes and sages functioned depended on their being learned. The most frequently used term that is translated "scribe" meant literally "one who knows things," a sage. Egyptian scribes supposedly studied everything, past and present. As in Mesopotamia, the training of scribes started with writing skills and the memorization and manipulation of written signs for language. For those headed into administrative positions in bureaucracy, army, temple, or court, more advanced and specialized training was necessary.[25] Scribal training was carried out mainly in the family, with father training son in the skills and ethos of scribal life.[26] A scribal household was also the school for "the children of others" who were given to a scribe "to be heirs as [his] own children."[27]

"Houses of instruction" beyond private scribal households did emerge in the First Intermediate Period. But there was no such specialized profession as "teacher." Rather, senior scribes directed fledgling scribes as apprentices; "fathers" taught "sons." Sources for the Middle Kingdom mention the *kap,* where orphans and other children apparently from nonscribal families might be trained for fundamental administrative functions.[28] Also mentioned is a royal school in the capital city, Memphis, in which student scribes may have become socialized into an obedient and cohesive cadre of royal servants. The expansion of the empire in the New Kingdom (ca. 1567–1085) required an expanded administration, with corresponding proliferation of scribal training.[29] In the first millennium "the priesthood became an ever more central locus for such education."[30] The "curriculum" in Egypt included more wisdom teachings and reflection, including the instruction of famous sages of the past, and fewer epic, historical chronicles and hymns than in Mesopotamia.[31]

As in Mesopotamia, the purpose of scribal training was not just literacy and learning, but also the shaping of a certain kind of person in a distinctive ethos of service. Scribes were drilled in moral instruction that emphasized living in conformity with *Ma'at,* the order established by the divine cosmic forces in primordial time. They were embued with and trained to conserve and transmit the collected knowledge of past generations. "An intelligent man is a [store]house for nobles. . . . *Ma'at* comes to the one well-strained in accordance with what the ancestors have said" (*AEL* 1.99). "Learned scribes" were socialized to serve the rulers with pride and obedience. Economically dependent on their superiors, they learned to use their knowledge in disciplined ways to help maintain the order established by the gods.

SCRIBES IN JUDAH-YEHUD-JUDEA

Increasing uncertainty about the circumstances in which the books that were later included in the Hebrew Bible were composed and further developed has led to extreme caution in their use as historical sources. The portrayal of the imperial-style monarchy that reached its climax under Solomon in 1 Kings 3–10 is now widely recognized as a later glorification. The most skeptical historians insist that the biblical books were not written until the fourth century BCE or later, and hence can yield information only about second-temple times; with regard to an earlier era, they merely project historical fiction.[32] The recent increase in archaeological evidence and its more systematic analysis now provides a sobering check on historical reconstruction from literary sources. This evidence suggests that even a small centralized monarchic state must not have emerged in Jerusalem until the eighth century.[33] Nevertheless, although they continued to develop during second-temple times (see chap. 6, below), biblical books included earlier materials. Thus, although the narratives in 1 Kings project a picture of a fully developed monarchy and royal administration back to the time of David and Solomon, that picture may well be much less an exaggeration of the monarchy's structure at the time of Isaiah and especially of Jeremiah.

References to "the scribe of the king" or the (principal) scribe at the royal court of David and Solomon, while probably projections onto an earlier time, thus seem to give a reliable picture of the Jerusalem monarchy in the eighth and seventh centuries.[34] As representations of scribal roles in the royal administration, they fit well into the fuller picture that can be derived from references to high-ranking scribes toward the end of the monarchy. The various names of "the scribe" at David's court (Seraiah, 2 Sam. 8:17; Sheva, 2 Sam. 20:25; Shisha, 1 Kings 4:3; Shavsha, 1 Chron. 18:16) look like they are derived from the Egyptian word for "royal scribe." That "Shisha's" sons, Elihoreph and Ahijah, are listed as scribes in Solomon's regime suggests that son(s) could succeed father in high office. The "scribe(s) of the king" stood among the top officials of the royal administration, alongside the priest(s), the recorder (also a professional scribe?), the head of the mercenary professional army, the head of forced labor, and the manager of the palace. That "the sons of David" are also included (as a separate item) in the list of "chief officers in the service of the king" (1 Chron. 18:16–17, alt.) suggests that "the scribe" and priests were not members of the royal family. Yet they stood among the members of the ruling family(ies) in the highest council of the monarchy, important for their special expertise and function. Under King Jehoash, "the scribe of the king" and the (high) priest took charge of donations to the Temple, from which they paid the workers who were repairing the building (2 Kings 12:9–16; cf. 2 Chron. 24:11). Under King Hezekiah, Shebna the scribe along with the palace manager and the recorder were sent as envoys to negotiate with the Assyrian officers besieging Jerusalem (2 Kings 18:18, 37; 19:2; Isa. 36:3, 22; 37:2).

We have a somewhat fuller picture for the reign of Josiah and the conflict between the prophet Jeremiah and the declining monarchy at the end of the seventh century. Shaphan, "the scribe," along with Hilkiah the high priest, played the central role in the discovery, reading, and validation (through the prophetess Huldah) of the law-scroll "found" in the house of the LORD (2 Kings 22:3–14;

2 Chron. 34:8–21). Shaphan's sons, Ahikam and Elasah and Gemariah, used their position to protect the prophet Jeremiah from the hostility of others in high position or to facilitate delivery of his prophetic messages that seemed subversive to many (Jer. 26:24; 29:3; 36:10). That Gemariah had a chamber in the upper court of the Temple near the New Gate may indicate that he had some supervisory role there. Shaphan's grandson, Gedaliah son of Ahikam, was appointed governor of the towns of Judah by the king of Babylon (2 Kings 25:22–25; Jer. 40). Son evidently followed father in the scribal profession, at least in high-level positions. Moreover, when a conquering empire removed the rulers, they entrusted administration of the area to such experienced professional administrators, who shifted their service (and obedience) from one set of rulers to another.

The book of Jeremiah (36:12, 20–21) also mentions Elishama in the office of "the scribe" along with other "officers" (*sārîm*) of the kingdom, including Gemariah son of Shaphan. This, along with the information that the Babylonians later appointed Gemariah's nephew Gedaliah as governor of Judah, suggests that there was more than one prominent scribe and scribal family among professional scribes at the highest level of administration. Among the highly placed scribes and scribal families there were alternatives, perhaps even rivals. It must have been well known that the other sons of Shaphan were protecting and cooperating with Jeremiah, who was insisting that the king of Judah "submit to the yoke of the king of Babylon." The king of Judah could appoint now one and now another as "the (royal) scribe," could replace Shaphan or one of his sons with Elishama. But Gemariah son of Shaphan continued to serve as one of the highest "officers," even when the vociferously protesting Jeremiah was seen as a threat to the regime. It may not be by accident that the conquering Babylonian rulers entrusted the administration of the towns of Judah to an experienced administrator whose family was identified with a prophet who had urged submission to their rule, thus representing the leading "loyal opposition" voices among royal counselors.

In addition to "the scribe of the king" who was one of the top counselors and administrators of the monarchy, there were other scribes serving at different levels of administration. The Deuteronomic account of the Babylonian conquest lists "the secretary [scribe] of the commander of the army who mustered the people of the land" among those executed by the captain of the guard (2 Kings 25:18–21; Jer. 52:25). It is possible that the "herald" (*mazkîr*) and "the [literate] officials" were also officers with (some) scribal training. Jeremiah's charge that "the false pen of the scribes has made [God's law] into a lie" suggests that there had been many scribes involved in the reform under Josiah (Jer. 8:8–9). Though most scribes must have served in some way in the administration of the monarchy or later temple-state, some may well have been at least semi-independent. Baruch, to whom Jeremiah dictated his prophetic oracles against the monarchy and temple and who then recited them in front of the people, the high officers, and then the king, certainly had the courage to risk his neck in delivering the unwelcome divine indictments.

Scribes in Judah thus served in many of the same range of functions as did scribes in Mesopotamia and Egypt, although our sources do not provide as complete a picture as we would wish. During the monarchy scribes had become an integral part of the royal administration in Judah. The phrase "skilled scribe" (*sôpēr māhîr*) became a standing idiom (Ps. 45:2; Ezra 7:6).[35] Alluding to that idiom, a traditional proverb indicates the political-economic position and role of scribes in Judah: "Do you see one skilled [*māhîr*] in work? He serves kings, not the common people" (Prov. 22:29, au. trans.). From the references just surveyed, it is clear that they were essential for correspondence, accounting and records (census and taxation), building projects, and at the highest level were involved in diplomacy and councils of state.[36] In contrast to their counterparts in Mesopotamia and Egypt, Judean scribes are not portrayed as specialists in magic or divination. The "prophets" (*nĕbî'îm*) who pronounced indictments and sentences on rulers and their officers for oppression of the people do not appear to have (also) been scribes. It is conceivable, however, that the "prophets of Baal" and "prophets of Asherah" at the court of Ahab and Jezebel in Samaria corresponded somewhat to the many scribal diviners at the court in Babylon.

From literature that reflects the Persian period the best-known figure is the "skilled scribe" and priest Ezra, a high-ranking Judean scribe in the service of the Persian imperial regime, who was sent to straighten out administration in the province Beyond the River (or at least in Judah/Yehud). This "skilled scribe" and priest became prominent in Judean culture as the great lawgiver who authorized the temple-state, and his memoirs became one of its foundational documents.

There are only a few references to other "scribes" in the books of Chronicles, Ezra, and Nehemiah.[37] Ironically, passing references may be the most informative. For example, to manage the distribution of tithes (and to block abuse of power by Eliashib and others in the priestly aristocracy), Nehemiah "appointed as treasurers over the [Temple] storehouses the priest Shelemiah, the scribe Zadok, and Pedaiah of the Levites" (Neh. 13:7–13). This indicates that Zadok was a prominent figure among a number of scribes attached to the Temple, who were supported by its resources from tithes. Evidently scribes continued to carry out certain functions for the central institution of the political economy of Judah-Yehud.

This is confirmed by the books of Chronicles, apparently composed to ground the temple-state in the Davidic monarchy. At many points the narrative indicates familiarity with scribes in service of the governing institution of Yehud (e.g., 1 Chron. 18:16; 27:32). The schematic recapitulation of the divisions of the priestly descendants of Aaron, duly recorded by "the scribe Shemaiah son of Nethanel, a Levite" (1 Chron. 24:6), in the presence of King David and the whole court, probably represents an important function of a high-ranking scribal administrator in the temple-state of the Persian period.

Shemaiah the scribe was also a Levite, and Ezra the skilled scribe was also a priest. There appears to have been significant overlap in these indications of status and position in the operation of the temple-state. This is stated explicitly in Josiah's deployment of the Levites to collect and disburse resources and supervise the laborers in the repair of the Temple: "some of the Levites were scribes [*sôperîm*], and [literate] officials [*shōṭěrîm*], and gatekeepers" (2 Chron. 34:8–13). Similarly, David's decree about the organization of the temple (1 Chron. 23–26) at two points includes among the Levites officers (*shōṭěrîm*) in charge of various Temple treasuries, and "officers and judges" for outside matters (*shōṭěrîm, shōpěṭîm*; 1 Chron. 23:1–6; 26:29–32). In texts portraying earlier times, as noted above, the functions of the last two were assigned to high-ranking scribes and priests, and the term *shōṭěrîm* in key contexts had connotations of "literate officials."[38] Later texts, moreover, certainly understood it this way, as illustrated in the Judean historian Josephus's paraphrase of 1 Chron. 23:1–6 (*Ant.* 7.363–365): the Levites were to be "scribes" (*grammateis*) as well as judges.

The *Testament of Levi* also knew that the Levites, "by [whose] word the sanctuary would be controlled," were to be "priests, judges, and *scribes*"; it has Levi exhort his sons to "teach your sons letters [*grammata*, writing and reading] that they might have understanding" (8:16–17; 13:1–2). We may also recall that the decree of Antiochus III reauthorizing the temple-state gave tax relief to the principal categories of people who presided over and operated the Temple: "the *gerousia,* the priests, the scribes of the Temple, and the temple-singers" (Josephus, *Ant.* 12.142). The books of Chronicles had simply included the latter two categories among the Levites.

It is thus evident that under Persian rule the administration of the temple-state included scribes who were supported from Temple revenues. Only some Levites were scribes, and it seems unlikely that all scribes were Levites. Nehemiah's administrative arrangement of disbursements from the Temple storehouses makes the scribes a separate group alongside the priests and Levites. There must have been different ways of designating the same scribal experts. That scribes were closely associated with priests and Levites enables us to understand many references in later texts to the scribes exercising functions that had been assigned to the priests in earlier literature. The scribal profession was hereditary, as exemplified in the list of the sons of Caleb, which includes "families of scribes who lived at Yabez" (1 Chron. 2:42–55).

On the position and functions of scribes later in the Hellenistic period, the information from Ben Sira, analyzed in chapter 3, can be supplemented from at least a few other references to scribes in Judean literature usually dated to Hellenistic times. "The Teacher" in the book of Ecclesiastes (dated around 300 BCE) is clearly a sage. Yet although he does not use the term "scribe," he has clearly had scribal training, is engaged in training others, and knows what it is like to deal with rulers. Along with "weighing and studying and arranging many proverbs, . . . he wrote words of truth" and knew only too well the tedium and futility of "making many books" and "much study" (12:9–10, 11–12). As Ben Sira later reflected, scribes were about the only people in Judean and similar societies who had the leisure, indeed the expectation and responsibility, to acquire such wisdom. "The Teacher" was well acquainted with an administrative hierarchy in which "the high official is watched by a higher, and there are yet higher ones over them" (Eccl. 5:8

[7 Heb.]. Only a scribe who had served in such an administration, in which he was dependent on his superior, knew that one cannot simply leave his post when "the anger of the ruler rises against you" (10:4; cf. 9:17). Whoever produced this book was very familiar with the position, role, and training of scribes in Judea.

Two works included in the book of *1 Enoch,* the Book of Watchers and the Epistle of Enoch, represent the hoary figure of Enoch as a professional "scribe," or "scribe of righteousness" (*1 En.* 12:4; 92:1). He has the requisite knowledge of formal communication and writing skill, as well as knowledge of how to proceed in the court of a great king, so that "the [rebel] Watchers" ask him to write their petition to the Lord of heaven for forgiveness (13:4–7). In the Book of Watchers he commands knowledge of the heavens and its divisions, as did Mesopotamian scribes, and is skilled in dream interpretation, as were both Mesopotamian and Egyptian scribes. "Enoch" presents his book as life-giving wisdom (82:1–3), and the Epistle of Enoch makes reference to "the wise" who seem to constitute his counterparts in the text (98:9; 99:10).

The books of 1 and 2 Maccabees, finally, both refer, however briefly, to scribes involved in the struggle against the Seleucid regime. Second Maccabees, an abridgement of a much longer history of the struggle under violent repression and the war against Antiochus Epiphanes, and strongly pro-Temple, includes an account of the martyrdom of "Eleazar, one of the scribes in high position, a man now advanced in age and of noble presence," who suffers a torturous death rather than eat swine's flesh in violation of the law/the traditional way of life (6:18–31). First Maccabees, composed to legitimate the Hasmonean dynasty by glorifying the great Maccabean heroes, has two references. First, when his army needed to cross a river, Judas "the hammer" "posted scribes of the people by the torrent" and commanded them to make sure the soldiers engage the battle (5:40–44, au. trans.). The second reference is unclear and has been the subject of much debate.

> Then a group [company] of scribes [*synagōgē grammateōn*] appeared in a body before Alcimus and Bacchides to ask for just terms. The Hasideans [*ḥāsîdîm*] were first among the Israelites to seek peace from them, for they said, "A priest of the line of Aaron has come with the army, and he will not harm us." Alcimus spoke peaceable words to them and swore this oath to them, "We will not seek to injure you or your friends." So they trusted him; but he seized sixty of them and killed them. (7:12–16)

Second Maccabees 14 portrays Judas himself as the leader of "the Hasideans," with the implication that this is the name of the whole resistance movement (v. 6). It is far more likely, however, that Hasideans are identical with "the assembly of scribes," and are also identical with the "assembly of Hasideans" in Maccabees 2:42. The "company of scribes" thus appear to have been some of the staff of the temple-state who joined the resistance movement after their positions were threatened by the Hellenizing "reform" (see chap. 2, above). First Maccabees portrays the scribes' trust of Alcimus as a mistake and has Judas keep up the armed struggle. Their "seeking peace" can be understood in either of two ways (7:12–16). Either these scribes, who had been professional servants of the temple-state in some capacity, having joined the revolt before, were ready to negotiate a settlement once the Seleucids moved to install a proper Aaronide to the high priestly office. Or Judas may have delegated the scribes as envoys to carry out the negotiations with Alcimus and the Seleucids—negotiation being one of the skills that they brought to high levels of administration (see 2 Kings 18:18). This may be the ruse that 1 Maccabees, as pro-Hasmonean propaganda, uses to avoid having the heroic leader Judas implicated in the misguided, premature overture of peace.

These three references in the books of the Maccabees thus attest the continuing importance of scribes in Judean society. As faithful servants of the temple-state, they would have been threatened by the Hellenizing "reform" of the 170s. So it is not surprising that they would have joined the resistance and served as officers in the popular militia led by the Maccabees or as envoys in negotiation with the Seleucids. And as guardians of the traditional culture and way of life, whose very raison d'être was being undermined by the reform, scribes would understandably have been prepared to undergo martyrdom rather than abandon that traditional way of life.

SCRIBAL TRAINING AND RANGE OF KNOWLEDGE

The sources for the monarchy in Judah offer even less information on the training of scribes than they offer on the various areas in which scribes may have had expertise. Much attention has been diverted onto the question of whether and when "schools" or a system of education developed in ancient Israel and Judah. Even those skeptical about early dates for schools believe that the existence of scribal and nonscribal schools can simply be assumed for the Hellenistic period and probably for the Persian period as well.[39] Debate on the question of education has been focused anachronistically on modern-style schools with professional teachers in separate buildings and open to the general public.[40] On the assumption that scribes in Mesopotamia and Egypt were trained primarily in such royal or temple schools, biblical scholars have simply drawn the analogy for the Davidic monarchy and/or temple-state. Recent studies of those two ancient civilizations, however, as noted above, find that while distinctive "royal schools" may eventually have developed, most scribal training was small scale and carried out in scribal households. Arguments for schools in Judah/Yehud have also worked from what may be questionable evidence. The supposed abecedaries (primers) and words scratched on ostraca may not attest the existence of schools but merely that someone in sites such as royal fortresses or industrial sites was practicing writing. These offer evidence for the practice of writing and perhaps education. But by themselves they do not attest the existence of schools.[41]

There may well be some good evidence for scribal training in certain texts of the Hebrew Bible, but it is minimal and does not necessarily point to separate schools for scribes or others. The sarcastic words in Isaiah 28:9–13 appear to mock the call-and-response drills of elementary training in alphabetic literacy:

> Whom will he teach knowledge,
> And to whom will he explain the message?
> Those who are weaned from milk,
> Those taken from the breast?
> For it is precept upon precept, precept upon precept,
> Line upon line, line upon line,
> Here a little, there a little.[42]

Several passages in Judean wisdom literature, the kind of proverbs and maxims used in elementary scribal training in Egypt, mention writing in connection with instruction and socialization into the scribal ethos, with "sages" in the role of the instructor. In the prologue to The Words of the Wise in Proverbs 22:20–21, the sage asks rhetorically, "Have I not written for you thirty sayings of admonition and knowledge, to show you what is right and true, so that you may give a true answer to those who sent you?" And as mentioned just above, the "Teacher," "being wise, . . . wrote words of truth plainly" (Eccl. 12:9–10). Often wisdom teaching or hymns take the form of alphabetic acrostics, useful for memorization (e.g., Prov. 31:10–31; Pss. 25; 34; 119; 145). As in Egypt, elementary training apparently involved serious physical "discipline" (*mûsār*), as attested in several passages in Proverbs. "Those who spare the rod hate their children" (13:24; cf. 26:3). "And you say, 'Oh, how I hated discipline! . . . I did not listen to the voice of my teachers" (5:12–14; cf. 22:15; 29:17).[43]

Texts later included in the Hebrew Bible do have references to "teachers," but they are few, and those in prophetic texts are not in concrete teaching contexts (Ps. 119:99; Prov. 5:13; Isa. 30:20; Hab. 2:18). Far more frequent in references to instruction are familial relations, father-son and mother-son:[44]

> Hear, my son, your father's instruction,
> And do not reject your mother's teaching.
>   (Prov. 1:8 RSV; 6:20)

Such passages, far from being merely rhetorical, reflect the concrete instructional context. Most scribal training probably occurred in households, with son apprenticed to father in preparation for entering the same profession. If small-scale household training was the principal context for scribal education in the great civilizations of Egypt and Mesopotamia, it would certainly have been dominant in a small kingdom such as Judah and a tiny temple-state such as Yehud.[45] Although ostensibly set in the Assyrian imperial court, the tale of Ahiqar illustrates how the training of scribes happened within the family setting. Since Ahiqar had no sons, he adopted his nephew Nadin, trained him, and proposed to king Esarhaddon of Assyria to appoint him as his successor.

I am old. I cannot work in the gate of the palace and do my service to you. Behold, my son, Nadin, is full grown. Let him take my place as scribe and counselor of all Assyria, and let him be seal-bearer to you. My wisdom and counsel I have taught him. (*Ahiqar* 2.17–21)

Instruction of kings and royal sons followed the same pattern. King Jehoash of Judah was instructed by the priest Jehoiada (2 Kings 12:2). In the court of the pretentious King Ahab in Samaria, all of the (supposedly seventy) sons of Ahab had guardians or tutors responsible for their education.

As in Egypt and Mesopotamia, the purpose of this family-based apprenticeship was to form a certain kind of character suited for a particular sociocultural role, service in the monarchy or temple-state. The learning of the requisite skills of reading and writing were basic. Yet the training of scribes also aimed to inculcate qualities of character necessary for their social-political functions, especially patience with detail for lower-level administrators, and personal discipline and obedience to higher authority. Parents admonished the younger generation repeatedly, by precept and example, to fear the Lord, guard their tongue, defer to their superiors, and to lead lives beyond reproach. In the process of this rigorous process of personal formation, moreover, as the scribes-in-training were shaped by the cultural heritage of their ancestors, they were shaped as the bearers of that elite culture in their society.[46]

Less clear in Judah/Yehud than in Egypt and Mesopotamia is the range of cultural heritage and expressions in which scribes were trained, the cultural repertoire that they may have cultivated. It has become standard in biblical studies to categorize literature into types and forms and then, more often than not, to assume that people with particular social roles or even particular "schools" produced and cultivated each of them somewhat separately. Sapiential teaching was perpetuated by sages, hymns composed and performed by musicians, the prophets' oracles by circles of their disciples, historical narratives by court historians.

This assumption, however, may not be warranted. The question of cultivating cultural heritage should probably be separated from that of original production. Many of the proverbs and maxims in the book of Proverbs, for example, may have stemmed originally from popular circles, but were then taken into the cultural lore perpetuated in scribal training. The singers among the Levites may have been those who performed psalms in the Temple, but Solomon, most renowned as the legendary producer and patron of wisdom, was also understood to have produced hymns, "a thousand and five" of them (1 Kings 4:32 [5:12 Heb.]). As often noted, moreover, many of the Psalms are "sapiential" and/or "instructional." And the "teaching" can be done by reciting the history of God's dealings with the people (e.g., Ps. 78). It thus seems unwarranted to associate wise scribes only with wisdom teaching, especially proverbial wisdom. As in Egypt and Mesopotamia, proverbial wisdom was particularly important at the elementary stages of their training. Yet their training and cultural competence was more extensive. As in both Mesopotamia and Egypt, scribes in Judah/Yehud were involved in the cultivation of the elite cultural heritage in a broader range of materials.

Just how much of a range of cultural materials Judean scribes/sages were trained to cultivate, however, is unclear, perhaps partly because the field of biblical studies has not rigorously pursued the question. Assuming that sages produced wisdom, prophets pronounced prophecies, and priests performed ceremonies and taught the law, we have not developed a historical sociology of cultural production and cultivation. That will require many focused studies over many years. Yet we can readily detect a few clues "on the surface" of our sources suggesting that the range of cultural materials in which Judean scribes gained expertise may have been similar to that of Egyptian and Mesopotamian scribes/sages.[47]

Most obvious is the scribes' cultivation of proverbial and other wisdom. The stereotypical characterization in Aramaic of the Judean scribe Ahiqar as "a wise and skillful scribe" (*spr hkym wmhir, Ahiqar* 1:1), "the wise scribe, counselor of Assyria" (*[s]pr' hkym' y'y 'trwr*, 1:12), and "the wise scribe and master of good counsel" (*spr' hkym' wb'l 'tt' tbt'*, 2:42) indicates that the scribe, by definition, was wise, a specialist in wisdom. The book of Proverbs exhibits the direct connection of scribes and proverbial wisdom in several ways. The overall book is the result of scribal activity. The rich sources for scribes in Mesopotamia and Egypt indicate that the collection and cultivation of proverbial wisdom was a scribal activity. The collection in Proverbs 25–29 is presented explicitly as the work of "the officials of King Hezekiah" (cf. RSV) from older, "Solomonic" proverbial wisdom: the product of scribes in the royal court. Many proverbs concern life among the ruling elite (e.g., 14:35; 16:12–15; 25:2, 6), and the clearly learned materials in 22:17–24:22 are thought to be dependent on the Egyptian wisdom in Sayings of Amenemope.[48] The latest section of the book, Proverbs 1–9, is clearly the product of learned scholars, presumably those with sophisticated scribal training. This wisdom takes the form of a father's instruction of his son, well known in Egyptian and Mesopotamian scribal training.

Judean scribes were also well situated to have been those who cultivated ancestral legends and history, somewhat as Mesopotamian scribes cultivated both myths and legends of the origins of their civilization. Insofar as we have already associated scribes with wisdom, it is easy to understand how they probably cultivated stories such as those about the culture-hero Joseph, a sage skilled in interpretation of dreams who became the Pharaoh's vizier. But scribes would also be good candidates to have cultivated and shaped legends of origin such as that of Adam and Eve as didactic materials. The royal scribes and their staff would presumably have been responsible for "the Book of the Annals of the Kings of Israel/Judah" (*sēper dibrê hayyāmîm lĕmalĕkê yĕhûdâ/yiśrā'ēl*) that are mentioned repeatedly in 1–2 Kings (as in 1 Kings 14:19, 29). And the sequence of longer or shorter accounts of the kings of Israel and Judah who "did what was good/evil in the sight of the LORD" (observed/did not observe the Mosaic covenantal law) in 1–2 Kings appears to be a series of historical examples used in instruction of scribes who serve kings and/or of the kings themselves.

Egyptian scribes adept at interpretation of dreams and Mesopotamian scribes as experts in divination compiled compendia of past predictions. In Israel and

Judah "prophets" were the experts in prophesying, some established at court, who "ate at the king's table," and some independent figures who delivered oracles, many of them directly against kings and their officers. Among the independent prophets, however, Jeremiah at least was in regular contact with high-ranking scribes in the king's council, and (twice) dictated his oracles to the scribe Baruch to write down on a scroll. The prophet Isaiah had earlier used the metaphorical language of a written scroll, to "bind up the testimony," in the instruction of his students (8:16–18), and then more literally of "inscribing it on a scroll" (30:8, au. trans.). These passages suggest that his prophecies were taught to students and were written on a scroll, perhaps at an early point. So who were the people who kept those scrolls and cultivated the prophecies of Isaiah and Jeremiah and other independent oracular prophets? Scribes were the (only) people trained to handle and copy scrolls and generally trained and expected to be the guardians of cultural legacy.

In biblical studies we have previously thought of collections of legal material in the Pentateuch in terms of "law codes" (the "Covenant code" in Exod. 21–23; the Holiness Code in Leviticus). Also, following explicit statements in biblical books, we have presumed that it was the priests' prerogative and responsibility to teach the law. Recent studies of collections of legal materials in Mesopotamia such as the laws of Hammurabi, however, conclude that they were not compiled as codes and were never "applied" by judges in concrete cases. Collections of legal materials were rather "scientific" compendia of "jurisprudence," the ancient counterpart of judicial philosophy. These new insights into the actual composition and function of ancient legal collections are leading some to rethink the legal material in the Pentateuch. The book of torah/law "found" in the temple that became the basis of the "reform" under King Josiah is thought to have been an early form of Deuteronomy. From the way the law scroll is received and verified—by the scribe Shaphan and high priest Hilkiah—and then used by the monarchy, it is clear that it was not a code of laws for application in the courts but a constitution-like document by which the monarchy and its program were authorized. That use by the monarchy and its scribal staff may well be what Jeremiah is objecting to with his rhetorical questions:

> How can you say, "We are wise, and the law/torah of the LORD is with us," when, in fact, the false pen of the scribes has made it into a lie? (8:8–9)[49]

It has long been observed that the book of Deuteronomy is heavily influenced by didactic wisdom, indeed that it virtually equated the law/torah of God with wisdom.[50]

In the second-temple period many of the scribes were the Levites, who were supposedly, with the priests, charged with teaching the law. In the scenario of Nehemiah 8, it is the skilled scribe Ezra, albeit an appointee of the Persians, who presides and reads from the law scroll, while the Levites interpret or translate to the people. If many scribes were Levites and some Levites were scribes serving in the Temple administration, then it will help us explain and understand why and how the teaching of wise scribes such as Ben Sira could feature the covenant/ torah/commandments so prominently, and how scribes could be so closely associated with the torah/law toward the end of second-temple times.

Coming again to Ben Sira, we can take another look at the curriculum he mentions in his famous passage on "the wisdom of the scribe" who "serves among the great [ones]" (Sir. 38:24–39:11). His expanded list includes "sayings of the famous, . . . parables, . . . proverbs" (39:2–3). Those are certainly the "sapiential" materials in which his own teaching concentrates. But the list begins more comprehensively:

> How different the one who devotes himself,
> And holds in mind the law [torah] of the Most High!
> He seeks out the wisdom of all the ancients,
> And is . . . [engaged] with prophecies.
> (39:1 [38:34–39:1E])

Nothing in these phrases suggests that Ben Sira is referring to a set of books. But the broad categories of torah, prophecies, and wisdom, which correspond to the three divisions into which the books of the Hebrew Bible were later organized (Torah, Prophets, Writings) indicate the wide range of materials that wise scribes included in their repertory of training and expertise.

In sum, this review of references to scribal roles and positions in Judah-Judea and in Mesopotamia and Egypt indicates that learned scribes served in royal and temple administrations. With wide-ranging expertise, they served a variety of functions for the rulers of their societies, ranging from composition of official documents and texts, political advice, interpretation of dreams and divination of future events, to the general cultivation of culture. This confirms the indications in Sirach that in second-temple times, certainly by the Hellenistic period, scribes were not simply and perhaps not primarily "wisdom teachers," but were intellectual "retainers" who served, sometimes at the highest level, in the administration of the temple-state. Evidence from Mesopotamia and Egypt, moreover, strongly supports Ben Sira's indications that, in their training and service, wise scribes devoted themselves to the cultivation of a wide range of cultural materials that included law and prophecy as well as proverbial wisdom. Ben Sira's own productions suggest that the range included hymnic and historical materials as well. Hence, not simply in addition to, but also in preparation for their service of the temple-state, wise scribes such as Ben Sira cultivated the Judean cultural repertoire in most or all of its forms and facets.

Chapter 5

Orality, Writing, and the Cultivation of Texts

My child, keep my teachings, write them on the tablet of your heart.

Proverbs

What if the traditum *existed in oral form? How different things would look from the description [in Michael Fishbane's magisterial analysis]. . . . My own study of ancient Israelite education suggests that Fishbane's approach to the dynamic process within the canon of interacting with earlier views rests on the highly dubious assumption of widespread literacy and ready access to written materials. Such convenient texts for consultation strike me as a figment of the imagination, given the agrarian society of Yehud and the limited population of Jerusalem in the Persian period.*[1]

That ancient "Judaism" was "a religion of the Book" has been one of the modern assumptions that has most determined the course of biblical studies. The Hebrew "Scriptures," sacred *writings,* comprise a set of books. We have simply assumed that biblical books were composed in writing, that copies of biblical books were readily available, and that ancient Judeans could read them. It should not be surprising, therefore, that scholars of "biblical" history would find confirmation of their assumption in recent archaeological finds. "The increasing number of inscriptions uncovered in excavations of Iron Age II–III sites in the land of Israel . . . testify that by the end of the eighth century Israelite society as a whole was literate."[2] Accordingly, we have then also assumed that the scribes, who were the specialists in writing, not only read and made additional copies of already-written texts, but also *wrote* new texts, somewhat like modern authors.

89

SCRIBAL INSTRUCTION AS ORAL

Reading and written texts are difficult to find, however, when we look at the teachings of the wise. Ben Sira knows about writing. He mentions that the sacred vestments of the prototypical high priest Aaron included "precious stones engraved . . . to commemorate . . . the [twelve] tribes of Israel" (45:11). He knows that ancestral figures had "composed musical tunes, or put verses in writing" (44:5). And he declares that he has "written" understanding "in this book." He presents his own teaching, however, as entirely oral, and the medium of his students' learning as aural. The "children" receiving instruction are to "listen" to their father and mother (3:1–3).

> Listen to me, my child, and acquire knowledge,
> And pay close attention to my words.
> (16:24–25; cf. 6:23; 31:22)

> For wisdom becomes known through speech,
> and education through the words of the tongue.
> (4:24)

The learning of scribes then continues by listening to spoken discourse.

> If you love to listen you will gain knowledge, . . .
> Stand in the company of the elders.
> Be ready to listen to every godly discourse.
> (6:23, 33–35; cf. 9:14–15)

> Do not slight the discourse of the sages, . . .
> because from them you will learn discipline
>   and how to serve princes.
> (8:8–9)

Wise scribes, moreover, carry out their role not by reading and writing texts, but by learning spoken words and, in turn, speaking wisdom. The prophecies, sayings, and parables that the wise scribes have "sought out" and "preserved" and "penetrated" comprise a repertory readily available in their memory, not inscribed on scrolls that they must consult (39:1–3). Ben Sira teaches in his "house of instruction" not by asking his students to open a book, but by "opening his mouth" (51:23–25). And in a more public role, the sage instructs his own people as "a skillful speaker" (37:16–26). But perhaps that was only fitting in a historical context where oral communication was dominant in the assemblies of rulers (11:7–9; 15:5; 21:15–17) as well as in the society at large (5:10–11; 5:13–6:1; 6:5; 14:1; 22:22, 27; 23:7–12; 27:11–15; 33:4; 37:16).

In earlier wisdom teaching, as in Ben Sira, learning is a matter of the children (students) listening to the voice or words of the father and mother (teachers) and holding the words in their heart (Prov. 4:1–5; 5:12–13). Wisdom is communicated by speech (12:18; 15:2; 16:21, 23). In the ethos of the sages, learning does not happen through reading and writing, but through oral communication (12:15; 15:31; 18:15; 23:12) or by observing the behavior of the wise teacher, as a positive paradigm, or that of the lazy and foolish, as a negative example (23:26; 24:30–34). Even in the section of "the words of the wise" where the teacher has "written" thirty sayings, learning happens by "inclining the ear" and having the words learned "ready on the lips" (22:17–21).[3] The only use of the verb *kātab* (to write) is metaphorical or symbolic, that their students should write their instruction on the tablet of their heart (3:3; 7:3).

These passages in Sirach and Proverbs suggest that scribes' instruction, like their service in the assembly of rulers, was conducted mainly in oral communication, however much they may also have consulted written scrolls.[4] Recent studies of scribal culture in Mesopotamia, Egypt, and (by implication) Judah have demonstrated that the teaching and learning of the wide range of cultural curriculum that scribal circles cultivated was done by oral recitation and repetition.[5] Yet these same scribes were the professional servants of court and temple responsible for written records and correspondence and the copying and perpetuation of written texts. How might we understand this situation that seems so anomalous on the assumptions of modern print culture? How was writing used, and what was its relationship with oral communication in ancient Judean society generally and in scribal circles in particular?

TOWARD AN APPROPRIATE APPROACH

Contrary to previous assumptions, literacy was not widespread in ancient Judea. As elsewhere in antiquity, literacy was limited to a tiny elite.[6] A recent survey of Jewish literacy in Roman Palestine provides extensive documentation that writing and reading were confined to the political-cultural elite, mainly to Herodian and Roman administrators, scribal and rabbinic circles, and other powerful people who used writing to enhance their own power and privilege.[7] If anything literacy would have been less widespread in Judean society toward the end of the monarchy.[8] In an agrarian society composed mainly of village communities in which most social interaction occurred face-to-face, there was little need for writing. Literacy was of interest mainly to rulers and their administrators in Jerusalem, to keep records of tax collection, to carry out official correspondence, and to enhance their culture.

Investigation of orality and literacy in ancient Israel and second-temple Judea is in a relatively elementary stage. We are only gradually learning what questions to ask and how to evaluate evidence—often from other fields that have dealt with the relations of oral and written communication for much longer.[9] Several recent studies, however, are bringing some sobering realism to the assessment of evidence for literacy in ancient Israelite and Judean society. Most fundamental, perhaps, is the recognition that there were different kinds and levels of literacy.[10]

This is true even in modern print cultures. Far more dramatic are the differences in literacies between modern print cultures and societies before the invention of the printing press, when written texts were cumbersome and difficult if not impossible to read—without already being familiar with the contents of the text. The development and uses of literacy depend on a number of closely related factors, such as customs and beliefs and the political-economic-religious structure of a given society. The development and uses of literacy, moreover, happen in close relationship with continuing oral communications.

An obvious first step toward an appropriate approach is a critical sense of our sources, of both the literary sources and the archaeological finds and what they provide evidence for. Graffiti and inscriptions by an unskilled hand, for example, do not provide evidence for a level of literacy at which people could compose literature. Abecedaries unearthed in remote, arid sites are not likely to have been schoolboy exercises, much less evidence of schools. The increase in the number of inscriptions and simple records in eighth-century Israel and Judah attest a growth of central administration rather than an increase in the general rate of literacy.[11]

The more important sources for our purposes are the written texts produced in Judea, some of which were later included in the Hebrew Bible. These are written examples of and sources for the cultural expressions and knowledge cultivated in second-temple Judea, which we will examine in the next chapter. They are also sources that mention writing of various kinds in their relation to oral communication on which we are focusing in this chapter. The first steps in assessment of these texts as sources of evidence for kinds and uses of writing would be to establish the meaning of key terms and carry out at least some elementary rhetorical criticism on the argumentative function of references to writing. For example, persons in a position of authority, such as a king, might be represented as "writing" or "reading" when they are really having someone (a scribe) "write" or "read" for them.[12] A sēper in Hebrew texts is not necessarily a book. Depending on the literary context, it could be a letter, a legal document, or simply a writing surface, such as a stone or a scroll. Moreover, references to a sēper where it does apparently mean a "book" (a written scroll), such as "the book of the covenant/torah" that Moses was reported to have written down on Sinai (Exod. 24:4–7), should not necessarily be taken "referentially" as indicating a book readily available in the royal or temple archives. Elementary rhetorical analysis suggests that such a reference may be an appeal to a written document for authority, without the book having been ready at hand for consultation.[13]

Any number of references to writing were almost certainly retrojections from a later to an earlier time and/or projections of elite cultural assumptions onto ordinary people. We can probably take at face value that Ezra was indeed "a skilled scribe," given his position of prominence in the Persian court before being delegated to appoint judges in the province Beyond the River. But the portrayal of Samuel as having written up "the rights and duties of the kingship" in a book (1 Sam. 10:25) is surely both retrojection and projection, as is the reference to the three recorders from each tribe appointed by Joshua (Josh. 18:4).

Taking note of the social location and role of those represented in our literary sources as doing the writing or reading indicates fairly clearly that literacy was virtually confined to the rulers, priests, and scribal, military, and other officials of the monarchy or temple-state in Jerusalem.[14] That ancient cultural literacy was confined to a tiny elite has been strongly confirmed by David Carr's extensive comparative study, arguing that the writing of texts was an integral aspect of ancient education that prepared a relatively privileged class of scribes and sages for administrative roles in service of the rulers.[15]

Especially illuminating has been Susan Niditch's more sophisticated and nuanced discussion of different kinds of writing and how they are related to oral communication in which they are embedded.[16] By drawing on studies of writing in other ancient and medieval societies, she explains how writing functioned in ways quite different from those assumed in modern print culture. For example, some ancient writing was more iconic or monumental than communicative, and the writing of legal texts or administrative records was done as "pledges to posterity" but not for future reference or consultation. Modern libraries and archives may have had no counterpart in ancient Athens or Jerusalem. Certain prominent kinds of writing in antiquity are so different from those that dominate in print culture because they are rooted in and related to the dominant oral communication. Niditch discusses these distinctive kinds of writing in terms of an oral-written continuum, in which some writings partake more of an oral mentality, while others are closer to a literate mentality. I am becoming convinced that virtually any example of or reference to writing in ancient Judean texts is intricately related to and embedded in oral communication.[17] Yet, while I have doubts about the concept of two distinctive mentalities (and a continuum between them), I sense that Niditch's discussion of various forms and functions of writing is compatible with such a shift in conceptualization and characterization.

We especially need to combine a focus on the different kinds of writing (in their relation with oral communication) with two important related questions: that of the social location and role(s) of the persons doing the writing, and that of for whom the writing is being done and with what effect. The following exploration of writing and its relation to oral communication in late monarchic Judah and early second-temple Judea will try to hold these questions together as we seek to understand the cultural ethos of the Judean scribes. The exploration proceeds in two steps. We first attempt to appreciate the different kinds of writing represented in Judean texts and evident in archaeological discoveries, their uses, and their relation to oral communication. Then we will examine the interrelated roles of orality and writing in scribal learning and cultivation of texts.

Because collections of narratives, poems, songs, and teachings often existed in memory and recitations instead of or as well as in documents, in the ensuing discussion we will use the term "text" for the substance while using the more specific "written text" or "written copy" or "document" to distinguish the text in the written medium.

KINDS OF WRITING AND THEIR USES

Recognition of the different kinds and uses of writing in ancient Judah/Judea can enhance as well as complicate our appreciation of the possible relationships that scribes may have had with written texts.

Simple Messages

Critical examination of short simple messages indicates that even simple "craft literacy" was confined largely to tax-collection and basic records. Toward the end of the seventh century BCE there was an increase in brief formulaic messages written on papyrus, rolled and sealed with impressions on lumps of clay, or "bullae." These documents, many of them clearly administrative and found in urban or fortress sites, were evidently drawn up by scribes, who knew the appropriate formulas, and the seals were often the artistic products of artisans.[18]

Jeremiah's "signing" (*kātab,* with his "mark," as in Job 31:35) and getting others as oral witnesses to "sign" a document (*sēper*) of a purchase of land from his next of kin in a procedure presided over by the scribe Baruch (Jer. 32:6–15) illustrates one typical meaning of writing in such brief documents. Baruch deposited both the sealed deed and the open copy in a storage jar for long-term storage. The document thus was clearly not intended as a record to be consulted or presented as proof of ownership.[19] It was rather like records in medieval England that M. T. Clanchy called a "pledge to posterity," an assurance of continuity under God's providence.[20] Jeremiah made the "permanent" writing of the deed into a prophetic sign, in the context of the imminent Babylonian conquest of Judah, a symbol of God's promise of continuity of Judean society and its tradition of ancestral land in each multigenerational family as a basis of livelihood. Another brief formulaic message that operated at a local level was a husband's signing/writing (*kātab*) a document (*sēper*) of divorce and placing it in his wife's hand and sending her out of the house (Deut. 24:1–4). The written renunciation was understood as particularly powerful and permanent, as writing was often viewed in a predominantly oral society.

Numinous Simple Writing

For people in a society dominated by oral communication, writing could have a mysterious, numinous aura.[21] A blessing or a curse pronounced orally carried the power to effect the pronouncement. Putting the blessing or curse in writing lent it all the more power, perhaps because it was permanent and had an objectified reality of its own. Certain written messages, however brief, were thus symbolic and iconic, with power to effect the message.

Such writing can be seen in its most visceral operation in the horrifying ritual curse designed to satisfy a jealous husband who accuses his wife of adultery but has no witness (Num. 5:11–28).[22] In the core of the ritual the priest writes out the curse to be suffered by the woman and washes it off into "the water of bitterness." She is then made to drink the water that now materially as well as "literally" contains the curse. Then the curse causes her bitter pain (presumably only) if she is guilty, entering her bowels and ruining her womb.[23]

The writing of God's commandments on the doorposts and gates of houses commanded in Deut. 6:4–9 also probably belongs among such numinous writings.[24] People did not need to be able to write or read to have commandments inscribed on their doorpost by someone with simple writing skills. The assumption as well as context was that the parents, with "the words commanded in their hearts," would "recite them to their children and talk about them at home and away, both night and day" (paraphr.). Such inscriptions on the doorposts were iconic talismans completely embedded in and reflective of a world of oral communication.

The ultimate case of numinous writing filled with power was that of God. The most vivid example of utterly mysterious, divine writing is the "fingers of a human hand . . . writing . . . on the wall" at the banquet of the Babylonian emperor Belshazzar in Daniel 5. The Aramaic words, "*MENE, MENE, TEKEL, PARSIN*" (5:25), which name units of weight and equivalent monetary values, "have a rhythmical, incantational quality when spoken, an assonance based on the repetition" of the -e- sound.[25] The message written and the context are thus oral communication, with the mysterious writing a terrifying omenlike medium of delivering God's message of doom against the Babylonian kingdom. The covenant commandments, "words" in short formulaic phrases, were not only delivered by Yahweh "in a loud voice," but also engraved on stone by the finger of God in the theophany at Sinai (Exod. 24:12; 31:18; 32:16; Deut. 4:13; 5:22; 9:10); these features gave them a utterly awesome, ultimate power and authority. The placement of these tablets written by God into the ark of the covenant made it electric with divine power. In a wide variety of references in the Hebrew Bible, further, God was understood as keeping a divine record book (e.g., Exod. 32:32; Isa. 4:3). The power inherent in the divine writing was determinative for peoples' lives and hence, for example, a powerful source of reassurance under imperial persecution (Dan. 12:1).

Letters and Decrees in the Royal Administration

Kings and queens had letters written, presumably by scribes toward the top of the royal administration, that were also accompanied by oral communication via envoys or messengers. Chronicles projects back letters accompanied by oral communication by official envoys as the medium by which the megadeal was arranged for Solomon to trade agricultural resources (from taxes) for the materiel and technical expertise to build the First Temple (2 Chron. 2:1–16).[26] King David is said to have used a secret letter to arrange for the "accidental" death of a militiaman, and Queen Jezebel to have used letters to judicially "frame" a recalcitrant Israelite who refused to give up his family's ancestral land to the king (2 Sam. 11:14–15; 1 Kings 21:8–14).

Royal and imperial regimes also used writing to circulate decrees. In what is probably a retrojection, King Hezekiah decreed, via letters and couriers who speak to the people, that all Israel and Judah should celebrate Passover in the Temple in Jerusalem (2 Chron. 30:1–9). Edicts and empirewide proclamations by the Persian emperors Cyrus and Darius formed the basis of authorization and legitimation on which the previously deported Judean elite established the temple-state and took control of the land (2 Chron. 36:22; Ezra 1:1; 6:1–5). Insofar as such decrees were written (in the various languages used in the provinces), they could easily have been deposited in the imperial archives. For purposes of communication of such decrees, however, the written copies were merely instrumental to wider oral communication carried out by the heralds. Imperial decrees are thus a vivid reminder of just how limited reading and writing were in ancient societies.

Lists and Annals in Royal Court and Temple-State

A kind of writing far more important than letters for the administration of the Judean temple-state was lists of lineages. The Levite scribe Shemaiah son of Nethanel is said to have recorded (*kātab*) the divisions of the sons of Aaron, evidently from the memory and oral testimony of King David, founder of the Temple, and his highest ranking priests (1 Chron. 24:5–6). Shemaiah's list, almost certainly a product of the early second-temple period, thus lent the authority of a written record of (supposedly) hoary antiquity to the longer list of the divisions of priests and Levites that controlled the Jerusalem temple-state in 1 Chronicles 23–26. The books of Ezra (2:1–61; 8:1–20) and Nehemiah (7:5–60; cf. 12:1–26, esp. 23) have lists with the similar constitutional functions of authorizing claims to the land and control of the temple-state by the returning priestly and Levitical families, other temple functionaries, and lay Israelites. In Nehemiah the list is used to exclude certain priestly lineages from the priesthood of the Temple (7:61–65). In that case the written list was being used to discredit and displace the claims backed by family tradition or memory, as orally communicated. "The document of matters/acts of the kings of Israel/Judah" and "the documents of the matters/acts of" prophets and seers to which the books of Kings and especially the books of Chronicles make numerous appeals appear to be a further development of such legitimating lists (1 Kings 11:41; 14:19; 15:31; 16:5; 2 Kings 21:17; 1 Chron. 29:29; 2 Chron. 9:29; 12:15; 16:11; 20:34; 27:7; 33:18).

These lists indicate a high regard for written documents and the authority they embody. Yet they should probably not be understood as analogous to "archives," in the modern sense of records for purposes of consultation. From a study of medieval English records, Clanchy concluded that making documents, keeping them as records, and consulting them as references were different activities, and that the one did not follow from the other.[27] There is little or no evidence that the Judean temple-state maintained "archives." Ancient Near Eastern collections of documents that have been labeled "archives" turn out to have been without principles of organization that would have made them useable for later consultation, and many documents were written on disposable materials.[28] Simply the making of lists of priestly lineages, however, or even the appeal to such lists having been written constituted a legitimation for those in charge of the Judean temple-state. And the function of "the documents of the acts of the kings" may have been primarily rhetorical, to supply veracity to the accounts in Kings and Chronicles.[29]

Books of the Covenant/Teaching (of Moses)

The most important "book" mentioned in Judean texts is "the document [sēper] of the covenant/teaching [běrît/tôrâ]" that plays such a prominent role in Exodus, Deuteronomy, Joshua, 2 Kings, and Nehemiah. In the covenant-making ceremony on Mount Sinai (Exod. 24:3–37), "Moses wrote down all the words of Yahweh, . . . took the document of the covenant, and proclaimed it in the ears of the people" (au. trans.). In this document full of divine power, the words of Yahweh have an independence of their own, standing over against the people. That they are written makes them all the more effective when proclaimed into the ears of the people ("all that Yahweh has spoken we will do"), a repeated emphasis in the subsequent references to "the document of the teaching." Again, after he had delivered an extended covenantal teaching (tôrâ), Moses "wrote down in a document the words of this teaching" and commanded the Levites to "place it beside the ark of the covenant of Yahweh . . . as a witness against you" (Deut. 31:24–26; cf. 28:58–61). As instructed (27:3–8), Joshua, leading a covenantal renewal ceremony, in Joshua 8:30–35, "wrote on the stones [of the altar he had built] a copy of the teaching of Moses, which he had written" (Josh. 8:31–32, au. trans.). Then "he recited all the words . . . according to all that is written in the document of the teaching" to the assembled Israelites (8:34, au. trans.; cf. 24:25–27).

As symbolized by its inscription on the stones, the "book" has figuratively as well as literally become a monument, permanent witness to the covenant with God.[30] Then as now, as Niditch states, "monuments are not to be read word for word to obtain information or to verify a date, but to point to, verify, and eternalize an event in a more holistic and symbolic fashion."[31] Even so, the covenant teaching deposited on the ark or written on stones was numinous monumental writing, inscribed as the ultimate legal document. Such a monumental writing of the covenant teaching externalized and eternalized the covenant between Yahweh and Israel, guaranteeing its continuing force. It was not (primarily) a text from which the people could learn the content of the statues and ordinances or which priests and scribes could later consult. Indeed, even its recitation to the people was not primarily to help them learn the particular laws but to commit them to the covenantal relationship with Yahweh in a ceremony that (re-)enacted the covenant.

In these accounts, moreover, the "documents" seem to have multiplied and become more complex and difficult to sort out. Joshua and his contemporaries are represented as having "a copy of the teaching of Moses which he wrote" (8:32), although that was presumably what Moses had received from God. "The document of the teaching of Moses" in Josh. 8:31 and perhaps also "the document of teaching" in 8:34, however, appear to be what were known to the later readers/hearers of the book of Joshua (not to Joshua and the Israelites in the covenant ceremony). Yet the latter cannot have been the same as the former. The copy that Joshua and the early Israelites had possessed had long since disappeared, both from the historical narrative after Joshua 8 and presumably from the ongoing life of Israel and the kingdom of Judah as well. Similarly, the covenantal "document" of God's teaching that Joshua writes (Josh. 24:25–26) is clearly different from the document(s) of God's covenantal teaching written by Moses (Exod. 24:3–7; Deut. 31:24–26). And certainly the covenantal teaching was undergoing some development and changes from document to document.

Both the monumental character of the writing and the continuing development of the teaching (torah) carry over into the ceremonial public recitations of "the book of the covenant/teaching" by King Josiah and Ezra the scribe. After a previously lost "book of the teaching" was found in the Temple by the high priest and recited to the king by the scribe, Josiah convened an assembly of all the people in which he "recited in their ears all the words of the document of the covenant [bĕrît]" (2 Kings 22:8–23:3, au. trans.). He then carried out a massive centralizing "reform, . . . as prescribed in this document of the covenant" (2 Kings 23:4–20, 21–23; cf. 23:24). "The document of the teaching" found in the Temple was anything but a dusty old manuscript. It presupposed, and was understood as a copy of, "the book of the teaching" written by Moses (and/or Joshua), which had been recited at earlier covenant ceremonies.[32] It was a powerful monumental writing whose very existence embodied and guaranteed the force of the covenant teaching inscribed, and it was a binding witness against the kingdom of Judah, which had not kept the covenant. This long-lost book of hoary antiquity was the legitimating authority for Josiah's reform.[33]

The Domesday Book of medieval England may provide a helpful analogy. As Clanchy has explained, its original significance was not as a record book, but as a symbolic, monumental writing, an awesome document of the majestic and unalterable Norman Conquest by William the Conqueror. Its earliest copies had elaborate multicolored embellishments, like a liturgical manuscript, suggesting a document that was sacred.[34] That "the book of the teaching" was found unexpectedly in the Temple suggests that such a covenant document and presumably other documents had been deposited in the temple precincts, but were not regularly consulted or brought out for periodic recitation to the assembled people.[35] This is only fitting for an iconic legal "monument for posterity." It is also in accordance with what we know from Egypt and Mesopotamia, where all sorts of writings were placed in temples, and similar to the earliest inscription of laws in the precincts of temples in Greece.[36]

A document of sacred power is also clearly evident in the account of Ezra's presentation, opening, and recitation of "the document of the teaching of Moses"

(Neh. 8). It is the central event in the highly formal ceremony before the assembly of Judeans who had been placed in charge of the temple-state. Ezra, flanked by other high-ranking figures, stood on a raised wooden platform constructed specially for the occasion. "Ezra opened the document in the sight of all the people, for he was standing above all the people; and when he opened it, all the people stood up" (8:4–5, alt.). In antiphonal blessing and praise, the people answered, "'Amen, Amen,' lifting up their hands," then "bowing their heads and worshiping Yahweh with their faces to the ground" (8:6, au. trans.). "The document of the teaching of Moses" is clearly a sacred object. Even its recitation is now full of mystery, requiring "interpretation" by the Levites (8:7–8; the document presumably was in Hebrew, but the people probably spoke Aramaic).[37]

Writing Dictated by Prophets

Prophets are usually represented as speaking. They declare "the word of Yahweh" that they have heard in the heavenly court. In rare instances Isaiah and Jeremiah are also represented as writing, or as having writing done.[38] Jeremiah is twice represented as sending "documents" as a means of conveying "the words of Yahweh" to some of the Jerusalem elite who had been deported to Babylon. In the first account (Jer. 29), the priest Zephaniah had to "recite in the ears of Jeremiah" a "document" from Shemaiah in Babylon; this suggests that Jeremiah himself could not read (29:24–29, au. trans.). In the second case (51:60–64) Jeremiah is portrayed as "writing in one document all the disasters that would come on Babylon" and instructing Seraiah, when he arrives in Babylon, "to pronounce [qārā] all these words so that . . . it [Babylon] shall be desolate forever" (au. trans.). The document is also to become a prophetic sign (or is it a numinous writing that effects the divine judgment, like the curse in Num. 5?): "Tie a stone to it, and throw it into the . . . Euphrates, and say, 'Thus shall Babylon sink.'"

The account of prophetic dictation in Jeremiah 36 (cf. 45:1–5) has long been thought to be an illuminating window onto the prophets and the writing of their oracles as the first steps toward the development of the prophetic books later included in the Hebrew Bible. It is even more illuminating of how writing was understood in relation to oral performance in ancient Judea, particularly prophetic performance of "the word of Yahweh." Yahweh instructed Jeremiah to "write on a document all the words I have spoken to you" since he had begun prophesying. Jeremiah, not being trained to write, called Baruch son of Neriah, who "wrote on a document from Jeremiah's mouth [dictation] all the words that Yahweh had spoken to him" (au. trans.). For many years Jeremiah had been pronouncing in public the many "words of Yahweh" he had received. Evidently he still retained them in his memory so that he could again speak them aloud for Baruch to write down. The reason for making a written copy of the pronouncements of judgment against Judah was to have Baruch pronounce them again publicly in the Temple precincts, from which Jeremiah had been banned as a subversive, in the hope that they would finally be heeded.

Hearing of the new performance, the highest ranking royal officers, some of whom were scribes and/or the sons of scribes and could have read the scroll themselves, had Baruch pronounce the oracles again in a private audience. Is this because they were not familiar with the words, hence could not recite the scroll, and/or because they did not want to be implicated themselves in pronouncing Yahweh's words of judgment against the monarchy? They also made a point of asking Baruch whether he had received the oracles from the prophet's own dictation. It was apparently the oral pronouncement of the oracles by the prophet himself, not the written copy, that made them genuine "words of Yahweh" that they had to worry about. The royal officers then had an assistant, Jehudi, recite the document to King Jehoiakim, who contemptuously cut off columns of the scroll and burned them.[39] In response, Yahweh instructed Jeremiah to make another scroll, which he again did by dictation to the scribe Baruch, all of the contents of the first scroll still being alive in his memory. Besides being available to enable yet another public pronouncement of the oracles, this dictation and writing of the second document has an addition that makes it also a prophetic sign of judgment against the contemptuous king.

Oral pronouncement and written document are in close relationship throughout this story. The writing, from dictation, is secondary to the original pronouncement of the words of Yahweh revealed to Jeremiah. And the writing appears to have mainly the instrumental function of making possible a new performance in a site where the prophet himself has been banned from speaking. Yet in a society where writing was so unusual, it often was infused with a kind of power of its own, and since in this case it was a writing of the divine words, the writing itself must have carried an ominous authority. The king was not simply burning some combustible material, but parchment on which the word of Yahweh stood written. Nevertheless, we get the impression that the oral performance of the word of Yahweh as revealed to Jeremiah is what carried the primary authority.

Written Copies of the Heavenly Tablets

Several Judean texts that survive from Hellenistic times purport to be written copies of heavenly books. The authority of such books is heightened by the claim that it is from primordial time. Some of these, such as *Jubilees* and the *Temple Scroll* (copies of both were found among the Dead Sea Scrolls), purport to be copies made by Moses of the Torah of God written on heavenly tablets and revealed to Moses by heavenly messengers, thus enhancing the authority of these alternative versions of the Torah of God. Sections of *1 Enoch* in effect combine the heavenly book with the prophet (like Jeremiah) who receives the word of God from heavenly visions or auditions with the scribe (like Baruch) who writes down those revelations in the scribal figure of Enoch. The latter, called a "scribe of righteousness" (12:3–4; 92:1), is instructed to "read what is on the heavenly tablets, . . . to learn everything written," then to "teach your sons, and write it down for them, and testify to all your sons," and to "recount and write" all the revelations, and give his son Methuselah "books about all these things" (81:1–82:1). As copies of numinous heavenly writing, the sections of *1 Enoch* have authority well above copies of prophetic oracles. Yet like most of the other kinds of writing just examined, they still involve a close interrelationship between writing and oral communication.

ORALITY AND WRITING IN SCRIBAL LEARNING, TEACHING, AND PRACTICE

From this examination of the kinds and uses of writing in ancient Judea, it is clear that virtually all writing and "reading" above the simplest graffiti was done by trained scribes, mainly those involved in the royal or temple administration. Scribes, as those trained in writing, would certainly have been the ones who produced the more complex written texts, such as "the documents of the acts of the kings," "the books of torah/covenant," and the scroll of Jeremiah's oracles. Yet the books of Sirach and Proverbs represent the teaching and learning of scribes as well as their professional functions as mainly oral, which accords with scribal practice elsewhere in the ancient Near East. Our problem then is to understand how writing and the reading of written texts may have been involved in what appears to have been the predominantly oral scribal learning and practice.

Most important as the basis for any further reflection on the issue is the recognition that writing was embedded in oral communication. Nearly all of the kinds of writing other than some administrative lists and annals were either extensions of oral statements or derived from oral communication, and most were written partly or mainly as instrumental to (further) oral recitation. This has implications for the scribes as well as the society in general. The people and often the king, high priest, and other officers were on the receiving end of the oral recitation. Scribes were responsible not only for transforming the spoken word into writing, but also for the recitation of the texts that had been written, as explicit in the cases of Baruch and the Levites who interpreted what Ezra recited. We need to inquire both about how the documents were produced and about how the text came to be recited. Although it is indirect, there is more evidence about the recitation of texts. We will therefore deal with recitation first in the hope that it will shed light on the production of texts.

Recitation of Texts

We are so accustomed to *reading* the translation of the ancient Hebrew word *qārā'* as "read" that it is difficult to cut through our deeply rooted assumption that written texts were physically read. But *qārā'* meant to proclaim or recite, not to read.[40] Studies of ancient scrolls and other manuscripts have noted that they would have been virtually impossible for anyone to read who was not already familiar with the texts.[41] But that does not mean that they had gained their familiarity with the text by physically reading from a scroll. Judging from the above survey of kinds of writing and other evidence from antiquity, there were a range of possibilities determined by a variety of factors.

First, since scribes were trained in writing and reading, they may well have relied on written texts for recitation in some cases. Some manuscripts themselves provide evidence that they may have functioned as aide-mémoire for scribes preparing for oral performance, although this cannot be stretched into evidence that they were the source of the performers' knowledge of the text in the first place. In the varying lengths and inclusions or omissions in the various written versions of Sumerian and Akkadian stories, "we should probably understand some of the abrupt changes of theme as bare skeletons which were fleshed out in practice by skilled narrators."[42] An early manuscript of the Hebrew prophets includes only the first word of each verse, followed by only the first letter of the succeeding words.[43] This manuscript would have been of use only to those already highly familiar with the Hebrew text of the prophets. It could have served as a useful reminder for fading memories and/or a prompt for those engaged in recitation. But there is little evidence in second-temple Judean texts that scribes were learning or reciting directly from written scrolls.

Second, several, indeed most kinds of documents were not written to be read. As noted above, many documents were written as "monuments" on which the text was duly "memorialized" in writing for preservation and display to certain people or to the gods. They were not for use by readers, certainly not in the same way as we today open a Bible or a textbook and read. So written copies of some texts may not have been readily available from which to learn (and memorize) a text by physically reading it. Of the kinds of writing where the text was to be recited to the people, "the book of covenant/teaching" used in Josiah's reform and the one presented by Ezra were monumental and sacred (deposited in the Temple), and were not accessible to scribes in general.[44] The writing of certain texts for political and religious purposes of administration, display, intimidation, or as perpetual offerings to God/the gods, quite apart from the ability of the literate to read them, has been referred to as "institutionalized unintelligibility."[45] So we cannot simply assume that manuscripts of such texts were readily available for the scribal teaching and learning that was being conducted mainly in familial contexts.

Third, evidence is beginning to build up that references to books in antiquity are mainly from memory, not by quotation from a written text. This was noticed a generation ago for the "quotation" of Jesus sayings in early Christian texts. Second-century literature does not quote Jesus sayings from Gospels that were composed and written down in the late first century.[46] Similarly, it appears that the apostle Paul was quoting the Jewish Scriptures in Greek by memory, and not from the standard written text (the Septuagint).[47] Lest those cases be dismissed as evidence from a popular movement with more limited literacy than in elite circles, the same was true among philosophers. Citation of earlier philosophers by later philosophers was by memory, not from written versions of their teaching.[48]

Fourth and most significant here, scribes may have known what was written on a document, or the gist of it, by means other than reading it. This appears likely

in several kinds of Israelite-Judean cultural materials that were composed and performed orally before and after being written down. Songs written in "the book of
Yashar" or in collections of psalms would already have been known from frequent
singing by scribes, Levites, and priests. Prophetic pronouncements of "the word
of Yahweh" were memorable words in memorable form addressed to memorable
circumstances. Baruch would have heard Jeremiah's pronouncements at least twice
by the time he wrote them on a scroll the first time, and at least three times by the
time he wrote them on a scroll again. Perhaps the act of writing them down helped
to fix them in his mind. But the later rabbis taught that once a student had heard
a teaching recited three or four times, he should remember it.[49] Prophetic oracles
would have been known and cultivated orally even after they were written down,
especially among "disciples" or admirers of particular prophets.

The "documents of covenant/torah" clearly stood in a tradition of covenantal
teaching. The one "found" in the Temple that legitimated Josiah's reform and the
one presented by Ezra to the Judeans returned from Babylon had both been
"updated" to serve as bases for, or were constitutive of, the new political arrangements. The scribes and/or priests and/or Levites involved in the production of these
documents would already have been well versed in covenantal teaching generally
and would have been involved in the innovative formulations. The Levites involved
in ceremonial recitation by Ezra did not need to have read the document of teaching in order to have "interpreted" it. The sayings of the wise may well have been
written down, as by "the men [scribes] of Hezekiah." But they continued to be
taught and learned orally-aurally, as is clear from the books of Proverbs and Sirach.

It is surely significant that at two points where modern scholars have assumed
that written copies of "the Torah/Law of Moses" were being used, the texts cited
as evidence do not support that assumption: Ben Sira's book, and the prescribed
procedure for group meetings in the *Community Rule* from Qumran near the
Dead Sea. In his reflection on the special role of the wise scribe, Ben Sira mentions the cultivation of "the torah of the Most High, the wisdom of all the
ancients, and prophecies" with no hint of writing and documents being involved.
And it has to be significant that in his "book," a collection of his wisdom the
principal emphasis of which is devotion and obedience to the covenant/teaching
of the Most High, he never quotes a single teaching or law from a written document of covenant/teaching.

According to the *Community Rule* from Qumran,

> where the ten are, there shall never lack a man among them who searches
> the torah [*dwrs btwrh*] day and night, concerning the right conduct of a man
> with his companion. And the many shall watch in community for a third
> of every night of the year, to recite the writing [*lqrw' bspr*] and to search the
> justice-ruling (*ldwrs mspt*) and to offer communal blessings [*lbrk byhd*].
> (1QS 6.6–8, my adaptation of the Vermes translation)

Contrary to standard scholarly translations of this passage, these gatherings were
not engaged in interpretive scholarly "study" of written texts. The three activities,

recitation, "searching," and uttering blessings, were all clearly oral. According to scholarly consensus, the *spr* being recited must have been a book of "Torah," although it is unclear from such a vague term precisely what text that might have been (Deuteronomy?). The latter is referred to as *spr* insofar as it existed in written form, which lent heightened authority. But the *Community Rule* itself, whether in this passage or elsewhere, gives no hint that the "writing" being recited was being read from a scroll.

Even if the recitation of a text involved the presentation of a written copy, the scribally trained reciters already knew the text.[50] It was inscribed on their memory as well as on a scroll. As a self-referential Egyptian satire says to a professional intellectual, "You are, of course, a skilled scribe at the head of his fellows, and the teaching of every book in incised on your heart."[51] The "incising" was probably not the result of physically reading a written copy of the book. "Egyptian sacred texts were typically memorized," while written copies were kept in a "house of life."[52] The training and professional practice of scribes was devoted to learning and cultivating in memory the various texts of the cultural tradition as well as cultivating an ability to recite those texts on appropriate occasions. If written texts were involved either as the source of scribal knowledge of a given text or as an aid in the recitation, they played a subsidiary role in a much more intensive process of oral learning, cultivation, and performance of cultural texts and their transmission to successive generations of scribes.[53]

Production of Documents

The survey of kinds of writing and their uses above suggests that documents were produced by writing from dictation. The king or a high military officer spoke, and a scribe wrote. Jeremiah recited the oracles he had received from Yahweh, and Baruch wrote them down on a scroll. Moses, represented as a scribe in Exodus and Deuteronomy, wrote the document of the covenant/torah from the "words" that Yahweh had spoken. In later times and other societies such as ancient Greece, the production of written texts was similarly by writing from dictation.[54]

The origins of the material that was dictated is a far more complex question. The concept of an author in the modern sense of an individual who creates narrative or poetry de novo is not appropriate to most of the literature included in the Hebrew Bible or the kinds of documents mentioned in its books. Perhaps even the term "composition" also is not appropriate to much of the cultural materials written in various kinds of documents, as suggested in the third factor above regarding the recitation of these materials. Most obviously, perhaps, traditional songs and liturgical psalms, far from having been composed de novo, were known in the collective social memory of the society in general and of the temple priests and Levites and singers, respectively. Poets/singers could then use their knowledge of the hymnic tradition to produce "new" hymns composed without direct use of writing.[55]

Similarly, much of the covenantal teaching and legal materials in the books of Exodus, Deuteronomy, and Leviticus as well as in earlier "documents of the covenant/teaching" were traditional. Those materials would have been further shaped and developed in cultivation (learning and recitation) by priests, Levites, and scribes. We might say that continuing "composition" happened in the process of such adaptation to and performance in developing social-political circumstances.[56]

Prophetic oracles are represented as composed in a special interactive way that did not involve writing. If we take seriously how prophetic experiences are represented in passages such as 1 Kings 22:15–23 and Isaiah 40:1–11 and what the oracles of an Amos or Isaiah or Jeremiah seem to presuppose, prophets were repeating Yahweh's indictments and judgments that they had overheard (or witnessed) in the heavenly council while in an ecstatic experience. Judging from the story of Jeremiah's dictating many such oracles to Baruch, these vivid "words of Yahweh" remained in the prophets' memories. And (the gist of) such short prophetic indictments and sentences mainly of kings and royal officers would have easily taken hold in the memories of a Baruch and other disciples caught in the political conflicts that became a regular feature of life under the monarchy and temple-state in Judah/Judea.

Such traditional orally cultivated materials (which may also have been written) then formed the basis for further development by the more creative scribes, which might be called composition. We can better imagine how this might have been done by Judean scribes from the way in which scribes seem to have worked with traditional materials in Mesopotamia. Mesopotamian scribes had learned, held in memory, and recited whole blocks of traditional material such as hymns, poetry, and epics. Creative scribes could then adapt, combine, or reconfigure those blocks of traditional materials in the process of creating a text that was both new and traditional.[57] Such composition probably did not require or involve writing in the course of composition, although the new text was eventually dictated and written. But even if it had involved writing in its composition, such a text recited periodically would have continued to function, to be learned and recited, apart from consultation of a written copy. Composition as adaptation and development of already-standard blocks of material (texts) originated and continued to exist primarily in the composition-in-performance and memories of the scribes, even when written copies (versions) of those texts existed.

Nevertheless, such composition, by combining, adapting, and reconfiguring traditional materials, involved literacy in various ways, some subtle and others more obvious. Both psalmic and instructional materials were occasionally organized in sequence of lines or verses by having the lines begin with successive letters of the alphabet (alphabetic acrostics, e.g., Pss. 25; 34; 119; Prov. 31:10–31). It is also likely that composition in writing played a role in certain connections, such as the arrangement of materials in books such as Isaiah, Deuteronomy, or Nehemiah. Many of us will find it difficult to believe that the composition of the books of Chronicles, including its adaptation of much material from the books of Kings, did not involve both a written text (of Kings) and composition in writing. Nevertheless, much of the continuing composition of texts that were then dictated and written down for certain purposes was done in the course of cultivating and performing traditional materials. Even more complex prose composition by later Greek and Latin intellectuals was commonly done in mental reflection on materials in one's memory, as Jocelyn Penny Small has documented.[58] The Latin "writer" Pliny explains how he composed in the solitude of his bedroom after awaking in the morning. Then he called in a secretary to take down the composition by dictation.

Conclusion

In discussion of the role of wisdom literature in ancient Israelite scribal education, Carr sketches an "oral-written" process in which, while the oral medium is primary, writing is still central.[59] In this regard wisdom literature had a place alongside other literature in a broader educational system similar to those in Mesopotamia, Egypt, and Greece. As in those societies, written texts were used "as part of a larger educational project of ensuring stable transmission of key traditions across time." "Scribal recollection of early traditions" in particular "was ensured partly through teaching students to read and reproduce written copies of the key traditions."[60]

It may well be that written texts played such a role in scribal learning and recitation of cultural traditions in Judea. But it is difficult to find evidence of it in Judean literature produced in earlier second-temple times, and it certainly does not seem to be true of the scribal training reflected in Ben Sira's wisdom or the book of Proverbs, as noted above. The "several wisdom texts" that Carr suggests "join textuality and memorization" use writing as a metaphor, for "writing on the tablet of the heart" (e.g., Prov. 3:3; 7:3). Teacher and students are clearly familiar with writing, or the metaphor would have no force. But no writing appears to have been involved in this process of memorization. Similarly in Proverbs 22:17–21, in which the claim to having "written thirty sayings" is part of the instructional rhetoric, the point is memorization by internalization into the heart and belly and establishment on the lips. "The material set down in writing" in the books of Proverbs or Sirach is indeed "well formed for memorization,"[61] but that is not because it was written. The material was taught orally before being written, and it continued to be taught and developed orally after it was written.

For Mesopotamia and Egypt there is indeed evidence for writing exercises on tablets at the elementary stages of scribal training and for scribal contact with written texts of major cultural texts. The abundance of tablets found in sites such as Nippur has enabled scholars to reconstruct how writing functioned in the elementary curriculum in two phases.[62] In the first, students copied a variety of lexical models to learn the writing system and vocabulary, then copied contracts for the simplest level of grammar. Toward the end of the first phase, they copied proverbs to learn the more complex grammar of complete sentences. In phase two they finally moved into literary texts for more complex constructions. If scribal training was similar in Judea, then students were probably put through similar stages of writing as a way of learning vocabulary and grammar at the elementary stages.

Even at the elementary stages, however, writing exercises were closely related to oral communication. Some of the evidence that Carr marshals to argue that the emphasis was on oral learning has the effect of diminishing the importance of written texts in the learning and recitation of texts. In Mesopotamia "numerous aspects of the lexical lists and exercises point to a largely oral process of instruction. . . . The school dialogues describe an educational process where oral dictation and accurate oral performance were central."[63] A range of Mesopotamian compositions, known to us because they were written down and preserved, call for their teachings to be memorized and "put in the mouth" of following generations, but apparently quite apart from the physical reading of the written text.[64] Similarly in Egypt, "most of the core texts appear to have been composed for oral performance, with use of metrical, episodic, and repetitive structures that would cue a performer seeking oral mastery of the text."[65] The purpose of scribal education was mastery of the cultural tradition, but that did not involve working with written texts on an everyday basis.[66] Egyptian wisdom literature prefigures later Judean wisdom in its emphasis on "hearing" and internalizing the instruction in "the heart."[67]

Scribal learning and practice at the time of Ben Sira thus would appear to involve writing in various ways. Scribes had presumably learned to write and to read writing, probably at an elementary stage of their training. Ben Sira himself claims to have written down his wisdom into a book. Scribes also knew of the existence of certain books and knew their contents; Ben Sira knew of the expectation of Elijah's coming that we are familiar with from Malachi.[68] But that does not mean that such wise scribes gained their knowledge of cultural tradition from reading scrolls. Most of the cultural tradition was oral in origin and continued to be taught and learned orally. Much of the professional role of scribes involved speaking, whether in public assemblies, advice to rulers, or teaching. We can only speculate that scribes may, on occasion, have been expected to deal in some way with documents that had been laid up in the Temple or to recite (or read) from documents such as lists and annals that had not been oral in origin and in continuing cultivation. In scribal practice in general, however, writing was deeply embedded in and instrumental to oral communication.

We have much more information from the parallel relation of writing and written texts to oral communications in Athens, and it may illuminate why the very specialists trained to write and read do not appear to use writing in their learning and professional service.[69] Evidence of both the incidence of literacy and of the use of writing increases from the fifth to the fourth centuries in Athens. At the same time, *grammata* (letters) intrudes on *mousikē*, the training in poetry, hymns, and other oral verbal art that composed the cultural complement to *gymnastikē* in traditional Athenian "education." Literacy became important as an elementary stage for the higher learning of traditional (oral) culture (poetry, song, prose, oratory) as well as for politics. In the *Laws* Plato expects that all would gain literacy, but "gives no indication that any of the later stages of education are performed through the written word."[70] Although in favor of acquiring basic literacy, intellectuals such as Plato, Xenophon, and Isocrates object that writing cannot produce virtue, that *grammata* is not the same as *logos*. "What they claim to teach, or know, without the aid of writing is in many cases something extremely sophisticated and specialized."[71] And it is this "higher" cultural education that prepares the well-born and wealthy to become political leaders. Writing and reading were elementary, instrumental and almost incidental to cultural education. Rhetoric may have presupposed, but did not directly involve writing or reading. "The written record of the classical period preserves no explicit reference to [written] texts being used for teaching."[72]

Like the classical intellectuals in Athens, although in a very different social location in a very different political-economic structure, Ben Sira and his fellow scribes were trained in literacy. But they learned and taught and played their political roles largely without direct use of written texts.

Chapter 6

The Cultural Repertoire of the Judean Scribes

Let us now sing the praises of famous men. . . .
those who gave counsel because they were intelligent;
those who spoke in prophetic oracles;
those who led the people by their counsels
and by their knowledge of the people's lore;
they were wise in their words of instruction;
those who composed musical tunes,
or put verses in writing. . . .

Ben Sira

In his prologue to the book of Sirach, Ben Sira's grandson declared that "my grandfather Jesus had devoted himself to the reading of the Law and the Prophets and the other books of our ancestors, and had acquired considerable proficiency in them." Taking the grandson's statement at face value, modern interpreters go even further, making Ben Sira into a veritable prototype of a modern Hebrew Bible scholar. "Ben Sira cites or alludes to" nearly all the "biblical" books, and "often bases his didactic discourse on a single text from the Torah."[1] A close inspection of his book, however, reveals that Ben Sira does not cite particular statements from the Torah, much less offer any explicit "interpretation." And the prophetic books appear to have left no significant mark on his instruction.

It is also striking that the "biblical" books do not leave a more direct and explicit imprint on Daniel and Enoch literature. Prophetic as well as sapiential features are evident in both. But Enoch literature appears almost to be avoiding the Torah. And while loyalty to the covenant is important in Daniel, the revelations in chapters 7–12 pay little attention to the Torah. According to their own self-characterization, the producers of this literature were scribes and sages. So how do we explain that these wise scribes, the very specialists who were professionally engaged in the cultivation of the authoritative texts of the Judeans, pay so little attention to the books of the Torah, and that Ben Sira fails to quote the Torah to which he is adamantly devoted?

The problem may be rooted in the limitations of established biblical studies. Given its roots in modern print culture and its dedication to the interpretation of the Scriptures (sacred *writings*), biblical studies tends to focus almost exclusively on written texts. We have tended to assume that Judean culture was virtually identical with the books of the Hebrew Bible. Unable to imagine a figure or a motif or a story that we know in a given book as having existed independently of that book (such as the legend of the giants in Gen. 6:1–4), we assume that its presence in a "later" text (such as *1 Enoch*) must be a reference to or an interpretation of the "earlier" or "biblical" text (such as Genesis). The appearance of figures such as Abraham, Aaron, Solomon, Elijah, and the Twelve Prophets, and so forth, in the praise of the ancestors in Sirach 44–50 must mean that Ben Sira knew most of the books of the Hebrew Bible.

Evidence of the existence and cultivation of these books is in fact minimal and fragmentary before the second century BCE. The most trusting biblical scholars nevertheless find in vague references such as those in Sirach 44–50 or Ezra and Nehemiah evidence that the books of the Pentateuch and many of the prophetic books existed, even in the form in which we know them, already toward the beginning of the second-temple period. The most skeptical scholars, on the other hand, holding out for more substantial evidence, argue that the "biblical books" as we know them were not even composed until late Persian and Hellenistic times. In both cases, however, the focus is on clearly defined written documents that we know as biblical.

The close relationship between writing and oral communication and the evidence that texts were inscribed on and recited from the memory of ancient scribes (explored in the previous chapter), however, suggest that the standard focus on written texts may be blocking rather than facilitating insight into the broader cultural process in which the "biblical" books were produced and cultivated. If wise scribes such as Ben Sira did not use written copies of texts in their learning and teaching (of wisdom and Torah and prophecies), then the existence and the particular contours of written texts may be of only relative importance in our approach to scribal knowledge and practice. Despite the concerns of modern biblical scholars to find stable, precisely definable writings, the realities of ancient cultural practices were evidently more fluid in their mixture of media, oral and written, and in the definition of what constituted texts, oral and written.

We may approach ancient scribal practice more appropriately if we think in terms of a rich repertoire of traditional culture of various distinctive forms that was cultivated (learned and recited and written) in transgenerational scribal circles. There would have been considerable continuity in the cultural repertoire, but there would have been moments of creativity as well, particularly at times of trouble and transition. Extant written texts constitute our only sources. Yet they are sources for the broader cultural repertory that was not confined to written texts, and the broader process of cultural production by which these written texts themselves developed. With this broadened approach, therefore, it may be possible to gain a clearer sense of the particular contours of the Judean cultural repertory that formed the context in which we can understand the production of Enoch literature, the book of Sirach, and Daniel literature.

While there is virtually no direct evidence and only contested evidence for the existence and contours of "biblical" texts during the centuries before Ben Sira and the scribes who produced Daniel and Enoch literature, we now have extensive evidence from the Dead Sea Scrolls discovered near Qumran in 1947 for late second-temple times. Information from the Dead Sea Scrolls can provide a later base line against which we can then assess the limited and indirect evidence for the availability and cultivation and development of texts in earlier second-temple times.

THE EVIDENCE FROM QUMRAN

A Wide Range of Texts—Still Developing

The scrolls found at Qumran included copies of nearly all the books that were later included by the Rabbis in the Hebrew Scriptures. Each book, such as Deuteronomy or Isaiah, was usually on a separate scroll. There are a few indications that these books were thought of in groups. A text evidently composed before the mid-second century CE makes reference to "the book of Moses, [and] the book[s of the Pr]ophets and in Davi[d and in the events] of the ages past."[2] If these were thought of as more than associative groupings of related books, however, the contents and limits of "the Prophets" and "David" were still somewhat undefined. The Psalms were thought of as prophetic at Qumran, as was the recently composed book of Daniel, later included among the Writings.[3]

The written texts of these books, however, were anything but standardized and stable. Eugene Ulrich has explained how the evidence challenges older assumptions about the protobiblical books, in two fundamental respects: (1) "Evidence from Qumran demonstrates that there were multiple editions of the biblical books in antiquity."[4] (2) These multiple textual traditions were unstable and still developing. Creative scribes were actively handing on the tradition, but they were adding to it, enriching it, and attempting to make it adaptable and relevant."[5] The same process involved in the composition of these texts from their beginnings was thus continuing all the way through the second-temple period.[6]

In addition to these protobiblical books in their unstable multiple versions, moreover, there were many other texts found at Qumran that were also clearly authoritative. One mark of their authority is the multiple copies of them found at Qumran, in some cases many more than for books that later became biblical. Psalms (36 manuscripts) and Deuteronomy (30) outranked all books, with Isaiah (21) and Genesis (20) next. But the book of *Jubilees* (at 15 copies), which includes alternative versions of some of the cultural tradition in Genesis and the first half of Exodus, rivaled Exodus (17) and Leviticus (14). The *Temple Scroll* and *Reworked Pentateuch* (5 each) were nearly as prominent as Numbers (8). The copies of (sections of) *1 Enoch* (12) outnumbered those of any prophetic book except Isaiah, such as Jeremiah and Ezekiel (6 each) and the Twelve (Prophets, 8) and Daniel (8). If we conclude that Exodus and Leviticus were authoritative at Qumran, then certainly *Jubilees* was also, and the recently composed sections of *1 Enoch* and the book of Daniel seem to have been as important as Jeremiah and Ezekiel.[7]

That the authority of the protobiblical books was only relative to and rivaled by many other books is further complicated by other texts found at Qumran. Even though it understood itself in terms of a new exodus and renewed covenant, the Qumran community evidently did not look directly to the Pentateuch for the rules and ordinances that guided its common life. Rather, the community generated new guidelines, evident in the *Community Rule* and the *Damascus Rule* and other texts. The "searching of the *mišpāṭ*" (presumably the community's own rulings) stands parallel to the "recitation of the book" (Deuteronomy?) and "group blessings" in an instruction for regular community ritual (1QS 6.6–8). The prophetic books contained important predictions, but they had to be supplemented with new books of "interpretation" that explained them (see further below). And while the Qumran community was virtually obsessed with "returning" to the Torah, they also valued and copied what appear to be other, alternative books of Torah that claimed even higher authority than the books of the Pentateuch.

The appearance of this wide range of written texts at Qumran, some of which were not produced by the community but brought there from elsewhere in Judea, both require and make possible a refinement of the terms and concepts we apply to second-temple Judean texts. "The Bible" and "biblical" are clearly anachronistic; there was no definitive widely recognized collection of books with a relatively stable text until much later. Using these terms in historical inquiry is not only anachronistic but teleological as well: it orients the investigation to the eventual outcome and tends to underestimate the importance of a wider range of texts in the Judean cultural repertoire. Using such terms thus also obscures the dynamic process by which some of the many "books" used in second-temple Judea came to be included in the "Hebrew Bible" centuries later. As Ulrich points out, "If we try to achieve a historical perspective on the text of the Bible, the first step is not to talk about a Bible."[8] We might add the corollary that we also drop the much later categories of "Apocrypha" and "Pseudepigrapha."[9]

We must evidently think in terms of a wide range of texts that had varying authority relative to one another, and texts that were still developing in a dynamic process of recitation and continuing composition and copying. To replace terms such as "biblical" the most satisfactory term would be "authoritative," which has the advantage of being flexible and analytical in the sense that it requires specification according to certain criteria.[10] Marks of texts' relative authority, in addition to the number of copies found at Qumran, would be explicit references to them ("as is written in the book of . . .") in other texts,[11] quotation of passages from them in other texts with or without introductory formulas, claims to being direct divine revelation, and claims to being a record of the very speech of God or a divine messenger.

Uses of Prophetic Texts

References to prophetic texts, like those to other authoritative texts such as the Pentateuchal books or *Jubilees,* are strikingly infrequent in the Dead Sea Scrolls, especially when compared with those in early Christian texts a century or so later. Citations of short passages from Isaiah or Ezekiel stand alongside those from Deuteronomy or Numbers, a reference to Nahum alongside some to Leviticus.

In connection with its own break with the incumbent high-priestly regime in Jerusalem as a fulfillment of prophecy, however, the Qumran community produced a uniquely new form of literature: a form of explicit interpretation.[12] These books of "interpretation" have a standardized structure. They are running commentaries on the text of prophetic books in successive steps of quotation of a few lines of text followed by an interpretation beginning with "interpreted, this concerns. . . ." Names in the prophetic declarations were taken as code for figures and groups of their own times.

The *Commentary on Habakkuk* indicates more precisely how the community understood the prophetic books and their direct application to the events in which it was involved (see esp. 1QpHab 2.6–10; 6.15–7.5). The prophets had written down, in cryptic terms, the events of the final generation, as revealed to them by God. But the revelation to the prophets was incomplete; God had not told them *when* what they wrote down would happen. Finally, however, God had made the mysteries known to the Teacher (founder of the community) so that he could interpret the word of the prophets. And the *interpretation* (*pesher*) indicated that the community itself was involved in the final events, which were now happening. Once the breakthrough revelation had been "put into the heart" of the Teacher (1QpHab 2.6–10), the community, now possessing the same "understanding," continued *interpretation* of the prophetic books along the same line.[13] The dissident scribal-priestly community at Qumran thus looked to the prophetic books as (potentially) authoritative for its withdrawal to the wilderness, in resistance to the dominant political order. The community's conflict with the Hasmonean high-priestly regime in Jerusalem and later the conquering Roman imperial forces had been predicted by the prophets as part of the now-revealed mystery of God's plan for the final generation. Other scribal circles still active in the temple-state in Jerusalem would presumably have known the prophetic materials and probably the prophetic books. However, not only the running commentary on authoritative books, but also the explicit and self-conscious "interpretation" of authoritative texts was unique to Qumran. Nothing like this appears in any Judean literature prior to the Qumran community.

Insofar as the running *pesharim* are confined to the prophetic books and Psalms at Qumran itself,[14] moreover, it is unwarranted to generalize from them to Qumran "interpretation of scripture" generally.[15] There appears to be a certain parallel between the knowledge given to the Teacher by God about the application of the prophetic predictions (see 1QpHab 2.8–10; 7.1–5 quoted just above) and "all that has been revealed" in relation to the Torah of Moses (1QS 5.8–10; 8.14–16; cf. 9.13).[16] Whatever the latter may have referred to, however, it does not seem to have led to explicit self-conscious "interpretation" of texts of Torah similar to those of prophetic passages, certainly not running commentaries on books of the Pentateuch. The uses of Torah appear to have been far more complex, subtle, and unreflective.

Uses of Texts of Torah

Much interpretation of the Dead Sea Scrolls has simply assumed that the Qumran community (like other priestly and/or scribal groups) related to the books of the Pentateuch primarily by study and interpretation. Scholars commonly translate the Hebrew term *qārā'* (recite) as "read" and the root *drš* (search) as "study," and seem to assume that the principal purpose of the "reading" and "study" of Torah texts was to "interpret" them—somewhat as modern biblical scholars proceed.[17] Emphasis on "the community's interpretive study of the Torah" is found in passages such as 1QS 8.12–16 and 5.8–10 and also in CD 19.33–20.13 and 6.2–11.[18] A closer look at these and other key passages, however, suggests a different relationship to and use of texts of Torah.

Not Study and Interpretation, but Community Action and Observance

The emphasis throughout the "Rules" of the Qumran community and/or the broader movement in its smaller communities falls on their collective action and group discipline in the historical crisis they discerned. Thus, in 1QS 8.12–16, the community was called

> to separate themselves from the settlement of the men of injustice and to go into the wilderness to "prepare the way . . ." [citation of Isa. 40:3]. This [way] is the searching [*midrash*] of the Torah w[hic]h He commanded through Moses, that they should act in accordance with all that has been revealed from time to time in accordance with what the prophets revealed by His holy spirit.

The "searching" here does not appear to be "interpretive study of the Torah" so much as an intense exposure to the Torah so that it will inform their community life.[19] The medium of revelation ("what the prophets revealed by His holy spirit"), moreover, seems to be understood more as oral (commandments and oracles) than as written.

The instruction for one who was ready to enter "the Covenant of God" in 1QS 5.8–10 has a similar emphasis on disciplined living in community. For this the inductee takes "a binding oath to return with all his heart and soul to all that has been commanded of the Torah of Moses." The instruction of youth and the examination of candidates and neophytes is focused on the laws of the covenant and the rules of the community in preparation for their close observance, not on interpretive study of Torah texts for esoteric knowledge (1QS 6.13–15; 1QSa 1.6–8).[20] The *Damascus Rule* also consistently emphasizes communal action and discipline in reference to the Torah. For example, the community/movement was called to "dig the well, that is, 'the well which the princes dug, which the nobles of the people delved with the scepter'" (CD 6.3–4; Num. 21:18). Again the "digging" and "searching" of the Torah is all about community action and discipline, "walking," guided by "ordinances." The emphasis falls repeatedly not on "interpretive study" but on "their collective dedication to the practice of God's will through their disciplined life."[21]

Torah (Books) Rarely Cited as Authoritative Writings

Despite the paucity of quotations from books of the Pentateuch, interpreters of the Scrolls often state that the laws and rules of the Qumran community were derived from the Torah in some way.[22] Qumran documents, however, simply do not support such a claim.

Citation of any text in sections of documents devoted to community rules is rare, confined largely to four columns in the *Damascus Rule* (CD 9.1–12.16). And in that short section citations from Nahum and Proverbs and even *Jubilees* crop up alongside two or three from Leviticus, only some references are explicit citations ("for it is written:"), and most function as proof texts rather than as "scriptural" texts from which community laws are derived.[23] Practice at Qumran parallels the general pattern observed in Judean texts until very late second-temple times: in legal rulings "there is almost no reference to Scripture," much less derivation of laws from the Torah.[24]

While the Qumran community produced laws and ordinances for its common life and ritual largely on its own authority, the occasional (re)citations of short "proof texts" from Leviticus, Nahum, or Proverbs are references to written texts as authoritative backing for their own legislation. This is further evident in *Some Observances of the Torah* (4QMMT), a nonpolemical text stemming evidently from the point at which the dissident priests and scribes were making their break from the temple-state authorities. In the seventeen or so matters of offerings, sacrifices, and purity about which they offer their rulings ("concerning X . . . we say . . . Y"), only four times is an appeal made to "it is written" (and in most cases no clearly definable citation is given). In the final exhortation (apparently to the Temple authorities) to return to "the books" and to follow the examples of the kings who were "seekers of Torah," however, it is evident that they understand their "observances of the Torah" to be in accordance with (the authority) and perhaps implementations of the Torah in a very general way.[25]

Ritual Recitation of Torah

The key terms as well as the context of one of the principal passages that has been translated and interpreted in terms of "reading" and "study" of the Torah (1QS

6.6 8) suggest a more likely alternative. This passage is part of a larger section of the *Community Rule* that gives instructions for formalized procedure (of eating, blessings, and deliberation) in meetings of (the council of) the community. In the middle comes an instruction for a nightly communal ritual.

> And the many shall watch together for a third of every night of the year, to recite the book [*liqrō' hassēper*], to search law/justice [*lidrōsh mišpaṭ*], and to bless together [*lebārēk běyaḥad*]. (1QS 6.6–8)

The nightly ritual had three parts. First was an oral recitation of what was presumably a book of Torah. Since members of the community, like other scribes and priests, were well drilled in knowledge of the text, they could recite from memory, even if an unwieldy scroll lay unrolled before them. Then they engaged in a "search of justice(-ruling)," presumably focused on their community rules. Finally they recited blessings together.

Such ritual recitation of torah, of course, was not unprecedented, as we are aware from the previous chapter. "The book(s) of the covenant/torah" mentioned in the covenant ceremonies in Exodus 24; Joshua 8 and 24; 2 Kings 22–23; and Nehemiah 8 all involved a ritual recitation of the words of the covenant/teaching before the assembled Israel. The instructions for the ritual reading at Qumran may even allude to God's instruction to Joshua: "Let this book of teaching not depart [be lacking, *lō'-yāmûš*] from your mouth, but recite [meditate on] it day and night, so that you will act in accordance . . ." (Josh. 1:8, au. trans.). The Qumran covenanters not only had a member who searched the Torah day and night (like Joshua, 1QS 6.6–7), but also in common "watch" every night recited the book of Torah (like Joshua).[26] The purpose of the communal ritual recitation at Qumran was surely the same as that stated in Joshua 1:8.[27] In this connection, particularly on the likelihood that the "book" recited was Deuteronomy, it is noteworthy that some of the manuscripts (ostensibly) of Deuteronomy found at Qumran were composed of excerpts and were apparently "used for liturgical purposes."[28]

The oral "recitation of the book" (of torah) at Qumran group meetings illustrates a way of appropriating scripture common in many societies and religious groups. Regular ritual recitation of revered texts is not only a common way of appropriating meaning that transcends the discursive level and works more at the affective level. Such recitation in groups also helps bind members of the group together in common ritual action and deeper emotional appropriation of the sacred text. And it also helps "internalize the values and norms implicit in the text, even if they are not grasped in a cognitive, intellectualized way."[29]

One important effect of regular ritual recitation of authoritative texts would have been directly related to the appearance of what seems like "biblical" phrases yet not what could be called "quotation" of particular passages in a stricter sense. Ritual recitation would have intensified the scribal-priestly participants' familiarity with the texts so that they were thoroughly imbued with the language of authoritative books. This and other ways in which scribes and priests cultivated (learned, taught, recited) various authoritative texts of Mosaic Torah would help explain why the language, for example, of Qumran's own *Community Rule* closely resembles "biblical" wording and style. Along with several other factors in the ongoing scribal cultivation of the legendary and legal aspects of the Judean cultural repertoire, it also helps to explain how newly composed texts of alternative Torah might appear to modern biblical scholars as mere "rewritten" versions of already authoritative older texts of Torah.

Books of Alternative Torah

Scholars have assigned a number of documents found in the caves near Qumran (such as the *Temple Scroll*) to the category of "rewritten Bible." This term had been applied to Judean literature such as *Jubilees,* Pseudo-Philo's *Biblical Antiquities,* and Josephus's *Jewish Antiquities,* which supposedly took as their literary framework the flow of the biblical text and, presumably for clarification, made changes by omission, expansion, and insertion.[30] The concept "rewritten Bible" and its variants "reworked Bible" and "parabiblical," however, are seriously problematic for historical understanding.[31] Since there was no clearly defined "Bible" yet in late second-temple times, application of the category "rewritten Bible" simply obscures the ways in which new compositions of Mosaic Torah may have drawn on traditional materials and authoritative texts of Mosaic Torah. The historically appropriate alternative would be an examination of the complicated relationship of texts such as *Jubilees* and the *Temple Scroll* to the still-developing books later recognized as biblical—while consciously trying to counteract the assumptions of modern print culture. Such an examination may have suggestive implications for how we understand the Judean cultural repertory, particularly the cultivation of Torah.

It is often said that the book of *Jubilees* takes its framework and much of its contents from the Pentateuch, specifically the narrative from the beginning of Genesis to the covenant scene at Sinai in Exodus 19.[32] But that is only a minimal and not a very determinative characterization of the book. While at points *Jubilees* appears to follow the wording of Genesis or Exodus (in a proto-Samaritan version) closely, at others it is hardly even a paraphrase or allusion. It does not include much that is contained in Genesis and Exodus. Yet it mentions matriarchs and other figures and places not included in Genesis, such as stories about Abraham that also appear in the *Apocalypse of Abraham*.[33] Such materials suggest that the legendary lore behind Genesis was much broader than what is known from the "biblical" book. From its materials on Enoch not known from Genesis (5:15–27) it is evident that *Jubilees* was familiar with several of the writings attributed to Enoch.[34] *Jubilees* also evidently makes use of the Hebrew tradition behind *Aramaic Levi* (in the DSS), and includes short passages of material also in Isaiah and the Psalms. *Jubilees* is thus drawing on other authoritative texts in addition to Genesis and Exodus and/or on those parts of the Judean cultural repertoire also used in those texts.[35]

Most significant perhaps, with regard to the torah texts that later became biblical, *Jubilees* systematically arranges legal materials according to its own distinctive ("historical") scheme. The producers of Jubilees placed materials familiar to us from the legal collections included in Leviticus, Numbers, and Deuteronomy at the points in its narrative of the patriarchs and matriarchs where the issues they address first appear. The ancestors before Moses thus receive revelation of and/or practice the laws of the Torah long before they were declared at Sinai (according to Exodus-Leviticus-Numbers). And in a book that insists on strict observance of Torah, those laws sometime include rulings that do not appear in any of the legislative sections of the Pentateuch.[36]

The *Temple Scroll* is a utopian charter for the final temple that God will construct and draws on various traditions of the wilderness tabernacle (Exod. 26; 35), Solomon's temple (1 Kings 6; 2 Chron. 3–4), and the schematic temple of Ezekiel (40–48). Its instructions for festivals and their sacrifices are similar to some of those in Numbers 28–29 and Leviticus 23, but include prescriptions for festivals not mentioned in pentateuchal texts, and follows the 364-day calendar known also in *Jubilees* and *1 Enoch* 72–82. The effect is to enhance festivals and sacrifices beyond what was prescribed in the Pentateuch.[37] The *Temple Scroll's* elaborate design for the ideal new temple implies that the existing temple needs to be replaced, and its revision of the codes included in Deuteronomy implies that this new code is a replacement.[38]

The continuing composition of new, alternative texts of Torah, such as *Jubilees* and the *Temple Scroll,* suggests strongly that the pentateuchal books had no monopoly on authority among texts of Mosaic torah. In fact, both the *Temple Scroll* and *Jubilees* claim higher authority than the pentateuchal books claim. The *Temple Scroll* has God speak in the first person, dictating the prescriptions for the temple and its sacrifices to Moses, who serves merely as God's amanuensis. In *Jubilees* the revelation disclosed to Moses on Sinai had already been written on heavenly tablets and was dictated to Moses by the angel of the (God's) presence.[39] The book of *Jubilees* thus claims to be a transcription of the ultimate in numinous writing, which has the power to make history happen. It also has much of the legal contents of the pentateuchal books revealed to patriarchs from the heavenly tablets, including in writing, long before they were revealed to Moses on Sinai, according to Exodus. Thus in the antiquity of their revelation, they have authority prior to the Mosaic legislation. At points *Jubilees* even makes a distinction between itself and "(the book of) the first law/torah" (2:24; 6:22; 30:12).[40] These books of alternative Torah thus relativize the authority of the pentateuchal books and downgrade the role of Moses.[41]

While the pentateuchal books may have been the principal sources of Mosaic torah, other books of Mosaic torah such as *Jubilees* and the *Temple Scroll* were being produced and becoming authoritative alongside the Pentateuch. And all of those texts were grounded in and were being further developed from a broader cultural tradition of Mosaic torah.

In sum, evidence from the Dead Sea Scrolls gives us a baseline from which to appreciate the uses of texts of Torah and prophetic books roughly in mid-second century BCE, just after the time that Sirach, Daniel, and the early texts of Enoch literature were produced. First, a wide range of cultural materials were cultivated in scribal(-priestly) circles such as the Qumran community. The range included (a) written and/or oral texts that had already reached distinctive form, some of which (while still developing) later became biblical, and others that rivaled them as authoritative, at least at Qumran; and (b) other orally cultivated cultural materials (evident, for example, in alternative texts of torah), some paralleled in books that later became biblical, and others not so paralleled. Second, texts of Torah were appropriated by intensive learning (presumably by recitation) and by regular ritual recitation, and not yet by "study" and "interpretation." But the Qumran community itself developed a distinctive mode of *interpretation* of prophetic texts that was unprecedented, yet not extended to texts of Torah and history. Third, texts, whether those that later became biblical or other revered, authoritative texts, underwent continuing development in the interaction of scribal learning, recitation, and copying.[42] Fourth, creative scribes, thoroughly acquainted with the broader repertoire of Mosaic torah and "historical" legends (and so forth), including material not in the pentateuchal texts and alternative versions of material that was, continued to compose alternative texts of torah. And fifth, creative scribes(-priests) in the Qumran community, thoroughly imbued with texts of torah, generated community regulations and composed new texts of "community rules" that use the same basic language (terms, phrases, figures of speech, and so forth) that are familiar to us from the books that later became biblical. These aspects of scribal use of texts should be kept in mind when we focus on the production of Sirach, Daniel, and Enoch texts (chaps. 7, 8, 9).

BEN SIRA'S RELATION TO TORAH AND PROPHETS

Scholars base their standard claim that Ben Sira knew "the Law and the Prophets"[43] on three or four key passages: the prologue by the grandson, the identification of Wisdom with "the book of the covenant of the Most High God" in 24:23, the reference to "the law of the Most High . . . and prophecies" in 38:34–39:1, and "the praise of the fathers" in Sirach 44–50. On closer inspection, however, the case is anything but clear or certain. The grandson's assertion two generations later that Jesus ben Sira had "read the Law and the Prophets and the other books of our ancestors" may well be a projection. It is not clear to what "the book of the covenant" and "the law/torah of the Most High" make reference (there is no indication that it is the Pentateuch), and "the prophecies" do not appear to refer to a book. And it is unwarranted to take the praise of ancestors that also appear prominently in the books of Genesis, Exodus, Joshua, Kings, and the prophetic books as an indication that Ben Sira was consulting those books.

Like that of the Qumran community, Ben Sira's relationship with "the Torah" was more complicated than modern interpreters have discerned, especially once we recognize that the Israelite cultural tradition was not reducible to the books that later became biblical. On the one hand, Ben Sira's instruction repeatedly

teaches obedience of the "covenant" and "commandments" of God, and his programmatic hymn glorifies the great ancestors. This stands in contrast with earlier
wisdom books (Proverbs, Job, and Qohelet), which had made virtually no reference to the distinctive traditions of Israel, such as Mosaic covenantal teaching or
ancestral legends or prophetic oracles. In addition to identifying "the book of
covenant of the Most High God" with Wisdom, Ben Sira often associates wisdom with the commandments.[44] At a few points Ben Sira even echoes a covenantal commandment (e.g., honor of parents in 3:1–6) or a social law included in
Deuteronomy (e.g., Sir. 4:1–6 on charity for the poor; cf. Deut. 15:7–11).

On the other hand, despite his frequent exhortations to obey the covenant or
the commandments, Ben Sira "does not cite biblical laws directly."[45] There is thus
no basis for arguing that he is engaged in the interpretation of the (books of) the
Pentateuch. Ben Sira's teaching "is neither legal proclamation nor legal interpretation."[46] There is only one passage in which the law is arguably the primary subject (32:14–24).[47] What might be characterized as echoes of stories or figures in
the book of Genesis occur, but mainly in "the praise of the fathers." Echoes of
covenantal teaching known mainly in Deuteronomy can be detected occasionally in Ben Sira's instructional speeches. But virtually no allusions, much less clear
references, can be found to the cultic and dietary laws of Leviticus.[48] The lack of
allusion to any sort of ritual laws leads us to suspect that "the book of the covenant
of the Most High God, the law/torah that Moses commanded us" (24:23), was
probably some version of Deuteronomy, which stood in a long tradition of "the
book of the teaching/covenant (of Moses)."

The book of Sirach thus offers evidence of a "book of the covenant of the Most
High God," although not of the books of the Pentateuch and not of a book of
Torah that he and other scribes read, cited, and interpreted. Indeed, in declaring
that this "book of the covenant" was the very embodiment of heavenly Wisdom,
which had been "established in Zion" (24:1–12, 23), Ben Sira seems to suggests
that, with its divine origins and sacred aura, it had a constitutional function in the
Jerusalem temple-state.[49] Although the "torah of the Most High" (in 38:34–39:1)
may not refer to a written scroll, it stands in first place among the several segments
of the Judean cultural repertory from which the wise scribes derive the wisdom
that enables them to serve with distinction among the rulers of the temple-state.
Yet Ben Sira and his students apparently did not engage in the reading and study
of law books as a basis for their own codes of prudential behavior or as a basis for
their service among the "great ones."

CULTIVATION OF TEXTS EARLIER
IN THE SECOND-TEMPLE PERIOD

The composition and cultivation of texts depended heavily on the political-
economic conditions in Judea under the dominant imperial regimes. If the population of Judea was much more limited than previously assumed (as noted in

chap. 1), there was an economic base to support only minimal scribal activity. If the population of Jerusalem was around 2,000 toward the end of the Persian period, it is difficult to imagine that there were more than a few score scribes, including some Levites. On the other hand, both the struggles to organize the new temple-state and the conflicts between rival priestly groups could have provided stimulus and occasion for cultural production, such as documents that would lend the authority of writing to one priestly group or another.

The interaction of multiple languages entailed in the imperial political-economic structure of the Persian Empire was also a major factor in the cultural processes of second-temple Judea. The majority of people, who had not been deported by the Babylonians, would have continued to speak a vernacular form of Hebrew. Prophetic oracles, psalms, proverbial instruction, and other oral and written forms of Judean culture were in a standardized form of Hebrew that scholars call "Classical" or "Biblical Hebrew." The Judean elite who had been deported and then repatriated to take charge of the temple-state, however, had learned Aramaic, the language of the dominant imperial culture.[50] This is what is presupposed in the story of Ezra's recitation of "the scroll of the torah of Moses" in the authorizing ceremony of the temple-state in Jerusalem. It was necessary for the Levites to "interpret" or "translate," so that the people in Jerusalem, no longer in command of Hebrew, would be able to understand (Neh. 8:8). In the course of the next several generations, Aramaic gradually became more prominent as a spoken language in Judea. And the linguistic situation was even further complicated under the Ptolemaic and Seleucid Empires, when Greek was the official imperial and dominant cultural language.

Texts in the Judean cultural repertoire, however, continued to be cultivated in Hebrew, and new texts were composed in "late biblical Hebrew." Only brief sections of the book of Ezra and the tales of Judean sages at the Persian court in Daniel 2–6 were composed in Aramaic. This means that Judean texts composed and cultivated by scribes and priests associated with the Temple constituted an elite culture. Yet, while Judean culture was in an archaic language no longer being spoken in the rest of society, it was nevertheless a local indigenous culture, in a language different from the dominant imperial language and culture.

Most of what we know as the books of the Pentateuch and Prophets must have taken their more or less definitive contours well before their appearance among the scrolls left at the Dead Sea, albeit in multiple versions or textual traditions that were all still developing. This must have happened, moreover, before their translation from Hebrew into Greek to form the Septuagint, presumably sometime in the third century BCE. They may well have taken more or less definitive shape during the Persian period, yet we lack evidence external to the books to demonstrate this. Internal to these books, however, are indications of some of the same features as in the Mosaic torah and prophetic segments of Judean cultural repertoire evident in the Dead Sea Scrolls: the Judean torah and prophetic repertories included a wider range of texts and general cultural materials than was contained in the books that later became biblical; books of torah and prophecy and the earlier texts that underlie their production were related to political struggles in Judea.

Torah/Legal Collections

It is commonly agreed that the books of the Pentateuch are a composite of several texts that developed in stages over several centuries. It has been standardly supposed that composition had been completed by the early Persian period and/or that Ezra, the prototypical scribe, had brought the Law (the Pentateuch) with him as central to his mission—to be the "constitution" or composite "lawbook" of the temple-state. Yet it seems highly unlikely that "the justice/order [dātā'] of your God/the God of heaven" (7:12, 14, 26) with which Ezra was charged is identified with "the torah of Moses/Yahweh" (7:6, 10) in Ezra 7.[51] In any case the books of Ezra and Nehemiah do not offer evidence for the existence of the Pentateuch.

It would be stretching things to conclude that Ezra and Nehemiah attest the existence of both the Deuteronomic Code and the Priestly Code, even if they had not yet been combined.[52] In the books of Ezra and Nehemiah certain actions are taken with an appeal to written authorization ("as it is written"). Those who produced Ezra and Nehemiah appear to have been familiar with some legal materials that were included in the Deuteronomic Code (such as exclusion from the community of people of certain ethnic origin, Neh. 13:1–2; cf. Deut. 23:3–4) and others that were included in the Priestly laws (such as the duties of priests and Levites, Ezra 6:18; cf. Exod. 29; Lev. 8). Yet the books of Ezra and Nehemiah also justify some of the actions taken by legal authority that have no recognizable parallel in any code included in the Pentateuch. The coercive divorces of native women to be carried out "according to the law" resemble nothing in the Pentateuch. The stipulated dates of certain cultic observances are different from those indicated in Leviticus or Numbers. And the legislation of the temple tax at the rate of one-third of a shekel (Neh. 10:32–33 [33–34 Heb.]) must precede the half-shekel in the Pentateuch (Exod. 30:11–16; 38:25–26), since taxes inexorably increase rather than decrease.

From exhaustive previous analysis of the Pentateuch over the last century or so, it is clear that several distinctive collections of legal material have been incorporated into one or more of the five books: the Covenant Code (Exod. 21–23), Deuteronomy, the Priestly collection (in Exod. 25–31; 35–40; Leviticus; Num. 1–10), and the Holiness Code (Lev. 17–26). That these various collections cover many of the same topics, yet make different and even mutually contradictory statements, suggests that some of them were rival collections, representing the interests of different groups. It thus seems likely that these different collections coexisted before being brought together at some point during the second-temple period in some sort of "compromise," although it is likely that they also continued to be cultivated separately by the different groups that had produced them.[53]

Recent study of ancient Near Eastern law collections suggests that the law collections included in the Pentateuch are misunderstood if likened to modern "law codes," in the sense of a comprehensive list of the laws that govern a given legal jurisdiction (such as English Common Law in the United Kingdom and most of the United States).[54] In Judea, as in most traditional societies dominated by oral communication, custom governed social-economic interaction and disputes, especially in local ad hoc courts. Ancient Near Eastern law collections, including those in the Pentateuch, are incomplete, with no coverage of whole areas of social-economic life. Records of actual court cases do not make reference to collections of laws, even where the latter include laws on those subjects. Laws were not binding on judges, nor did judges decide cases by applying or making reference to law collections.

Recent studies of ancient Mesopotamian and other law collections conclude that they were not law codes, but rather what might be called documents of ancient jurisprudence, hence understandably remote from the concrete social interaction. They were learned documents that described the law but did not prescribe it. They were "academic" representations of justice as a political ideal abstracted from contingent circumstances irrelevant to their universal applicability, in the form of a list of dozens or hundreds of conditional "If . . . , then . . ." examples of various topical areas of law. Collections of laws, like omen literature that classified the various meanings of the livers of sacrificed animals or medical texts that described and categorized diseases, were the "scientific" product of scholars, learned scribes.[55]

Such collections of laws, moreover, were used for political propaganda, to legitimize a regime. The prime example is Hammurabi's "Code." It was not a law code, and its purpose was not to proclaim the law of the land. The stela on which the "laws" were inscribed, which shows the god giving Hammurabi (not a set of laws but) a rod and ring as symbols of justice and authority, was erected as a monumental declaration that the king had established justice in his realm.[56]

Comparative materials suggest that legal scholars among the Judean scribes collected and formulated these legal materials. The use of law collections in Mesopotamia and elsewhere to legitimate a monarchy or a temple suggests that legal collections in second-temple Judea functioned as legitimating documents. Just as "books of torah/covenant" (possibly an early version of Deuteronomic materials) were found or kept in the Temple and proclaimed to the assembled body politic (2 Kings 22–23; Neh. 8; as noted in the previous chapter), so other collections of laws may have served to ground the authority of rival priestly groups. In one telling feature, only in the Priestly collection is a sharp distinction drawn between Levites and priests proper, who are limited to the descendants of Aaron, while in Deuteronomic laws all Levites are also priests. This suggests that the Priestly collection could have been the authorizing document to which the Aaronide priesthood appealed to legitimize its position as dominant, while relegating the Levites to subsidiary functions and authority. These collections of laws and eventually the whole Pentateuch were likely written on scrolls as monumental or constitutional writings on which the authority of the established priesthood or rival priestly factions was based.

Meanwhile, the kinds of materials included in the various legal collections were presumably being cultivated in the ongoing life of the groups that produced them. For example, the variant formulations of the covenantal Decalogue in the different collections were rooted in the respective traditional recitation of priestly groups or scribal circles. The different rules for the observance of certain rituals stemmed from varying practices of different priestly groups and/or evolving practice in the Temple. At certain points there would also have been innovation and "legislation." At some point presumably the priestly aristocracy in power "raised taxes" from a third to a half-shekel, which then was duly inscribed in the latest "edition" of a sacred book that was laid up in the Temple, thus authorizing the latest "traditional" rate of temple taxation, along with other matters needing the authorization of constitutional writing.

While these collections were thus probably not originally formulated as curriculum for teaching and learning, such a usage may have developed later. Since scribes needed to know legal collections and/or "the law/torah of the Most High" for their service in the temple-state, such texts must have become central in their training. Among legal collections, the book of Deuteronomy, as we know it, is the most instructional in its presentation. This highly idealized "constitution" for a society in which the king has been stripped of most of his authority, which has been distributed among priests and others (Deut. 16:18–18:22),[57] presents a renewed Mosaic covenant and extensive covenantal teaching. As often noted, many features of the instruction (torah) in Deuteronomy closely resemble instructional wisdom in books such as Proverbs and Sirach. Moreover, while the fact that it is written is important for its authority as covenantal instruction from God, Deuteronomy is oral-aural in its presentation and appropriation. Accordingly, while it existed in written form probably from an early date (at least early second-temple times), the covenantal teaching of Deuteronomy was cultivated (recited, taught, learned) orally. In both oral and written form, moreover, the text of Deuteronomy would have continued to develop as it continued to be recited and recopied.

Such considerations may help to explain why there is little or no evidence prior to the documents from Qumran of any study and interpretation of long-authoritative written texts of torah. The authority of a given text lay more generally in the document as a whole, for example in its monumental constitutional function for the temple-state and/or as a sacred text of a traditional way of life, not in its particular statements. It is also at least conceivable that ritual recitation of specially authoritative texts (such as Deuteronomy) in communal settings was not an innovation of the Qumran community, but was already practiced in priestly and scribal circles.

History Books and Prophetic Books

The report in 2 Maccabees 2:13–14 that Judah the Maccabee "collected all the books lost on account of the war" claims that he was following the model of

Nehemiah, who had "collected the books about the kings and the prophets, and the writings of David, and the letters of kings about votive offerings." Though the concept of a "library," especially in a book produced in Egypt (see 2 Macc. 2:19–32), may have been patterned after the great library established in Alexandria, this reference to Nehemiah's collection is striking for its omission of the Law, which was listed first in the tripartite grouping in the Prologue to Sirach. The (to us) unexpected "letters of kings about votive offerings," however, gives the list a certain archaic ring of authentic historical memory. Such letters, paralleled among the documents laid up in temple or palace "archives" in Mesopotamia, must have been either from the late Davidic kings or from the Persian or Greek emperors. They suggest the range of documents known to have been deposited in the Temple.

More familiar are "the writings of David" and "the books about the kings and prophets." Assuming that the former referred mainly to psalms, this may be an indication that psalms were not just sung in the Temple rituals, but already gathered in written collections earlier in second-temple times. "The books about the kings and prophets" could be simply the books of the Deuteronomistic History. Just as easily it could refer to both history books and prophetic books, both of which, by implication, were deposited in the Temple in the Persian period.

The Deuteronomistic History, or at least the books of Samuel and Kings, must have taken a definable form by the middle of the Persian period, because the books of Chronicles follow its text closely in many passages.[58] It must not have proved satisfactory to the dominant scribal-priestly faction(s), however. Chronicles does not simply offer a revisionist history; it also replaces the Deuteronomistic narrative[59] with one clearly composed to ground the authority of the Temple and priesthood in a more glorified portrayal of David and Solomon—a "constitutional" text especially important for the "library of Nehemiah." Although we have no evidence regarding its use in later second-temple times, we can surmise that it would have useful in defending the established high priesthood at least in the first crises under the Ptolemies (see chap. 2, above).

We have nothing but internal evidence for the composition and use of the prophetic books. By critical scholarly consensus, most of the prophetic books grew by addition of new material. Large blocks of later oracular material were added to Isaiah. The book of Jeremiah was developed by addition of Deuteronomic materials, and then developed in at least two different textual traditions. Books such as Micah and Amos were supplemented with material that "updated" them for the situation of the second Temple under Persian rule. Most of the prophetic books either in their initial collection (Ezekiel, Haggai, and Malachi) or in their development (Isaiah, Zechariah) serve to authorize the Temple and its priesthood. In both cases the role of literacy and scribes will have been relatively greater in their composition.[60] Some sections of prophetic books reflect some of the conflicts in the temple-state (Isa. 56–66; Zech. 9–14).[61] Insofar as prophetic materials were oral in origin, it may be less difficult to imagine that scribes may have continued to cultivate them in oral recitation while supplementing and adapting them to apply to new circumstances and making expanded written versions.

KINDS OF WISDOM

Missing so far from this discussion of the Judean cultural repertoire has been the segment most associated with learned scribes, wisdom. Proverbs had been collected by the wise scribes themselves, for example by "the officials of King Hezekiah" (Prov. 25:1–29:27). While many proverbs pertained to scribes' relations with the rulers, their patrons, collections of proverbs apparently did not play a role in the legitimation of the temple-state. Wisdom texts were collections and compositions of, by, and for the wise scribes themselves, whether primarily for training and character building (Proverbs), in debate about cruel fortunes of life (Job), or in cynical reflection on the frustrations of scribal life itself (Ecclesiastes).

That scribal circles were engaged in vigorous cultivation of a rich repertoire of wisdom, however, is more evident in Sirach and Daniel and the sections of *1 Enoch* than it is in earlier wisdom books. Ben Sira's expansion in his proud summary of the sage's curriculum (torah of the Most High, wisdom of all the ancients, and prophecies) focuses on sayings, parables, and proverbs (38:34–39:3). But that list pertains to only one among several kinds of wisdom actively cultivated by his scribal contemporaries. At other points, however, he gives clear indications that he is fully aware of and even conversant with several distinguishable types of wisdom. And both Enoch and Daniel literature, which is produced by people who identify themselves and/or the figures who ostensibly composed the literature as professional scribes, exemplify several of those types of wisdom.[62] That the wise scribe Daniel and his Judean scribal companions serving in the Babylonian imperial court had become "versed in *every branch* of wisdom" may well be a pointer to the several kinds of wisdom in the Judean and ancient Near Eastern scribal repertoire.

1. There are proverbs aplenty scattered through the book of Sirach. Unlike Proverbs 10–22; 25–29, however, Sirach is not simply a collection of proverbs and other sapiential sayings. The bulk of the book consists of *instructional wisdom* on various topics, primarily topics of intrafamily relations and social relations, speeches generally more elaborate than the presumably earlier ones collected in Prov. 22:17–24:34; 31:1–31. These include speeches on the more general theme of seeking wisdom (Sir. 4:11–19; 6:18–37; 14:20–15:10; somewhat similar to many such speeches in Prov. 1–9) and on "the fear of the Lord" as "the beginning of wisdom" (1:11–30).

2. Overlapping somewhat with instructional wisdom is *reflection* or speculation *on* the nature of *wisdom* in general, and where and how wisdom can be found. Wisdom becomes not only generalized and abstracted, but also personified and, in effect, divinized. Ben Sira has two speeches on Wisdom, her relation to God, and how she comes to be known by Judean sages (1:1–10; 24:1–22, 23–34). Reflection on wisdom had already become a standard feature of scribal culture, as can be seen in Prov. 8:22–31 and Job 28, and was continued by later sages (cf. Bar. 3:1–4:4; Wis. 6–9). It also had much earlier antecedents in reflection on Ma'at by Egyptian scribes.

3. Also distinguishable, though related to the previous two types of wisdom, is *knowledge of* and appeal to the divinely created *order of the universe.* Sirach includes some relatively long passages of this *cosmological wisdom,* in 16:26–17:24; 39:16–35; 42:15–25; 43:1–33. Ben Sira again stood in a well-established tradition of such knowledge, as evident from Job 38–41. Cosmological wisdom could take different forms, such as the ostensible dialogue in Job 38–41 or the hymns of praise in Sirach 39:12–35 and 43:1–33. Included in this type of wisdom is astronomical knowledge based on centuries of observation, as in the Book of Luminaries and sections of the Book of Watchers in *1 Enoch* 72–82 and 1–36, respectively. This type of wisdom has strong roots in Mesopotamian scribal circles. Such knowledge was of considerable importance in the determination of the calendar (for agricultural and ritual cycles), hence also a potential source of conflict depending on whether authority was attributed to the pattern of the sun or that of the moon (see Sir. 43:2–5, 6–8, 9–12; *1 En.* 72–82). Other typical features of this type of wisdom are appeals to the constancy and dependability of the divinely created order in contrast to human sinfulness (Sir. 16:27; more elaborately in *1 En.* 5), and reflection on how God's providence can be reconciled with the vagaries and injustices of historical-political experience (as in Sir. 39:16–35; 42:15–25). The personification of natural elements with wills to take certain actions (see 39:31; 42:16–17; 43:17) reminds one of the similar "mythic" features in other literature, such as the Book of Watchers, in *1 Enoch* 1–36.

4. Also, especially well developed in Mesopotamia was *mantic wisdom.* Dream interpretation was a standard specialization among Judean sages and teachers, as we shall see in the treatment of Daniel and *1 Enoch* (chaps. 8 and 9, below). And interpretation of omens crops up in the tale about the hand writing on the wall in Daniel 5. The wise and righteous scribes and sages who projected their wisdom onto the prototypical sages Enoch and Daniel produced several "historical visions" (*1 En.* 83–84, 85–90; Dan. 7; 8; 10–12), which recount the sweep of events that lead up to, result in, and bring resolution to the historical crisis in which they are living. That Ben Sira is fully aware of the wisdom gained through dreams, divination, and omens can be seen in his blunt rejection of it.

> Divination and omens and dreams are unreal. . . .
> Unless they are sent by intervention from the Most High,
>   pay no attention to them.
> For dreams have deceived many,
>   and those who put their hope in them have perished.
> (34:5–7)

Despite his rejection of mantic wisdom, however, Ben Sira certainly knows and apparently agrees with the basic assumption of such dream interpretation, God's foreknowledge: "Whatever he commands will be done at the appointed time," since "from the beginning to the end of time he can see everything" (Sir. 39:16–21; 42:18).

Yet another kind of wisdom has been identified as *secret but revealed.* It is unclear, however, whether this is another type of wisdom or a mode by which some wisdom is known. The substance of what has been included in "revealed" wisdom is difficult to distinguish from dream interpretation and cosmological wisdom.[63] Ben Sira gives what appear to be mixed signals on "hidden wisdom." On the one hand, he makes statements such as the warning about seeking "what is hidden, . . . too difficult, . . . and beyond your power" (3:21–24). It is not clear whether this refers to knowledge of the divine world or to speculations about what he considered the unknowable, the future (cf. 42:18–19; 43:32–33). Yet on the other hand, he refers several times in a more positive tone to the revelation of secrets and knowledge about things to come. The figure of Wisdom was thought to "reveal her secrets" to the wise, who "ponder her secrets" (4:18; 14:21). In his praise of the divinely created order, Ben Sira says more suggestively that God "discloses what has been and what is to be, and he reveals the traces of hidden things" (42:19). At the end of his account of the wondrous works of God, he asserts that "many things greater than these lie hidden," with the implication that they also may be made known to the godly who have wisdom (43:32–33). Both "Daniel" and "Enoch" are actively engaged in receiving revelation of hidden wisdom. The very point of the tales in Daniel 1–6 was that he had received his remarkable wisdom of dream interpretation from God. The wisdom about past and future in both Daniel 7–12 and the historical surveys in *1 Enoch* is revealed in visions and interpreted by angels. And the Book of Watchers presents an elaborate development of cosmological wisdom in the form of "Enoch's" revelatory journeys into the heavens and far regions of the earth.

CULTURAL REPERTOIRE AND NEW COMPOSITION

By the time of Ben Sira, around 200 BCE, the Judean cultural repertoire cultivated by learned scribes included a wide range of Mosaic torah, prophetic traditions, and modes of wisdom. At the center of the repertoire were many still-developing torah and prophetic texts that existed also in written copies. These included recently composed texts that were authoritative in addition to the texts that later became biblical, which existed in multiple versions. Just as writing was embedded in oral communication, however, so written texts were embedded in a broader cultural memory. The Judean cultural repertoire was far richer than the sum of its extant documentary parts. It included alternative versions of historical legends and legal materials that were not incorporated in the books that became biblical.

This cultural repertoire provided a rich reservoir from which more-creative scribes-sages composed new texts. The evidence from the Scrolls found at Qumran suggests that the escalating crisis of rival factions in the aristocracy and the Hellenizing reform became the occasion for creative scribal activity. The crisis of authority in Jerusalem may be what led some creative learned scribe(s) to compose books of alternative torah, such as *Jubilees* or the *Temple Scroll,* that claimed authority higher than that of the pentateuchal books. The crisis may also have led some scribal circles to more intense cultivation of Isaiah and other prophetic materials, an intense preoccupation with which may have led to the production of the *pesharim* at Qumran. In chapter 7 we will explore how Ben Sira not only continued to train fledgling scribes but also drew on the covenantal/torah, historical, and prophetic segments of the Judean cultural repertoire in attempts to bolster a traditional ideology of the Temple and high priesthood. In chapters 8 and 9 we will explore how Daniel and sections of *1 Enoch* drew upon the prophetic segment of the cultural repertoire as well as mantic and cosmological wisdom to gain revelatory understanding of the escalating historical crisis and God's solution to it.

Chapter 7

The Wisdom of Jesus Ben Sira

Do not slight the discourse of the sages,
Because from them you will learn discipline
and how to serve princes.

Wisdom praises herself: . . .
And so I was established in Zion,
And in Jerusalem was my domain.

He made an everlasting covenant with [Aaron],
And gave him the priesthood of the people.
                                        Ben Sira

Ben Sira was not a "writer," contrary to what has often been assumed by modern interpreters. His teachings and hymns have been compiled into a book. But he repeatedly represents the teaching and learning of wisdom as oral-aural (as noted in chap. 5, above). It would thus be anachronistic to conceive of Ben Sira in modern terms as a "writer," as if he were "authoring" original aphorisms, "treatises," or hymns. Similarly, Ben Sira was not an interpreter of the Torah/law of Moses or other "Scripture." He does not even cite particular laws much less offer explicit interpretations of them (as noted in chap. 6, above). Instead, he repeatedly calls for devotion to the covenant and keeping the commandments.

Ben Sira instead was a wise scribe engaged in service of the temple-state and high priesthood. As a scribe he was also a scholar deeply embedded—albeit far more creatively than most—in a wide range of Judean culture. In the programmatic discourse on the vocation and cultural-political role of the wise scribe, he characterizes the prominent sage as deeply devoted to learning a broad traditional cultural repertoire in its three major segments: "the teaching [torah/law] of the

Most High, . . . prophecies, . . . [and] the wisdom of all the ancients" (38:24–39:3, au. trans.). As indicated in the ensuing parallel clauses, the emphasis is clearly on the wisdom of all the ancients, focused on their sayings, parables, and proverbs.[1] Such wisdom was also apparently "international" (39:4b). Although Ben Sira's book focuses on instructional wisdom, it is clear from the contents of his book that he also seriously cultivated both reflective and cosmological wisdom, and was well acquainted with, while suspicious of, mantic wisdom. It is thus a serious oversimplification to categorize Sirach as "wisdom" literature as opposed to Daniel or *1 Enoch* as "apocalyptic" literature, or as exemplifying "wisdom" theology in contrast to "apocalyptic" eschatology. That dichotomy of synthetic scholarly constructs simply does not fit the realities of Ben Sira or contemporary scribal practice. It is appropriate rather to discern how Ben Sira relates to the overall Judean cultural repertoire and, within that, how he relates to the spectrum of various kinds of wisdom.

The principal purpose of the scribe's learning, according to Ben Sira, was preparation for service among the rulers of the temple-state and personal devotion to the Most High (39:4–5). The final section of this programmatic discourse maintains the same double focus of the wise scribe's political and religious role and responsibility. "He will show the wisdom of what he has learned," and for this "he will be praised in the assembly," and he will "give thanks to the Lord in prayer" (39:6–11, au. trans.). Yet in this principal speech about the vocation of the wise scribe, he does not mention the role of teaching.

Ben Sira also understands the wisdom of all the ancients that the sage learns as derived from (and identical with) Wisdom as a personified heavenly figure. In this regard he is again thoroughly rooted in the previous scribal tradition of reflection on the origins and divine qualities of wisdom that we discern in and behind texts such as Prov. 8:22–31. Several poems or hymns of praise about Wisdom and speeches about searching for wisdom frame the instructional speeches in Sirach, especially in the first half of the book (1:1–10; 4:11–19; 6:18–37; 14:20–15:10; 24:1–34). As a universal divine force, the firstborn of all creation, she sought a home among peoples as well as devotees (esp. 1:1–10; 24:1–12).

Among these poems and speeches, several phrases or statements indicate that the divine Wisdom is available and known precisely in "the wisdom of all the ancients." Wisdom herself is involved in the teaching and discipline by which the sage acquires knowledge and comes to political prominence (4:10–19). "She will feed him with the bread of learning, and give him the water of wisdom to drink" (15:3). It is Wisdom herself who "will open his mouth in the midst of the assembly" and bring him renown (15:5–6). Yet the way by which the wise come to know wisdom is to listen attentively to the discourse of the elders and sages and to meditate on the commandments of the Lord (6:32–37), in a pairing precisely parallel to the key sources of the sage's knowledge in the programmatic speech about the wise scribe's special role and responsibility (38:34–39:2; cf. further 8:8–9; 9:14–16).

INSTRUCTIONAL WISDOM SPEECHES

While service among the rulers is evidently the primary role of the wise scribe, he is also a teacher. In an extended metaphor Ben Sira portrays Wisdom as a great flowing river of instruction and understanding, with the sage like a "canal" through which wisdom is "channeled" into his "garden." By tapping into that vast cultural stream of wisdom, through devoted study and learning of the wisdom of all the ancients, the sage is then able to bring forth instruction for future generations of students who seek wisdom (24:30–34).

Most of the materials included in the book of Sirach appear to be derived from this instruction that Ben Sira "brought forth" as a teacher of student scribes. That he conceives of his instruction as flowing from the stream of transcendent Wisdom, which is the divine source of the wisdom of the ancients, is surely one of the keys to understanding his teachings. They are not interpretations of particular statements of the Pentateuch, as noted above, and they are not newly composed maxims or aphorisms. Nor do his teachings present statements for meditation, reflection, deliberation, and perhaps debate—although the students are called to reflection on life. Nor do Ben Sira's teachings, in contrast to what is often said about proverbial wisdom, appear to be proverbs based upon and calling for the recognition of the fundamental nature of the creation and social experience. His teachings are rather primarily commands and admonitions, primarily about social and political life, to be heeded, internalized, and obeyed. Their authority is that of divine wisdom and of the previous teaching of all the ancients, along with the teaching (torah, commandments, covenant) of the Most High. Ben Sira's teachings, like much of the instruction of Egyptian scribes, were primarily admonition or exhortation to be internalized as a personal disposition and assimilated as the social ethos of those who served the rulers/aristocracy of the Jerusalem temple-state.

Variable Patterns in the Traditional Form of Instructional Speeches

The deeply ingrained habit in biblical studies of focusing on individual verses reinforces the assumption that wisdom literature consists mainly of individual sayings. Interpreters thus tend to identify the "literary" genre of the instructional materials in Sirach narrowly as the *mashal,* or proverb, aphorism, maxim, saying.[2] Commentaries may be organized according to clusters of sayings grouped into stanzas of lines. Yet most interpretation, generally heavily weighted to the theological and ethical, still proceeds verse by verse, saying by saying.[3]

Virtually all of the instruction presented in the book of Sirach, however, takes the form of short poetic speeches focused on particular topics. It is often claimed that Sirach was modeled on the book of Proverbs.[4] But the model would not have been the sections in Proverbs 10–22 and 25–29, which consist of one proverb after another, with no obvious topical grouping. Such collections of proverbs are

merely lists, not forms of interpersonal communication. To function in communication, a proverb or maxim must be applied in some literary or social context.
The instruction in Sirach rather resembles that in Proverbs 1–9; 22:17–24:34;
and 31:10–31, which also consists of speeches.

In most of the speeches in Sirach and Proverbs 1–9, moreover, an argument
is easily discernible.[5] The teaching employs certain rhetorical devices to make a
case to the listeners. The particular structure of the argument may be different in
nearly every speech. But the speeches have certain common typical features that
can be readily detected, enabling us to appreciate how their respective arguments
proceed. Most basic may be an admonition followed by a motive clause (as in
Prov. 24:21–23). The admonition and/or the motive clause may be multiplied,
and a similar, parallel admonition may form an inclusio at the end of the speech.
Often a proverb or maxim functions as an admonition or a sanctioning motive
clause (as in Prov. 23:22–25). A speech can be constructed of several proverbs,
one serving as a motive statement (e.g., Prov. 24:3–6). Illustrative examples and
maxims or proverbs may be used to reinforce the basic point made in the admo-
nition(s). And a proverb or other saying can provide a sanctioning promise of
reward or threat of punishment, often at the end of the speech.

The collections of instructional materials included in the book of Proverbs
include both short, simple speeches (22:17–24:34) and longer, more complex
speeches (1–9). Many of the latter are introduced by a "call to listen to/obey" the
teaching of the father (teacher) to the child/son (student). In a series of admonitions with lengthy motive clauses, the main body of the instruction is followed
by maxims or proverbs that state the consequences of wise or foolish behavior. In
Proverbs 5:1–23, for example, we can hear the call to listen, with motive clauses
that announce the topic (5:1–2, 3–5), then after a brief renewed call (5:7), two
statements of programmatic admonitions with extensive motive clauses (5:8–14;
5:15, 16–19), followed by a rhetorical question and proverb (5:20, 21), and concluded by a double parable about the fate of the wicked (in third person).[6]

Ben Sira thus stands in a tradition of wise scribes who delivered their instruction in speeches composed of various combinations of admonitions, motive
clauses, and maxims. The contours of particular speeches of varying length are
discernible in most of the book, in some cases placed next to speeches on closely
related issues. The coherence as well as the variation in patterns can be illustrated
from speeches on various issues,[7] some of which we will examine again with
regard to the particular language devoted to particular issues.

In the speech on honoring one's father/parents in 3:1–16, the admonition to
"honor your father by word and deed" is not stated explicitly until the middle (3:8).
The speech opens with an appeal to "listen" to the "father" (teacher) coupled with
an appeal to the children's self-interest (3:1), followed by a maxim as a motive clause
(3:2). Three parallel bicola (two parallel lines, usually synonymous) of maxims in
the form "those who honor/respect their father/mother" (3:3–7) then set up the
central admonition to "honor your father" and the ensuing motive statement
(3:8–9). Then come another admonition with motive clause (3:10) and a maxim

that functions as a further motive statement (3:11). Attached to this general exhortation to honor parents is a shorter speech calling for more specific care (3:12–16). It begins with a relatively complex, detailed admonition to "help your father in his old age" (3:12–13), followed by a similarly complex motive statement (3:14–15), and concludes with a double "whoever" maxim as a divine sanction (3:16).

A speech on responding to the poor and hungry has the fairly simple structure of two sets of multiple admonitions with a motive clause attached to the last items in the sequences (4:1–5, 6, 7–10a, 10b). Two maxims, on almsgiving and repaying favors, function as a preface to this speech (3:30–31). Another speech on helping the poor (29:8–13) consists of a sequence of admonitions, the first three pertaining to giving, the second three providing the motives.

The speech on seeking wisdom (choosing discipline) in 6:18–37 is one of several with twenty-two bicola (the number of letters in the Hebrew alphabet). The overall speech develops in three parts, all marked by the opening address to "my child" (6:18–22, 23–31, 32–37). It is conceivable that the first two parts were originally a complete speech, insofar as the multiple motive statements in 6:28–31 form a fitting climax or payoff from the discipline called for in 6:18 as well as her "fetters" and "bonds" in 6:24–25. The third part forms a complete speech on its own, exploring the discipline that leads to wisdom, yet the statement in 6:37 forms a suitable conclusion to 6:18–37 as a whole, with "wisdom" as an inclusio corresponding to the goal of the discipline in 6:18. The first part moves from opening admonitions and motive clause (6:18–19) to maxims that provide counterinstances to the maxim (6:20–22). The second part, after an appeal to "listen" (6:23), stacks up admonitions (6:24–27), followed by motive clauses. The third part, starting with parallel admonitions in conditional form (6:32–33), gives two examples of how to become wise (6:34–37a), the latter of which leads to the concluding payoff of wisdom granted (6:37b).

A speech about association with the wealthy and powerful, Sirach 13:1–13, begins with a warning proverb that sets up the general admonition not to associate with one more powerful, then illustrates the danger with another proverb (13:1–2), and follows with a proverbial illustration and several other illustrations of the exploitative behavior of the rich (13:3–7). After several more illustrative admonitions, followed by a motive clause (13:8–11), come another maxim and a concluding general admonition sanctioned by a warning motive clause (13:13).

Discerning these variable but clear patterns in Ben Sira's speeches should enable us better to appreciate that they were delivered orally.[8] Yet there are clear signs that such poetic speeches, a fundamental expression of scribal culture, were influenced by literacy. Principal among these is the fact that some of the speeches in Sirach (such as the speech on seeking discipline sketched above, in 6:18–37; cf. 1:11–30), like many in Proverbs 1–9, were composed in twenty-two lines or bicola. Other features, however, mark Ben Sira's speeches as oral communication. These are the frequent assonance, alliteration, and rhyme evident in the Hebrew, and often discernible even in the Greek and English translations (examples evident in the speeches outlined just above would be words and sounds in 6:19; 13:1–2). Chiastic patterns are occasionally evident (e.g., in 6:22, 37). And the repetition of a key term or an idea in both the opening and closing lines often constitute an inclusio.[9]

That most of the book of Sirach consists of short speeches on particular topics means that it is inappropriate to take sayings or "verses" in isolation, separated from the speeches of which they are integral components. Ben Sira's speeches were designed to persuade. It is incumbent on interpreters to appreciate their rhetoric. It is doubtful that a proverb taken by itself, as it appears in a list such as Proverbs 10–22, functions as a unit of communication. But a proverb used in a speech has a rhetorical function in the speech as a whole, which interpreters misunderstand if they attempt to interpret it as if it had a meaning in itself. To appreciate the rhetoric of instructional speeches, moreover, it is necessary to have some sense of the social roles and relations involved, especially since most such speeches focus on topics of familial and social relationships. Statements in Sirach have often been taken more or less at face value (literally). The rhetoric of Ben Sira's speeches, however, often has a subtle tone that can be appreciated only with a better understanding of the social relations in which he was embedded and the cultural traditions in which he was immersed (see chap. 3, above).

Registers of Speech Dedicated to Topics of Instruction

Completely tied up with the structure of Ben Sira's instruction as short speeches is its other major feature. The instructional speeches collected in the book of Sirach are, for the most part, each devoted to a particular topic or issue. The topic can be indicated at different points in different speeches, at the outset (as in 38:1–15, on honoring the physician), both at the beginning and end (as in 5:1–8, on [dishonest] wealth), or in the middle (as in 3:1–16, on honoring one's parents).

This major feature of instructional wisdom, of short speeches each devoted to a particular topic, is not unique to Ben Sira's instruction. Major sections of the book of Proverbs consist of collections of speeches, some as long as twenty-two lines/bicola, as in 1–9 and 31:10–31, and some quite brief, as in 22:17–24:34. It thus seems clear that short speeches, each devoted to a particular topic, were a standard traditional feature of instruction.

Both Sirach and Proverbs, moreover, contain two or more speeches on many topics. In many cases the multiple speeches by Ben Sira on a given topic display many of the same images, motifs, and phrases and even similar lines. In cases where Proverbs has speeches on the same topics as Sirach, those speeches also display many of the same images and motifs and even variant versions of the same proverbs, maxims, or admonitions.

These features of instructional wisdom in Proverbs and Sirach lead to an important recognition about instructional practice. Instruction proceeded according to standard topics. Wisdom teachers such as Ben Sira, who had learned instructional wisdom in the form of speeches devoted to particular topics, then in turn gave instruction in that form themselves. And, the crucial point, there was a particular traditional set of language for each topic of instruction.

This is similar to what sociolinguistics has observed about communication in general. Spoken or written language is keyed to particular typical contexts of communication. The one major variable, determined by social location or class, is usually called "dialect." The speech or language of an upper class differs from that of a lower class, of urban workers or rural peasants. There are also local and regional dialects, although these can disappear in some modern societies under the influence of mass media. The other major variable is the style of speech determined by the typical situation or activity or set of relations to which speech is addressed. Sociolinguists refer to this as the "register."[10] Others might use the term "discourse."

More important than the terms is the concept, which can be explained best perhaps by illustrations. In modern higher education different sets of language are devoted to particular academic fields, such as psychology or physics. A distinctive language is dedicated to sports and sports broadcasting, in contrast to the language of concert music criticism. Within the general sports register, further, particular sets of language are devoted to particular sports, such as baseball or basketball. An announcer would not communicate much about a baseball game using the register of speech devoted to football. More analogous to ancient instructional wisdom may be the different register of speech (and music) we recognize in particular religious contexts, such as funerals or weddings or Easter sunrise services.

In a similar way speeches of instructional wisdom on particular topics were articulated in distinctive sets of language appropriate to their topics and typical communication context. Each of these particular registers of speech or types of discourse, moreover, was rooted in its own deep tradition. Particular registers included proverbs and standard admonitions that focused on typical familial and social relations, such as husbands-wives, parents-children, rich-poor, or particular concerns of scribal culture, such as acquiring wisdom, speaking, or relations with powerful patrons. Much of the imagery and idiom thus depended on the particular relationship in focus. Generations of experience had generated a store of illustrative examples of the consequences of certain behavior in those basic relationships, often formulated in proverbs and maxims. And insofar as all such relationships or concerns belonged to a larger context of relations with the Divine and traditional culture in which such relations were symbolized, given speech registers had developed typical sanctions or motive clauses that fit particular topics.

Ben Sira's instructional speeches on typical topics and their distinctive language registers bear a certain resemblance to what have been called *loci communes* (commonplaces) in classical rhetorical culture. As Walter Ong has reminded us, Greek and Latin orators cultivated a plethora of formulaic phrases and sayings and examples appropriate to a wide variety of topics such as honesty, loyalty, treachery, or "things-are-going-to-hell," grouped for easy recall around typical social relations and topics.[11] Individual orators such as Cicero formed set pieces out of the general cultural store of these topical registers on a whole range of topics in advance and stored them in their mind for use in public orations or court cases.

To better appreciate how instructional wisdom exhibits a rich range of traditional registers of speech (sets of language), we can examine speeches on several different standard topics. It is possible to do this only insofar as we have parallel speeches in Sirach itself and/or a parallel speech or proverbial wisdom on a given topic in earlier/other wisdom literature, such as Proverbs or comparative Egyptian instructional texts. After gaining an appreciation of the particular sets of language devoted to several different topics for which we have multiple speeches and/or other sapiential materials, we can then begin to sense how speeches on other topics are similarly rooted in and carry forward certain distinctive sets of language. What we are trying to do with Ben Sira's instructional wisdom is to move beyond the (often purely) formal analysis standard in biblical studies to an analysis of communication (such as teaching) in which the typical context is as important as formal aspects. We aim to appreciate how, when Ben Sira moves from topic to topic, he shifts into the distinctive traditional registers of language appropriate to the topics. We can thus begin to appreciate how the general repertoire of instructional wisdom that he had learned and was now teaching himself was subdivided into and constituted by a range of different discourses or registers of speech.

Friendship

The book of Sirach includes several speeches on *friendship* that exhibit easily discernible similar features (6:5–17; 12:8–18; 22:19–26; 27:16–21). All of these speeches feature the same key terms, concepts, and portrayal of contingent relationships: for example, the rich have friends, the poor are friendless; friends stand by in adversity, false friends do not; a true friend is like one's kin; be on guard with/test friends, keep away from enemies. Two of these speeches also share the themes of reviling/betraying a friend and the possibility of reconciliation. The focus on these same terms and relationships in many proverbs (Prov. 14:20; 17:9, 17; 18:24; 19:4, 7; cf. Job 19:19–21) indicates that they belong to the same traditional set of language pertaining to friendship. This suggests that when Ben Sira composed several different speeches on friendship, he clicked into a standard register of language dedicated to the topic.

Seeking Wisdom

Similarly, Sirach contains several speeches on *seeking and finding wisdom* (4:11–19; 6:18–37; 14:20–15:10; cf. 51:13–30). While each of these speeches displays distinctive features, they all draw on the same motifs, images, and phrases and combine them in similar ways, and they share those common motifs and phrases with the similar speeches in Proverbs 1–9. Among the most prominent are the following: wisdom as teacher/mother/bride/wife, the wise as students/children; the ways/paths of wisdom; the wise as seekers; the wise love wisdom, know her secrets; discipline/toil/yoke/torment/listening; the wise exalted/crown/glory/honor/name, and inherit wisdom; contrast with fools/sinners, and their ruin/destruction; and the commandments/torah (see further the chart of parallel themes and motifs in these speeches, in Appendix A). Again the common language shared by several different speeches on seeking wisdom, in Proverbs 1–9 as well as Sirach, indicates that there must have been a standard traditional discourse dedicated to the topic on which Ben Sira drew in his composition.

Each speech, of course, develops the common motifs of seeking wisdom in particular ways. In the speech in 6:18–37 (the form of which was examined just above), the opening address of each of the three sections ("my child/listen my child") immediately signals the register of "seeking wisdom," just as it does in the parallel speeches in Proverbs 1–9. Only on the assumptions of modern print culture would we imagine that Ben Sira "was modeling himself on" a particular "verse" such as Proverbs 4:10, for admonitions such as "Listen, my son, and take my advice" had long since become the standard opening of such instruction. Virtually all of the ensuing images and motifs are derived from what must have been the standard register of speech devoted to seeking wisdom. This speech downplays the toil and harshness of the discipline that the wise choose, displacing them to the fools, who are the standard foils in such discourse (6:20–21). The next step of the speech, again adapting standard images, acknowledges the typical difficulties of wisdom's discipline, but insists that the search will result in rest and peace; the fetters will become a defense and the collar a glorious robe, indeed a royal cord and crown (6:23–31). In the final step Ben Sira indicates more specifically—and perhaps more specific to the line of instructional wisdom in which he stands—the substance that the discipline of wisdom consists of gaining knowledge from the discourse of the wise and meditating on the commandments of the Lord (6:32–37). And again the images and terms are all standard in such discourse. In fact, 6:32–33 ("My child, . . . If you love to listen you will gain knowledge, and if you pay attention you will become wise") sounds like Ben Sira's more elaborate version of what must have long been a standard admonition, as in Proverbs 8:32–33 ("And now, my children, listen to me. . . . Hear instruction and be wise").

Economic Relations: Wealth and Poverty, and Responding to the Poor

Yet another set of topics that appear to have been standard in instructional wisdom concerns wealth and poverty (Prov. 10:15; cf. 14:20; 18:23). Traditional proverbs provide the content of the speech on the rich and the poor in Sirach 13:15–24 (Prov. 10:15; 14:20 [reformulated in Sir. 13:21]; 18:23). The proverbs included in this speech emphasize the direct relationship between wealth and poverty: "Wild asses in the wilderness are the prey of lions; likewise the poor are feeding grounds for the rich" (Sir. 13:19; cf. 13:17, 18, 21–22). Sirach also has two parallel speeches warning against the temptation of pursuing wealth (5:1–8; 40:18–27). While the tone is a bit different in the two speeches, the theme and basic message are the same. In 40:18–27 the series of traditional proverbs seems to acknowledge various positive aspects of wealth and the security and delights it makes possible. Yet each of the proverbs adapted into this speech, hinging on an adversative ("but . . ."), offers a better alternative, the "treasure" of finding wisdom, giving good counsel, and giving alms (cf. the older proverbs in Prov. 11:28; 13:11). The concluding maxim here (Sir. 40:27) is recognizable as an adaptation or another version of the proverb that we know from Prov. 15:16 (Prov. 16:8 is another version of same proverb; cf. also 22:7, 8, 16). A series of admonitions in the speech in Sirach 5:1–8 (which is in effect sharpening embellishment of Prov. 16:8) states the same message on the same topic. The conclusion of the speech in Sirach 40:18–27 makes clear that wealth is incompatible with the fear of the Lord (as does the juxtaposition of the two versions of the parable in Prov. 15:16 and 16:8). The parallel speech in Sirach 5:1–8 formulates the implications pointedly, as stated simply in the concluding admonition: "Do not depend on dishonest wealth, for it will not benefit you on the day of calamity." Both these particular proverbs and the admonitions belong in a standard discourse devoted specifically to the issue of not being tempted by the pursuit of wealth.

The book of Sirach also provides two parallel speeches, 3:30–4:10 and 29:8–13, exhorting the hearers to give alms and otherwise aid the poor, suggesting that this was yet another (sub)topic on which sages such as Ben Sira drew on a traditional speech register. Again the book of Proverbs provides a window onto the tradition of proverbial wisdom devoted to this topic. "Whoever is kind to the poor lends to the LORD, and will be repaid in full" (Prov. 19:17; see also 14:21, 31; 17:5; 21:13; 28:27). The core of both speeches in Sirach consists of a series of admonitions:

Sirach 3:30–4:10 (4:1–4)	Sirach 29:8–13 (29:8–9)
Do not keep needy eyes waiting, . . . or delay giving to the needy,	Do not keep [the humble] waiting for alms.
Do not reject a suppliant in distress . . .	Do not send [the poor] away empty- handed.
Give a hearing to the poor,	Help the poor for the commandment's sake.

The two speeches also have highly similar motive clauses, the one at the start ("Almsgiving atones for sin," 3:30), the other at the conclusion ("Store up almsgiving in your treasury, and it will rescue you from every disaster," 29:12–13). Both draw the connection with covenantal commandments (4:6; 29:9, 11). And both speeches are linked with or advocate active steps to aid or rescue the neighbor, even to "rescue the oppressed from the oppressor" (29:1–7, 14–20; 4:9, 10–11; cf. Prov. 31:8–9).

Scribes' Relations with the Rulers

For scribes engaged in service of the temple-state, their relations with their wealthy and powerful patrons ("the great/rulers" et al.) was an important topic of instruction. Along with many passing comments on this subject (e.g., Sir. 4:7, 27; 7:4–7; 8:1–2; 9:13; 20:27–31), Ben Sira has speeches both on the general topic of association with the great and on the more particular subtopic of behavior at banquets (dining and drinking) hosted by the wealthy and powerful. In both cases it is evident that these speeches are rooted in deep traditions of instructional speech devoted to these particular subjects.

The speech on relating to rulers in Sirach 13:1–13 (whose form we examined above) combines proverbs, admonitions, analogies/similes, and proverbial illustrations that arise from a traditional speech register.[12] This can be seen in both earlier individual proverbs (Prov. 14:35; 19:12 = 20:2; 22:11) and earlier shorter speeches (24:21–22; 25:[2–]6–7). The formulations in Sirach 13:8–10 are addressed to the same situation and its perils as indicated in Proverbs 25:6–7, and give virtually the same advice.

> When [a ruler] invites you, be reserved,
> and he will invite you all the more insistently.
> Do not be forward, or you may be rebuffed;
> do not stand aloof, or you will be forgotten.
> (Sir. 13:9–10)

And the concluding admonition (picking up the illustrations of 13:3–4, 7) repeats the same ominous concern as Proverbs 20:2 (cf. Sir 9:13).

> Be on your guard and very careful,
> for you are walking about with your own downfall.
> (Sir. 13:13)

Sirach includes a far more elaborate speech on behavior at banquets sponsored by patrons among the aristocracy, in 31:12–32:13. In addition to traditional proverbs and short speeches on the dangers of scribes' (and kings') excessive drinking (Prov. 20:1; 21:17; 23:19–22, 29–35; 31:4–5), Proverbs includes a short speech warning about the potential risks involved in "sitting down to eat with a ruler" (23:1–3). Such speeches by earlier Judean scribes had deeper roots in the instructional speech of Egypt, where banqueting with rulers was a standard topic in several extant collections.[13] Ben Sira's speech stands directly in this tradition of discourse on the topic. The first long section (Sir. 31:12–18, or perhaps 12–24) is an elaboration, mainly in admonitions, of speeches such as Proverbs 23:1–3, warning hungry sages against appearing greedy at the table of the great (Ben Sira does add the practical suggestion that, should one overeat, "get up to vomit," 31:21). Besides the standard traditional Judean and ancient Near Eastern proverbial wisdom on the importance of moderation in wine-drinking (31:25–31), Ben Sira addresses the possibility of a scribe being made "master of the feast"—which requires all the more moderation along with a diplomatic humility (32:1–2). The ensuing advice first to the more senior sages and then to the more junior, indicating a situation in which guests talk during the music,[14] again draws on a traditional idiom of Judean instruction, on moderation in speech (32:3–12)—and concludes with a nod to God, as the source of such blessings (32:13).

Recognition of the existence of these many standard traditional registers of language dedicated to particular topics, juxtaposed with recognition of the variable standard form of instructional speeches, enables us to appreciate how Ben Sira proceeded in delivery of instructional wisdom. Having mastered the many traditional discourses or language registers of instructional wisdom, he could tap into standard motifs, images, phrases, and proverbs, depending on the particular topic. His creativity lay in how he combined and reconfigured traditional language according to the people and situations he was addressing. We modern "readers" would probably have to be much more familiar with a wider range of such speeches to appreciate the subtleties of particular twists and emphases that Ben Sira made in particular speeches on a given topic as he trained students for their service of the temple-state in the early second century CE.

HYMNS OF PRAISE

Ben Sira presents three kinds of content in hymnic style. In both his hymns of cosmological wisdom and his hymns of reflective wisdom it is evident, either from comparison of parallel hymns in Sirach or from comparison of Ben Sira's hymns with other Judean hymns, that Ben Sira draws upon the standard motifs, images, and themes of traditional language registers. The third kind of hymnic material, the praise of the ancestral officeholders, is unique not only in extant wisdom literature but also in any of the kinds of literature that were later included in the Hebrew Bible. It is thus difficult to judge whether and how Ben Sira may have been drawing on traditional language devoted to praise of ancestors.

Hymns on the Created Cosmos

Ben Sira articulates his cosmological wisdom largely in hymnic form. The parallel images and motifs in the creation hymns in Sirach 16:24–17:24; 39:12–35; and 42:15–43:33 (18:1–14?) are evident enough on cursory examination. Many of the same images and motifs are paralleled at points also in prophetic books such as Isaiah. Particularly striking are the terms and motifs paralleled in the Psalms, to which scholarly commentaries frequently draw attention (e.g., Ps. 104 for Sir. 16:26–30). With an awareness of how the various aspects of the Judean cultural repertoire were cultivated orally as much or more than by physically reading cumbersome scrolls, we can recognize that in cases of close similarities, Ben Sira was not drawing his terms directly from a written scroll, but from a register of language devoted to the subject of creation.

Hymns to Wisdom (Sir. 1:1–10; 24:1–34; cf. Job 28; Prov. 8:22–31; Bar. 3:15–4:4)

That reflection about the origins and accessibility of wisdom took a standard hymnic form is evident from wisdom's self-praise in Proverbs 8:22–31. Ben Sira's two hymns about transcendent wisdom, in 1:1–10 and 24:1–22 (–34) are thus clearly rooted in yet another particular "register" of language, one dedicated to reflection about wisdom. Later but less elaborate versions of the same kind of speech appear in Job 28 and Baruch 3:15–4:4. Since so much analysis and interpretation has been devoted to such "wisdom speculation," perhaps it suffices for our purposes here simply to chart the principal images and motifs shared by these hymns (along with relevant earlier proverbs), while also indicating certain distinctive features of the one or the other.

Concepts, motifs, themes	Sir. 1:1–10	24:1–22	Job 28	Prov. 8:22–31	Bar. 3:15–4:4
Wisdom speaks/praises herself		24:1–2		8:22–31	
From/with the Lord	1:1	24:3	(implied)	(implied)	
Wisdom created (by God) first	1:4	24:9		8:22–23	
Eternal	1:1	24:9			
Wisdom role in creation				8:30	
Relation to creation/cosmos	1:2–3	24:4–6	28:14, 24ff.	8:23–29	3:32–34
Wisdom as tree(s)		24:13–17			
To whom revealed? (no one)	1:6		28:12–22		3:29–31
Only God knows her	1:8		28:23–27		3:32, 36
God revealed her	1:9				
To all/those who love him	1:9–10		28:28	(8:31)	
To Israel/Jerusalem/Temple		24:8, 10–12			3:36; 4:2–4
Possession		24:20			
Food and drink		24:21			
Identified with Torah		24:23			4:1
Instruction/teaching		24:29, 30 34			

Interpretation of Sirach 24 has emphasized its similarities to aretalogies of the Egyptian goddess Isis as well as its affinities with Proverbs 8.[15] It has several distinctive features not found in Sirach 1:1–10 and Proverbs 8:22–31: a lengthy characterization of wisdom as great trees and the motifs it shares with speeches on seeking wisdom (possession, food and drink, identification with the Torah, and instruction; see above). Yet it is striking that it shares virtually all the principal images and motifs that appear in both Sirach 1:1–10 and Proverbs 8:22–31, using a particular register of language for hymns of wisdom speculation.

Praise of the Ancestors

The praise of ancestors in Sirach 44–50 finds no precedent in the cultural repertoire of Judea. The genre is praise, but in contrast to the Psalms, here Ben Sira praises men, not God. The hymn focuses on several characters who figure prominently in the accounts of the history of early Israel and of Judah, but it is not a narrative of historical events similar to either the historical accounts in the Pentateuch or those in the Deuteronomists' or Chroniclers' histories. It touches briefly on several prophets but does not cite their prophecies, unlike prophetic texts. It follows the chronological sequence also assumed in Judean cultural tradition, but does not follow or reference the accounts in what later became biblical books—in fact it often disagrees with particulars in those accounts. Nor do analogies drawn from other cultural repertoires, such as the lengthy poetic epics of the Greeks, offer precedents that Ben Sira or his teachers could have adapted.[16] Certainly no genre of Greek or Latin literature offers a prototype for praise of holders of the distinctively Israelite offices of prophecy, priesthood, and kingship.[17] It cannot be categorized as historical narrative on any familiar model, since it does not narrate historical events.

Rather, this material praises the ancestors because of their significance for the temple-state. The focus is on the offices they occupied. And the emphasis is clearly on Aaron, along with Phinehas, and Simon son of Onias, and "the everlasting covenant of priesthood" (cf. 45:7, 15) that God made with Aaron and his successors. It is surely significant that in the only interruption of the sequence of ancestral praise, there is a blessing following the section on Aaron and Phinehas (45:26), and then at the end, after Simon (50:22–24).[18] Thus, however unprecedented this praise of ancestors is in Judean cultural heritage, it does belong in a book of materials produced by a scribe closely associated with the Jerusalem Temple and the Aaronide priesthood.

All of these observations, however, do not lead us to conclude that, in composing the praise of ancestors, Ben Sira did not draw on traditional cultural materials of various sorts. Although there may not have been a well-established register of language dedicated to such praise, it is evident at several points that Ben Sira was drawing on standard themes and motifs with regard to particular figures or offices. Certain psalms have shorter sets of lines in celebration of the contributions of a Moses or a David. That Elijah would "restore" the tribes of Jacob (48:10), for example, is familiar from Malachi 4:5–6. That David played a role in the establishment of the Temple cult (Sir. 47:9–10) is emphasized in Chronicles even if not in 2 Samuel. That Jeremiah was called from the womb to build up as well as break down was a familiar motif prominent also in the book of Jeremiah. Yet there is no indication that Ben Sira was looking at written texts (e.g., books of the Pentateuch, 2 Samuel, 1 Kings) and more likely that in composition of the praise of ancestors he was drawing on the broader general repertoire of Israelite heritage.

Ben Sira's other principal reference to figures and events of Israelite legendary or historical tradition is also in a hymn. In the hymn of Sirach 16:24–17:24, following admiration of the created cosmos, he makes a short poetic recitation of the creation of humanity (with similarities to and differences from Genesis 1 and 2) and the giving of the covenant and its commandments, before moving to Israel as a people directly under God's own kingship (but note the ethical-penitential conclusion). He also marshals key incidents from Israel's (legendary) history as paradigms of judgment, as with the "ancient giants" and "the neighbors of Lot" (Sodom and Gomorrah) in Sirach 16:7–8 (but note the individualized divine judgment in conclusion, 16:12–14).

BEN SIRA AND THE POLITICS OF THE SECOND TEMPLE

The materials compiled into the book of Sirach are integrally related to the politics of the Jerusalem temple-state. Some of them pertain specifically to the struggles among aristocratic factions and their implications for scribes in the early second century BCE. Even some of the instructional speeches offer hints of Ben Sira's and presumably other scribes' concern about aristocratic exploitation of the poor and their own vulnerability to the rulers on whom they were dependent.

The Tension between the Role of Retainers and Commitment to the Commandments

Closer examination of Ben Sira's instructional speeches just above strongly reinforces the impression that wise scribes were ambivalent about their own position in the temple-state. His speeches on relations with rulers, together with his programmatic speech on the role of the wise scribe, leave little doubt that they served the "great ones" of the temple-state as what historical sociologists would call intellectual retainers (as outlined in chap. 3, above). Yet those same speeches and others focused on economic relations clearly articulate their feelings of vulnerability to the power of their patrons. Some of the speeches on economic relations, moreover, indicate that Ben Sira and other scribes saw their role as including attention to the plight of the poor. This concern is explicitly linked to the commandments of God (29:9, 11). Covenantal ideals appear to underlie other admonitions in Ben Sira's instruction, such as not to show partiality to the wealthy and powerful, and even to actively intervene to "rescue the oppressed from the oppressor" (4:9).

That same commitment to covenantal commandments may also account for the strong words of condemnation of those who oppress the poor (34:21–27). The sharpness of this warning is all the more striking because it is grouped with a speech on dutiful religious-economic support of the Temple and priesthood (34:21–31; 35:1–26). That Ben Sira was a strong advocate of dutiful support of the Temple and priesthood is clear from a shorter admonition on the obligation to render up tithes and offerings (7:29–31). The first three lines boldly articulate the basic ideology that held a temple-state together and supposedly motivated the people's economic support necessary to its operation: fear of the Lord entails honoring the priest with material support. The ensuing three lines specify the obligations for firstfruits, shoulders, sacrifices, and portions, as commanded. Dutiful payment of taxes for support of the priesthood is the material manifestation of religious devotion to God and honoring the priests. Encouragement of support of the Temple and priesthood may well have been among the responsibilities of scribes. And self-interest was involved insofar as they depended on their aristocratic priestly patrons for economic support.

The center section of the longer speech on support of the Temple and priesthood (35:6–13) features strong admonitions on tithes, offerings, and sacrifices grounded in the same ideology of the temple-state serving God as well as in fulfillment of the commandment. The immediately preceding speech on God's concern for the poor is almost prophetlike in its condemnation of and warning against oppression of the economically vulnerable, and the ensuing section of the speech about tithing articulates similar warning.

> If one sacrifices ill-gotten goods,
>   the offering is blemished.
> The Most High is not pleased with the offerings of the ungodly,
>   nor for a multitude of sacrifices does he forgive sins. . . .
> To take away a neighbor's living is to commit murder;
>   to deprive an employee of wages is to shed blood. (34:21–27)
> [The Lord] will not ignore the supplication of the orphan,
>   or the widow when she pours out her complaint. . . .
> The Most High . . . does justice for the righteous, and executes judgment. . . .
>   [He] breaks the scepters of the unrighteous; . . .
>   he repays mortals according to their deeds.
>
>   (35:17–24)

In the tiny temple-state of Judea the wealthy, warned in these lines specifically about the relation of exploiting the poor to sacrifices, would have been members of the priestly aristocracy or their close associates. Ben Sira and other scribes were clearly capable of criticizing abuses by the very elite on whom they were dependent.[19] It is not difficult to see how this speech could have addressed the increasing exploitation of the Judean peasantry under the rigorous tax-collection by the Tobiad Joseph and the struggle for power that it exacerbated in the Jerusalem aristocracy (chap. 2, above).

Despite the ambivalence that Ben Sira expresses about the role of scribal retainer, however, he also gives eloquent expressions to an ideology that helped authorize the temple-state and legitimated the Oniad high priesthood at a point when it desperately needed to shore up its power. These can be seen respectively in his praise of Wisdom in Sirach 24 and in his praise of the ancestors in Sirach 44–50. In both cases these are hymns intended for a wider audience (although pitched primarily to the priests and others in the Temple), not instruction more narrowly focused on aspiring scribes.

Wisdom Established in the Jerusalem Temple

Sirach 24:1–22 is far more than a hymn of Wisdom's self-praise in a tradition known through the earlier reflective praise of Wisdom in Proverbs 8:22–31. If the hymn jumped from Sirach 24:1–6 to 24:19–22, it would conform more closely to the combination of wisdom's divine origins at the creation with an invitation to possess and consume wisdom found in Proverbs 1–9 or Sirach 1:1–10.

The significance of the hymn also reaches beyond Ben Sira's identification of Wisdom with the torah that Moses commanded, in 24:23.[20] More important in the historical context is the crucial application made in 24:8–12 that is often overlooked. In other hymns in praise of Wisdom, she is more universally distributed, "poured . . . upon all the living" (Sir. 1:9–10). The hymn in Sirach 24, however, articulates something far more specific, more political, or rather more political-religious. After Wisdom "sought a resting place among"—a better translation might be "had held sway over"—every other people (24:6–7), the Creator of all things assigned her to make her dwelling place in Jacob/Israel. Not only that, she also was established in (the Temple in) Zion, assumed authority/power in Jerusalem (24:8–12). The Creator has assigned the divine ordering force in the creation of the universe to have its domain in the Jerusalem temple-state. This declaration grounds the political-religious order in Jerusalem in the divinely established order of the universe. It would be difficult to find a stronger statement of the absolute authority of the Jerusalem temple-state as a way of legitimating the established political order.

The images in 24:13–17, moreover, confirm that this hymn of Wisdom is pitched to the culture of the wealthy elite in Jerusalem, the priestly aristocracy who preside in the Temple. Only they and the sophisticated scribes who worked among them, not marginal Judean villagers, would have appreciated the exotic flora of Palestine such as the date palms of En-gedi along the Dead Sea, with their featherlike leaves and delicious dates, or the pleasures of relaxation among the luxuriant palm trees and rose gardens of Jericho, in the ever-warm Jordan valley (24:14). Only the priestly aristocrats would have had direct experience of the exotic plants and shellfish from which the exotic perfumes and incenses were made that were used in conduct of holy rites in the Temple (tent; 24:15).[21]

Cultural legitimation of the established order in the temple-state was surely one of the important functions of leading scribes working for the priestly aristocracy. Yet it is clear that Ben Sira's use of traditional hymnic reflection on the origin and nature of Wisdom to bolster local political power relations was a deliberate step, not an inevitable one. As we shall see in Enoch texts, other scribes had become sharply critical of the Jerusalem high priesthood.

The declaration that divine Wisdom had been established in authority in the Temple seems all the more remarkable when we juxtapose it with the historical context. After all, the Jerusalem temple-state remained subject to the Seleucid regime, which had only recently taken control of Syria-Palestine. Factions of the priestly aristocracy, Oniads, Tobiads, or others, would have been under no illusion about the concrete political power arrangement under which the temple-state operated. And sages such as Ben Sira would also have known that the Oniad high priesthood in Jerusalem continued to be dependent on Seleucid favor. Surely, as one of those "scribes of the Temple" who had received tax breaks, he knew that the principal source of funding by which Simon II had "repaired and fortified the Temple" was the Seleucid regime (50:1–4). So to what audience was he addressing the praise of Wisdom that installed her in the Temple? Perhaps in the circumstances in which the imperial power relations were all the more concretely evident, it was important to scribal circles who served the ruling aristocracy, as well as to the more tradition-minded priestly aristocrats themselves, to shore up their belief that the temple-state had its authorization in the installation of Wisdom in the Temple by the Most High God.

Praise of the Ancestors

The praise of the ancestors in Sirach 44–50 leads persistently to its climax in the praise of Simon son of Onias and "all the sons of Aaron in their splendor."[22] The sustained praise of ancestors thus provides a sort of charter for the Judean temple-state. All of the great offices and officeholders, the most important of which is the high priesthood, flow into and are embodied in the high priesthood headed by Simon. Moses, the prototypical prophet, ordained Aaron to the office of high priesthood. The kings, David and Solomon and their successor Hezekiah, and later Zerubbabel and Jeshua and Nehemiah, instituted the temple cult, built the Temple, and/or fortified the city of Jerusalem. Aaron and his descendants took over the teaching of the commandments to the people. Only Aaron received the "everlasting covenant," that of the priesthood, to be continued among his descendants "as long as the heavens endure" (45:7, 15). That covenant was reaffirmed in the covenant of friendship to Phinehas, "that he and his descendants should have the dignity of the priesthood forever" (45:24). That the covenant with David was to continue in his offspring was, in effect, transferred to priesthood, so that "the heritage of Aaron is for his descendants alone" (45:25).[23] Not only are Aaron and his successors to bless the people and minister to the Lord, but also only the priests Aaron and Simon are [said to be] head of the people or to judge or deliver the people (45:26; 50:24). The welfare of Jacob/Israel is thus more dependent on the priests in the Temple than on the great prophets such as Moses and Samuel and the kings such as David and Solomon. Clear markers of this are the blessings that interrupt the sequence of praise and that are delivered only on Aaron(-Phinehas) and then, at the end of the whole paean of praise, on Simon (45:26 and 50:22–24).

Ben Sira's praise of the ancestors, addressed to his own contemporaries, thus presents Aaron's descendants as specially anointed with holy oil to serve the Lord and bless the people, offering sacrifices, incense, and atonement for the people. They also have authority to teach the torah. Any rebellion against them is sanctioned by the Lord's wrath against the company of Korah. And the Aaronide priesthood is endowed with the sacralized economic support of firstfruits, bread, and sacrifices in lieu of having land of their own (45:15–22). The same is portrayed in the ceremony at the Temple altar in the praise of Simon, as he and "all the sons of Aaron" offer sacrifices to the Most High and then pronounce God's blessings on the people (50:12–21). When we recognize that the everlasting priesthood was the only office that continued into the second-temple period, it becomes clear that the lengthy elaboration of how Aaron was "clothed in perfect splendor and strengthened . . . with the symbols of authority" (45:7–13) had a contemporary resonance that Joshua's brandishing his sword and David's playing with lions and bears did not. For Simon in Ben Sira's own day was also arrayed in a glorious role and clothed in perfect splendor, and wore those same symbols of authority as the head of the priesthood and people in Temple ceremonies.

If the praise of wisdom in Sirach 24 was a legitimation of the temple-state in general, the praise of the ancestors was a blatant endorsement of (propaganda for) a particular branch of the priesthood as authorized to dominate its affairs. As discussed in chapters 1 and 2 (above), rival factions of the priesthood struggled for influence, position, and dominance in the Jerusalem temple-state. The struggle was exacerbated by rival Hellenistic imperial regimes' struggle for influence in and control of Syria-Palestine, and escalated to crisis proportions when the Seleucid regime finally succeeded in taking control of Jerusalem. After the sustained conflict between the Oniad dynasty and the Tobiads, the position of Simon II was sorely in need of shoring up. That is surely what the idealizing portrayal of Ben Sira's praise of Simon, set up by the sustained praise of the ancestors, is all about. We can imagine either that Ben Sira had already been a protégé of the Oniads (more likely) or saw the opportunity for influence and honor in becoming an enthusiastic supporter of Simon II. In any case, his praise of the ancestors, far from disinterested poetry honoring the great historical heroes of Israel, was pro-Simon propaganda.

It may also have had an additional agenda in the struggles of priestly factions for power. The section on Aaron and Phinehas provides legitimation specifically for Aaron and his descendants, to the apparent exclusion of the (other) Levites.[24] Were the Levites in effect being demoted? Near contemporary Judean literature such as *Aramaic Levi* (in the DSS) makes the case for the legitimacy and higher position of the Levites.[25] Judging from Josephus's accounts of priestly status in Herodian times, however, they must have lost further ground (*Ant.* 20.216–18). It is puzzling that Ben Sira's hymn of praise makes no mention of the Zadokites, particularly considering that the Oniads were ostensibly of Zadokite lineage.[26] Perhaps one way of shoring up support for the continuing prominence of the Oniad family was for it to seek fuller cooperation with the wider circle of "the sons of Aaron," in effect to the detriment of the Levites.

Like the praise of Wisdom in Sirach 24, the praise of the ancestors exhibits a studied naïveté about the real political situation of the temple-state's dependence on Seleucid imperial favor and, as soon happened, the instability of the Jerusalem ruling aristocracy vis-à-vis the needs and intrigue of the imperial regime. To help explain how indigenous intellectuals such as Ben Sira could produce hymns so oblivious to their own political situation, it is tempting to draw analogies from the cultural elite of other subject cities and peoples. For ostensibly ruling elites who are themselves politically subject to outside rulers, the cultural dimension becomes all the more important as the only feature of their society that they still control. Scholars of "the Second Sophistic," the literary movement among early-second-century CE intellectuals of the Greek cities long subject to Roman imperial rule, have observed that the Greek elite seemed to be living as if in the glory days of classical Greece.[27] Something similar may have been happening with Ben Sira and others of the Judean cultural elite. Precisely when they had to face their political impotence, to maintain any pretence of independence from a more interventionist imperial rule, they more actively memorialized the glories of their great prophets, kings, and priests of old. In particular they imagined their own priesthood, which was in fact politically subject to imperial rule, as replicating the splendor of the ancestral priests of hoary antiquity, Aaron and Phinehas.

Chapter 8

1 Enoch

And I saw a lofty throne; . . .
And its wheels were like the shining sun . . .
And the Lord called me: . . .
"Go and say to the watchers of heaven . . .
The spirits of the giants do violence, make desolate, and attack . . .
You will have no peace."

Book of Watchers

And they raised up that tower . . . and they placed a table before that tower,
and all the bread on it was polluted and not pure.

Animal Vision

Woe to those who build their houses not with their own labors, . . .
Woe to those who reject the . . . eternal inheritance of their fathers.

Epistle of Enoch

What has become known as *1 Enoch* consists of at least five different books, all attributed to the antediluvian figure of Enoch.[1] Originally written in Aramaic,[2] the texts that constitute *1 Enoch* were translated into Greek, and eventually from Greek into Ethiopic, from which they became known in the nineteenth and twentieth centuries. Each of the "Enoch" books is a composite of forms, and each was still developing in antiquity.

The Book of Watchers (chaps. 1–36), after an introductory oracle of judgment based on the regularity of the created order (1–5), features the myth of the heavenly Watchers' generation of the warlike giants that does not involve Enoch (6–11)[3] and an account of Enoch's divine commission as a prophet of judgment in a vision (12–16), followed by a juxtaposition of Enoch's two journeys through the heaven (17–36). Although some of its traditions are older, the book dates to mid-third century BCE.

The Book of Parables (chaps. 37–71) is a series of heavenly tableaux of the judgment over which a figure named variously as Righteous One, Elect One, Anointed One, and Son of Man presides. This latest of the various sections of *1 Enoch* is dated to the late first century BCE, thus falling outside the period of our focus.

The Book of the Luminaries (chaps. 72–82), the oldest of Enoch traditions, with roots in the Persian period, is a collection of separate astronomical descriptions of the movements of the sun, moon, and stars, as revealed to Enoch.

The fourth "book" presents two visions: the first is of the world's destruction in the flood (chaps. 83–84). The second (chaps. 85–90) is a sustained vision of animals that allegorically represents the history of Israel under attack by foreign enemies, with resolution in divine judgment. The present form of the text appears to stem from the time of the Maccabean Revolt, around 165 BCE.

The Epistle of Enoch (chaps. 92–105), beginning with a sweeping visionary rehearsal of history, presents a series of prophetic woes against the sinners and reassurance of the righteous in anticipation of the divine judgment. With no obvious indications internal to the text, it could stem from the early second century.

Four of these component books of "Enoch" are some of the most important Judean texts of the third and early second centuries BCE. Along with the teaching of Ben Sira and the components of the book of Daniel, they arose out of and addressed the escalating political crises in Judea under Hellenistic imperial rule.

GENERAL ASPECTS OF ENOCH TEXTS AND CONSIDERATIONS OF APPROACH

Wisdom Literature Produced by Scribes

Enoch literature is usually categorized as apocalyptic. Yet the books that constitute *1 Enoch* all represent their own contents as wisdom and present the figure of Enoch as a sophisticated scribe, who both writes the contents and teaches them orally.

In the Book of Watchers, for example, Enoch is "the scribe," "righteous scribe" (12:3–4), and "the scribe of truth" (15:1), who knows how to function in a royal court (13:4–7; cf. 15:2). As in Sirach, the recipients of the message are characterized as wise scribes who have received wisdom (5:8; cf. 32:3–6; 82:2). A difference from Ben Sira is that Enoch has received his wisdom in multiple celestial media of communication, having heard the words of heavenly figures and read the heavenly tablets. While representing Enoch's communication of wisdom as oral testimony and teaching, as in Sirach, the Book of Watchers also places emphasis on the writing of the wisdom received. In what was probably the concluding stanzas of the Book of Watchers (apparently displaced to the end of the Book of the Luminaries, 81:1–6; 82:1–2), Enoch "reads what is written" on the "heavenly tablets" of all deeds of all humankind, and is then to "make everything known," both orally and in writing, to his son Methuselah, so that he in turn can communicate them both orally and in writing (81:1–6; 82:1–2; cf. 85:2; 91:2, 18–19).

Again in the Epistle, Enoch is "the scribe" who writes a letter to all his sons (92:1; 100:6) and communicates its contents orally (93:1, 3; 94:1, 3; 94:10; etc.). And the recipients of Enoch's wisdom are again represented as "the wise" who can read the words of Enoch's written letter (100:6; 104:11–13). From what we know of scribal culture in Judea and other ancient Near Eastern societies, it would be a reasonable surmise that these portrayals of Enoch as a wise scribe who communicates both orally and in writing reflect the way in which the producers of the "books" of Enoch literature were communicating their contents.

Types of Wisdom—and History and Prophecy

While the various texts included in *1 Enoch* represent themselves as wisdom written and spoken by a prototypical scribe, they draw upon and present kinds of wisdom different from the instructional wisdom that dominates in Sirach. In contrast to a common impression, even the Epistle of Enoch has little instructional wisdom beyond the introductory admonition to "love righteousness" (94:1–5). Cosmological wisdom, including astronomical, meteorological, and other kinds of knowledge about aspects of the universe, dominates in the Book of Watchers as well as the Book of the Luminaries, and plays a role in the Epistle, somewhat like its limited appearance in Sirach. Mantic wisdom, which Ben Sira rejected, specifically dream interpretation, plays an all-important role in the Book of Watchers and in the Visions. Much of the cosmological wisdom in the Books of the Watchers and the Luminaries and the review of history in the Apocalypse of Weeks is also presented as previously hidden wisdom that was revealed to Enoch by heavenly figures (13:8; 14:2, 8, 24; 93:2).

As for the broader repertoire of Israelite-Judean culture, like the wise scribe Ben Sira, the righteous scribe "Enoch" is well acquainted with the historical traditions of Israel and is heir to the prophetic tradition. "Enoch," however, through his latter-day creators, not only draws far more heavily on the prophetic tradition than does Ben Sira, but even assumes a prophetic role. In a vision he receives a commission, patterned after that of prophets such as Jeremiah or Ezekiel, to prophesy to the Watchers (12:3–6) and receives oracles to deliver to them and to the hearers/readers in general (1:4–5:9). Much of the Epistle, moreover, consists of series of prophetic woes in performative speech patterned after a tradition familiar from Amos, Isaiah, and Habakkuk. Striking by its absence in these Enoch texts is Mosaic torah.[4]

The Figure of Enoch

Enoch emerged as an important figure to whom revealed wisdom was attributed for several reasons. His legendary features included in the Priestly genealogy in Genesis 5 indicate some of them. "Enoch walked with God" (v. 22)—so he must have received revelation directly from the divine source. Since "God took him" (v. 24), moreover, he must have been resident in heaven and accessible as a source of wisdom, perhaps through mantic techniques, in which some scribes were trained.

Also in the Priestly ancestral genealogy in Genesis, Enoch is the seventh in the sequence of ten antediluvian figures, and he is "taken" by God at a remarkably young age for one of the primordial ancestors, at 365. The latter suggests that he was associated with the solar calendar of 364 or 365 days. And the former invited comparison with the role of Enmeduranki in Mesopotamian culture. Enmeduranki was usually listed in Mesopotamian texts of late second and first millennium BCE as the seventh antediluvian king and as king of the city of Sippar, whose deity was Shamash, the Sun-god. Other Mesopotamian texts attribute to him the origin, in Sippar, Nippur, and Babylon, of divinely revealed divinatory techniques of obtaining omens, in particular the observation of oil on water and the use of a liver tablet. This was part of Enmeduranki's role in Mesopotamian culture as the founder of the *baru* guild, high-ranking scribes specializing in divination and interpretation of omens, including dreams.[5] These similarities in cultural motifs suggest that the figure of Enoch in Judean scribal culture was associated with astronomical observation and divination, which in turn may have been influenced by or rooted in Mesopotamian astronomical and divinatory wisdom.

The angel-narrators of the second-century BCE *Jubilees* confirm precisely this, that Enoch was the prototypical scribe whose specialty was astronomy and knowledge of the future by means of visions:

> He was the first among men . . . who learned writing and knowledge and wisdom and who wrote down the signs of heaven according to the order of their months in a book, that men might know the seasons of the years according to the order of their separate months. And he . . . recounted the weeks of the jubilees, and made known to them the days of the years, and set in order the months and recounted the Sabbaths of the years as we made them known to him. And what was and will be he saw in a vision of his sleep, as it will happen to the children of men throughout their generations until the day of judgment; and he saw and understood everything, and wrote his testimony, and placed the testimony on earth for all the children of men and for their generations. (*Jub.* 4:17–19)

In the books that constitute *1 Enoch,* astronomical wisdom and revelations through visions are the most prominent parts of the repertoire of wisdom that Enoch commands as the primordial scribe. It almost goes without saying that in this representation of Enoch, the "Enoch" scribes are also portraying their understanding of their role and repertoire.

Composite Texts and the Question of Genre

The composite character of the different books that make up *1 Enoch* resists categorization according to genres as defined by modern scholars. It is not clear that it helps us understand the texts any better to assert that the framing genre of several sections of *1 Enoch* is an "apocalypse" or a "testament" as determined from later Judean documents when the components of those sections are prophetic oracles or astronomical wisdom or visions.[6] In the composition and cultivation of Enoch texts, we may be seeing a creative process of the mixing and transformation of materials standard in the Judean scribal repertoire (including prophetic forms of which they had become the heirs) into new combinations and composite forms. The different sections of the Book of Watchers assume several composite cultural forms, presenting cosmological wisdom framed by prophetic oracle of judgment, narrative myth as embellishment of traditional legend, prophetic commissioning juxtaposed with prophetic oracle, astronomical wisdom juxtaposed with heavenly journey. In the Epistle of Enoch the outer testamentary framing does little to determine the judgmental tone and condemnatory substance of the series of prophetic woes.

Texts in Process of Development

Fragments of several different manuscripts of four of the sections that form *1 Enoch* were found among the Dead Sea Scrolls, thus indicating that these books were recognized as authoritative in some way, at least by the people at Qumran. The differences between copies of the same section of *1 Enoch* and the further differences between the Aramaic and the Greek and the Ethiopic versions, moreover, indicate clearly that the text of all of these books continued to develop.[7] Apparently all of them were being "cultivated" and continually developed, orally and in successive written manuscripts. This continuing development, combined with the composite character of each of these books, suggests that it is inappropriate to think in terms of individual "authors" having "written" them.

Continuity of an Enochic Scribal Circle

The producers of the later Enoch texts evidently knew and further developed material in the earlier Enoch texts. The Book of Watchers, which dates from the end of the third century, clearly presupposes and works with the same astronomical wisdom that appears in the earlier Book of the Luminaries. Both the Animal Vision and the Epistle of Enoch appear to have known the Book of Watchers, or at least the kinds of material used in it. The later Parables book clearly knows and depends on the Book of Watchers. Such "intertextual" relations strongly suggest that these Enoch texts were produced by a succession of scribes with considerable continuity over several generations.[8] There was apparently some sort of circle of "Enoch" scribes who cultivated and developed a succession of interrelated texts of "Enochic" wisdom over a period of a century or more. Judging from the prominence of Enoch literature at Qumran, moreover, this succession of "Enoch" scribes had considerable influence in later scribal circles.

BOOK OF THE LUMINARIES (*1 ENOCH* 72–82)

Most of the contents of this book appear to be an early second-temple development of cosmological wisdom derived from early Mesopotamian scribal culture
(with little or no Greek influence), where astronomical and meteorological observations were one of the bases of divination.[9] It was believed that the divine powers (gods) that determined human life left clues to predictable occurrences that
could be "read" or interpreted by those who possessed the appropriate knowledge.
Elaborate records were kept of scribal experts' observations and predictions.
Among the massive number of tablets recovered in Mesopotamia are seventy
tablets of astronomical and meteorological omens, the great *Enuma Anu Enlil*
compendium.[10] The astronomical wisdom of the Book of Luminaries strongly
resembles that in the *Enuma Anu Enlil* collection, in which schematic "scientific"
arrangements often do not accord with empirical observations.

Aside from *1 Enoch* 80:2–8 and 82:4–8,[11] the astronomical and meteorological materials in this book read like a scientific treatise, with no application to particular circumstances. This text of astronomical wisdom and the Mesopotamian
texts that its contents resemble seem somewhat analogous to the collections of
laws, the texts of "jurisprudence" such as the Code of Hammurabi (see chap. 6,
above). Such cosmological wisdom thus seems to be a subject of instruction, albeit
advanced instruction, to be mastered by scribal specialists.[12] That such astronomical and meteorological knowledge had become standard in the repertoire of
Judean scribal wisdom can be seen in a variety of texts ranging from psalms (Ps.
148) to reflective wisdom (Sir. 1:1–10) to later "apocalyptic" literature (*1 En.*
41:3–7; 43:1–2; 60:11–22; *2 Bar.* 59:5–11). Precisely because such knowledge
had become part of the standard scribal repertoire of wisdom in Judea as well as
in Mesopotamia, its components were cataloged in lists, and those lists could then
be used in various connections.[13]

In Judean culture, of course, the heavenly bodies and natural forces that constituted the fundamental conditions of life and the objects of such knowledge
were all understood as the works of God. Accordingly these creatures (angels,
sun, moon, stars, deeps, fire, hail, snow, wind), along with animals, fish, and
birds, which were also the objects of scribal knowledge, were called upon to
praise their divine orderer, as in Psalm 148. The difference between a simple list
recited in a psalm and scribal knowledge about the patterns of heavenly bodies
and natural forces can be seen in the hymn about the works of the Lord in Sirach
43:1–22. Ben Sira not only knows such cosmological wisdom but also knows
that this kind of wisdom really belongs to God, who must display it in his works
and otherwise reveal it so that it can be known, even by scribal sages (1:1–10;
42:15–25). Yet because he is hesitant about the "greater things that lie hidden"
(43:32), he tiptoes around the question of just how much other than sun, moon,
stars, and winds can be known, even though God "discloses what has been and
what is to be, and reveals traces of hidden things" (42:18–19; cf. Job 38; *1 En.*
93:11–14).

The "Enoch" scribes, however, boldly claimed such knowledge, by divine revelation. In the Book of Luminaries, all the regular movements of the heavenly bodies are revealed by the divine messenger Uriel. Later Enoch literature and other later "apocalyptic" and "wisdom" texts assert, almost matter-of-factly, that God has revealed such knowledge to figures such as Enoch or Moses. And they expand the list of the revealed knowledge to include not only the height of heaven, the breadth of the earth, and the number of raindrops, but also the abyss, the mouth of hell, judgment, and worlds to come (*1 En.* 41:3–7; 43:1–2; 60:11–22; Wis. 7:17–22; *2 Bar.* 59:5–11; *4 Ezra* 4:5–7).

The function or purpose of (learning) this type of wisdom, however, would not have been simply instructional, but political-economic-religious as well. As seen in more polemical texts (such as *Jub.* 6:32–38), astronomical wisdom was the basis of the calendar and festivals of the agricultural cycle, which affected the economic base of any ancient agrarian society. This political-economic function can even be seen in the emphasis throughout the book on the sun, moon, stars, and winds maintaining orderliness and adherence to fixed positions and patterns, so that the seasons, festivals, months, and days are secure in the 364/5-day solar calendar. This is very clear in both the judgment against sinners in 80:2–8 and the brief polemic on right and wrong calendrical practice in 82:4–6. The next Enoch book to be examined, about the Watchers, uses such knowledge for further revelations about the results of political conflict and about future judgment.

BOOK OF WATCHERS (*1 ENOCH* 1–36)

The superscription in *1 Enoch* 1:1 clearly indicates the purpose and substance of the Book of Watchers: "Enoch's words of blessing on the chosen and righteous ones at the divine judgment when all the[ir] enemies are removed." Right at the outset, the book indicates its imperial-political situation and anti-imperial stance. Drawing on the tradition of the Blessing of Moses (Deut. 33) and other such prophetic blessings pronounced on Israel, "Enoch" addresses new circumstances in which the people of Israel are again struggling under foreign enemies, evidently the Hellenistic empire(s).

The introduction in *1 Enoch* 1:2–3 identifies the discourse Enoch is about to deliver as (from) a prophetic vision of the Holy One of heaven and the words of the Watchers. As widely recognized, the language and form of the announcement resemble those of the oracles of (the diviner) Balaam (Num. 22–24; esp. 24:3–4, 15–17).[14] The latter, a professional diviner in Pethor, on the Euphrates River (22:5; the Hebrew word *ptr*, of Mesopotamian derivation, also means "dream interpreter"),[15] was being paid by a foreign king to pronounce curses against Israel, but God repeatedly constrained him to pronounce blessings instead. This clearly suggests a political role of the Enoch scribes: they saw themselves as the heirs of diviner-prophets such as Balaam, and as constrained by God to prophesy against their aristocratic patrons, the heads of the Judean temple-state.[16]

Enoch's Oracle of Judgment and Blessing

The first section of the Book of Watchers, 1:3c—5:9, serving as the introduction to the book, takes the form of a prophetic oracle of blessings on the righteous and of curses on the sinners. Patterned somewhat as a prophetic lawsuit, the oracle proceeds in four steps: an opening announcement of God's appearance, which shakes the created order (1:3c–7); a preliminary announcement of God's blessings and destruction (1:8–9); an indictment of the disobedience of the sinners ("you"), in contrast to the obedient "works of heaven" and earthly cycle of seasons (2:1–5:4); and finally the pronouncement that the sinners will be an eternal curse, while the chosen will inherit the earth and receive wisdom (5:5–9).

The oracle is deeply rooted in the traditional Judean prophetic repertoire. The appearance of God with armies of holy ones from or upon Sinai to deliver blessings on the people/Israel, while removing enemy forces, is influenced by the Blessing of Moses (see esp. Deut. 33:1–2, 27, 29; cf. the early victory song in Judg. 5:4–5). This is not a case of an "Enoch" author referring or alluding to a particular "biblical" passage, but rather of "Enoch" scribes thoroughly familiar with a particular register of prophetic speech. The portrayal of the earthshaking effects on the created order caused by God's appearance in judgment derives from the related but different standard Israelite prophetic register dedicated to the theophany of the divine Warrior, which often appears in more complete oracles that announce God's judgment on oppressive rulers or on the foreign kings who have conquered his people (Mic. 1:2–7; Jer. 25:30–31, 32, 34–38).[17] The scribes who produced the Book of Watchers were thoroughly familiar with such prophetic oracles and could compose in such specific prophetic registers of language. In earlier interpretation of "apocalyptic" literature, this hyperbolic language of theophany was taken in a literal sense as predicting "cosmic catastrophe," the destruction of the created order.[18] But that was a misunderstanding of such "apocalyptic" language, which stands in continuity with the traditional prophetic register of language dedicated to theophany. Far from cosmic dissolution, the Book of Watchers is concerned with the restoration of the heavenly order.

The point of the earthshaking pyrotechnics of God's appearance, in heightened metaphoric and hyperbolic language, was to symbolize how terrible and terrifying the appearance of God in judgment will be. The whole tradition of such oracles (including Mic. 1:2–7; Jer. 25:30–38) was sharply political, pronouncing condemnation of oppressive domestic or foreign rulers and their defeat by God acting as divine Warrior with heavenly armies—and/or the people's deliverance from such rulers. The prophetic oracle in Isa. 24:17–23 even includes the "host of heaven" along with "the kings of the earth" in the divine punishment, a step toward the focus on judgment against the rebel Watchers in the rest of the Book of Watchers.[19]

While the dominant form of this section as a whole and most of the imagery in the theophany and pronouncement of judgment and salvation derive from Judean prophetic culture, prophecy here has been shaped by scribes. The indictment section of the oracle, moving from poetry to prose and from third- to second-person address, is composed of astronomical and meteorological wisdom. The particular list of the passage's natural phenomena derives from a standard topic of astronomical-meteorological wisdom and its language register, in which the obedience of the heavenly bodies constitutes a foil for the disobedience of humans (as can be seen, for example, in Sir. 16:26–28; *T. Naph.* 3:2–4:1 and *Ps. Sol.* 18:10–12).[20]

Story of the Watchers

The next section of the Book of Watchers (*1 En.* 6–11) tells a story about rebellious Watchers' generation of destructive giants and does not even mention Enoch. Like other sections of Enoch literature, this story also focuses on natural forces, only the forces are now more dramatically personified, semidivine forces (Star-god, Thunder-god, Rain-god, Sun-god, et al.; 6:7–8), with wills of their own, which some of them use to rebel against the divine order.[21] Sons of heaven led by Shemihazah, desiring human women, took wives and produced great giants, who devoured the labor of humans, then the humans themselves, and then devoured one another. They and Asael introduced weapons of war (and mining/ metalworking), magic spells, and cosmetics into human society. Concerned about the violence and bloodshed, the heavenly messengers Sariel, Raphael, Gabriel, and Michael approached the Lord of ages, the King of kings, who then delegated them, respectively, to warn Noah, to bind Asael and Shemihazah and the other rebel Watchers until the day of judgment, to destroy the giants by inducing them to war against each other, and to cleanse the earth from impurity so that the righteous can live in peace, enjoying God's blessing.[22]

The focus and principal concern of the story is on the origins of violence, particularly the expropriation of people's produce and the destruction of human life by the giants, who have military forces—and the assurance that through the heavenly messengers God is still in control and will eventually execute judgment on the destructive forces and make genuinely humane life possible. George Nickelsburg has suggested that the giants who devour one another with weapons of war point to the wars of the Diadochoi, the successors of Alexander the Great who battled one another for imperial position in the late fourth century BCE.[23] The list of weapons in 8:1 surely matches the Hellenistic armies of Alexander and his successors: swords of iron, shields, and breastplates.

The actions of the giants, however, probably pertain to the effects of Hellenistic rule more generally, Ptolemaic rule in Judea more particularly, and the periodic warfare between the Ptolemies and the Seleucids for control of Syria-Palestine. As suggested by the increasingly more vicious beasts in the dream-vision of Daniel 7, Hellenistic rule was experienced by Judeans as more heavily exploitative and destructive than previous imperial rule. The Ptolemies are well known for trying to exploit the areas they ruled for maximum revenues from the agrarian economy, "devouring the labor of all the sons of men, and men were not able to supply them" (*1 En.* 7:3). The giants' killing people and devouring one another, and the repeated theme of the giants' violence and bloodshed upon the earth (9:1, 9; 10:15) could pertain to the repeated wars between the imperial regimes (see chap. 2 above). The extreme destruction wrought by repeated Hellenistic imperial warfare and the severe economic exploitation by the Ptolemaic regime were inexplicable to Judeans such as the Enoch scribes in simple traditional (Deuteronomic) terms of disobedience to divine commands. To explain the origin of such extreme imperial violence and oppression, they resorted to the story of the rebel superhuman heavenly forces.

The story of the rebel Watchers also reflects the imperial situation with which the Enoch scribes were struggling in a more subtle way. The universe is represented as a great empire over which stands the God of gods as the great emperor, "the King of kings." But since this Lord of lords, like the Persian emperor, is remote from what is happening in his vast empire, responsibility for governing has been delegated to multiple satraps and other functionaries, who have been assigned responsibility for certain areas and aspects in the cosmic governance. The Lord of lords is sufficiently remote that it is necessary for some of the highest-ranking officers of the imperial regime to bring to his attention the rebellion by Watchers that has brought such violence to the distant region of the earth (9:1–11). Only when these officers approach the imperial "King of kings" about the rebellion of his other officers does he then delegate them to bind the rebels and destroy their destructive sons, the giants. The message is that, although remote, God is ultimately in control. Judgment and deliverance are not imminent, but they are certain.

Enoch's Prophetic Commission to Announce Judgment on the Rebel Watchers

Returning to the prophetic role of "the scribe of righteousness," the next section, *1 Enoch* 12–16, expands on God's judgment of the rebel Watchers whose mating with women has led to violence and destruction of people on earth. In form and substance it is a commissioning of Enoch as a prophet in a vision to announce God's judgment to the rebel Watchers. In a scenario using the legend that Enoch "was taken" into the divine world as its point of departure (12:1–2; cf. Gen. 5:24), he is commissioned as a prophet in several steps. The climax comes in an elaborate account of Enoch's visionary ascent through great heavenly houses to the very throne of the Great Glory (*1 En.* 14:8–23).[24] There the Lord charges him with his message of indictment of the rebel Watchers for the violence and desolation they have unleashed and, briefly, a reiteration of their punishment (14:24–16:4).

The long final step of the vision in which Enoch is commissioned with his prophetic role and message corresponds particularly closely to the visions and/or calls of prophets such as Micaiah ben Imlah (1 Kings 22:19–22), Isaiah (6; 40), and especially Ezekiel (1–2). It also has close parallels with Daniel 7.[25] This prophetic commissioning in a vision of God the King holding judgment in the heavenly court establishes Enoch's primary role in the Book of Watchers as a prophet who has a direct vision of the divine judgment and then communicates the message. As he receives the prophetic commission, however, he is already established in the role of a scribe (13:4–7; 15:1). And he carries out the prophetic commission in scribal form, producing a "book of the words of truth" (14:1–7; etc). In their representation of Enoch's prophetic commissioning, the scribal producers of this text must also indicate that they see themselves not only as the heirs of the Israelite prophetic repertoire, but also as the heirs of the prophetic role. Whether simply working creatively from the tradition of revelatory prophetic commissioning and visions, or in visionary experiences that provided the source of such creativity as well, they were called to deliver messages of God's judgment from the divine court.[26]

The expanded indictment in the oracle that Enoch is charged with delivering to the rebel Watchers, finally, brings us to the message toward which this section has been driving (15:2–16:4). They are charged with having defiled themselves with women, having begotten with the blood of human beings, and lusted with the blood of people (15:3bc, 4b).[27] The principal concern of the indictment, however, is what all of the lusting and mating with women led to: the begetting of the giants who caused desolation (15:3, 5–7). But the oracle that Enoch is to pronounce then moves beyond the story of the Watchers in chapters 6–11. The destruction of the giants resulted in their souls having become "evil spirits upon the earth" (15:8; 16:1), which has proved to be disastrous for people because "the spirits of the giants lead astray, do violence, make desolate, and attack and wrestle and hurt upon the earth, and cause illnesses" (15:11).

This constitutes a revelation about the historical situation through which the addressees of "Enoch" are living. In the previous section the story of the rebel Watchers' production of the giants toward the beginning of history explained the origin of imperial warfare and economic expropriation of agricultural produce, which had become so devastating to human life. Enoch's prophetic vision that the spirits of the destroyed giants have become evil spirits who continue the giants' devastation of human life is the explanation of Judeans' situation of continuing to suffer under the Ptolemaic regime's rule, with its rigorous economic exploitation of the peoples it controlled ("make desolate"), its periodic warfare in Syria-Palestine against the rival Seleucids ("violence, . . . attack"), its seduction of the indigenous elite to compromise the traditional Judean way of life ("lead astray"), and the debilitating effects of all of these on Judean social-economic and personal life ("hurt . . . and illnesses"). The spirits of the giants are driving the imperial kings to the same destructive actions that the giants perpetrated in Enoch's time.

Enoch's Journeys to the Northwest and East

The rest of the Book of Watchers, virtually half of it (chaps. 17–36), continuing the dream-vision(s) of the previous section, is devoted to Enoch's journeys through the universe. The largely prose accounts are rooted in and draw upon astronomical, meteorological, and geographical "science" similar to what appears in the (older) Book of Luminaries. The journey narratives use particular facets of this spatial knowledge of the universe to give further assurance to the addressees that, although they are suffering devastation as a result of the rebel Watchers' actions, everything is in ultimate control under the divine governance. While the previous sections of the Book of Watchers focused on the control of the rebel Watchers and the violence of the giants, the visionary journeys give relatively more attention to the geography and topography of the earth with regard to the fate of humans.[28] Included are the mountain where the spirits of the dead (righteous and sinners) are sent (chap. 22); the mountain with the tree of life, the fragrance of which will enliven the righteous with longevity (24–25); the deep valley where the cursed will be gathered (26–27); and the mountain location of the tree of wisdom, from which the primordial father and mother ate and learned wisdom (28–32). The climax of the journey to the high mountain whose peak is like the throne of God indicates that all of this assurance is directed specifically to the "Enoch" scribes in Jerusalem (and whatever audience they may have reached).

Interpreters often overplay the "eschatology" of the Book of Watchers,[29] perhaps because it is usually classified as Judean "apocalyptic" literature. Yet the sections of the book do not seem to have a strong sense of urgency. They do display what might rather be called an "eschatological" *perspective*. In the journey section, for example, the spirits of the Watchers who mated with women will bring destruction on people "until the great judgment" (19:1). And at the judgment, God will visit the earth in goodness (25:3–4). But nothing in the narrative suggests that God is poised to act imminently. The principal message revealed in the journeys section, as in other sections of the Book of Watchers, is that cosmological wisdom revealed by the highest-ranking officers of God's universal government indicates that things are still ultimately under the control of the King of kings.

Perhaps it would help to distinguish the judgment of the rebel Watchers from the future "great judgment" in the Book of Watchers. The judgment (binding/ imprisonment/burning with fire) of the rebel Watchers for propagating the giants who caused such destruction has already been enacted, is permanent (10:11; 18:14–16; 19:1; 21:5, 10; 23:4), and will last at least until the day of judgment/ consummation (10:12; 18:14). The judgment of the giants, the sons of the rebel Watchers, has already taken place. They have been destroyed, partly by a mutual war of destruction (10:9, 15)—although now their spirits perpetuate the violence and desolation of people on the earth (15:8; 16:1). The souls of the dead, moreover, are already placed in the respective mountain hollows (chaps. 24–27).

The other expressions of judgment, future judgment that consists of blessings on the righteous and curses on the wicked, prominent in the introduction and the story of the Watchers' rebellion, are not much different from those in late prophetic texts such as Isaiah 65. The earth will be restored to productivity so that the righteous will live long lives, with no more sinning. The imagery in *1 Enoch* 5:5–9 and 10:11–11:2 or that of the fragrance from the tree of life is no more fantastic than that in Isaiah 65 or Jeremiah 31. The message is one of hope and perhaps consolation in difficult circumstances. But there is less of a sense of urgency or imminence than what emerges later in texts such as Daniel 7 and 10–12, where the empire is beastly in its brutal attacks and the scribes are being martyred for their resistance.

ANIMAL VISION (*1 ENOCH* 85–90)

Enoch's vision in *1 Enoch* 85–90 is ostensibly about predatory animals' and birds' attacks on sheep and the sheep's relationship with their lord. But these are signs transparent to the "real" (intended) referents in the history of Israel-Judeans' repeated experience of attacks by other nations, and the ups and downs of their relationship with God. The Animal Vision is similar to other visions in contemporary Judean texts. The Epistle of Enoch includes a briefer vision of Israelite/Judean history from its origins through destruction and perversion to glorious restoration in ten "weeks" (93:1–10; 91:11–17). And the book of Daniel includes several dream-visions of the sequence of empires focused on the violence suffered and the restoration experienced by Judeans (chaps. 2; 7; 8; 10–12). These overviews of international and/or Israel's problematic history leading to a final utopian outcome are all revelations, mainly via a seer's dream-vision. In most of the visions in Daniel a human or heavenly interpreter applies the dreams to historical events. The vision included in the Epistle of Enoch is presented simultaneously as "the words of the Watchers and holy ones" and what Enoch found written on heavenly tablets as well as what he saw in a vision (93:2). The vision of the animals, like that of the flood, is so transparent that it requires no interpreter.

In the broader Judean cultural repertoire, it is difficult to discern any texts that might have provided a model on which these visions of a broad sweep of international historical events were patterned. No instructional, reflective, or cosmological wisdom is present, unless we count the rebel stars and heavenly "shepherds," the objects of cosmological knowledge. The form of vision (with its interpretation) derives from mantic wisdom. It is possible that the older Mesopotamian divination by dream interpretation and by projection of future events based on accounts of past events (*vaticina ex eventu*) had an influence in Judean scribal circles concerned with current malaise and future deliverance.[30]

Beyond that, the influence from segments of traditional Judean culture appears to have been more indirect and general. Books such as Exodus, Joshua, and Judges presented the people's origins and identity in terms of historical struggles for life independent of foreign rule. Prophetic oracles established a connection between Judah's and Israel's rulers' failure to adhere to the covenantal principles in domestic political-economic life and attacks by foreign rulers.[31] Prophetic oracles in the collections of Jeremiah and Ezekiel also announced God's judgment against "(rulers of) the nations" for violence against conquered peoples and each other. Especially influential on later texts were the prophecies of "Isaiah" that represent God as the overall ruler of historical events and international relations, particularly as they bear on Israel/Judea. Prophets also presented images of God holding judgment over the nations (foreign rulers) and of the restoration of Zion/ Jerusalem.

Some key assumptions and procedures typical of standard biblical studies may not be appropriate to the Animal Vision. First, since the books later included in the Hebrew Bible were only some of the texts in a wider repertoire of Judean culture cultivated by professional scribes, we should not assume that the allegory is drawing its details as well as its general sequence of events from "biblical books."[32] The versions of history that we know from biblical books may, however, provide comparisons that help us discern the emphases in the Animal Vision's narrative. By such comparisons, for example, we notice that the primordial couple's disobedience of God's command and the Mosaic covenant at Sinai are missing. Second, since the Animal Vision has considerable narrative coherence as a sustained sequence of events, the significance of particular episodes depends on their function in the overall story. Indeed, key questions of interpretation would be the main problems that the story addresses, how they originated, and how they are resolved. Comparison with "biblical" parallels would be of secondary, ancillary importance.[33]

The problem on which the vision focuses is political: the imperial subjugation and exploitation of Judeans/Israel (to which the "blindness" of Judeans has contributed). The beasts and birds of prey signify the imperial rulers who have attacked Israel and Judeans militarily and oppressed them economically—in recent history the Babylonians, the Macedonians, specifically the Ptolemies and Seleucids (89:66; 90:2, 4, 11), and earlier the Egyptians and Philistines (89:15, 42).[34] In its opening section on primordial history, the vision explains the origin of violence as less from acts of disobedience by humans, as in Genesis 2–4, and mainly from superhuman heavenly forces. In the Enochic tradition of the Book of Watchers (esp. chaps. 6–11), the allegory attributes the origin of imperial violence to the descent of superhuman heavenly forces ("stars") to mate with women, producing predatory forces (elephants, camels, asses) that attack and devour people (86:1–6). Even though these predators are supposedly destroyed in the flood (89:6), violence and exploitation have thus been unleashed, now in attacks by powerful rulers against people over whom they wield power.

Closely related to imperial violence and oppression is the relation between the sheep/Israel and their Lord, particularly the blindness and straying of Israel/ Judeans. Insofar as religion is inseparable from political-economic relations prior to modern Western societies, the relation of Israel and its Lord should not be construed in narrowly religious terms. The vision focuses the relationship between the sheep and their Lord in their "house." The "house" of the sheep (89:40) does not refer to the temple in Jerusalem. The latter is clearly signified by the "large and high tower built on the house for the Lord of the sheep" (89:50, 54, 56, 66; cf. the other tower, high above the earth, 87:3). Insofar as the tower was built on the house (89:50) and the house is destroyed when the tower is burned (89:66), it evidently refers to the city of Jerusalem.[35] The reference, however, seems to be broader than the city.[36] The house appears to signify the "house" of the people, of Israel, originally established by the sheep-become-a-man, who signifies Moses (89:36).[37]

The recurrent theme of the sheep alternatively opening their eyes and seeing and then being blind and straying (from the path or from their house) indicates that Israel was supposed to adhere to the covenantal path that Moses had shown them (89:28–32; although no explicit reference is made to the covenant in connection with the Lord's appearance at Sinai.[38] As attested earlier in oracles of Amos, Micah, Isaiah, Jeremiah, this is what the prophets were sent to accuse the rulers of disobeying, clearly the reference in 89:51–53.[39] And it is the rulers' violation of covenantal principles for which God unleashes foreign imperial rulers to punish them, apparently the references of the sheep's abandonment of the house and the tower and of the Lord's abandonment of their house and tower in 89:54–58.

The two interrelated themes of the superhuman origins of violence and the relationship between God and Israel virtually merge in the vision's explanation of the extreme violence and oppression to which Judeans have been subjected under Babylonian and especially Ptolemaic and Seleucid imperial rule. The Lord of the sheep, who is also the imperial Lord of history, has abandoned his sheep (because they abandoned their house) and placed them under the rule of a sequence of seventy "shepherds" and their subordinates (89:59).[40] That is, superhuman heavenly forces that stand behind and give orders to the beastly imperial regimes are responsible for the extreme imperial violence. As in the Book of Watchers, moreover, God has here become a heavenly emperor so remote that he is no longer in control of his empire and must rely on a secret informant who audits the extent to which the imperial satraps abuse and destroy his subjects (89:61–64).

The climactic crisis of history comes in the fourth period under the shepherds, under Seleucid rule. The allegorical narrative suddenly moves into relatively specific references to groups and struggles. These almost certainly were involved in the events surrounding the Hellenizing reform under Antiochus IV, the resistance to it, and Antiochus's attempts to suppress the resistance that turned into rebellion. Insofar as the narrative identifies with the "lambs" who began to open their eyes and cry out to the sheep and thus precipitate the crisis (90:6), it seems likely that they were scribes, perhaps a circle who identified with the Enoch tradition in which the allegorical vision itself stands. If we follow the sequence of the allegorical narrative, the "lambs" who opened their eyes and other "sheep"[41] were active prior to the Hellenizing reform in 175 BCE. The deaf and blinded sheep (90:7) were probably the aristocratic faction(s) who spearheaded the reform. The Seleucid regime took violent repressive measures (90:8). But that only led to the group's armed resistance, which evoked even heavier imperial repressive measures (90:8–9). The big horn that sprouted on one of the sheep was almost certainly Judas the Maccabee, and a large number of others responded to his leadership in armed resistance, including some of the "lambs" who started the resistance (90:9–10). In response the Seleucids, urged on by all other Hellenistic forces, mounted a fuller war to suppress the rebellion (90:11–16).

At this point reference to historical events gives way to the anticipated action of God (90:17–27). That the blinded sheep who had opposed the awakened lambs were thrown into the abyss along with the overly destructive heavenly powers responsible for violence on earth (90:26–27) indicates just how serious their actions had been in the eyes of the producers of this vision. This condemnation of the priestly aristocracy in control of the Temple may have originated in the crisis touched off by the Hellenizing reform. But the intensity of the judgment against them may have run very deep in the Enoch circle of scribes. Earlier in the vision was a resounding declaration that the very establishment of the temple-state had been illegitimate. Besides the sheep having been blind, the tower they raised was only "called the high tower," and the bread on the table before it "was polluted and not pure" (89:72b–74).

At the end of the vision, moreover, the rejection of the Temple and high priesthood continues in the fantastic restoration and revitalization of the people, centered on the symbol of the house. After the old house was folded up and removed, "the Lord of the sheep brought a new house, larger and higher than that first one, and erected it on the site of the first one" (90:28–29). That the restored house of Israel is erected on the site of the old house (presumably in Jerusalem, at the center of Judea/Israel) makes it all the more striking that it has no temple. The original house in which the sheep all stood, in the time when the Lord was directly involved in their life, had no tower (89:28–36).[42] The new, enlarged and higher house that the Lord erects at the end has no high tower. With God now directly involved in the restoration of the people (God is "present" in "his" house, 90:33–36), there is no need of a temple.[43] That the vision imagines the renewal of Israel without the Temple confirms the impression given by the condemnation of the second temple as polluted, that its scribal producers went beyond opposition to the incumbent high priests to a rejection of the legitimacy of the second temple at the head of the Judean people.

THE EPISTLE OF ENOCH (*1 ENOCH* 92–105)

The "ten-week" vision in 93:1–10 and 91:10–17 frames the ensuing woes against the wealthy and encouragement to the righteous with an overview of history from origin to fulfillment. Absent the origin of imperial violence in superhuman heavenly forces and any mention of sin by primordial parents, "deceit and violence" arise in the second week (93:4) after the original righteousness until Enoch's time in the first week (93:3). In the third week history focuses on Israel (93:5). "A covenant for all generations" made in the fourth week (93:6) is the only explicit mention of the Mosaic covenant in the different texts that compose *1 Enoch*, although it seemed implicit in the Animal Vision. "The house of glory and kingdom built forever" in the fifth week suggests the people of Israel in their land around Jerusalem as much as the Temple (93:7). Its burning with fire in the eventful sixth week, on the other hand, alludes to the burning of the Temple by the

Babylonians (93:8). That the people stray from "wisdom" after the covenant was given suggests a scribal association of the two, as in the Deuteronomic tradition and Ben Sira's scribal circle. The mention of the man who ascends here as well as in the Animal Vision indicates that Elijah was an important figure in the "Enoch" circle as well as Ben Sira's.

Like the Animal Vision, the "ten-week" vision focuses on the historical polit-ical crisis, only the conflict is now with the high-priestly aristocracy instead of with the imperial rulers. "The chosen as witnesses of righteousness from the eter-nal plan of righteousness" who receive "sevenfold wisdom" in the climactic sev-enth week are surely the circle of Enoch scribes themselves (93:10). The "perverse generation" who arise first in the seventh week, after the burning of the house and the dispersion, appear to be the founders and heads of the temple-state, which the "Enoch" scribes reject here, as in the Animal Vision, in almost absolute terms ("all of its deeds are perverse," 93:9).

That the chosen who receive the sevenfold wisdom "will uproot the founda-tions of violence and the structure of deceit in it to execute judgment" here (93:10; 91:11; 4Q212 4.13–14), as in the Animal Vision, suggests that the "Enoch" people had launched some sort of serious resistance to the incumbent heads of the temple-state. And that there is no hint of a larger uprising or of Judas the Maccabee suggests that they began serious resistance before the Maccabean Revolt, and probably even before the Hellenizing reform. The "sword given to all the righteous to execute righteous judgment on all the wicked" in the eighth week (*1 En.* 91:12; 4Q212 4.15–16) suggests a significant new development: a more widespread revolt. That the wicked "will be delivered into their hands" (*1 En.* 91:12; 4Q212 4.17) suggests that the revolt is just underway, or else that it is being anticipated with eager expectation. If only anticipated, it would fit nicely with the woes and anticipated judgment articulated in the Epistle of Enoch.

The bulk of the Epistle consists of six discourses[44] that move from long series of woes against the wealthy for oppressing people, alternating with brief statements of hope to the righteous in the first and second (*1 En.* 94:6–96:3; 96:4–98:8); to long statements of reassurance to the righteous, interrupted by brief further woes against the sinners in the sixth (102:4–104:8). In between come a long series of woes against sinners for false teaching, with a warning about the judgment in the third discourse (98:9–100:10); a series of woes repeating the indictments of the wealthy for oppressive actions, with a description of the judgment in the fourth (99:11–100:6); and three woes followed by a long statement about the judgment in the fifth (100:7–102:3). The principal message of the whole sequence of woes and descriptions of judgment is to reassure the righteous that despite their suffer-ing God will eventually vindicate and restore them, while punishing the rich sin-ners, who stand under divine curse and condemnation.

That the Epistle is scribal-sapiential in its ethos and production is evident par-ticularly in the focus on writing and books in the conclusion (104:9–105:2) as well as the opening ("Written by Enoch the scribe . . . ," 92:1; cf. further empha-sis on books; 97:6; 98:7–8; 103:2; 104:1). In the fifth discourse, the kind of astronomical and meteorological wisdom that forms the main content of other Enoch texts is used in portraying judgment for sinners (100:10–102:3).

In these discourses, however, the scribal producers have taken over the traditional prophetic form of (series of) woes that first state the indictments against the ostensible addressees and then pronounce the corresponding sentence/punishment: "Woe to you who have done X . . . , for you shall receive Y . . . ."[45] Most of the examples of prophetic woes are found in the earliest layers of the books of Amos, Micah, Isaiah, and Habakkuk. The woes are indictments for violating Mosaic covenantal commandments and are followed by a statement of sentence/punishment. They thus seem closely related to prophetic covenantal lawsuits and are rooted in Mosaic covenantal tradition as it appears, for example, in Deuteronomic torah. The woes are pronounced against rulers or their representatives for their exploitation of peasants. While some are single woes/indictments plus statements of punishment (e.g., Isa. 5:8 + 8–9; 5:11–12 + 13; Mic. 2:1–2 + 3–5; Hab. 2:6 + 7–8), most come in sets of two, three, or four, followed by a statement of punishment (Isa. 5:18–19, 20, 21, 22–23 + 24; Amos 6:1–3, 4–6 + 7; Hab. 2:9–11, 12, 15 + 16–17, [and another woe] 19). In the discourses of the Epistle of Enoch, the woes come mostly in series of three to eight, each of which combines an indictment and a sentence, with some in sequences of four or five woes capped by a sentence.

The sequence of discourses in the Epistle of Enoch continues not just the form of the prophetic woes but the substance as well, especially of the indictments for closely related facets of economic and political oppression. "Enoch's" indictments are reminiscent of passages in prophetic books. For example, that the rich sinners "build their houses with sin/not with their own labor" (94:7; 99:13) calls to mind Jeremiah's indictment of King Jehoiakim: "Woe to him who builds his house by unrighteousness, . . . Who makes his neighbors work for nothing" (22:13). Insofar as scribes were cultivating the prophetic repertoire of Judean culture (as Ben Sira states), the "Enoch" scribes would have been familiar with this distinctive "register" of prophetic speech, from which they could formulate new woes against the wealthy in their own situation.

This is the best explanation for the dramatic similarities of themes and images that appear when we examine whole sets of woes in the Epistle of Enoch (and purposely do not isolate particular words, phrases, and motifs) and compare them with complete woe-passages and related oracles in the prophetic books with which the "Enoch" scribes were presumably familiar.[46] A particularly concise and explicit case is Micah 2:1–2, 3–5.

> Woe to those who devise wickedness and evil deeds on their beds!
> When the morning dawns, they perform it, because it is in their power.
> They covet fields, and seize them; houses, and take them away;
> They oppress householder and house, people and their inheritance. (alt.)

As illustrated explicitly in the third and fourth lines just quoted, the actions for which the rulers and their officers are indicted are violations of the command-

ments and mechanisms of the Mosaic covenant ("You shall not covet/steal," etc.,
and expropriation of inalienable God-given family inheritance, articulated, e.g.,
in Exod. 20:3–17 and Lev. 25).[47] The declaration of punishment (the "sentence"
of the covenantal lawsuit pronounced by the prophets) that follows this indictment in Micah 2:1–2, 3–5 also provides the most vivid illustration of how "the
punishment fits the crime" in these prophetic woes.[48]

The indictments in "Enoch's" woes, while often stated in somewhat more general terms, build upon and reflect just this prophetic tradition. The woes are
against the rich, who have acquired gold and silver (*1 En.* 94:7–8; 96:4; 97:8–10;
103:5–6). The wealthy are also the powerful (96:8). Their great wealth, the goods
in their houses, and the houses themselves have been acquired unjustly, by iniquity and violence, as they exploited their neighbors (94:6; 95:5; 96:7–8). They
have acquired the "finest of the wheat" that they "devour" and the fine wine that
they drink from bowls by plundering and stealing, by sin and deceit (96:5;
100:9). As with those indicted by Amos and other prophets, the wealthy accused
by "Enoch" have covetously schemed to defraud the lowly (lying awake plotting)
by manipulating oaths and both witnesses and weights in making loans (95:6).
Having forced the impoverished peasants into debt-slavery (98:4), they have even
managed the building of their houses with the labor of debt-slaves (94:6–7;
99:11–15). A striking case of how the punishment in store for the oppressors
matches what they have done to afflict their neighbors can be seen in the "burning with fire" in the opening woes of the fifth discourse (100:7–9; cf. 95:5).

That the wealthy sinners who engaged in such oppressive actions are also
accused of perversion of "the eternal covenant" and a rejection of "the foundation and eternal ancestral inheritance" (99:2, 14) may be yet another aspect of
the traditional prophetic indictments, which are rooted in criteria of the Mosaic
covenant. While "the eternal covenant," synonymous with "the true words," is
almost certainly broader in its reference than the Mosaic covenant, it includes
Mosaic covenantal law, judging from the blessing of those who do "the commandments of the Most High" (synonymous with "the words of the wise") that
concludes the discourse (99:10).[49] Despite the apparent avoidance of Mosaic
torah in Enoch texts, virtually all of the oppressive acts of the wealthy sinners in
the Epistle of Enoch are violations of covenantal commandments or mechanisms.
And (in contrast to the Animal Vision) the Apocalypse of Weeks that precedes
the sequence of woes in the Epistle of Enoch includes the giving of the (Mosaic)
"covenant for all generations" (93:6).

The "perversion of the eternal covenant" points to what is perhaps the most
significant development beyond the traditional prophetic indictments: "Enoch's"
emphasis on rejection of true, covenantal teaching. One set of woes in Isaiah
(5:18–24) charged the wealthy with falsehood as well as iniquity, with calling
"evil good and good evil," being "wise" in their own eyes, and rejecting "the
instruction of the Lord of hosts," as well as depriving the innocent of their rights.
The Epistle of Enoch devotes a whole series of woes to indictment of the
fools/sinners for "not listening to the wise" (*1 En.* 98:9–99:2). But they are not

simply violating the torah of God, as in Isaiah. They are more programmatically
"altering the true words." Indeed, they even engaged in scribal activity of producing books ("write lying words") and teaching ("lead many astray with their lies
when they hear them," 98:15). Assuming that those indicted in the woes in
the whole sequence of discourses are more or less the same people, the "wealthy/
sinners/fools" include scribes who cultivate legal teaching. The explicit emphasis
on true covenantal teaching versus lies suggests that rival scribes were associated
with the wealthy and powerful whom the Enoch scribes were condemning.

In the punishments connected with the indictments in the woes as well as in
the warnings to the sinners and the reassurances to the righteous come various
portrayals of judgment. That the oppressive wealthy and powerful will be
destroyed or have no peace (94:6; 96:8; 97:1; 99:16; 103:8) or that fathers and
sons will come into conflict (100:1–2) had become standard in earlier layers of
the repertoire of prophetic oracles.

That the nations would be thrown into confusion (99:4) and that judgment
and the associated theophany would include disruption of the luminaries and
weather patterns (100:10–13; 101:1–19; 102:1–2) are derivative from the later
prophetic repertoire—making it unnecessary and inappropriate to label them
"apocalyptic" features, as often done. That the righteous would participate in the
punishment of the sinners appears to be a scribal contribution to the scenario of
judgment (94:3; 98:12). New and distinctive in Enoch texts (and to the last section of Daniel) are the portrayals of the vindication and restoration of the righteous to "shine like the luminaries of heaven, . . . have great joy like the angels of
heaven, . . . and be companions of the host of heaven" (104:2–6). Such imagery
would appear to be a creative contribution of scribes whose own repertoire of wisdom included astronomical knowledge that they had used in explaining imperial
subjection of Judeans (further discussion in chap. 9).

With its woes and portrayals of judgment, the Epistle of Enoch provides the
best indications among the "Enoch" texts of the political conflict in which their
scribal producers were involved. The woes and judgment scenes of the Epistle have
previously been seen as involving two opposed groups, the wealthy sinners and the
righteous pious. It may be possible to delineate the conflict more precisely through
a careful analysis of the discourses against the backdrop of the historical situation
sketched in chapter 2 and the political-economic-religious structure of Judean
society gleaned from information in Sirach in chapter 3.

Consistently across the six discourses, the sinners indicted for acts of oppression and threatened with punishment are portrayed as the wealthy, the very
wealthy, with silver and gold, fancy houses, and lavish food and drink (94:7–8;
96:4–6, 8; 97:8–10; [98:1–3] 98:11; 99:12–13; 102:9; 103:5–6). They are also
the powerful (96:8) and, closely connected with "the rulers," they are able to
manipulate the courts to their own advantage (94:7; 97:8, 10; 103:14–15). One
suspects that some among the wealthy were also the rulers, including the judges,
as in Ben Sira's representation of the Judean aristocracy and in ancient Near Eastern societies in general.

In the third discourse the sinners are not only wealthy (with "good things to eat and drink," 98:11) but also engaged in scribal activity of teaching and writing (98:15). Insofar as such scribal activity was closely associated with the priests in charge of the Temple, scribes often being themselves priests or Levites and in any case engaged in the service of the temple-state, the sinners would appear to be aristocratic priests along with their scribal protégés. That the same, mainly priestly elite can be represented as wealthy and powerful in most literary contexts and then represented as priestly in another literary context in the Epistle of Enoch is merely a mirror image of the dual representation in Sirach. One further indication that the sinners condemned by the scribes who produced the Epistle were priests is the form in which they will be destroyed: "swallowed up in the earth" (99:2). This is a clear allusion to what happened to Korah, ancestor of the Levitical clan, who had challenged the Aaronide priesthood (Num. 16:23–35). This allusion suggests that at least part of the issue underlying the conflict was control of the priesthood among rival priestly factions. The Enoch scribes were attacking a faction of the wealthy priestly aristocracy (along with their scribal protégés)—and apparently the incumbent high-priestly family currently enjoying "honor and glory"—for "altering the true words and perverting the eternal covenant" (99:1–2).

Rhetorically the discourses address encouragement to "the righteous" in alternation with the woes against "the sinners." In order to determine whether "the righteous" are identical with those who are being oppressed and/or the wise, however, closer analysis of the indictments is necessary.

It seems fairly clear that "the wise" whom the sinners do not listen to (98:9) are (the associates of) the "Enoch" scribes who composed and cultivated the Epistle of Enoch. While "the wise among men who will see the truth" in 100:6 would appear to be a different, broader group of people than the "Enoch" scribal circle, the oath to "the wise" appears to be an aside addressed directly to the producers' circle, a tidbit of wisdom that stands out in contrast to the exhortations to the righteous to "fear not" or "be hopeful" elsewhere in these discourses (94:3; 96:1–3; 102:4–103:4). So who are "the righteous," and what is the relationship between "the wise" and "the righteous"?

Most of the specific and general indictments of the wealthy sinners do not identify their victims as "the righteous." Judging from some of the specific indictments, such as those about building their luxurious houses with unpaid labor, they were exploiting the peasants. And the peasantry made up the vast proportion of the population and would have been the people whom the wealthy and powerful could have manipulated into indebtedness and debt-slavery.

"The righteous" appear as victims of the wealthy and powerful in only a few instances. On the basis of the two instances in the third discourse, where the sinners "rejoice over the troubles of the righteous" and "annul the words of the righteous," the latter seem to be identical with the wise, whose words the fools do not heed (98:9, 13–14). And it would be understandable if the scribes articulating the indictments of the wealthy sinners were eager to be among "the righteous," to whom the sinners would be delivered to be slaughtered (98:12). On the other hand, the sinners' "persecution of the righteous" in the first discourse stands parallel to such actions as manipulating the scales in making fraudulent loans to peasants (95:4–7). And in the second discourse the wealthy sinners' "oppressing the righteous one" is parallel to acts such as using their power to "devour the finest of wheat," while "treading on the lowly," again evidently victimizing the peasants (96:4–8). Most problematic for taking "the righteous" as identical with the wise scribes is the concluding discourse. Since they are certain to be vindicated and restored by God, they are exhorted not to perpetually complain about their oppression, saying that they were "consumed," "destroyed," "powerless," and (most tellingly) were "not masters of their own labor" and became "food of the sinners," whose "yoke" weighed upon them (etc.; 103:9–12). All of these images suggest the typical relations of peasants and their lords, who use their power to exploit their labor and manipulate them into greater dependency, vulnerability, poverty, and servitude.

If the reference to "the righteous" is primarily to the lowly peasants, who were exploited in multiple ways by the wealthy, then it appears that the discourses in the Epistle of Enoch involve a three-way political-economic-religious relationship. The scribes, addressing other wise scribes in their circle, proclaim severe indictments and pronounce severe punishments against the wealthy and powerful for their merciless oppression of Judean peasants.[50] This is the same relationship evident in Ben Sira's instructional wisdom about almsgiving, the relations between rich and poor, and the relations of scribes and their wealthy aristocratic patrons. Like Ben Sira and his students, the "Enoch" circle of scribes may well see themselves as culturally superior to the peasants in their possession of special wisdom. And in their economic dependency these scribes are also vulnerable to the political power of aristocratic figures. Yet they are concerned about the ways in which the poor are exploited by the wealthy and powerful and feel a sense of responsibility to address such oppression. The wise scribes of the Epistle of Enoch even seem to identify themselves with "the righteous" oppressed, at one point referring to themselves with the same term (98:12–13).

In that sense, scribes of the Enoch tradition have become a great deal more alienated from the aristocracy than was the propagandist for the high priesthood of Simon son of Onias. Ben Sira encouraged his students to intervene on behalf of the poor when possible. The scribal producers of the Epistle of Enoch, drawing on the prophetic tradition of which they are the heirs, pronounce condemnation on the wealthy oppressors. Like the Ben Sira speeches, the Enoch woes accuse the wealthy of "murder" in so oppressing their neighbors that they take away their very life (99:15; cf. Sir. 34:25–27). Far beyond the rhetoric of Ben Sira, however, the Enoch woes declare that in the judgmental turning of the tables, the righteous will cut off the necks of the wealthy sinners. While Ben Sira discusses the issues in a more detached and reflective manner, the wise of the Epistle of Enoch take considerable satisfaction in anticipating the future destruction of the rich and the restoration of the righteous to the good life that the sinners deprived them of in the days of their tribulation.

Chapter 9

Daniel

After this I saw in the visions by night a fourth beast, terrifying and dreadful and exceedingly strong. It had great iron teeth and was devouring, breaking in pieces, and stamping what was left with its feet.

The wise among the people shall give understanding to many; for some days, however, they shall fall by sword and flame, and suffer captivity and plunder.

Daniel

The book of Daniel is all about imperial politics and how the wise scribes who produced such literature are caught in the middle of it.[1] This is more obvious in the tales and visions of Daniel than in the books that constitute *1 Enoch*. The introductory tale about Daniel and his associates and the final few steps of the closing vision in the book of Daniel vividly illustrate many of the main points already discussed in previous chapters.

First, literacy, the cultivation of a repertoire of high culture, and the production of literature were socially located and politically operative in circles of learned scribes. These intellectuals served as advisers and administrators in the imperial regimes of the ancient Near East, both in the central administration and in local institutions, such as the Jerusalem temple-state. "Daniel" and his Judean colleagues brought to Babylon from Judah were trained to take their places alongside other wise scribes "serving in the king's palace," and were supported economically by the regime (Dan. 1:4–6, 8, 19). Toward the end of the book's last section, the *maskilim,* "the wise among the people" who "give understanding to many," take the lead in opposition to the Judeans "who forsake the covenant" in alliance with the emperor (Dan. 11:30–35). The *maskilim* were thus apparently dissident retainers who came into conflict with the aristocratic faction that controlled the temple-state.

Second, these professional scribes were trained in a wide range of culture, including different kinds of wisdom. The young Judeans became "versed in every branch of wisdom, endowed with knowledge and insight," were thus "competent to serve in the king's palace," and were "taught the language and literature of the Chaldeans" (1:4).[2] Among the "branches" of wisdom was the skill in interpreting dreams and visions, which becomes central in the tales and visions that follow; Daniel proves to be more adept (in his God-given wisdom) than all "the dream interpreters and exorcists" of Babylon (1:17, 20; again in 5:12; cf. Sir. 39:1–2).[3]

Third, however, insofar as the imperial regimes encouraged or allowed the cultivation of indigenous Judean (Israelite) culture (including relations with the God of Israel), the scribal custodians of culture developed expressions of their own people's distinctive political-religious identity that conflicted with the culture and practices of the empire. And insofar as the learned scribes were the professional custodians of such culture, they developed a sense of their own authority separate from and independent of their authority as representatives of the rulers. Daniel and the other Judeans insisted on observing their distinctive purity code with regard to food (1:8–16). The final long vision in Daniel 10–12 illustrates how Judean sages who had cultivated dream interpretation in the interest of Judeans rather than the imperial regime understood the historical crisis in which they were involved.

Fourth, Judean scribes could use their own indigenous forms of wisdom, such as cosmological knowledge and dream-interpretation (often in combination with prophetic traditions), to give expression to the political-economic interests of the subjugated Judeans that conflicted directly with the interests and power of the ruling empire. Indeed, in a crisis of authority, dissident scribes were capable of mounting stubborn resistance to the oppressive and repressive practices of the empire and/or its client regime in Jerusalem. The *maskilim* stood firm in the covenant against the dominant aristocratic faction that, in collusion with the imperial regime, abandoned it (Dan. 11:28–35).

The rest of the tales and visions in Daniel, along with the introductory and concluding ones, indicate how learned scribes used some of the kinds of wisdom they cultivated and the prophetic tradition of which they were the heirs in resistance to imperial domination.

THE TALES IN DANIEL 1–6

The tales in Daniel 1–6 resemble court legends found in other scribal cultures subject to Eastern empires. Perhaps the most interesting parallels are the cycles of court legends focused on Croesus that circulated under the Lydian and Persian empires, as known through Herodotus and other Greek sources.[4] As in the legends in Daniel 1–6, a conquered nobleman becomes a wise administrator/adviser to a succession of kings. Stories of his wise deeds and sayings were cultivated by fellow members of his ruled ethnic group in a cycle of legends. These tales, told from the perspective of the ethnic scribal group subject to empire, assert the wisdom and exploits of their cultural hero, and the values and identity of the subject people.[5] The Persian court appears to provide the background context and "local color" detectable in several of these tales, both Judean and Lydian.[6] Professional scribes from subject peoples are known to have served in the Persian court and imperial administration. The occurrence of the term "Chaldeans" as signifying astrologers and diviners (Dan. 2:2–5, 10; cf., e.g., Diodorus Siculus 2.29–31), however, along with indications that the fourth empire in Daniel 2 must refer to the Hellenistic empire(s), suggests that the court legends of Daniel 1–6 as we have them date from the Hellenistic period.[7]

In the cycle of court legends in Daniel 1–6, the tales are of two subtypes: court contest and court conflict. Tales of conflict, Daniel 3 and 6, tell of rivals manipulating the culture hero (or heroes) into danger from which he (they) escapes by divine action. In the tales of contest, Daniel 2, 4, and 5, after rival wise men fail to interpret the king's dream or the writing on the wall, Daniel succeeds and is then exalted (or restored) to high(er) position. Within the common pattern, particular tales may emphasize different aspects.

The tales in Daniel 1–6, however, are all composite creations. The court contest in Daniel 2, for example, includes both a report and an interpretation of a dream, a political oracle, and a hymnic doxology. The contest story in Daniel 5 includes a prophetic indictment and a *pesher* (interpretation) of mysterious numinous writing instead of a dream. Most significantly, the interpretation of the statue in Daniel 2 announces God's termination of all empires, and the legends in Daniel 3, 4, and 5 all announce judgment of some sort against the emperor(s), which is not generally part of tales of court conflict.[8] In the Daniel tales, the genre of court legend has been combined and transformed with several other forms that all revolve around political conflict. The tales have creatively combined these traditional Israelite and/or ancient Near Eastern forms to present prophetic criticism of arrogant imperial rule from the Judean perspective of the universal rule of God. The various "additions" to Daniel and the variant versions of the book in ancient manuscripts offer abundant evidence of the continuing development of these court legends as "unstable" texts.[9] Earlier versions, moreover, exhibit even more intense political conflict than the apparently adjusted Masoretic version.

Considering that the cultivation of the elite cultural repertoire was carried out almost exclusively by scribes and the tales' focus on royal administrative skills and ideals, it is most likely that the tales were part of the lore specifically of scribes and scribes-in-training.[10] Insofar as they portrayed the conflict built into the power relations between Judean scribes and the dominant imperial culture, as represented by the king, the tales would have continued to resonate with scribes in the Jerusalem temple-state under the Hellenistic empires. We can explore the function of the tales in the imperial context by looking particularly for the principal message and the political conflict(s) (criticism of and accommodation to the king/empire) that each story articulates.

In Daniel 2, Daniel interprets Nebuchadnezzar's dream of the statue—with head of gold, chest of silver, middle of bronze, legs of iron, and feet of iron and clay, destroyed by the huge stone—to mean a succession of four empires that will be crushed by the coming kingdom of God. The tale makes two interrelated points, that God is ultimately in control of the empires that appear to control the lives of subject peoples, and that God reveals the overall plan for the course of history. As Nebuchadnezzar declares at the end of the tale, "Truly, your God [of Israel] is God of gods and Lord of kings and a revealer of mysteries" (2:47). The same two points are also articulated earlier in the doxology (2:21):

> [God] changes times and seasons,
>   deposes kings and sets up kings;
> he gives wisdom to the wise,
>   and knowledge to those who have understanding.[11]

The mystery of the dream, God's plan behind the succession of empires ruling the peoples of the earth, which God finally reveals to Daniel, is that God's own kingdom will finally destroy all the imperial kingdoms.[12]

The king's dream appears to have combined two different ancient Near Eastern schemes of a succession of empires. Ancient texts later than Daniel attest what was apparently a widely known scheme of four successive empires succeeded by a fifth, a scheme that originated prior to the tales of Daniel. The scheme was apparently used among several subject kingdoms under the Hellenistic empires as a sign of hope that they might finally regain their sovereignty.[13] The other scheme, whose imagery of four metals dominates here, was also widely known in the eastern Mediterranean.[14] The imagery of the metals signified a declining sequence of world ages, beginning with the age of gold, and pointed to a better age to come. Combined with the four-kingdoms scheme, the imagery signifies a declining sequence of empires to be replaced by a new golden age. The adapted scheme in Daniel 2 represents the Macedonian empire(s) as bringing a sharp escalation in violence against subject peoples, as it "crushes and smashes everything" (Dan. 2:40). And the stone that smashes all the metals would be the kingdom of the God of the Judeans, who would presumably be regaining their independence. Far from being "almost incidental to the message of the chapter,"[15] the political content of the dream and interpretation are another expression of the God of the Judeans as the true sovereign of history. "He deposes kings . . . ; he gives wisdom to the wise."

The ending of the tale in Daniel 2, following the pattern of a court contest, does not fit the interpretation of the king's dream. The lack of fit may be significant for understanding the tale's message. Because Daniel's God has revealed the meaning of his dream, Nebuchadnezzar worships and promotes Daniel to the highest scribal-administrative office in Babylon and confesses that Daniel's God is the Lord of kings. But, as the tellers and hearers of the tale know well, if he had been listening to Daniel's interpretation of his dream, that the Lord of kings was about to crush his empire along with all the others (2:44–45), the Babylonian emperor who had conquered and destroyed Jerusalem would have had Daniel executed for treason. In contrast to those who tell and hear the tale, the king does not seem to recognize that his kingdom is doomed. But to portray the king as clueless at the end of the story fits the sharply negative portrayal at the outset, where the king is utterly irrational in refusing to disclose his dream so that the magicians and exorcists can interpret it and then flies into a violent rage (2:4–12).[16]

What modern scholars call idolatry was not merely a religious matter. Idols were symbols of divinized forces (sun, moon, storm, et al.) that people were not just worshiping but also serving in a political-economic sense. The colossal golden statue that Nebuchadnezzar erected in Daniel 3 was a symbol of his imperial rule. This could not be clearer when he summons all of the imperial officers of every level in all the provinces to its dedication and then has the herald proclaim that all the subject peoples and nations are to do obeisance, even by prostrating themselves before the statue (note the elaborate list; 3:2–6). This is a highly symbolic ceremonial act of loyalty to the emperor, inseparably political and religious.[17] But affirming religious-political loyalty and service of imperial kingship is precisely what the Judean scribal administrators of Babylon refuse to do. The Chaldeans who denounce them, moreover, point out exactly where the conflict lies: "They do not serve your gods," meaning the gods of the empire (3:12; cf. Esth. 3:8); that is, they are disloyal subversives. The Judeans have no defense. Because they serve their own God (sovereign over all kings/kingship), they cannot serve his gods, and they refuse to worship the symbol of his arrogant and totalitarian imperial rule (3:16–18, 28). The story of the fiery furnace, which in tone is a comic parody of a blustering old tyrant, does not have the king punished for his presumptuous imperial arrogance. But it does condemn arrogant imperial rule and encourage firm resistance to imperial institutions designed to induce and enforce the Judean sages' loyalty to the empire.[18]

The imperial arrogance of King Nebuchadnezzar is also the focus of the tale in Daniel 4, only this time the king is punished by a divinely decreed sentence until he acknowledges the sovereignty of the Most High. The theme of God's sovereignty recurs throughout the tale, in the king's hymnic confession at the beginning and the end (4:3, 34–35, 37), in the sentence given by the divine council of watchers/holy ones in the king's dream (4:17), and in the interpretation of the dream (4:25). The point about the repeated assertion of the divine sovereignty, however, is that God humiliated the arrogant king for his pretentious expansion of his own imperial rule (4:22).

The king's dream about a tree at the center of the earth that reaches to heaven and its cutting down (4:10–12, 14–17) on which the story focuses is deeply rooted in Israelite prophetic tradition. The image of a great tree as a symbol for empire is widespread in the ancient Near East; Babylon is thus compared to a great tree in the Building Inscription of Nebuchadnezzar.[19] Late Judahite prophecy turns the image against the empires in oracles of judgment.[20] Also derived from the prophetic tradition is Daniel's oracular admonition to the king that he atone for his sins with righteousness and for his iniquities with mercy to the oppressed (4:27; cf. Isa. 1:17).

The humiliation of Nebuchadnezzar, who was famous for his building projects (4:30; possible only with forced labor), inverts the earlier prophetic image that God had "given him even the wild animals of the field to serve him" (Jer. 27:6; Dan. 4:25, 33). The king is transformed into the most docile and obedient of his previous subjects, eating grass like an ox (a beast who labors under the lash in agriculture and in construction of royal buildings). Recent research suggests that Nebuchadnezzar's transformation into a beast turns the Mesopotamian myth of a primordial human figure on its head. In Mesopotamian mythic tradition, a primordial animal-like human (e.g., Enkidu, in the Gilgamesh epic) is transformed into the founder of civilization, the apex of which is the king of Babylon, builder of cities (as in Nebuchadnezzar's ideology).[21] The tale in Daniel 4 portrays the exact reverse: the great builder of cities, especially the magnificent Babylon as imperial capital, obsessed with his imperial power and glorious majesty (4:29–30), is made to eat grass like an ox. Understood against this background, the tale is an even more pointed condemnation of imperial rule.

The courtly contest legend in Daniel 5 is scarcely more than an ill-suited framework for a prophetic indictment and sentencing of Belshazzar. It is also the Judean story/text closest to the prominent Babylonian scribal practice of interpreting omens, in this case "the hand writing on the wall" (5:5–6, 24). In this tale Daniel interprets an omen instead of a dream. Yet his interpretation sounds more like a prophetic lawsuit of the Hebrew prophets than an omen interpretation of Babylonian diviners. After reciting previous history of God's favor and the previous king's (Nebuchadnezzar's) oppressive violence against his subjects (5:18–21), Daniel then delivers an indictment against Belshazzar for similar arrogance (5:22–23). The interpretation of the words written on the wall finally pronounces the sentence: God has brought his rule to an end, the king has been found guilty, and his kingdom is to be divided and given to others (5:24–27).

Again in the story of "Daniel in the lions' den" in Daniel 6 the conflict with the imperial regime and its institutional forms is severe, even though the king himself, Darius the Mede (historically a Persian emperor), is favorably disposed to Daniel. As in the story of the fiery furnace (Daniel 3) the imperial regime claims the highest authority, enforced by the requirement that subject people pray to and otherwise express exclusive ritual loyalty to the emperor, even if the emperor himself does not insist on it. The point of vulnerability for Daniel was his determination to observe "the law of his God" (6:5, 10–13). The tale in Daniel 6 provided a model of the great sage who remained unflinchingly faithful to his God despite the threat of death—with the fantasy-resolution that the emperor himself came to recognize that the God of Daniel was the true, eternal sovereign.

If we had any doubt that these tales are not just about issues of religion but are also about imperial politics, we need only consider the importance of dreams and omens to ancient Near Eastern emperors. Dreams and omens were understood as the means by which the divine powers that determined political-economic affairs were communicating about present and future events. That is why imperial regimes maintained a large staff of professionally trained experts among their scribal retainers to interpret both dreams and omens. In these tales generally the prototypical Judean dream interpreter, by his God-given wisdom, turns the tables on the usual interpretation of dreams and omens in the imperial court, declaring that because of imperial overreach, the emperor is to be humiliated or killed and/or that the empire is to be destroyed.[22]

The legends of the great Judean scribal hero Daniel (and his companions) provided Judean scribes with a model of unflinching trust in their God, even in circumstances where they were under intense pressure to compromise their traditional way of life and give complete allegiance to the emperor.[23] Daniel-stories also offered a paradigm of "speaking truth to power" on the basis of the wisdom God revealed to them, even when it would presumably evoke violent repression from the emperor. And the tales of Daniel gave a message of hope that their God was still ultimately in control of history (and would eventually judge the empires) even in circumstances of imperial power relations that forced them into serious accommodation to imperial rule. These legends would thus surely have bolstered the determination of some of the dissident Jerusalem scribes who eventually broke with the dominant faction in the Jerusalem aristocracy in the early second century.

THE VISIONS IN DANIEL 7–12

Despite his portrayal as a wise scribe in the tales, Daniel was understood as a prophet in late second-temple times. Josephus pronounced him "one of the greatest prophets," because he not only prophesied events of future deliverance, but also announced when the events would take place (*Ant.* 10.11.7; cf. Matt. 24:15; 4QFlor 2.3–4).

This understanding of Daniel as a prophet is entirely appropriate since the visions in Daniel 7–12 are a development of prophetic tradition. The symbolic vision form has deep roots in Israelite prophetic tradition, judging from the visions in Amos 7:1–9; 8:1–3.[24] In the more elaborate visions of Zechariah 1–6 (and Ezekiel, esp. 40–48) a heavenly messenger appears to interpret the significance of the images to the prophet. Substantively, moreover, the visions-and-interpretation in Zechariah 1:7–17; 2:1–4 (1:18–21E); and 6:1–8 are international in scope, and the basic message is of divine succor and protection of a Judea still devastated by imperial armies.

The accounts in Daniel 7 and 8 begin with elaborate visions (7:2–14, continued in 7:19–22), the "interpretation" of which is then given by "one of the attendants" (in the heavenly court; 7:16–18, continued in 7:23–27) or the divine messenger Gabriel (8:19–26). The "word" revealed to Daniel in the account in Daniel 10–12 also entails understanding "received in the vision," but consists mostly of Gabriel's narrative from "the book of truth" (10:21; 11:2–12:3). The vision in 7:2–14 includes a vision of the throne of God and the divine court sitting in judgment (7:9–10), a scene that had long become standard in prophetic tradition (e.g., Micaiah's vision in 1 Kings 22; Ezek. 1; Isa. 40:1–12). The

accounts in Daniel 8, 9, and 10–12 also include "appearances" by a divine messenger (8:15–17; 9:21–23; 10:5–14), with features that resemble appearances of
God ("theophanies") coming in judgment in prophetic oracles. The human
appearance of the divine messenger is also a continuation of prophetic tradition
(Ezek. 1; 8:2; 10:2; Zech. 1:10–11; 2:1–5).

The visions with interpretation in Daniel 7–12 also have "clear affinities" with
Babylonian dream interpretation. Most obvious is the framing of the dream and
interpretation by indicating the circumstances in which the vision was received
and the disturbed reaction of the visionary at the beginning and end of the
account.[25] The substance of the revelation in the interpretations in Daniel 7–12,
moreover, takes the form of predictions after the fact (*ex eventu* prophecies) of
the rise and fall of kings and kingdoms/empires. Much of this predictive material has the stereotyped form of "a king shall arise."[26] This form of "dynastic" or
"regnal prophecy" is also quite familiar from collections of Akkadian prophecy.
A significant example from Hellenistic Babylon is the Dynastic Prophecy.[27] This
Babylonian background is only fitting for "Daniel," the prophet-sage who is
receiving these visions, since he had supposedly lived and worked in the Babylonian imperial court.

The broad spectrum of the Judean cultural repertoire included texts that
sharply criticized dreams (e.g., Deut. 13:2–6 [1–5E]; Jer. 27:9–10; 29:8–9).
Some, perhaps many among scribes contemporary with the *maskilim* who cultivated Daniel lore, were suspicious of dream interpretation (e.g., Ben Sira, in Sir.
34:1–8). Even the *maskilim* who produced Daniel 7–12 distinguished themselves
from Babylonian and other dream interpretation by insisting that dreams were
not understood by human interpretation, but only by divine disclosure, wisdom
given by God and/or communicated through a divine agent.

It may be impossible to determine whether visionary experiences underlie the
vision accounts in Daniel 7–12, which are deeply rooted in Judean prophetic tradition long cultivated in scribal circles. The portrayal of the vision in Daniel 10,
for example, which is partially modeled on Ezekiel's visions, has features charac-
teristic of visionary experiences in other societies, some of which do not appear
in Israelite prophetic visions, such as mourning, fasting, and falling into a deep
sleep. These are particularly striking insofar as comparative cases show that
visionary experience tends to flourish in historical circumstances where subject
peoples are being oppressed and/or their traditional way of life suppressed by outside forces. The crisis of Hellenizing reform by the Jerusalem aristocracy and
Antiochus Epiphanes' attempt to suppress the traditional Judean way of life probably placed many of the scribes dedicated to cultivation of the traditional Judean
way of life in an impossible dilemma.

Although the Animal Vision and the "ten-week vision" in *1 Enoch* surveyed
history from its origins to its glorious fulfillment, the vision-and-interpretation
accounts in Daniel 7–12 limit their scope to the second-temple period. This may
simply be a function of the *maskilim* having had the figure of Daniel, whom legends placed in the Babylonian and Persian courts, as the source of the visions. It

might also suggest that the *maskilim,* who identified with Daniel as the proto-typical sage, thought mainly in terms of the Judean people under one empire after another in second-temple times. Although the visions or interpretations refer to "the law" and "the holy covenant," they give little or no indication that those are the Mosaic law or covenant, and Mosaic torah plays no role in the visions or reviews of history. Similarly, although the visions are developments of traditional prophetic forms, no prophet or prophetic book plays a role except that of Jeremiah about the seventy years, which had become well known, apparently, in second-temple times.

The visions-and-interpretations are all struggling to understand the crisis of Antiochus Epiphanes' attacks on Jerusalem and the Temple.[28] The sequence of the four visions matches Antiochus Epiphanes' escalation of the attacks on Jerusalem and the resistance by the *maskilim* themselves. The vision in Daniel 7 focuses on Antiochus's violent attack on the holy ones, including his attempt "to change the sacred seasons and the law." Yet since it does not mention an attack on the Temple offerings and sacrifices, it may be dated after Antiochus's attacks in 169 and 168 BCE, but before his more systematic attempt to suppress the operation of the Temple. Correspondingly, its message of hope is a general one, that the God will destroy the unprecedently violent imperial regime and give sovereignty to the Judean people. The vision in Daniel 8 (two years later; 8:1) and the interpretation of the seventy years in Daniel 9, both of which mention the suppression of the regular burnt offering and the abomination that desolates, were evidently responding to the escalated crisis (cf. 1 Macc. 1:41–61; 2 Macc. 6:1–6). The principal question that both address is "how long" the imperial violence against the people and the institutional observances that constitute their traditional way of life will last (8:13–14, 25; 9:24–27). The final survey of imperial history also focuses on the escalated crisis of abolishing the burnt offering and setting up the desolating abomination (11:31) and the martyr deaths of *maskilim* who have engaged in steadfast resistance to the imperial violence (11:32–35). Indeed, the envisaged resolution to the crisis now focuses mainly on what will happen to the martyred *maskilim* (12:1–3). We limit discussion to Daniel 7 and 10–12.

Daniel 7

In his thorough research into the wider cultural context of the visions in Daniel 7–12, John Collins finds the key to Daniel 7 in Canaanite myth. The beasts "are embodiments of the primeval power of chaos symbolized by the sea."[29] The basic meaning of the dream is thus that "creation is threatened by the eruption of the beasts from the sea, but the threat will be overcome by the rider on the clouds." Although the beasts do symbolize kings/kingdoms, the dream "assimilated a historical situation to a mythic pattern."[30]

The significance of the dream, however, presumably arises from its most prominent images and from how the narrative unfolds. After mentioning in only one phrase that the beasts arose from the sea, the narrative gives an elaborate description of each of the beasts, with escalating emphasis on their extremely destructive violence and ravenous appetite. The portrayal of the fourth beast and its little horn is twice as long as that of the previous three beasts and as long as the whole ensuing judgment scene. The destructive and devouring warlike beasts are the controlling images of the dream. The interpretation of the dream laid out in 7:17–18, 23–27, moreover, is explicitly political. The "attendant" tells Daniel explicitly that the four great beasts are the great empires that had ruled Judea and the ancient Near East,[31] and that the "little horn" coming up out of the severely violent fourth beast is the emperor who was threatening the Judean temple-state and its law (7:17, 25). The dream account is less "a powerful portrayal of chaos unleashed"[32] than a vivid portrayal of the political and military power of the imperial kings whose domination of Judea had become increasingly violent under the Hellenistic regimes.[33]

Representation of imperial kings as predatory beasts was already well established in Israelite prophetic tradition. In Hosea (13:7–8) Israel's own king, Yahweh, threatens to step into the role of a ferocious lion, leopard, or bear. Ezekiel (34) attests an already standard portrayal of Israel's imperial rulers as predatory animals. More directly to the point of the imagery in Daniel 7, prophecies in Jeremiah represent the Assyrian Empire and/or the Babylonian Empire as lions who destroy nations, lay waste the land, devour the sheep (Israel) and gnaw its bones (4:5–8; and esp. 50:17–20, where God will punish the king of Babylon and restore Israel!). Horns, such as those on the severely destructive fourth beast in Daniel's dream, also symbolized imperial power and violence. Coins of the first Seleucid emperors display the royal heads wearing horned helmets.[34] In early second-temple texts, one of Zechariah's visions deals with the horns that had "scattered Judah, Israel, and Jerusalem" (2:1–4; 1:18–21E).

The sequence of beasts/empires and their escalating violence and destruction climaxes in the fourth beast and "the little horn." It was "terrifying and dreadful and exceedingly strong" (Dan. 7:7). Its "great iron teeth" along with "its claws of bronze" in the continuation of the dream (7:19) symbolized not simply strength, but also an insatiable appetite for violent destruction that was utterly out of control, "devouring, breaking in pieces, and stamping what was left with its feet" (7:7, repeated in 7:19).[35] On the basis of comparison with contemporary textual references, it is clear that the little horn is Antiochus Epiphanes. His arrogant speech surely referred to his attacks on Jerusalem, a city specially sacred to God, but probably also his treatment of other gods and sacred institutions (referenced in Dan. 11:36–39). The climactic image, that the little horn "made war with the holy ones and was prevailing over them" (7:19–21), refers to his attack on the temple-state in Jerusalem.

The dream shifts dramatically to the heavenly court of judgment and the destruction of the terribly rapacious and devastating fourth beast. The portrayal of the throne of God as the focus of a wider scene of the heavenly court[36] in 7:9–10, like the closely parallel one in *1 Enoch* 14:8–23, is rooted in long prophetic tradition that emerges in such texts as 1 Kings 22:19; Isaiah 6; 40:1–11;

Ezekiel 1–3. Both portrayals attest a considerable further development of the previously standard register of language dedicated to prophetic visions of the heavenly court.[37] The throne of God was thus an integral part of the scene in which a prophet received a commission from God to proclaim an oracle, as in *1 Enoch* 14–16 (cf. Isa. 6; 40:1–11; Ezek. 1–3), and/or of the scene of judgment in the heavenly court, as in Daniel 7:9–10 (cf. 1 Kings 22).[38] Thus in Daniel 7:9–10, as in *1 Enoch* 90:20–27, the sight of the throne set up signals that God is finally arriving in a court of judgment, where the oppressive and destructive imperial rulers will be destroyed.[39]

That the judgment begins with the opening of the books lends a distinctively scribal touch to what is otherwise a prophetic vision (Dan. 7:10). Scribes knew writing as an instrument by which rulers kept records that were used in controlling their peoples. Thus, like the "Enoch" scribes who produced the Animal Vision (*1 En.* 89:61–64), so too the "Daniel" scribes could project numinous writing into the heavenly imperial court, where God, while seemingly not in control at present, had been keeping records of earthly imperial oppression that would eventually be used in judgment. Heavenly books, moreover, have here expanded their function from intra-Israelite social-economic relations to "international" political-economic relations between Judeans and their imperial rulers. In the judgment not only is the superviolent fourth beast destroyed, but the other beastly empires also are disempowered, their dominion taken away (7:11–12).

In the final scene of the dream (7:13–14) "one like a human being coming with the clouds of heaven" comes before the Ancient One and receives an everlasting sovereignty. Although the image of "coming with the clouds of heaven" resembles "rider of the clouds,"[40] the representation of the humanlike figure in Daniel's dream stands in contrast rather than similarity to that of the Canaanite Lord Storm. The latter is a violent warrior who defeats and slays Sea, and threatens violent destruction to any who challenge the order he imposes. The humanlike figure, on the other hand, emerges in the dream narrative as a pointed contrast with the violent beasts, whom Lord Storm of Canaanite myth resembles. The humanlike figure, like Lord Storm, receives an everlasting sovereignty. But nothing in the dream indicates that this figure has any role in the defeat and killing of the fourth beast who arises from the sea. The beast is put to death before the humanlike one appears (7:11, 13). If anything, the humanlike figure is a pointed contrast with Lord Storm, who may have been lurking in the cultural background of the Syrian Ba'al Shamem/Zeus Olympus to whom Antiochus Epiphanes was devoted[41]— something of which the *maskilim* would have been aware.

In the ensuing interpretation of the dream by the heavenly attendant (7:17–18) "the humanlike figure" to whom sovereignty was given is taken to indicate "the holy ones of the Most High." These must be the same "holy ones (of the Most High)" that the little horn attacks in 7:21, 25 and that receive the kingdom in 7:22. In the elaborated interpretation "the humanlike figure" who receives the kingdom and dominion is said to be "the people of the holy ones of the Most High" (7:27). According to the traditional interpretation, "the holy ones of the Most High" were simply the faithful Jews, who were under attack. In a survey of Judean texts earlier than and contemporary with Daniel (including the Dead Sea Scrolls), Collins has argued that "the holy ones (of the Most High)" refer rather to celestial beings, albeit heavenly figures "associated with God and with faithful Judeans.[42] Those other Judean texts, however, also indicate that these "celestial beings" played an important role in the Judean cultural understanding of God's governance of history.

In prophetic literature, when Yahweh comes to deliver or to punish Israel, he commands a heavenly "host." In the later prophecy of Zechariah (14:5; cf. Deut. 33:2), these "holy ones" assist Yahweh in battle against would-be imperial conquerors. Enoch literature has "the holy ones" parallel to or identical with "the Watchers," who are charged with assisting God in governing the universe and human affairs, with special attention to Judea, including mediation of privileged knowledge to Enoch (1 En. 1:2; 93:2; 106:19; cf. Dan. 4:13–17). Certain figures among those heavenly forces have special responsibility for or give special attention to Judea, even to communication with scribes such as Enoch, to be written down for later generations. Daniel 7 portrays "the holy ones of the Most High" as sharing God's special attachment to and concern for the Judean temple-state in Jerusalem. With "the Ancient One" having become relatively distant in exercise of ultimate control in governance of the universe, "the holy ones" had become the more immediate heavenly forces representing the Judean temple-state. Indeed they appear almost to be the heavenly reflection or counterpart of Judean society.[43]

Thus in Daniel 7 when the "little horn," Antiochus Epiphanes, arrogantly challenges the divine governance of history that operates through the heavenly beings and attacks the Jerusalem temple-state, he is also making war on the holy ones. In the dream imagery, when the Ancient One finally acts in judgment to destroy the violent beast and gives dominion to the "humanlike" figure, it is clear that the holy ones have been given sovereignty.[44] And since they represent the (faithful) Judeans, this also means that the latter as "*the people* of the holy ones of the Most High" are (also) to receive the kingdom.

The imperial attack on the temple-state in the dream and its interpretation, finally, is far broader than religious persecution. The imagery of the dream symbolizes the political-economic dimensions of military violence and the extreme devastation of human life and its material basis. Yet to some biblical interpreters (of 7:25), to "speak words against the Most High" seems like mere "blasphemy," and to "change the times [NRSV: sacred seasons] and the law" (RSV) seems to be "religious innovation," "disruption of the cultic calendar."[45]

Once we recognize that the religious and political-economic dimensions were inseparable in Daniel 7 as in the Jerusalem temple-state, however, we can better appreciate the full import of the phrases in 7:25. "Speaking words against the Most High" was tantamount to declaring war against "the head of state" and the divine symbol of the temple-state—who in this case was the God of Israel, who Judean visionaries believed presided over history. "Changing the times and the law" meant changing the very "constitution" of the society and temple-state. To "wear out [afflict] the holy ones of the Most High" was to attack the heavenly forces that represented and were guardians and defenders of the Judean temple-state and its people. That Antiochus had "power over them" (lit., "They will be given into his hand") sums it all up: a foreign ruler had brought them under his power, which means they were no longer directly and exclusively under the power of their God, as well as their guardian celestial forces and their own "constitution." This is the desperate situation that the dream and its interpretation in Daniel 7 are struggling with.

Daniel 10–12

Far from Daniel 10–12 having an otherworldly orientation, as previously often claimed about apocalyptic literature in general, it is concerned directly with the events of history, specifically the history of imperial rule of Judea. The narrative comes with a threefold authority: it originated in a vision, it is narrated by a heavenly messenger, and it comes from the numinous heavenly "book of truth"—and Daniel himself records the revelation in a sealed book (10:1, 21; cf. *1 En.* 93:1–2). The detailed narrative of events is a remarkably accurate sketch of the wars between the Ptolemies and the Seleucids leading up to Antiochus Epiphanes.[46] As with the other visions, the focus is on Antiochus Epiphanes' attack on Jerusalem and the Temple, which occupies more than half of the narrative. At height of the crisis and at the divine judgment, the focus widens to include the Judeans who are resisting the imperial attacks, especially the *maskilim* who produced (and were addressed by) these visions (11:31–35; 12:1–3).

Since the narrative's principal concern is the series of events leading to the current crisis, it moves quickly from the early wars between the Ptolemies ("king of the south") and the Seleucids ("king of the north") into the campaigns of Antiochus III (the Great) to take over Syria-Palestine and Judea (11:14–19). While the dream images of Daniel 7 and 8 emphasized the violence and destructiveness of the imperial forces, the portrayal in Daniel 11 repeatedly stresses their irresistibility (e.g., 11:15–16). The contemptible, scheming, and deceitful Antiochus Epiphanes' use of military force is utterly overwhelming (11:20–22). Desperate for revenues, but also needing to consolidate his hold on subject cities, Antiochus plundered temples in some cities in order to lavish gifts on others (11:24).

In its account of Antiochus's invasion of Jerusalem, intrigue with the reform party, and attacks on Temple and resistant Judeans, the narrative refers repeatedly to "the covenant." While covenant was discussed primarily in terms of obedience to Mosaic torah in Sirach, "the holy covenant" in the narrative of Daniel 11 refers more to the "constitution" of Judean society broadly conceived:[47] the bond(s) that hold the people together with God and each other and the institutions of the temple-state, high priesthood, and Temple. Thus "the chief(tain, *nāgîd*) of the covenant," whom Antiochus kills (11:22), is the high priest, God's regent in Judea; "those who violate [forsake] the covenant" (cf. 11:32; and 11:23, "a small party") are those who cut the deal with Antiochus to depose Onias III and to transform the constitution and culture of Jerusalem; and in the emperor's intent to subvert and "take action against the covenant" (11:28, 30), "covenant" represents the Judean body-politic and its constitution, which Antiochus attacks after he is defeated by the Romans in Egypt.

Interwoven with the narrative's focus of Antiochus's attack against the holy covenant is a second focus on the roles of various groups of Judeans involved in the climactic events of the crisis (11:30–35), especially the *maskilim*.[48] Those who forsake and violate the holy covenant (11:30, 32) must have been primarily the dominant faction among the priestly aristocracy, who with the backing of Antiochus had transformed Jerusalem into a polis. Since he had backed the "reform" and then Menelaus's seizure of power from Jason, Antiochus's control of Jerusalem depended on the success of Menelaus and his faction in maintaining power. It is conceivable that the occasion of the king's listening to their advice (11:30) was their desperation to maintain control of the city against Jason's attempt to take over while Antiochus was waging war in Egypt—and/or their struggles against resistance by other groups, such as "the sheep whose eyes were opened," who had already taken up resistance (*1 En.* 90:6–9). Keeping an aristocratic faction in some semblance of control in Jerusalem would have required some mutual manipulation ("seduce . . . with flattery," 11:32 RSV). Just at this point the narrative refers to the steps Antiochus took to assert his own and his aristocratic allies' control, measures that the king may have taken over two years' time (168–167 BCE): he attacked the Temple, which was fortified (hardly just a "religious" institution); discontinued the traditional cultivation of rituals in honor of God, centered in the daily offerings; and set up the "desolating abomination" (au. trans.), which was apparently an alien altar erected on the great altar of the Temple.

"The people who are loyal to their God" (11:32) were apparently all of those who remained faithful to the traditional way of life and central institutions. In prophetic tradition "knowing God" refers to keeping or being obedient to the covenant with God (cf. Isa. 1:2–3). That they "stand firm and take action" clearly suggests that they were resisting the invasion and repressive measures of Antiochus. It is inappropriate to use the violent revolt led by the Maccabees as a foil here, since it may not have started yet at the time Daniel 10–12 was produced. The Hebrew verb ("stand firm") ranges in usage from "be strong/resolute" to "engage in battle" (1QM 10.5–6). The action that the people loyal to God were taking would certainly appear to have been more "resolute" than passively waiting until some form of persecution came to them.

The "wise among the people" (*maskilim*), who "gave understanding to many," are usually identified as those who produced and identified with the visions of Daniel 7–12; they must have been a circle of scribes, somewhat like the ancient hero they identified with in the tales (Dan. 1–6). Learned scribes ordinarily communicated their wisdom among other scribes. Given the crisis in which precisely the dominant aristocratic faction had "abandoned the holy covenant," however, they attempted to explain to others the revelation they had received about what was happening in the violent imperial attacks. Given the political-economic structure of Judean society, the vague term "the many" most likely refers to ordinary (nonscribal) Jerusalemites, such as artisans, whose livelihood was dependent on the Temple and high priesthood (but not peasants in outlying villages). Not only would the Jerusalemites have been familiar to the *maskilim* in a small city such as Jerusalem, but also their social role and livelihood, like those of the scribes, would likely have been threatened by the transformation of Jerusalem into a Hellenistic polis.[49]

That the *maskilim* "for some days . . . fall by sword and flame, and suffer captivity and plunder" indicates that their resistance was steadfast and persistent, and that they were being hunted down, captured, and executed—becoming martyrs (cf. 1 Macc. 1:63). Most modern interpreters have taken "(a) little help" in Daniel 11:34 as a reference to the Maccabean leaders. The Maccabean Revolt, however, had probably not begun yet when Daniel 10–12 was composed. The statement says rather that when the *maskilim* fall, they will receive little help from anyone,[50] which fits better with the ensuing assertion that many will join them insincerely. Other scribal circles at least did join in resistance of some sort, whatever their motives and differences in intentions from the *maskilim*. A group of "Enoch" scribes (the "lambs who began to open their eyes" toward the end of the Animal Vision) began resistance, apparently well before Antiochus's attacks on Jerusalem. And the *Hasidim* (*ḥāsîdîm*, or Hasideans, as in 1 and 2 Maccabees) began resistance before the Maccabean Revolt. Throughout this summary of imperial repression and Judean resistance in Daniel 11:24–35, the principal focus is clearly on the *maskilim* themselves. And the martyrdom of those who were martyred had an important effect: refining, purifying, and cleansing them.

In response to the resistance of the *maskilim* and other Judean scribal circles, Antiochus escalated his measures to secure control of Jerusalem.[51] His honoring "the god of the strongholds" and acting on behalf of "those who fortify strongholds" and his "honoring people of a strange god who rule over the many and divide the land as their wages" (11:36–39, au. trans.) are references to the religious and political-economic aspects of garrisoning the Akra (citadel) fortress with military colonists to maintain military control over the city (1 Macc. 1:33–40). This was a further blow to the *maskilim* and other Judeans who now had Syrian troops watching over them and taking control of their lands.

The resolution of the crisis, which begins with a judgment scene, has a twofold focus, one on the people as a whole and one on the *maskilim* martyrs. The general concern, addressed in 12:1, is what is going to happen to the Judean people who have been suffering through the attacks by Antiochus Epiphanes. That "at that time Michael, the great prince, the protector of your people, shall arise" anticipates that he will act as advocate for the Judean people in the divine court and/or as the one who executes the divine judgment.[52] That "your people shall be delivered" anticipates that, as in Daniel 7, the Judeans are to be delivered as a people, presumably to gain their independence of imperial rule.

Of particular concern in Daniel 10–12, however, is what will happen to the *maskilim* who have been martyred in the struggle against Antiochus, addressed in 12:2–3. This is usually discussed in terms of "resurrection," even though the term does not occur in 12:2–3 (or in the parallel adduced from *1 En.* 104:1–6). John Collins concludes his extensive "Excursus" on the concept with a question about "the stereotypical assumption that resurrection in a Jewish context was always bodily."[53] His discussion suggests even more: that the synthetic theological concept of resurrection may not be applicable to Daniel 12:2–3.[54]

Two particular terms in the narrative, "the covenant" and "righteousness," may point us to what is driving the anticipation of the *maskilim* in 12:2–3. It was utterly baffling as well as intolerable that those who were keeping the covenant in loyalty to their God were being attacked and martyred by the imperial forces. Standing in the tradition of Israelite prophets, the *maskilim* looked to God's judgment for justice, especially for vindication of the heroes of righteousness. That they were "making many righteous" (12:3, au. trans.) is an allusion to the servant of Yahweh known in Isaiah 52–53, from which the *maskilim* took their name.[55] In fact, the whole pattern in Daniel 10–12 is similar to that in Isa. 52:13–53:12. Those who have steadfastly pursued righteousness are vindicated in the divine judgment over against the kings who have violently attacked them. In the prophetic tradition of Isaiah 52–53, Daniel 12:2–3 declares the vindication of the righteous who experience violence, even martyrdom, by imperial rulers. Different from Isaiah 52–53, the vindication of the wise in Daniel 12 is understood as an aspect of the broader restoration of the Judean people after their oppression by imperial kings.

The narrative of the judgment and restoration in Daniel 12:1–3 imagines the vindication in two basic images, both of which we should understand in the context of the restoration of the people announced in the previous statement. The one is awaking from sleep, meaning resuscitation to life for the judgment and reward of "everlasting life." The latter is a vague term, appropriately so in imaging an uncertain, indefinite, uncharted future; it probably means something more like "long life" than "eternal life."

The second image of vindication, and the one that dominates the context, is that the wise/righteous will be exalted so that they will shine *like* the heavenly bodies (12:3). The language is metaphorical, with similes that are also hyperbole. The thought world is the same one in which a prophet has a vision of hearing voices of heavenly beings in the divine court; "the holy ones of the Most High" are heavenly forces that have a special protective and interactive relationship with "the people of the holy ones"; and the arrogant violence of the emperor against Jerusalem rivaled "the host of heaven" and "threw some of the stars down to the earth" (7:15–27; 8:9–14). The wise scribes who cultivated the Israelite prophetic repertoire were steeped in a culture in which there was an affinity and close interaction between the heavenly forces and the people of Judea, especially the prophets and wise scribes. Somewhat the same pattern as well as the same images appear also in the closely contemporary Epistle of Enoch, where the messengers in the heavenly court of judgment defend them before the Great One and they "will shine like the luminaries of heaven . . ." (*1 En.* 104:1–6). This suggests that we are seeing here an issue, with an already-standard register of speech, familiar to two different circles of scribes in the same circumstances of imperial attack.[56]

THE *MASKILIM* IN THE POLITICAL CRISIS

All of the visions and interpretations of Daniel 7–12 focus on the crisis of the imperially approved Hellenizing reform of the constitution of the Jerusalem temple-state and the violent attacks on the city, the Temple, and the people by imperial military forces. Interpretations rooted in biblical studies often identify the problem in Daniel 7–12 as "religious persecution," taking its cue from the description of the killing of faithful Jews for refusing to eat pork and the stories of martyrdom in the books of the Maccabees. It is difficult, however, to find an allusion much less an explicit reference to persecution in the accounts in Daniel 7–12, unless it be the brief reference to the fate of some of the *maskilim* in 11:33. The conflict portrayed in Daniel 7–12 is indeed cultural-religious. But the conflict is inseparably also political-religious, for example in the transformation of the polity of Jerusalem, in which the controlling aristocratic faction abandoned the covenant (11:30).

The accounts in Daniel 7–12 focus broadly on the sustained crisis, fully political and inseparably political-religious, that began with the transformation of Judean polity by the dominant aristocratic faction and escalated in successively more drastic violent measures taken by Antiochus Epiphanes to suppress the resistance and retake control of Jerusalem. Not just the longer summaries of these events (8:9–12, 24–25; 11:22–35), but also the shorter summaries as well (7:25; 9:26–27), portray the crisis and imperial attacks in such broad terms. In addition to the reform, the execution of the last faithful high priest of the temple-state, and military attacks on Jerusalem and Judeans, three of the accounts also feature attacks on the Temple, including the removal of the burnt offering (8:11; 9:27; 11:31). And the accounts represent those attacks as also attacks on "the holy ones" and even "the prince of the host/the princes" (8:10–12, 24–25; 11:36). For the ancient Judeans and other ancient Near Eastern societies, however, those institutions and heavenly forces and those attacks were inseparably political-economic as well as religious.

The visions and interpretations of Daniel 7–12, moreover, place the Seleucid emperor's attacks on Jerusalem and the Temple in the broader context of the whole sequence of violence by a succession of empires against subject peoples. The visions, like dreams generally, involve many "mythic" elements such as images of beasts and celestial beings. The interpretations in Daniel 7 and 8, however, explicitly state that the terrifyingly destructive beasts in the visions are not mythic symbols of primordial chaos but represent the sequence of empires that dominated Judeans and other subject peoples, and that the Hellenistic empires are the most violent and destructive of all. The account in Daniel 11 clearly summarizes the imperial wars of the Ptolemies and the Seleucids for control of Palestine, and their effects on Judea. All of these narratives recount the escalating violence of the succession of empires as the context out of which comes the most extreme imperial violence of all: Antiochus's attacks that are destroying the constitutive institutions of Judean society, the covenant, the city of Jerusalem, and the Temple.

The narratives in Daniel 7–12, further, see the solution to the crisis in divine judgment in which the empire/emperor will be destroyed and the Judean people will be restored. In addition to the Hellenistic empire or Antiochus Epiphanes being destroyed (7:11, 26; 8:25d; 9:27; 11:45), other empires will be terminated (7:12). Biblical scholarship sometimes underplays the restoration of the Judean people to sovereignty by focusing the restoration on "the holy ones," understood as the angels, and/or by taking the imagery in 12:2–3 as signifying a general concept of individual resurrection and afterlife. The interpretation in 7:27 and the narrative in 12:1, however, belong in a long-established tradition of prophetic hope that God would restore the people of Judea. And part of that restoration (12:2–3), based in the closely related prophetic tradition of the servant of Yahweh, was the vindication of the *maskilim*.

In the visions and interpretations of Daniel 7–12, as in the tales in 1–6, the overarching issue is sovereignty, which has become an issue of extreme urgency in a situation of military attack designed to assert the sovereignty of the Seleucid empire/emperor. The only way that second-temple Judean scribes could reconcile the ideal of God as the true and exclusive ruler of the people of Judea under the covenant was that God had temporarily granted rule to a king, dynasty, or empire. But God retained the ultimate sovereignty. And when imperial rulers became so pretentious, as to demand exclusive or absolute sovereignty and to exercise their power in ways excessively destructive of their subjects, God could and did terminate their rule (Dan. 2–5). When imperial domination became so extremely destructive, as under Antiochus Epiphanes, God would destroy that imperial rule, restore the people, and restore sovereignty to them, understood as living directly under God's rule, with no intermediary imperial rule.

Closely interrelated to the sharp condemnation of and resistance to imperial domination expressed in the accounts of Daniel 8–12 was the sharp opposition to the Hellenizing aristocratic faction that had seized control of Jerusalem. Daniel 11:30–32 explicitly states what is a bit vague in 8:23–25, that the priestly aristocrats who led the Hellenistic "reform" had forsaken and violated the holy covenant (with God and the people). Wise scribes' service of the Jerusalem temple-state included cultivation of authoritative Judean cultural traditions such as covenantal torah and prophetic appeals for justice. They would have been understandably concerned about the special deals that some of their aristocratic "patrons" were making with imperial officials and the increasing influence of Hellenistic social-political culture in Jerusalem. Their own influence would have been diminished correspondingly.[57] The transformation of Jerusalem in the direction of a Hellenistic city was not only a threat to the traditional Judean way of life of which they were the custodians, but also eliminated their role (and livelihood!) in the temple-state.

Thus threatened, they evidently mounted resistance in Jerusalem, which would initially have been to "those who had forsaken the covenant." The account in 11:29–35 gives the impression that their resistance, like that of the Enoch scribes "who began to open their eyes" in the Animal Vision, had started before Antiochus's invasions to suppress the revolt and his attacks on the Temple. It was then, in the circumstances of imperial attacks and steadfast resistance by "the people who are loyal to their God" with more or less aggressive "action," that the *maskilim* were trying "to give understanding to many," and some were captured and executed (11:32–33). Their opposition to the dominant aristocratic faction, those who abandoned the covenant, must have been an irreconcilable break, judging from their conviction that the violators of the covenant would be punished at the judgment with "shame and contempt" (12:2; cf. the judgment of the wealthy in the Epistle of Enoch; see chap. 8, above). Their resistance does not appear to have involved armed revolt, unlike that the *Hasidim* who were allied with the Maccabean rebellion, at least for a time.

The attitude of the *maskilim* toward the Temple is as unclear, at first glance, as their opposition to empire is clear. The vision but not the interpretation in Daniel 8 and the interpretation in Daniel 9 (like the account in 11:29–35) mention the suppression of the burnt offering in the Temple and the abomination that makes desolate. The key question of "how long" also focuses on the cessation of "the regular burnt offering" in both Daniel 8 and 9 (8:13; 9:27). We would expect scribes, like priests and anyone else closely associated with the Temple, to be struck with horror at such a sacrilege as the attack on the key ritual in the temple service of God. Also, the accounts in 9:26 and 11:22 see a significant marker of the escalating imperial attacks against the temple-state in the killing of Onias III, the last of the faithful high priests. On the other hand, the imagery and interpretation of the restoration of the people do not explicitly include a restoration of the Temple or the offerings or the high priesthood. The anticipation of the restoration in 9:24 includes "a holy place" along with the broader social-political realization of "everlasting righteousness." But it is unclear whether this vague phrase refers to restoration of the Temple, the city, or even the land, as suggested in the NRSV translation "place" (in contrast to the more precise "sanctuary" to be destroyed, in 9:26). Perhaps it is significant that in the historical summary in 9:25–27, the restoration and rebuilding of Jerusalem in the sixth century BCE is mentioned, but not that of the Temple. The stance of the *maskilim* toward the Temple is thus ambivalent at best. They are shocked at its violation but do not appear to put much stock in its restoration.

The conclusion of the book of Daniel may allow us to discern one more aspect of their attitude toward Temple and high priesthood by "reading between the lines." The principal transaction conducted in the Temple ritual had been atonement. At the time of the visions in Daniel 8 and 10–12, however, the Temple and its altar had been profaned and the offerings suppressed and replaced. Nevertheless, "many shall be purified, cleansed, and refined," while "the wicked shall continue to act wickedly" (12:10). How can purification and atonement happen without Temple sacrifices? As suggested by the reference back to the martyrdom in 11:33–35, atonement now happens by the faithful, righteous resistance and martyrdom of the *maskilim*.[58]

Conclusion

Understanding Texts in Contexts

In the chapters above we have considered the production of Sirach, early Enoch texts, and Daniel in the three interrelated contexts of the historical situation, the structure of Judean society under Hellenistic imperial rule, and the wider Judean cultural repertoire. This multicontextual consideration has led to the questioning of some standard assumptions, approaches, and concepts previously key to interpretations of these texts, and has introduced some new questions and issues. Taking these interrelated contexts into account complicates but also enhances our appreciation of the circumstances and concerns of the Judean intellectuals who produced these texts as they responded to the deepening crisis of the Judean temple-state under Hellenistic imperial rule.

THE BROADER CONTEXT OF THE SOCIAL
STRUCTURE AND ROLES

All three of these books represent their producers as wise scribes. Being a scribe, however, was not just one possible occupation or profession among many. On the basis of information in Sirach and historical sociological studies of other agrarian societies, it is possible to see how scribes were situated in the overall political-economic-religious structure and dynamics of second-temple Judea. In historical sociological terms, scribes served the temple-state as advisers and administrators, or intellectual "retainers." Their learning of a wide spectrum of elite culture, including proverbs, legends, legal torah, prophecy, and dream interpretation, was professional preparation for their service among the rulers. To have the leisure to acquire wisdom, they did not labor with their hands, like peasants and artisans, but were economically dependent on the patronage of the aristocracy. As the professional intellectuals who cultivated the Judean cultural heritage, however, they had acquired an authority of their own, semi-independent of the rulers of the temple-state.

The scribes who produced Sirach, Daniel, and *1 Enoch* were thus "caught in the middle" in the structural conflicts of the tributary system of the temple-state. As the custodians of the Judean cultural heritage who were also personally committed to Mosaic torah and prophetic oracles, learned scribes were aware of the contradiction involved as the powerful exploited the poor, and they felt some responsibility to defend the poor. They were also vigilant about their own vulnerability to their superiors. Because of their position and role in the overall structure of the society, scribes were politically engaged, but they were also conservative and cautious.

The potential for conflict was compounded by the temple-state's function as an instrument of imperial rule over Judea, and it was further exacerbated by the rivalry between the Ptolemaic and Seleucid regimes for control of the area. The continuing position of power and privilege of the Judean aristocracy was dependent on the backing of the imperial court, which was concerned to guarantee stability and revenues. The opportunities for mutual manipulation between powerful figures in the Judean aristocracy and imperial regime increased with the rivalry between Hellenistic empires. Judean aristocrats seeking economic gain and/or assimilation into the dominant Hellenistic political culture took advantage of such opportunities. Judean scribes were thus even more "caught in the middle" in the resulting crisis in the early second century BCE, between their economic dependency on and loyalty to their aristocratic patrons one one hand, and on the other hand their commitment to the Judean cultural heritage of which they were the authorized custodians.

THE BROADER CONTEXT OF JUDEAN CULTURE

Understanding Sirach, *1 Enoch,* and Daniel can be enhanced by moving from a narrower focus directly on "wisdom" and "apocalyptic" literature to a broader focus on the wider repertoire of Judean culture in all its segments. Biblical studies standardly classifies texts by type (and often "genre") according to the three divisions of the Hebrew Bible (Torah, Prophets, and Writings), with further division into ancestral legends and Mosaic torah, books of history and books of prophecy, and books of psalms and books of wisdom. Sirach is classified as a book of wisdom, like Proverbs. Daniel, however, having initially been understood as prophecy and then classified among the writings by the Rabbis, later came to be classified as "apocalyptic," a classification strengthened by the modern discovery of seemingly similar books such as *1 Enoch*. Working on the basis of these categories, interpreters have attempted to define "wisdom" and "apocalyptic" in a synthetic abstract way derived from and applicable to a variety of texts from a wide range of times and places.

Recent study of many Judean texts has recognized that they do not fit neatly into such categories. The prototypical book of Mosaic Torah, Deuteronomy, displays many features of wisdom. Many prophetic books seem "Deuteronomistic." "Apocalyptic" texts show continuity with prophecy and share elements with "wisdom" texts, with which they were previously contrasted. More recently evidence from the manuscripts of biblical and other books discovered among the Dead Sea Scrolls indicates that virtually all Judean texts were undergoing development through at least the end of the second-temple period. Previously unknown texts also discovered among the Dead Sea Scrolls, moreover, reinforce previous indications of continuing composition of texts of Torah, texts that do not fit any of the categories of biblical literature, and texts that cut across or combine those categories. This plethora of texts, moreover, indicates that multiple versions of legends, historical accounts, legal collections, and other textual types were being cultivated. It is clear that in late second-temple times, Judean culture was much broader and deeper than the sum of its textual parts.

We can more appropriately think of all these texts as having belonged to a wide-ranging Judean cultural repertoire. The overall spectrum of texts and wider culture can be loosely categorized in the segments of Mosaic torah, history, prophecy, psalms, and wisdom. Those segments of culture included different types of material. Collections of laws, collections of prophetic oracles, and historical narratives were all distinctive kinds of cultural material. But there were no walls between them, and they were being developed with varying degrees of influence across the different segments.

The wisdom segment included at least four different kinds of wisdom:[1] instructional, reflective, cosmological, and mantic. Each of these kinds of wisdom was distinctive, although there was overlap and mutual influence, particularly between instructional wisdom and reflective wisdom. Each kind of wisdom appears to have taken a particular standardized form (or forms): speeches for instructional wisdom, hymns for reflective wisdom, hymns or a kind of "scientific" description for cosmological wisdom, dream account plus interpretation for mantic wisdom. Each kind of wisdom, moreover, had its social-political-religious function: the training of fledgling scribes into the ethos of service at court (instructional); the formulation of the agricultural and liturgical calendar and the grounding of the political-economic order in the cosmos/creation (cosmological); the knowledge of the anticipated unfolding of "international" affairs (mantic). All of these kinds of wisdom, their forms, substance, and functions, moreover, were inherited and adapted by Judean scribes from traditional scribal practices and cultures in the dominant ancient Near Eastern civilizations, particularly Egypt and Mesopotamia.

Thinking about the variety of Judean texts in terms of a broader cultural repertoire is strongly reinforced by the recent recognitions that literacy was limited largely to the professional scribes who served the temple-state as advisers and administrators, and that scribes cultivated (learned and recited) texts orally as well as in written form. The implications of these recognitions are far-reaching.

Not only were scribes (and priests) the people in Judean society who cultivated texts. They were also the only people who would have composed and further developed the texts that were written down and survived, some to become "biblical" and others "noncanonical" as known today—although they often used cultural materials originally from nonscribes, such as ancestral legends, prophetic oracles, popular proverbs, or customary "common law."

Scribes learned and cultivated all segments of the cultural repertoire of texts and other, oral materials. Studies of scribal culture in other ancient Near Eastern societies have shown that scribes learned and copied texts of all sorts, from collections of laws and omens to psalms to myths and legends, and not just "wisdom." Ben Sira says explicitly that the exemplary scribe learned the torah of the Most High and prophecies as well as sayings, proverbs, and parables. This provides a more historical sociological grounding to the production and cultivation of texts than the previous tendency in biblical studies to think of legal materials as produced by priests, prophetic books by prophets, and wisdom texts by sages. This social location of the cultivation of the texts in all segments of the cultural repertoire also enables us to appreciate how particular kinds of texts developed. If the scribes cultivated texts of Mosaic torah as well as instructional wisdom, for example, then it is not difficult to understand why and how the book of Deuteronomy exhibits so much influence from "wisdom."

Approaching Sirach, *1 Enoch,* and Daniel from this broader perspective of the wide-ranging Judean cultural repertoire enables us to move beyond the limits of previous discussions of "wisdom" and "apocalyptic(ism)." All of these texts indicate that they were composed by wise scribes. And they all give indications that their composers were at least acquainted with different kinds of wisdom. They all also indicate that their composers were familiar with and/or drew upon other segments of the Judean cultural repertoire. The effect of these recognitions is not to break down the categories of cultural materials, but to appreciate that the scribes who produced Sirach and the sections of Daniel and *1 Enoch* all had available a wide spectrum of cultural materials and drew upon various traditional forms and substance from different segments of the cultural repertoire, often in creative combinations.

Ben Sira is the least innovative, staying mostly within the standard wisdom segment of the cultural repertoire. He knows and uses some of the content of the Judean legendary and historical tradition and knows what is evidently becoming a standard list of prophets. But he does not utilize historical or prophetic forms. Most of his book consists of speeches on standard topics of instructional wisdom, often with two or more speeches on given topics. At many points he identifies this instructional wisdom with obedience to Mosaic torah. He also composes discourses of reflection on wisdom in its traditional hymnic form and standard language register. And though suspicious of mantic wisdom, he draws on long-standard cosmological wisdom in its usual hymnic form. In his most distinctive and creative composition, he draws on knowledge of historical tradition in the elaborate hymn of praise of the ancestors.

The scribes who produced the texts included in *1 Enoch* were deeply rooted in cosmological and mantic wisdom, but drew little from instructional wisdom. They may have known reflective wisdom, but reflection on heavenly wisdom does not appear in Enoch literature until the later Book of Parables (*1 Enoch* 42). The Enoch scribes, however, in addition to their knowledge of Israelite histori-cal tradition, were also deeply rooted in prophetic tradition and even appear to be assuming a prophetic role. The Book of Luminaries is apparently standard astronomical and meteorological wisdom derived from a Mesopotamian back-ground, part of the Judean wisdom repertoire that does not appear in the books that later became biblical. In the Book of Watchers, the scribal producers adapt the traditional prophetic forms of commissioning of "Enoch" as a prophet in a vision of the heavenly court and throne of God and the reception of oracles directly from God; they expand both oracles and heavenly journeys with elabo-rate cosmological wisdom. The Animal Vision, drawing its outer form(s) from mantic wisdom and prophetic tradition, exhibits deep knowledge of Israelite his-torical tradition, some of it juxtaposed with cosmological wisdom. The Epistle of Enoch, after its brief survey of history, is largely a continuation of the prophetic tradition of woes of judgment against the wealthy and powerful. None of the Enoch texts appears to know much about Mosaic torah.

The *maskilim* who composed Daniel represent their hero as thoroughly edu-cated in all branches of wisdom in his training for service at court. Special exper-tise and concern, however, are focused in mantic wisdom, the interpretation of dreams. The first six chapters consist of court legends, which must have been yet another standard form of cultural material cultivated by second-temple Judean scribes serving under imperial rule. Daniel 7–12 takes the form of visions-and-interpretation, similar to those in Enoch literature, which have been influenced by both Judean prophetic forms and mantic wisdom. The interpretations of the visions recount Judean history under a sequence of empires, but display little or no interest in earlier Israelite historical tradition or the Mosaic torah.

Taking this broader approach to Sirach, *1 Enoch,* and Daniel thus makes possi-ble much greater precision in our use of the concept "wisdom." In contrast with the tendency in biblical studies to use "wisdom" primarily with reference to prover-bial wisdom, we can distinguish the different kinds of wisdom with simple quali-fying adjectives. Sirach can be discerned as an anthology of speeches of instructional wisdom, reflective and cosmological wisdom in hymnic form, and a hymn of praise to the great ancestral officeholders. The Book of Luminaries would be most appro-priately described as cosmological (or even more precisely astronomical and mete-orological) wisdom. Other sections of *1 Enoch* can be discerned to draw more or less heavily on cosmological wisdom to flesh out prophetic visionary forms. It might be considered, further, whether the court legends in Daniel 1–6 belong with the wisdom segment of the Judean cultural repertoire. And mantic wisdom influences the development of prophetic visions-and-interpretations both in Daniel 7–12 and in the Animal Vision and Vision of Weeks in *1 Enoch*.

Whether the concept of "apocalypse/apocalyptic" is useful is a much more complicated matter, partly because the concept has usually been so vague, synthetic, and abstract. It should be readily apparent that the concept does not fit the Book of Luminaries or the Epistle of Enoch or the tales in Daniel 1–6. The visions-and-interpretations in Daniel 7–12 and the Animal Vision, Vision of Weeks, and the Book of Watchers, however, are still categorized as apocalypses/apocalyptic.

Separating "historical apocalypses" from "otherworldly journeys," John Collins lists symbolic vision as the most common form of revelation among their distinguishing characteristics.[2] Symbolic vision, which often included a heavenly messenger as interpreter, however, was already a well-established form in the prophetic repertoire, hence is hardly a distinctive feature that would help distinguish the visions-and-interpretations in Daniel 7–12 and *1 Enoch* as "apocalyptic" rather than a continuation of prophetic tradition.

Another feature of the "historical apocalypses" that Collins identifies is "eschatological predictions," which "invariably fall into a pattern of crisis-judgment-salvation."[3] In the narratives of Daniel 7; 8; 9; 10–12; *1 Enoch* 85–90; and 93:1–10 + 91:10–17, however, the crisis, judgment, and restoration of the people are the last, climactic, reassuring steps in the vision and/or interpretation, and not a distinctive, separable form. The crisis, moreover, is not "eschatological prediction," but a summary of the agonizing recent events. It is difficult to see how the judgment and "salvation" focused on the restoration of the Judean people in these texts "transcend the bounds of ordinary history." The judgment in the Daniel and Enoch visions-and-interpretations is of the historical empires and is not cosmic in scope.[4] It is also difficult to discern what is "eschatological" in the imagery at the climax of these visions in Daniel (and Enoch). In all of them the focus is the resolution of the historical crisis, violent oppression by imperial forces, through a divine judgment that both destroys the empire and restores the people. Again the visions-and-interpretations in Daniel and Enoch texts are developments of the prophetic tradition along lines already clear in Isaiah 40–55, 56–66; Isaiah 26–29; and Zechariah. Similarly, in Daniel 12 the vindication of the martyrs who died while resisting imperial designs is also a development on the basis of Isaiah 52–53, and the utopian image of all peoples living in peace in the Animal Vision appears to be a development of prophetic tradition, as in Isaiah 11:1–9.[5]

Where Collins recognizes the similarity and continuity in forms between "apocalyptic" and prophetic texts, these texts nevertheless exhibit "a shift in emphasis" and "important departures." First, while "the activity of angels is not peculiar to the apocalypses, . . . the increased interest in the angelic world . . . marks a shift in emphasis . . . over against the older prophetic writings."[6] But the interest in heavenly forces in Daniel 7–12 appears rather to be more or less on the same level as in the prophetic books, and where heavenly figures play roles, they are similar to and/or developments of those in the prophetic repertoire.[7] The shift in role from a heavenly voice overheard to a heavenly messenger who interprets a vision happened already in Ezekiel and Zechariah. Different from prophetic texts is not the extent of interest in or the roles of heavenly figures, but the extent to which they play those roles in a way semi-independent of the divine sovereign. The latter appears to be related to the shift from the prophets' context in a semi-independent monarchy to the wise scribes' context under imperial rule, with its complex imperial governance headed by a remote emperor.

Second, Collins also sees in Daniel 7–12 a "new departure" from prophetic tradition not so much in literary form as in "the use of pseudonymity and extended *ex eventu* prophecy," which, he claims, express "a new worldview," one of "determinism."[8] But pseudonymity had long been practiced in the prophetic tradition in the collection of the prophetic oracles of Isaiah and the "adaptation" of Amos and Hosea and Micah after the destruction of Jerusalem. Moreover, it is not clear how different "Daniel's" and "Enoch's" *ex eventu* prophecy is from the attribution of the prophecies in Isaiah 26–29, 40–55, and 56–66 to Isaiah, or the prophecies of future restoration to Amos, Hosea, and Micah. It is difficult to see how these features make the visions of Daniel or Enoch any more deterministic than the oracles of Micaiah ben Imlah, Isaiah, or Zechariah (or any prophetic oracles), where human events are (already) known in the heavenly council of Yahweh and declared as "the word of Yahweh," sometimes as the judgment of Yahweh on oppressive rulers.

Third, Collins sees the "crucial difference from biblical prophecy" in "the expectation of personal reward or punishment after death."[9] But the supposed "resurrection," as distinguished from the restoration of the people, occurs only in Daniel 12 (and *1 Enoch* 104), and there the imagery refers to the vindication of the *maskilim* who had been martyred by Antiochus's suppression of resistance in Jerusalem, and that (as Collins notes) in the context of communal restoration. This is not yet an expression of "a basic shift in worldview," of "individual salvation over and above the collective salvation."[10]

The concept "apocalypse/apocalyptic," even as refined by Collins and others, thus does not appear to distinguish the visions-and-interpretations in Daniel 7–12 and *1 Enoch* 85–90 as texts from prophetic texts. Continued application of the concept to Daniel 7–12 and the Animal Vision and Vision of Weeks, moreover, runs the risk of continuing to project aspects of the synthetic modern construct of "apocalyptic(ism)" that are inappropriate to them. It would be more appropriate (adapting the concept "historical apocalypse") to refer to these texts as *historical visions*: "visions," to designate their common form of vision-and-interpretation and also to suggest their continuity with the same or similar form in late prophetic texts and the influence of mantic wisdom; and "historical," to indicate the contents of the interpretation, sometimes but not always given by a heavenly messenger.

Collins classifies the Book of Watchers as an "otherworldly journey."[11] More recently, however, Nickelsburg has demonstrated that precisely where the journey leads—into the heavenly court to the very throne of God—the dominant forms are those of prophetic vision to obtain God's commission as a prophet and to receive an oracle of God (in continuity with 1 Kings 22; Isa. 6; 40; and Ezek. 1–3). The heavenly forces and holy ones now have more specific functions, but this is also a development of, not a departure from, the multiple "voices" of "the sons/children of God" in the court of the divine King in 1 Kings 22 and Isaiah 40. The core of the message is also prophetic (judgment of the perpetrators of violence and oppression and reassurance to the faithful), which is fleshed out with cosmological wisdom. The source of violence and oppression suffered by Israelites/Judeans is now located in the rebellious actions of heavenly "watchers" rather than in foreign kings. But this also seems more of a development than a departure from the prophetic tradition, where in defeating the foreign kings, Yahweh was also battling their gods—and all divine forces are now ultimately under the control of the divine King.

Different from the prophetic predecessors of the Book of Watchers are the temporal perspective, from primordial time to the eventual divine judgment, and the heavenly-and-earthly "geographical" scope of the implementation of the divine judgment. The sweeping temporal perspective is again a development of the prophetic tradition, as evident in Isaiah 40–55. The universal "geographical" scope results from the combination of cosmological wisdom with the visionary-prophetic perspective. Perhaps a special term is needed to refer to this apparently new combination.

Yet to use the term "apocalyptic," with all its features that do not fit the Book of Watchers or other Enoch texts and Daniel 7–12, might distract attention from the creative combination of prophetic vision and cosmological wisdom. An example would be the common generalization that apocalyptic texts express a dualism.[12] It is difficult to detect a temporal dualism, such as that between the old age and a new age, in any of these texts. Instead, all of them climax in an end of the historical crisis of second-temple times, and/or the long history of violence and oppressions at the hands of foreign empires, and/or rebel heavenly powers—an end through divine judgment and restoration of the people (or all peoples). Nor do these texts exhibit some sort of unprecedented "periodization of history." The Enoch texts follow the stages of history already explicit or implicit in the historical and/or prophetic segments of the Judean cultural repertoire; and the Daniel texts, focused on second-temple times, follow the sequence of empires (also articulated in the four-empire scheme). Nor do these texts exhibit a "spatial dualism" that is different from that integral to Judean cultural materials, especially prophetic texts. Both in Daniel and Enoch texts and in prophetic texts, historical affairs are in regular interaction with divine or heavenly powers.

The concept "apocalypse/apocalyptic" thus does not seem very appropriate or helpful in understanding Daniel and Enoch texts, in which some developments that may have led to later documents classified as "apocalyptic" may have begun. Perhaps the concept can be refined in ways that will make it applicable and useful to those later texts.

THE BROADER CONTEXT OF HISTORICAL
CRISIS IN JUDEA

In producing Sirach, *1 Enoch,* or Daniel, finally, different scribes or scribal circles were responding to the escalating crisis of rival aristocratic factions struggling for power and position in Jerusalem in relation to rival imperial regimes. The Enoch scribes, like the *maskilim* who produced Daniel, were probably more than a few individuals, yet probably numbered no more than a few dozen, given the tiny area and population of second-temple Judea. At acute points of crisis they may have developed a following, but they did not become or lead larger movements. Different kinds of wisdom had always had certain political-religious functions, just as prophetic oracles or legal collections or monumental texts had particular political-religious uses. In all these books the different sections and materials are directly related to stages or aspects of the historical crisis in which they were produced, and we cannot understand them adequately unless we discern that relationship.

As a servant of the Judean temple-state, as one with an acute sense of his own authority, and as a scribe obedient to the torah of the Most High, the learned scribe Ben Sira was clearly an advocate of the incumbent Oniad high priesthood. Like his predecessors, he cultivated and taught instructional wisdom to fledgling scribes, in effect socializing them into the conservative ethos of obedient service to the temple-state, so that they were content with their mediating role in Judean power relations. Fully aware of the problems in those power relations, however, his instructional wisdom is also cautiously critical. He urges his listeners to defend the poor against the predatory practices of wealthy aristocrats. And he cautions fledgling scribes to "watch their back" while carefully managing their economic dependency on their aristocratic patrons.

Also like his predecessors, Ben Sira actively cultivated the broader Judean cultural repertoire as preparation for service in the temple-state. He used some of those other cultural materials, specifically, reflective wisdom and historical knowledge, to bolster the temple-state and its incumbent high priesthood, which apparently was under threat from the pull by others in the aristocracy to assimilate to Hellenistic imperial culture. In the hymnic self-praise of wisdom (Sir. 24), he pointedly had the personified heavenly figure of Wisdom find her resting place and domain in Zion, giving divine authorization to the Temple in Jerusalem. And in the sustained praise of the great ancestral officeholders (Sir. 44–50), he had the authority of all their offices flow into that of the current Oniad high priesthood of Simon II. Ben Sira, however, appears to purposely avoid any nod to the Seleucid imperial regime that provided the Oniads' more concrete political authorization.

The scribes who identified with the antediluvian figure of Enoch appear to have been dissidents in the earliest text we have from their hand, the third-century BCE Book of Luminaries. Here they used their "scientific" cosmological wisdom to advocate a solar calendar, evidently over against the official lunar calendar. The solar versus lunar calendar continued as a central issue of conflict among scribal and priestly groups into the next centuries, as evident in the book of *Jubilees* and some Qumran texts. Well before the end of the third century BCE, in the Book of Watchers, the Enoch scribes had become acutely aware of the destructive effects of Hellenistic imperial domination. Drawing on their cosmological wisdom as well as prophetic tradition, they explained Hellenistic imperial violence and exploitation as due to heavenly forces who rebelled against the ultimate imperial governance of God, while prophetically reassuring eventual blessings for the righteous and condemnation for the warlike giants. The use of cosmological and mantic wisdom in the Book of Watchers and subsequent Enoch texts to interpret imperial violence and condemn its perpetrators forms a striking contrast with the uses of such kinds of wisdom in earlier Mesopotamian scribal circles, from which it probably derived, where it was used in support and legitimation of imperial incumbents and their practices.

Judging from references in the Animal Vision and the Vision of Weeks, the Enoch scribes themselves moved into active resistance against Seleucid domination, perhaps in response to the transformation of the temple-state into a Hellenistic polis (175 BCE). The Animal Vision offers a prolonged criticism of imperial violence as due to superhuman heavenly forces who rebel against God's ultimate governance. And the Animal Vision in particular indicates that Enoch scribes rejected legitimacy of the second Temple, suggesting that their criticism has much deeper historical roots in earlier second-temple history. In any case, the active resistance of the Enoch circle to Seleucid imperial rule and its client regime in Jerusalem had begun well before the outbreak of the wider Maccabean Revolt. In a way that moves far beyond Ben Sira's criticism, finally, the Epistle of Enoch, in a series of prophetic woes, declares God's condemnation of the wealthy and powerful aristocratic families for their exploitation of the poor.

The *maskilim* who produced Daniel cultivated legends of Judean scribes (Dan. 1–6) in the service of Babylonian kings as a way of reinforcing scribes' commitment to their indigenous Judean culture in circumstances where they were serving directly or indirectly under foreign imperial rule. Daniel provided a paradigm of the scribe trained in all kinds of wisdom, especially dream interpretation, who remained faithful to his God even when subject to imperial arrogance and overreach. With the special wisdom revealed by God, the scribes remained steadfast in the knowledge that God continued to hold the ultimate sovereignty in history and would condemn and terminate abusive imperial kings.

In the visions-and-interpretation (Dan. 7–12) the *maskilim* were responding to the transformation of Jerusalem into a polis and then Antiochus Epiphanes' attacks on Jerusalem to support his client rulers, whom he had placed in power there. Like the Enoch scribes, the *maskilim* articulated an indictment and condemnation of imperial rule over the Judeans during the second-temple period, using mantic wisdom (dream-interpretation) against rather than in support of the rulers. They represented Hellenistic rule as a dramatic increase in destructive violence. Although they give no indication of rejecting the legitimacy of the second Temple, the *maskilim* did come into direct conflict with those who abandoned the covenant. Their resistance to the latter and/or to Antiochus's attempts to control Jerusalem, however, was so active and effective that they were hunted down, tortured, and executed (11:33). And they saw themselves as helping others to understand the situation, presumably also in order to resist, like the Enoch scribes, before the emergence of the more widespread Maccabean Revolt.

Different circles of Judean scribes, all of whom were acquainted with different kinds of wisdom as well as the other segments of the Judean cultural repertoire, thus deployed themselves in different ways, depending on the circumstances they were addressing. Ben Sira used cosmological and reflective wisdom along with historical knowledge to support the incumbent high priesthood against Hellenizing threats. Enoch scribes, however, used cosmological wisdom to flesh out their prophetic protest and condemnation of imperial domination. And for both Enoch scribes and the *maskilim*, mantic wisdom, which previously functioned in support of kings, influenced prophetic forms used to pronounce God's judgment against imperial violence and oppression. All of these scribal circles responded to the historical situation not by interpreting already-standard texts, but by creating new ones. In the Book of Watchers the Enoch scribes created what appears to be a new combination of prophetic vision and oracle with cosmological wisdom. In the *historical visions* both the Enoch scribes and the *maskilim* created significant elaborations of the prophetic form of vision-and-interpretation. This was their creative response to historical circumstances in which they were desperate for revelation regarding the imperial violence threatening to destroy the traditional Judean way of life and/or constitution of the temple-state.

The active resistance to the assimilating aristocracy and their imperial sponsor by Enoch scribes and the *maskilim* makes all the more credible the reconstruction of the *Hasidim* as yet another scribal circle. There may well have been some continuity from the former to the latter. In any case, judging from the brief accounts in books of the Maccabees, the *Hasidim* appear to have been a group led by or consisting mainly of scribes who joined the wider revolt led by the Maccabees (hence their characterization as "mighty warriors," 1 Macc. 2:42). Yet some among them, committed to the basic form of the temple-state and eager to see it restored to a "legitimate" basis under Seleucid imperial rule, may have entered negotiations with an imperial officer—only to be taken captive and executed (7:12–16).

FURTHER IMPLICATIONS

We come back to key concepts that have determined the standard picture of late second-temple "Judaism" in biblical studies, especially the concepts of "wisdom" or "wisdom theology," and "apocalypticism" or the "apocalyptic worldview." Sirach, Daniel, and *1 Enoch* do not seem to provide evidence of these concepts, much less of historical realities to which they might apply.

Of the different kinds or branches of wisdom, instructional or reflective wisdom would appear to be the only ones that might suggest a particular worldview. Instructional wisdom was an important part of the socialization of fledgling scribes into the scribal ethos. But devotion to Mosaic torah appears to have been almost as important for Ben Sira. More to the point, the scribal ethos of obedient service to the temple-state was cultivated in particular social forms, such as the "discipline" of training in the scribal family, enforced by (the threat of) physical punishment. This ethos was particular to scribal training and scribal service. "Wisdom sayings" would not, by themselves, have transmitted this ethos to artisans or peasants, who were not immersed in the accompanying social forms.

Reflective wisdom was surely central to the scribal piety of Ben Sira. It could also be used to lend ideological support for the Jerusalem Temple. But in Sirach it was not yet developed into the kind of mystical devotion to heavenly Wisdom that emerges later in the Wisdom of Solomon and Philo of Alexandria. In Wisdom of Solomon, moreover, it is combined with reflection on the suffering righteous ones (chaps. 1–5) and moral-religious lessons drawn from exempla in Israelite tradition (chaps. 11–18).

Cosmological wisdom was adaptable: for hymns that supported the established order, in support of either a solar or a lunar calendar; to flesh out a prophetic indictment; or to help explain imperial violence. Mantic wisdom, after being developed in elaborate ways by earlier Mesopotamian scribes in support of imperial control and aggrandizement, was combined with prophetic forms by the Enoch scribes and the *maskilim* behind Daniel to explain and condemn imperial violence and oppression. Neither, however, articulates a distinctive worldview of its own, but rather belongs to a common worldview of the system of superhuman heavenly powers that participate in the divine governance of the world and influence historical affairs.

Daniel and the texts of *1 Enoch* do not attest an "apocalyptic worldview," much less an "apocalyptic movement." Again, these texts are scribal products and belong to a scribal ethos and address the difficult situation in which Judean scribes were caught in the historical crisis of the early second century BCE. It would be unwarranted to imagine that Judean peasants or Jerusalem artisans were somehow inspired by the visions in Daniel and Enoch texts to form a wider movement or resistance or rebellion.[13] The Enoch scribes and the *maskilim,* moreover, were small groups (hence the term "circles"), not large enough to call a movement. The *Hasidim,* who were also evidently scribes, joined a wider movement in the Maccabean Revolt, but there is no evidence that this wider rebellion was inspired by "apocalyptic" visions.

Even for the limited "circles" of the scribes who produced the Daniel and Enoch texts, it seems questionable to project or posit an "apocalyptic worldview" as something that is new and distinctive. The architecture of the heavenly court in the historical visions is merely a development of that in prophetic visions, as noted just above. The traditional language register of theophany, full of metaphoric and hyperbolic language articulating how awesome and terrifying God's sudden advent in judgment would be, is hardly a basis on which to posit a belief that the world is about to be destroyed in an imminent cosmic cataclysm. The interpretations of Daniel 7–12 translate terrifying dream images into historical terms. To argue for a distinctive "apocalyptic worldview" and especially a movement, we would need some other indications, such as statements in certain Dead Sea Scrolls that the Qumran community had taken the drastic action of withdrawing to the wilderness in anticipation of an imminent divine deliverance and judgment (but that might not qualify as "apocalyptic," since it lacked the "cosmic catastrophe").

Although they do not appear to attest an "apocalyptic worldview," both the book of Daniel and early Enoch texts fairly quickly commanded authority in other scribal circles, at least in the Qumran community. These books underwent continuing development, judging from the multiple copies found among the Dead Sea Scrolls, the citation of Enoch in *Jubilees,* the eventual inclusion of Daniel in the Hebrew Bible, and the later translation of Enoch books into other languages such as Ethiopic. Some passages that have been taken as quotations of or allusions to Daniel or *1 Enoch* in later texts are instead probably evidence of the continuing oral (and written) cultivation of some of the developing language registers devoted to particular issues and themes that appear in the earlier Enoch texts and Daniel. And the Enoch scribal tradition was continued in the first-century-BCE Book of Parables.

The investigation of the social location and role of the scribes who produced different texts in early second century BCE may also have some implications for how we understand continuing social conflict in the final two centuries of second-temple Judean history. Sources such as Josephus, rabbinic texts, and the Gospels mention several groups in conflict with each other and/or the rulers under the Hasmonean high priests, the Roman client King Herod, and the priestly aristocracy in the last decades of the second Temple. Josephus discusses the Essenes, the Sadducees, and the Pharisees (and the "Fourth Philosophy") as "parties" (*haireseis*) and as "philosophies" analogous to the Hellenistic philosophies. Modern biblical scholarship has constructed these as Jewish "sects," by analogy with the Protestant "sects" over against the state "church" in modern Europe. This conceptualization is a poor fit, and all the more so once we recognize the political-economic-religious structure of the Judean temple-state.

The same fundamental structure continued in Judea after the Maccabean Revolt, except that the Hasmonean high priesthood was relatively independent of foreign imperial rule until the advent of Roman and Herodian rule, which kept the temple-state intact. Once we discern the existence of several different circles of scribal retainers in the late third and early second centuries BCE, including the dissident circles of scribes who produced Enoch texts and Daniel, we have the historical precedent of the Pharisees, Sadducees, Essenes, and the Fourth Philosophy. The Pharisees appear to have been a rather sizeable faction of scribal retainers who served the temple-state throughout late second-temple times, except under Alexander Yannai (Jannaeus), when the Sadduccees came to prominence. The Essenes, thought by most to be the same as the Qumran community and its satellite communities, look like a combination of scribes and priests who broke with the established high priesthood and formed a utopian community in the wilderness. The "teachers" and "Pharisees" of the Fourth Philosophy were dissident retainers who agitated against direct Roman rule and the tribute. Only the Qumran community might appropriately also be characterized as a "sect." The others were larger or smaller scribal circles that maneuvered for positions of influence in the Hasmonean and later high priesthoods and affairs in Judea.

It is difficult to know whether the absence of evidence (of "wisdom" and "apocalyptic" texts) indicates the evidence of absence (of such texts) among these scribal(-priestly) circles in late second-temple times. The only text that stands in direct continuity with either Sirach, early Enoch texts, or Daniel is the Book of Parables, and that was apparently produced by "Enoch" scribes who appear to stand in continuity with earlier Enoch texts. The Pharisees concentrated on oral cultivation and continuing production of Mosaic torah and its application. The Fourth Philosophy was a smaller circle of Pharisees (Saddok) and other scribal teachers (Judas of Gamla; cf. Acts 5:37) who took a radical stance against direct Roman rule in 6 CE. The Qumranites evidently valued and even revered both Daniel and Enoch texts. And the discovery of the "Sapiential" fragments at Qumran indicates that Qumranites of other circles continued instructional wisdom somewhat similar to that evident in Sirach. The Qumran community, however, presents the seeming anomaly of the one group that could be called an "apocalyptic" movement and yet did not produce an "apocalypse" among the many texts composed in and for the community.

Later texts that have been labeled as either "wisdom" or "apocalyptic" literature could be said to have been produced in ways similar to the production of Sirach, Enoch texts, and Daniel, only in even less stable social-political contexts and in a far more complex multicultural repertoire. Wisdom of Solomon, for example, is a composite of texts that drew on, and developed much more elaborately, material from the Judean cultural repertoire, specifically reflection on the suffering righteous ones, reflective wisdom, and reflection on historical exempla—but all in a multicultural situation heavily influenced by Platonic philosophy and in historical circumstances of Roman-Hellenistic subordination even of diaspora Judean elites. And the scribes who produced *2 Baruch* and *4 Ezra*—on the basis of torah, prophetic materials and forms, and historical traditions as well as cosmological wisdom and Danielic visions-and-interpretations—struggled to understand the Roman imperial destruction of Jerusalem and the second Temple, a crisis far more severe than that faced by Enoch scribes and the *maskilim*.

Appendix A

Shared Motifs/Images/Themes in Speeches on "Seeking Wisdom"

Motif/image/theme	Sirach 4:11–19; 6:18–37; 14:20–15:10	Proverbs
Wisdom as teacher (mother), wise as students/children	4:11a; 6:32; 15:2	3:11
ways/paths of wisdom	(4:17, 19) 6:26b; 14:20, 22	4:11–14,18–19, 26–27
Wisdom as house/tent		7:6ff.; 9:1
Waiting by gates/doors, gazing in windows	14:22–24	
Wisdom as mother, bride, wife	6:32; 15:2	cf. 1:20–33; 7:4
giving bread and drink	15:3	9:2–6
Sir. 1:16 inebriates, 1:17		
wisdom as tree	14:26f.	
Sir. 24:13–17; Prov. 3:18 tree of life		
wise as children	4:11; 6:18, 23, 32; (15:2–4)	
wise as seekers	4:11b, 12; 6:27a; (14:22ff.)	
wise love her	4:12ff.	3:16, 18; 8:17, 35
secrets	4:18b; 14:21	
discipline, toil	6:18f., 32	5:12
yoke/fetters	6:24f., 29f.	
torture, torment	4:17; 6:20a, 21a	
listen	6:33f., 35	
the wise exalted/crown/glory/name	4:13a; 6:29–31	4:8–9
Sir. 1:18, 19		
inherit/obtain wisdom, etc.	4:16; 6:18b, 33, 37; 15:1 (7)	
fruits	6:19bd	
eloquence in assembly	15:5	
Sir. 1:30		
contrast with fools, sinners, etc.	4:19a; 6:20–21; 15:7–9	
ruin/destruction/Hades	4:19b	
relate to Wisdom, relate to God	4:14	8:35
ordinances/commandments	4:17; 6:37	
the law/torah	15:1	
fear of the Lord	15:1	

Notes

Introduction

1. This can be seen in many critical introductions to the New Testament. To cite just one magisterial introduction, see Helmut Koester, *Introduction to the New Testament,* vol. 1, *History, Culture, and Religion of the Hellenistic Age* (Philadelphia: Fortress, 1982), esp. 230–34, 243–46. These standardized portrayals of the dominant theologies in Judaism, especially of apocalypticism, persist from the influential introduction of Norman Perrin, *The New Testament: An Introduction* (New York: Harcourt Brace Jovanovich, 1973), 65–74; to that of Bart D. Ehrman, *The New Testament: A Historical Introduction to the Early Christian Writings* (New York: Oxford, 1997), 215–17.
2. For example, Dale C. Allison, *Jesus of Nazareth: Millenarian Prophet* (Minneapolis: Fortress, 1998); Bart D. Ehrman, *Jesus: Apocalyptic Prophet of the New Millennium* (Oxford: Oxford University Press, 1999).
3. This has been systematically developed by the Jesus Seminar, and most impressively and influentially laid out in John Dominic Crossan, *Jesus of Nazareth: The Life of a Mediterranean Jewish Peasant* (San Francisco: HarperCollins, 1991).
4. On the sections of *1 Enoch*, see especially George W. E. Nickelsburg, *1 Enoch,* part 1, Hermeneia (Minneapolis: Fortress, 2001); Patrick A. Tiller, *A Commentary on the Animal Apocalypse of 1 Enoch,* SBLEJL 4 (Atlanta: Scholars Press, 1993).
5. Many of the papers from the early years of the group were printed in the *Society of Biblical Literature Seminar Papers* for 1994 and subsequent years (Atlanta: Scholars Press). A selection of those papers is in Benjamin G. Wright III and Lawrence M. Wills, eds., *Conflicted Boundaries in Wisdom and Apocalypticism* (Atlanta: SBL, 2005).
6. This is true not only of the work of the great R. H. Charles, who edited many of the recently discovered texts classified as apocalyptic, but also of key interpreters at midcentury, such H. H. Rowley, D. S. Russell, and Klaus Koch with their emphasis on the key constitutive motifs of "apocalyptic."
7. E.g., Nickelsburg, *1 Enoch,* part 1; Tiller, *Animal Apocalypse;* John J. Collins, *Daniel,* Hermeneia (Minneapolis: Fortress, 1993).
8. John J. Collins, ed., *Apocalypse: The Morphology of a Genre,* Semeia 14 (Missoula, MT: Scholars Press, 1979), esp. the introduction.
9. A recent installment on a long-running debate can be seen in the magisterial commentary by Nickelsburg, *1 Enoch,* part 1; and the reviews by Patrick Tiller, John Collins, and James VanderKam in *George W. E. Nickelsburg in Perspective: An Ongoing Dialogue of Learning,* ed. Jacob Neusner and Alan J. Avery-Peck (Leiden: Brill, 2003), 365–86. On the tales in Dan. 1–6, see Lawrence M. Wills, *The Jew*

    in the Court of the Foreign King: Ancient Jewish Court Legends, HSM 26 (Minneapolis: Fortress, 1990).

10. Richard A. Horsley, "Nickelsburg and Other Scribes of Righteousness," *Review of Rabbinic Judaism* 8 (2005): 250–54.

11. See Sarah J. Tanzer, "Response to George Nickelsburg, "Wisdom and Apocalypticism in Early Judaism," in Wright and Wills, *Conflicted Boundaries,* 41–45.

12. Benjamin G. Wright III, *No Small Difference: Sirach's Relationship to Its Hebrew Parent Text,* SCS 26 (Atlanta: Scholars Press, 1989); summary of advances in knowledge of the Hebrew text in relation to the Greek and Syriac versions in Patrick W. Skehan and Alexander A. DiLella, *The Wisdom of Ben Sira,* AB 39 (New York: Doubleday, 1987), 51–62.

13. Jack T. Sanders, *Ben Sira and Demotic Wisdom* (Chico, CA: Scholars Press, 1983); Martin Hengel, *Judaism and Hellenism* (Philadelphia: Fortress, 1974); J. Marboeck, *Weisheit im Wandel: Untersuchungen zur Weisheitstheologie bei Ben Sira* (Bonn: Hanstein, 1971).

14. T. R. Lee, *Studies in the Form of Sirach 44–50* (Atlanta: Scholars, 1986); Burton L. Mack, *Wisdom and Hebrew Epic: Ben Sira's Hymn in Praise of the Fathers* (Chicago: University of Chicago Press, 1986).

15. See especially Kenneth G. Hoglund, *Achaemenid Imperial Administration in Syria-Palestine and the Missions of Ezra and Nehemiah,* SBLDS 125 (Atlanta: Scholars Press, 1992); Jon L. Berquist, *Judaism in Persia's Shadow: A Social and Historical Approach* (Minneapolis: Fortress, 1995); Joseph Blenkinsopp, "The Judean Priesthood during the Neo-Babylonian and Achaemenid Periods: A Hypothetical Reconstruction," *CBQ* 60 (1998): 25–43; Charles E. Carter, *The Emergence of Yehud in the Persian Period: A Social and Demographic Study,* JSOTSup 294 (Sheffield: Sheffield Academic Press, 1999); and Lisbeth S. Fried, *The Priest and the Great King: Temple-Palace Relations in the Persian Empire,* BJS 10 (Winona Lake, IN: Eisenbrauns, 2004).

16. George W. E. Nickelsburg, "Social Aspects of Palestinian Jewish Apocalypticism," in *Apocalypticism in the Mediterranean World and the Near East,* ed. David Hellholm, 2nd ed. (Tübingen: Mohr, 1989), 646. See also Philip R. Davies, "The Social World of Apocalyptic Writings," in *The World of Ancient Israel: Sociological, Anthropological, and Political Perspectives,* ed. R. E. Clements (Cambridge: Cambridge University Press, 1989), 251–71.

17. Otto Plöger, *Theocracy and Eschatology* (German ed., 1959; Richmond, VA: John Knox, 1968; followed by Martin Hengel, *Judaism and Hellenism: Studies in Their Encounter in Palestine during the Early Hellenistic Period,* 2 vols. (Philadelphia: Fortress, 1974).

18. Paul D. Hanson, *The Dawn of Apocalyptic* (Philadelphia: Fortress, 1975), simply pushes the same or similar conflict into early second-temple times.

19. See further Philip R. Davies, "Hasidim in the Maccabean Period," *JJS* 28 (1977): 127–40.

20. See further Jonathan Z. Smith, "Wisdom and Apocalyptic," in Smith, *Map Is Not Territory: Studies in the History of Religion* (1975; repr., Leiden: Brill, 1978), 67–87; Philip R. Davies, "The Social World of Apocalyptic Writings."

21. See now Benjamin G. Wright, "Putting the Puzzle Together: Some Suggestions concerning the Social Location of the Wisdom of Ben Sira"; and Richard A. Horsley, "The Politics of Cultural Production in Second Temple Judea: Historical Context and Political-Religious Relations of the Scribes Who Produced *1 Enoch,* Sirach, and Daniel," both in Wright and Wills, *Conflicted Boundaries,* 89–112 and 123–45.

22. Hengel, *Judaism and Hellenism.*

23. Hengel, *Judaism and Hellenism*, following Victor A. Tcherikover, *Hellenistic Civilization and the Jews* (repr., New York: Atheneum, 1959), 149.

24. Little headway could thus be made on what Philip Davies called the "long overdue task" of "rescuing" either apocalyptic writings in particular or second-temple Judea in general "from theological dogmatics and amateur sociology" (Davies, "The Social World of Apocalyptic Writings," 269).

25. Many of the papers presented to this group have been published in Philip R. Davies, ed., *Second Temple Studies*, vol. 1, *Persian Period*, JSOTSup 117 (Sheffield: Sheffield Academic Press, 1991); Tamara Eskenazi and Kent H. Richards, eds., *Second Temple Studies*, vol. 2, *Temple Community in the Persian Period*, JSOTSup 175 (Sheffield: Sheffield Academic Press, 1994); and Philip R. Davies and John M. Halligan, eds., *Second Temple Studies*, vol. 3, *Studies in Politics, Class, and Material Culture*, JSOTSup 340 (Sheffield: Sheffield Academic Press, 2002).

26. There are some exceptions. Interest in the distinctive hypothesis of Joel Weinberg, *The Citizen-Temple Community*, JSOTSup 151 (Sheffield: Sheffield Academic Press, 1992), proved unproductive, yet it provoked critical rethinking of the political-economic-religious structure of the temple-state established under the Persians; see Joseph Blenkinsopp, "Temple and Society in Achaemenid Judah," 22–53; and Richard A. Horsley, "Empire, Temple, and Community—but No Bourgeoisie! A Response to Blenkinsopp and Petersen," 163–74; both in Davies, *Second Temple Studies*, vol. 1. On Judea in the Hellenistic period, see Richard A. Horsley and Patrick Tiller, "Ben Sira and the Sociology of the Second Temple," paper presented to the Sociology of the Second Temple Group at the SBL 1992 Annual Meeting, now in Davies and Halligan, *Second Temple Studies*, 3:74–107.

27. See especially the extensive surveys of evidence in William V. Harris, *Ancient Literacy* (Cambridge, MA: Harvard University Press, 1989); and Catherine Hezser, *Jewish Literacy in Roman Palestine* (Tübingen: Mohr-Siebeck, 2001).

28. See especially the sophisticated study of Susan Niditch, *Oral World and Written Word*, Library of Ancient Israel (Louisville, KY: Westminster John Knox, 1996).

29. Explained in David M. Carr, *Writing on the Tablet of the Heart: Origins of Scripture and Literature* (Oxford: Oxford University Press, 2005); and Martin Jaffee, *Torah in the Mouth: Writing and Oral Tradition in Palestinian Judaism, 200 BCE–400 CE* (New York: Oxford University Press, 2000).

30. See especially the conclusions based on close analysis of manuscripts in Eugene Ulrich, *The Dead Sea Scrolls and the Origins of the Bible* (Grand Rapids: Eerdmans, 1999).

Chapter 1. Origins of the Judean Temple-State under the Persian Empire

1. Joseph Blenkinsopp, "The Judean Priesthood during the Neo-Babylonian and Achaemenid Periods: A Hypothetical Reconstruction," *CBQ* 60 (1998): 25–43, and texts cited there.

2. See further Jon L. Berquist, *Judaism in Persia's Shadow: A Social and Historical Approach* (Minneapolis: Fortress, 1995), chap. 2; Charles E. Carter, *The Emergence of Yehud in the Persian Period: A Social and Demographic Study*, JSOTSup 294 (Sheffield: Sheffield Academic Press, 1999); and Oded Lipschits, *The Fall and Rise of Jerusalem* (Winona Lake, IN: Eisenbrauns, 2005), esp. 360–78.

3. Recent years, moreover, have produced a far more critical and circumspect scholarly treatment of Persian imperial practices and the history and literature of the Jerusalem temple-state, which has challenged the oversimplified previous assumptions. In addition to the volumes of Berquist and Carter (note 2), see especially

Kenneth G. Hoglund, *Achaemenid Imperial Administration in Syria-Palestine and the Missions of Ezra and Nehemiah,* SBLDS 125 (Atlanta: Scholars Press, 1992); Lisbeth S. Fried, *The Priest and the Great King: Temple-Palace Relations in the Persian Empire,* BJS 10 (Winona Lake, IN: Eisenbrauns, 2004); the wealth of recent articles by specialists in Oded Lipschits and Joseph Blenkinsopp, eds., *Judah and the Judeans in the Neo-Babylonian Period* (Winona Lake, IN: Eisenbrauns, 2003); Oded Lipschits and Manfred Oeming, *Judah and the Judeans in the Persian Period* (Winona Lake, IN: Eisenbrauns, 2006); and the survey of sources and recent scholarship in Lester L. Grabbe, *A History of the Jews and Judaism in the Second Temple Period,* vol. 1, *Yehud: A History of the Persian Province of Judah* (London: T&T Clark, 2004).

4. On these sources see, e.g., Tamara C. Eskenazi, "Current Perspectives on Ezra-Nehemiah and the Persian Period," *Currents in Research: Biblical Studies* 1 (1993): 59–86.

5. See, for example, Peter Frei, "Persian Imperial Authorization: A Summary," and the other articles in response in *Persia and Torah: The Theory of Imperial Authorization of the Pentateuch,* ed. James W. Watts, SBL Symposium Series 17 (Atlanta: SBL, 2001).

6. See the recent reconstruction of possible steps by Fried, *Priest and Great King,* 157–77. Cf. Peter R. Bedford, *Temple Restoration in Early Achaemenid Judah,* JSJSup 65 (Leiden: Brill, 2001); and Diana Edelman, *The Origins of the "Second" Temple: Persian Imperial Policy and the Rebuilding of Jerusalem* (London: Equinox, 2005).

7. Berquist, *Judaism,* chap. 9, 131–46, esp. 141. See also Hoglund, *Achaemenid Imperial Administration.*

8. On Persian imperial policy and practice, see M. Dandamaev and V. Lukonin, *The Cultural and Social Institutions of Ancient Iran* (Cambridge: Cambridge University Press, 1989); Pierre Briant, *From Cyrus to Alexander: A History of the Persian Empire* (Winona Lake, IN: Eisenbrauns, 2002); idem, "The Seleucid Kingdom, the Achaemenid Empire and the History of the Near East in the First Millennium BC," in *Religion and Religious Practice in the Seleucid Kingdom,* ed. Per Bilde et al. (Aarhus: Aarhus University Press, 1990), 53–60.

9. Fried, *Priest and Great King,* 20–30, 63–67.

10. Ibid., 184–87.

11. Berquist, *Judaism,* 136.

12. Ibid., 57.

13. On both see Fried, *Priest and Great King,* 193–96, who argues that these Persian troops were no mere "armed escort" with travel guides. See also Oded Lipschits, "Achaemenid Imperial Policy and the Status of Jerusalem," in *Judea and the Judeans in the Persian Period,* ed. O. Lipschits and M. Oeming (Winona Lake, IN: Eisenbrauns, 2006), 34–35.

14. Fried, *Priest and Great King,* 193–99.

15. Ibid., 215–17.

16. A variety of bullae, seals, and stamped jar handles used to mark measures of taxes taken in kind bear the names of people identified as officials, including "governor" of the province, as laid out by Seth Schwartz, "On the Autonomy of Judaea in the Fourth and Third Centuries B.C.E.," *JJS* 45 (1994): 160, nn. 13–16 and references there.

17. Joachim Schaper, "The Jerusalem Temple as an Instrument of the Achaemenid Fiscal Administration," *VT* 45 (1995): 528–39; Christopher Tuplin, "The Administration of the Achaemenid Empire," in *Coinage and Administration in the Athenian and Persian Empires,* ed. I. Carradice (Oxford: British Archaeological Reports, 1987), 109–66; Lipschits, "Achaemenid Imperial Policy," 38–40;

Hoglund, *Achaemenid Imperial Administration,* 213; Carter, *Yehud,* 281. Grabbe, *History of the Jews and Judaism,* vol. 1, supplies detailed discussion and documentation, and separates his analysis according to the modern categories of administration (chap. 7), economy (chap. 9), and religion (chaps. 10–11), without attempting to discern how these were inseparable in the ancient world. A survey of references to the high priesthood, council, and related matters such as David Goodblatt's *The Monarchic Principle* (Tübingen: Mohr/Siebeck, 1994) can reach such dramatically different conclusions about the Judean temple-state because it abstracts its subjects from the historical context of empire, including the concrete political-economic relations in which they were embedded.

18. Supplementing the central storerooms in the Temple were public grain storage facilities, some of which have been discovered in Neo-Babylonian and/or Persian sites; Carter, *Yehud,* 252–53.

19. The invention of coinage did not replace in-kind payments of taxes and tribute. It is unlikely that the local economy in the Near East was ever monetized until quite recently. Even Ottoman taxation records from Syria-Palestine indicate that in-kind payments in barley, wheat, and other agricultural products were the primary means of extracting surplus from the peasantry. See further ibid., 271–72. Coins were used in Persian trade and by the Persian military (ibid., 281).

20. Ibid., 304–6; Richard A. Horsley, "Empire, Temple, and Community," in *Second Temple Studies,* vol. 1, *Persian Period,* ed. Philip R. Davies, JSOTSup 117 (Sheffield: Sheffield Academic Press, 1991), 163–74. In ancient Judea as in ancient Near Eastern civilizations generally, there would have been no independent commercial sector of the economy, since trade was managed by and for the benefit of the ruling elite. Archaeological explorations indicate a correlation of distribution of foreign wares and local imitations with major urban centers, the residence of the wealthy, e.g., at En Gedi, Jericho, Tell en Nasbeh, and Jerusalem. See Carter, *Yehud,* 256–58, 285.

21. Schaper, "Jerusalem Temple," 529–39, with detail of officials and taxes. Berquist, *Judaism,* 135.

22. Norman K. Gottwald, *The Politics of Ancient Israel* (Louisville, KY: Westminster John Knox, 2001), 110. In what is surely a mark of previous irregularities he confronted, Nehemiah established a regular supervision of collections and disbursements by a panel consisting of one priest, two representatives of the lower clergy, and a certain Zadok, who was apparently his own representative (Neh. 13:13; cf. 2 Macc. 3:5–6, 10–12; Josephus, *War* 6.282; *Ant.* 14.10–13).

23. Joseph Blenkinsopp, "Temple and Society in Achaemenid Judah," in *Second Temple Studies,* 1:49.

24. Carter, *Yehud,* 249, and the charts of archaeological surveys; Oded Lipschits, "Demographic Changes in Judah between the Seventh and the Fifth Centuries B.C.E.," in Lipschits and Blenkinsopp, *Judah and the Judeans in the Neo-Babylonian Period,* esp. 364–67; Kenneth G. Hoglund, "The Material Culture of the Persian Period and the Sociology of the Second Temple Period," in Philip R. Davies and John M. Halligan, *Second Temple Studies,* vol. 3, *Studies in Politics, Class and Material Culture,* JSOTSup 340 (Sheffield: Sheffield Academic Press, 2002).

25. Carter, *Yehud,* 199–201, 246.

26. Ibid., 201, 288.

27. Ibid., 259, 289.

28. Ibid., 289.

29. Berquist, *Judaism,* 135–36.

30. "These immigrants were distinct ethnically and culturally. . . . Immigration became Persia's chief means for exerting state influence upon Yehud." Ibid., 133,

136, 140; Philip R. Davies, *In Search of "Ancient Israel": A Study in Biblical Ori-gins*, JSOTSup 148 (Sheffield: Sheffield Academic Press, 1992), 117–118, puts it even more starkly: "a new ethnic entity" (85) and a "colony." Berquist's read-ing of Isa. 56 (*Judaism*, 153), that the immigrant group from Babylon is arguing that "the foreigner attached to Yahweh" should be accepted in the temple-community, suggests serious ethnic differences between those who had stayed on the land and the immigrants installed by the Persians. If, on the other hand, 56:3–4 represents the voice of the indigenous Yehudim against the immigrant group, 56:3–4 still indicates serious ethnic differences. Two suggestive recent analyses of the immigrant "Judeans" in relation to the question of Judean "iden-tity" are Jon Berquist, "Constructions of Identity in Postcolonial Yehud," 53–66; and John Kessler, "Persia's Loyal Yahwists: Power Identity and Ethnicity in Achaemenid Yehud," 67–90; both in Lipschits and Oeming, *Judah and the Judeans in the Persian Period.*
31. David J. A. Clines, "Haggai's Temple, Constructed, Deconstructed, and Recon-structed," in *Second Temple Studies*, vol. 2, *Temple Community in the Persian Period*, ed. Tamara Eskenazi and Kent Richards, JSOTSup 175 (Sheffield: JSOT Press, 1994), 60–87.
32. Blenkinsopp, "Temple and Society," 44–47, drawing somewhat on the work of Joel Weinberg, whose articles are now collected in *The Citizen-Temple Commu-nity*, JSOTSup 151 (Sheffield: Sheffield Academic Press, 1992); cf. the critical dis-cussion in Horsley, "Empire, Temple, and Community."
33. Robert P. Carroll, "The Myth of the Empty Land," *Semeia* 59 (1992): esp. 79, 81, 85, 88; Hans M. Barstad, *The Myth of the Empty Land: A Study in the History and Archaeology of Judah during the "Exilic" Period* (Oslo: Scandinavian Univer-sity Press, 1996); cf. B. Oded, "Where Is the 'Myth of the Empty Land' to Be Found? History versus Myth," in *Judah and the Judeans in the Neo-Babylonian Period*, ed. Lipschits and Blenkinsopp, 55–74.
34. Hoglund, *Achaemenid Imperial Administration*, 234–40.
35. On the exclusion of the native population, see further Carter, *Yehud*, 296, 311; Davies, *In Search*, 84, 116.
36. Berquist, *Judaism*, 149.
37. Cf. Davies, *In Search*, 118–19. As political theorist John Kautsky points out, "aris-tocratic empires" such as those in the ancient Near East cannot be called "soci-eties," since imperial regimes often pull many different peoples under their rule. Given the imperially commanded movement of peoples and ruling aristocracies subject to imperial regimes, it would not be surprising if even a tiny province such as Yehud included groups with some cultural and ethnic differences.
38. See esp. the cross-cultural study by James C. Scott, *The Moral Economy of the Peas-ant* (New Haven, CT: Yale University Press, 1976).
39. Recent studies of the priestly groups in Joseph Blenkinsopp, "The Judean Priest-hood during the Neo-Babylonian and Achaemenid Periods: A Hypothetical Reconstruction," *CBQ* 60 (1998): 25–43; Risto Nurmela, *The Levites: Their Emergence as a Second-Class Priesthood*, SFSHJ 193 (Atlanta: SBL, 1998); and building carefully on previous studies, Joachim Schaper, *Priester und Leviten im achaemenidischen Juda*, FAT 31 (Tübingen: Mohr Siebeck, 2000).
40. Blenkinsopp, "The Judean Priesthood."
41. Nurmela, *The Levites.*
42. The implication of the probing analysis of priestly genealogies in Gary N. Knop-pers, "The Priestly Genealogies and the High Priesthood," in Lipschits and Blenkinsopp, *Judah and the Judeans in the Neo-Babylonian Period*, 109–34.
43. B. Porten and J. C. Greenfield, *Jews of Elephantine and Arameans of Syene: Ara-maic Texts with Translations* (Jerusalem: Hebrew University, 1974), 90–93.

44. It is conceivable that the differences of position evident in Isa. 56–66 represent different priestly groups vying for influence, thus offering offer evidence for considerable and sustained conflict between rival claimants to influence and legitimacy in Judah at the beginning of Persian rule. See Berquist, *Judaism.*

45. The latter also appears as the father of the donor of a silver vessel dated to around 400 BCE: "Qainu bar Geshem, king of Qedar," which makes him roughly a contemporary of Nehemiah, as explained by William Dumbrell, "The Tell El-Maskhuta Bowls and the 'Kingdom' of Qedar in the Persian Period," *BASOR* 203 (1971): 33–44; A. Lemaire, "Un nouveau roi arabe de Qedar," *RB* 81 (1974): 63–72; Fried, *Priest and Great King,* 202–3.

46. On the silver coin, see Dan P. Barag, "Some Notes on a Silver Coin of Johanan the High Priest," *Biblical Archaeologist* 48 (September 1985): 66–68; idem, "A Silver Coin of Yohanan the High Priest and the Coinage of Judea in the Fourth Century B.C.," *Israel Numismatic Journal* 9 (1986–87): 4–21; Lisbeth S. Fried, "A Silver Coin of Yohahan Hakkohen," *Transeuphratene* 26 (2003): 65–85. On the letter from Elephantine, see B. Porten and J. C. Greenfield, *Jews of Elephantine,* 90–93.

47. On nationalism as a modern phenomenon/concept (hence inapplicable to ancient political life), see Benedict Anderson, *Imagined Communities: Reflections on the Origin and Spread of Nationalism* (London: Verso, 1983).

48. Goodblatt, *The Monarchic Principle,* chap. 1, argues for a priestly monarchy.

49. The implication of Goodblatt's analysis in ibid., chap. 4, if not his conclusion.

50. Cf. ibid., 11–12.

51. Carter, *Yehud,* 311–12.

52. Cf. Berquist, *Judaism,* 133–40.

Chapter 2. The Judean Temple-State under the Hellenistic Empires

1. Summaries in Peter Schaefer, *The History of the Jews in Antiquity* (Luxembourg: Harwood, 1995), 15, 18, 21–24; and Lester L. Grabbe, *Judaism from Cyrus to Hadrian,* vol. 1, *The Persian and Greek Periods* (Minneapolis: Fortress, 1992), 212–14.

2. Dov Gera, *Judaea and Mediterranean Politics, 219 to 161 B.C.E.* (Leiden: Brill, 1998), 28–31.

3. Victor Tcherikover, *Hellenistic Civilization and the Jews* (New York: Jewish Publication Society, 1959); Pierre Briant, "The Seleucid Kingdom, the Achaemenid Empire and the History of the Near East in the First Millennium BC," in *Religion and Religious Practice in the Seleucid Kingdom,* ed. Per Bilde et al. (Copenhagen: Aarhus University Press, 1990), 59; Roger S. Bagnall, *The Administration of the Ptolemaic Possessions outside Egypt* (Leiden: Brill, 1976), 14–15, 219; cf. Grabbe, *Judaism,* 1:190–91.

4. David Goodblatt, *The Monarchic Principle* (Tübingen: Mohr/Siebeck, 1994), 29–35.

5. Frances H. Diamond, "Hecataeus of Abdera and the Mosaic Constitution," in *Panhellenica: Essays in Ancient History and Historiography in Honor of T. S. Brown,* ed. S. M. Berstein and L. A. Okin (Lawrence, KS: Coronado, 1980), 77–95; Doron Mendels, "Hecataeus of Abdera and a Jewish 'Patrios Politeia' of the Persian Period (Diodorus Siculus 40.3)," *ZAW* 95 (1983): 96–110.

6. Schaefer, *History,* 13–18, even projecting "state capitalism" and a "Greek bourgeoisie"; Grabbe, *Judaism,* 1:189–92.

7. Bagnall, *Administration,* 3–10, 11–24; Victor Tcherikover, "Palestine under the Ptolemies," *Mizraim* 4–5 (1937): 9–90.

8. Bagnall, *Administration,* 19–20.

9. Victor Tcherikover and A. Fuks, *Corpus papyrorum Judaicarum,* 3 vols. (Cambridge, MA: Harvard University Press, 1957–64), 1: nos. 4, 5.

10. Daniel Schwartz, "Josephus on the Jewish Constitution and Community," *SCI* 7 (1983/84): 30–42; Dov Gera, "On the Credibility of the History of the Tobiads," in *Greece and Rome in Eretz Israel,* ed. A., Kasher, U. Rappoport, and G. Fuks (Jerusalem: Israel Exploration Society, 1990), 21–38.

11. Martin Hengel, *Judaism and Hellenism,* 2 vols. (Philadelphia: Fortress, 1974), 1:27–28, 268–71; even by Tcherikover, *Hellenistic Civilization,* who repeatedly emphasizes its legendary features.

12. Versus Gera, "Credibility," 30; idem, *Judea,* 49.

13. As explained by Tcherikover, *Hellenistic Civilization,* and admitted by Gera, "Credibility," 34, n. 58; idem, *Judea,* 53–55, nn. 73, 76–78.

14. Often paraphrasing the translation of *Ant.* 12.156–191 by Ralph Marcus in the Loeb Classical Library.

15. Tcherikover, *Hellenistic Civilization,* 64, as part of a much more complete discussion of Tobiah and the historical context indicated in the Zenon papyri.

16. The assumption that *prostasia/prostatēs* referred to an office that Onias presumably relinquished and Joseph obtained has more to do with modern scholars' assumptions that there must have been formal political positions or offices than with any sources that might indicate that. See Daniel Schwartz, "Josephus on the Jewish Constitution," 30–52, esp. 40–44; followed by Seth Schwartz, "On the Autonomy of Judaea in the Fourth and Third Centuries B.C.E.," *JJS* 45 (1994): 164.

17. E.g., Tcherikover, *Hellenistic Civilization,* 129; Schaefer, *History,* 19. To speculate further that Onias or even a larger "party" within the Jerusalem elite had developed some sort of pro-Seleucid ideological position, however, is unwarranted.

18. Cf. the suggestive observations made in his elaborate and detailed but speculative argument reconstructing the "original story" of the Tobiads, by Jonathan A. Goldstein, "The Tales of the Tobiads," in *Christianity, Judaism, and Other Greco-Roman Cults: Studies for Morton Smith at Sixty* (Leiden: Brill, 1975), 94–98.

19. *P.Tebt.* 8 11.15–16; Michael Rostovtzeff, *The Social and Economic History of the Hellenistic World,* vol. 1 (Oxford: Clarendon, 1953), 335, 338.

20. *UPZ,* col I, 112, 1.1; Claire Preaux, *L'economie royale des Lagides* (Brussels: Édition de la Fondation égyptologique rein Élisabeth, 1939), 451 n 2.

21. *Ant.* 12.177–178; G. M. Harper Jr., *Aegyptus* 14 (1934): 269–85; Preaux, *L'economie royale,* 452–57.

22. *Ant.* 12.181, 183; *OGIS* 59; *SEG* 9:5, 11, 46–71. Preaux, *L'economie royale,* 450–59.

23. Bagnall, *Administration,* 3–24.

24. Pace Schwartz, "Autonomy of Judea," 163, 167.

25. See the discussions in Tcherikover, *Hellenistic Civilization,* 127–42, 153–74; and Hengel, *Judaism and Hellenism,* esp. 1:267–83, and references there.

26. A combination of information from Polybius about his military career with the Ptolemies and recently discovered inscriptions mentioning his father and grandfather as Ptolemaic governors leads to this conclusion. The precedent had been set by the defection of many Ptolemaic officers in 218 BCE, following a reorganization of the army, as mentioned by Polybius. Further discussion and references in Gera, *Judea,* 28–32.

27. Suggestive discussion by Gera, *Judaea,* 20–34.

28. Grabbe, *Judaism,* 1:240–41, 246; David Goodblatt, *The Monarchic Principle* (Tübingen: Mohr Siebeck, 1994), 15.

29. In some publications Elias Bickermann concluded that the temple-state was aristocratic at the start of Seleucid rule, with the high priest becoming supreme with the Hasmoneans, although Bickermann changed his mind in *God of the Maccabees* (Leiden: Brill, 1979), 37–38. See Goodblatt, *Monarchic Principle,* 16 n. 30.

30. Cf. the careful, measured argument of Goodblatt, *Monarchic Principle*, 16–20, walking through Bickermann and Tcherikover, and leaning on Will and Orrieux. Yet these arguments hardly amount to support of his conclusion. Schaefer, *History*, 32, places too much weight on Ben Sira in Sir. 50.

31. The most careful analysis of this escalating crisis in Judean history, especially for the circumstances and motives of Antiochus IV's attack on Jerusalem, is Erich Gruen, "Hellenism and Persecution: Antiochus IV and the Jews," in *Hellenistic History and Culture,* ed. Peter Green (Berkeley: University of California Press, 1998), from which I take many cues in the following summary reconstruction.

32. While the Greek codices of 2 Macc. 3:4 have Simon as "of the tribe of Benjamin," the Old Latin and Armenian MSS preserve what must have been the original reading, "Balgea." The Mishnah (*Sukkah* 5.8c) offers a legend that illuminates the memory of representatives of this priestly family: "The priestly family of Bilga was excluded from offering sacrifice for all time because of its conduct in the religious distress under Antiochus IV," as laid out by Martin Hengel, *Judaism and Hellenism,* 279; and Tcherikover, *Hellenistic Civilization,* 403–4.

33. Cf. Hengel, *Judaism and Hellenism*; Schaefer, *History*; Grabbe, *Judaism*, 1:277.

34. Similarly Tcherikover, *Hellenistic Civilization,* 160.

35. Robert Doran, "Jason's Gymnasion," in *Of Scribes and Scrolls: Studies on the Hebrew Bible, Intertestamental Judaism, and Christian Origins Presented to John Strugnell,* ed. Harold W. Attridge et al. (Lanham, MD: University Press of America, 1990), 99–109, is a careful, thorough study, with citations from key texts.

36. Ibid., 105, 108; Tcherikover, *Hellenistic Civilization,* 163. The *gymnasion* and *ephēbeion* had become the institutions by which the citizens of the cities established by Macedonian colonists and indigenous elites (who adopted the Hellen[ist]ic political-cultural forms) distinguished themselves from the native populace, who comprised the rest of the residents of the cities and the peasants of the surrounding villages. So Getzel M. Cohen, *The Seleucid Colonies: Studies in Founding, Administration and Organization* (Wiesbaden: Steiner, 1978), 36–37.

37. Josephus's account uses the same terms, also making clear the Hellenistic imperial context, in which the constitution of a city was authorized by the emperor: the Jerusalem aristocratic party that initiated the project "wished to abandon their ancestral laws [*tous patrious nomous*] and the constitution/way of life [*politeia*] prescribed by them and to follow the imperial laws and have a Greek constitution [*Hellēniken politeian*]" (*Ant.* 12.240).

38. Hengel, *Judaism,* emphasizes the cultural transformation; Tcherikover's statement (*Hellenistic Civilization,* 164), that "the complete abolition of the existing constitution and its replacement by a new one" is surely an overstatement. Grabbe, *Judaism,* vol. 1, downplays the religious-cultural change; Doran, "Jason's Gymnasion," says that this was mainly an educational innovation.

39. Fergus Millar, "The Phoenician Cities: A Case-Study," *Proceedings of the Cambridge Philological Association* 209 (1983): 55–71; Seth Schwartz, "The Hellenization of Jerusalem and Shechem," in *Jews in a Graeco-Roman World,* ed. Martin Goodman (Oxford: Clarendon, 1998), 37–45, who emphasizes that establishing a "Greek" public life effected the privatization of traditional native culture.

40. In the same period Phoenician cities continued to be ruled by their traditional "judges" (*dikastai*), as indicated by Millar, "Phoenician Cities," 62, 67.

41. Similarly Tcherikover, *Hellenistic Civilization,* 166.

42. Similarly ibid., 169.

43. Although Josephus's account has him presiding over a temple in Leontopolis in Egypt, *War* 1.31–33.

44. Grabbe, *Judaism,* 1:282–84.

45. Schaefer, *History,* 13; Hengel, *Judaism,* 53, 106.
46. Hengel, *Judaism,* 53. In contrast to this modern scholarly treatment, the Tobiad romance, moreover, portrays Joseph as brutally ruthless in his methods of expropriation.
47. So also Schaefer, *History,* 17–18.

Chapter 3. Ben Sira and the Sociology of Judea

1. Hengel, *Judaism and Hellenism,* 2 vols. (Philadelphia: Fortress, 1974), is still followed in standard interpretation of Sirach and other texts, as for example by John J. Collins, *Jewish Wisdom in the Hellenistic Age,* Old Testament Library (Louisville, KY: Westminster John Knox, 1997), 23–25.
2. Victor A. Tcherikover, *Hellenistic Civilization and the Jews* (repr., New York: Atheneum, 1959), 149.
3. It simply had not occurred to Hengel and others who shared the standard orientation of biblical studies to ask certain questions of social location about a very different historical structure. For example, what he sees as "merchants" and "traders" were mainly agents of the Ptolemaic imperial regime. The vast majority of coins were found at Samaria, Shechem, and Scythopolis, outside of Judea, or at Beth Zur, site of a military garrison, hence hardly evidence for the monetarization of the economy in general. The wine jars from Rhodes in the Aegean Sea were found at Phoenicia on the coastal plain, outside Judea, and only at military garrison sites in Judea, again hardly evidence of a commercialization of Judean society in general.
4. In classical studies as well as biblical studies, much of the standard picture of ancient Judea as of the Hellenistic social and economic world was based on the monumental research and reconstruction by the great scholar Michael Rostovtzeff, who projected into ancient times the evolving capitalism of his native Russia in the early twentieth century. See Michael Rostovtzeff, *The Social and Economic History of the Hellenistic World,* 3 vols. (Oxford: Clarendon, 1941).
5. In recent years biblical interpreters have begun to ask some pointed sociological questions of Judean literature and history—for example, in the programs of the Sociology of Second Temple Group in the SBL and their publications such as *Second Temple Studies,* vol. 1, *The Persian Period,* ed. Philip R. Davies (Sheffield: JSOT Press, 1991); *Second Temple Studies,* vol. 3, *Studies in Politics, Class, and Material Culture,* ed. Philip R. Davies and John M. Halligan (Sheffield: Sheffield Academic Press, 2002). Such investigations have enriched as well as complicated interpretation of the second-temple period. Having an archaeologically informed sense of just how small the population of Judea was in the Persian period brings a sobering caution about hypotheses of high literary productivity among Jerusalem intellectuals at that time. Studies focused on such particular social issues, however, have not yet been combined into a critically formulated overall picture of the structure and dynamics of Judean society under the Persian or the Hellenistic Empires.
6. See especially Gerhard E. Lenski, *Power and Privilege: A Theory of Social Stratification* (New York: McGraw-Hill, 1966).
7. See, for example, Anthony J. Saldarini, *Pharisees, Scribes, and Sadducees: A Sociological Approach* (Wilmington: Glazier, 1988).
8. Gerd Theissen, *The Sociology of Early Palestinian Christianity* (Philadelphia: Fortress, 1978); criticized by John H. Elliott, "Social Scientific Criticism of the New Testament and Its Social World," *Semeia* 35 (1986): 1–33; and Richard A. Horsley, *Sociology and the Jesus Movement* (New York: Crossroad, 1989).

9. It is especially important to avoid two related pitfalls in some recent use of social science models on biblical materials. One is the imposition of a sociological model on ancient texts and history that may obscure some of their key features, and the other is to focus on the model and then use Judean "data" from ancient sources merely to flesh it out.

10. The following is heavily dependent on the research and analysis that I did some years ago together with Patrick Tiller, now published in "Ben Sira and the Sociology of the Second Temple," in *Second Temple Studies*, vol. 3. I am deeply indebted to Pat Tiller particularly for his philological expertise and his close critical analysis of key passages in Sirach.

11. How we use an ancient document critically as a source depends on who it is addressing as well as the social location of its producer. In previous readings the vague sense of Ben Sira's audience (the broad sections of the population, sometimes "the wealthy": Tcherikover, *Hellenistic Civilization,* 149) reflects interpreters' failure to consider the particular social structure of Judea. Much of the book focuses on the substance and transmission of wisdom itself, with the instruction addressed to "my children," which had become a standard idiom for scribal students (see chap. 4, below).

12. Although this verse is not extant in Hebrew, the original must have read *bemoshlim bmwshlym,* which was misread by the Greek translator as *bemashalim bmshlym = parabolai,* as Patrick Skehan has shown (Patrick W. Skehan and A. A. DiLella, *The Wisdom of Ben Sira* [Garden City, NY: Doubleday, 1987], 448).

13. Most frequent are the three Hebrew terms that occur together in 10:24: *sar, shophet,* and *moshel* (in Greek *megistan, krites,* and *dynastes,* respectively; NRSV: "prince, judge, and ruler"). *Sarim* in Hebrew "biblical" literature refers to magnates/nobles/rulers/"princes," usually officers of the monarchy subordinate to the king. In the Greek text of Sirach, it is translated in different passages by *megistanes* ("great ones/magnates"), *dynastes* ("nobles, power holders"), *hegoumenoi* ("rulers"), and *presbyteroi* ("elders"). *Moshel* (qal participle of *mashal*) is translated in Sirach by the same Greek terms, *megistan, dynastes,* and *hegoumenos,* as well as *kyrios* ("lord"), seems to refer to anyone who rules or has authority over others. The *shophet,* consistently translated with the Greek *krites* and into English as "judge," also seems to overlap with the others in the people to whom it refers. In what appears as another synonymous term, Ben Sira also refers to a *nadib,* translated with *dynastes* in 7:6, which in the Hebrew Bible refers to one who rules or has power over. Other terms for rulers in Sirach are the "master of the city" (*shl ton 'ir, megistan,* 4:7), before whom one should bow one's head, the "head" of a city (*rosh,* 10:2), and the "chieftain" (*nasi', hegoumenos,* 41:17) before whom one should be ashamed of falsehood. See further Horsley and Tiller, "Ben Sira and the Sociology of the Second Temple," 81–83. A similar pattern of language usage is discernible in Ben Sira's references to "the poor/poverty" in contrast to "the wealthy/wealth," with several somewhat interchangeable terms in Hebrew, translated by different Greek terms that also appear somewhat interchangeable. See Benjamin G. Wright III and Claudia V. Camp, "'Who Has Been Tested by Gold and Found Perfect?' Ben Sira's Discourse of Riches and Poverty," *Henoch* 33 (2001), 154–55; and for earlier proverbial wisdom, see J. David Pleins, "Poverty in the Social World of the Wise," *JSOT* 37 (1987): 63–72.

14. Since *sārîm* frequently occurs in the plural in Hebrew texts, suggesting that such "princes" or "nobles" operated in a group, *presbyterōn* in 7:14 would be an understandable translation in Greek.

15. "V 2ab is in synonymous parallelism with v 1; as is usually the case, the rich are also the great" (Skehan and DiLella, *Wisdom of Ben Sira,* 211).

16. Ben Sira also mentions that the sage "instructs his own people," although it is difficult to discern whether this means the people generally, the Jerusalemites generally, or his own circle of disciples. If the former, then we might suspect that this special teaching function would also be part of the sage's service of the ruling aristocracy: instructing the Jerusalemites and/or peasants in the ideological basis for the priestly aristocracy (as in the "praise of the ancestors" in Sir. 44–50).

17. In his magnification of Ben Sira's criticism of merchants and trading, for example, Hengel focused on 11:10–19; 13:24–25; 21:8; and 31:3–9. But nothing in Ben Sira's speeches contrasting the rich and the poor, wealth and poverty, in 11:14–19; 13:13–24; and 31:1–11 suggests that he has merchants in mind. And the line about "building one's house with other people's goods" in 21:8 sounds more like a wealthy creditor taking advantage of his desperate debtors.

18. See Lenski, *Power and Privilege,* 191 n. 5a.

19. Ibid., 215–16.

20. Ibid., 154–55.

21. John H. Kautsky, *The Politics of Aristocratic Empires* (Chapel Hill: University of North Carolina Press, 1982).

22. For example, Hengel, *Judaism and Hellenism,* 1:26.

23. Lenski states the relationship of the peasantry and their rulers bluntly: "In short, . . . the political elite sought to use the energies of the peasantry to the full, while depriving them of all but the basic necessities of life" (*Power and Privilege,* 270).

24. Ben Sira (in Sir. 34:24–27) sounds like the prophet Amos (in 2:6–8) when he suggests that powerful creditors were taking advantage of vulnerable peasants who had fallen heavily into debt.

25. Lenski, *Power and Privilege,* 278–79.

26. Ibid., 250. Lenski's discussion of the merchant class draws mainly on medieval European life, even nascent capitalist evidence, and on agrarian societies that had been affected by early modern mercantile or modern capitalist systems.

27. Already in the Persian period Phoenicians and Greek traders may well have been operating in Jerusalem, although their trade would still have been primarily in luxury goods and items desired by and paid for by the ruling elite. The Ptolemaic regime would have been powerful enough to limit the number of Greek or Phoenician traders, except of course for when they were serving the Ptolemaic interests.

28. There must have been other retainers in the temple-state. Since the imperial regime would have kept a monopoly on military force, there were presumably no military forces at the command of the priestly aristocracy. Yet maintenance of the temple compound called for temple guards or "doorkeepers." The "physicians" admired by "the great ones" for their skills with healing and medicines (38:1–8) may have been more like retainers, serving the aristocracy directly, and less like the artisans, who were less directly in service to the elite. The regular priests and Levites would seem to have functioned somewhat as did the retainers Lenski describes in other agrarian societies, mediating between the high-priestly rulers and the common people, including "effecting the transfer of the economic surplus from the producers to the political and religious elite" (Lenski, *Power and Privilege,* 246).

29. Ibid., 244.

30. See especially the extensive and insightful analysis of Claudia V. Camp, "Understanding a Patriarchy: Women in Second Century Jerusalem through the Eyes of Ben Sira," in *Women Like This: New Perspectives on Jewish Women in the Greco-Roman World,* ed. Amy-Jill Levine (Atlanta: SBL, 1991), 1–39.

Chapter 4. Scribes and Sages: Administrators and Intellectuals

1. Jonathan Z. Smith, "Wisdom and Apocalyptic," in *Map Is Not Territory: Studies in the History of Religion* (original essay, 1975; Leiden: Brill, 1978).
2. Ronald F. G. Sweet, "The Sage in Mesopotamian Palaces and Royal Courts," in *The Sage in Israel and the Ancient Near East*, ed. John Gammie and Leo Perdue (Winona Lake, IN: Eisenbrauns, 1990), 103.
3. A. Leo Oppenheim, "The Position of the Intellectual in Mesopotamian Society," *Daedalus* 104 (1975): 39–46, offers a compact overview of the functions of scribes in Mesopotamia, although with his anachronistic sense of a nascent capitalism in first-millennium Mesopotamia, he projects an unlikely life as "independent expert" for some scribe-scholars (43–44).
4. Oppenheim, "Position of the Intellectual," 41.
5. Ibid., 40–41.
6. Raymond Westbrook, "Biblical and Cuneiform Law Codes," *RB* 92 (1985): 247–64; Martha Roth, *Law Collections in Mesopotamia and Asia Minor* (Atlanta: Scholars Press, 1997); Lisbeth S. Fried, *The Priest and the Great King* (Winona Lake, IN: Eisenbrauns, 2004).
7. Fuller analysis and documentation of divinization appears in A. Leo Oppenheim, "Divination and Celestial Observation in the Last Assyrian Empire," *Centaurus* 14 (1969): 123–35.
8. Ronald F. G. Sweet, "The Sage in Mesopotamian Palaces and Royal Courts," in Gammie and Perdue, *The Sage*, 105.
9. Ibid., 105–7.
10. Recent research into the rich supply of tablets recovered from Mesopotamian civilizations gives us a fairly clear sense of that training, starting with the Old Babylonian period, as laid out in an illuminating synthetic summary of the ancient Mesopotamian "educational system" by David Carr, in *Writing on the Tablet of the Heart: Origins of Scripture and Literature* (Oxford: Oxford University Press, 2005), chap. 2.
11. For the following, see esp. Eleanor Robson, "The Tablet House: A Scribal School in Old Babylonian Nippur," *Revue d'assyriologie et d'archeologie orientale* 95 (2001): 39–66.
12. This paragraph summarizes some of the discussion in Carr, *Tablet of the Heart*, 23–25.
13. See Petra D. Gesche, *Schulunterricht in Babylonien im erstern Jahrtausend v. Chr.*, AOAT 275 (Münster: Ugarit-Verlag, 2001), 81–152, 174–83; Niek Veldhuis, *Elementary Education at Nippur* (Groningen: Styx, 1997), 134–36; and idem, "Mesopotamian Canons," in *Homer, The Bible and Beyond: Literary and Religious Canons in the Ancient World*, ed. Margalit Finkelberg and Guy Stroumsa (Leiden: Brill, 2003), 9–28, esp. 113–14.
14. As cited in Carr, *Tablet of the Heart*, 17, 31.
15. Ronald J. Williams, "The Functions of the Sage in the Egyptian Royal Court," in Gammie and Perdue, *The Sage*, 96.
16. "Just as the core elite is identified with literacy, both it and the remainder of the scribal subelite are identified with administrative office. There is no evidence of scribes with careers separate from office." John Baines, "Literacy and Ancient Egyptian Society," *Man*, NS, 18 (1983): 584.
17. Williams, "The Functions of the Sage," 97; similarly Ronald J. Williams, "The Sage in Egyptian Literature," in Gammie and Perdue, *The Sage*, 26.
18. Williams, "The Sage," 25 n. 9.
19. All in Williams, "The Functions of the Sage," 96.

20. Williams, "The Sage," 27; "The Functions of the Sage," 96–97.
21. Williams, "The Sage," 28 n. 21.
22. Ibid., 28.
23. Ibid., 27; Carr, *Tablet of the Heart,* 79.
24. Williams, "The Sage," 26.
25. Ibid., 26–27.
26. Carr, *Tablet of the Heart,* 65–67, 82.
27. Translation in ibid., 67 n. 15.
28. Ibid., 67.
29. Williams, "The Sage," 22.
30. Carr, *Tablet of the Heart,* 77.
31. Carr, *Tablet of the Heart,* 69, 77.
32. See the survey of pertinent studies by Gary N. Knoppers, "The Vanishing Solomon: The Disappearance of the United Monarchy from Recent Histories of Ancient Israel," *JBL* 116 (1997): 19–44.
33. For how archaeological findings bear on scribes and schools in ancient Judah, see David W. Jamieson-Drake, *Scribes and Schools in Monarchic Judah: A Socio-Archaeological Approach,* JSOTSup (Sheffield: Almond, 1991).
34. That even a small kingdom such as Judah would have had at least a small administrative apparatus that included scribes is indicated by sources for other monarchies in the area, in previous centuries or contemporary with Judah. The diplomatic correspondence between kings of city-states in Syria and Canaan and the Egyptian imperial court known as the Amarna Archives provide evidence of at least a few scribes in high administrative positions many centuries before the emergence of the kingdoms of Israel and Judah. The lists of kings and scribes in Akkadian sources found in the royal palace at Ugarit in Syria are especially informative, about the (sometimes conflictual) relations between king and his top scribal administrators, as well as about the position and role of the scribes. See Anson F. Rainey, "The Scribe at Ugarit: His Position and Influence," *Proceedings of the Israel Academy of Sciences and Humanities* 3 (1969): 126–46, here 144–45. Here are "expert scribes" functioning as "counselors/friends of the king" and even as the vizier. In some cases son succeeds father in office, as with Yasiranu and Husanu. The kings supported their high scribal administrators by granting them estates ("cities/towns," from the revenue of which they lived comfortably). But on occasion king and scribal counselor/vizier would come into conflict. For example, the king transferred the estate of Yasiranu to one of his chariot warriors, who was also "a friend of the king." But the next king restored both father and son to their positions and granted Yasiranu another estate. The inscription left by Mesha, king of Moab, and that by the Aramean king of Damascus in Dan provide evidence that small kingdoms contemporary and in conflict with the kingdom of Israel had "royal scribes" at their court. And the Aramean King Bar-Rakib in northern Syria left a relief portraying himself on the throne and being approached by a scribe. See William M. Schniedewind, *How the Bible Became a Book* (Cambridge: Cambridge University Press, 2004), 40–45, and other references in his notes.
35. Michael Fishbane, *Biblical Interpretation in Ancient Israel* (Oxford: Clarendon, 1985), 26.
36. On royal correspondence, see E. Lipinski, "Royal and State Scribes in Ancient Jerusalem," 158–59; and Denis Pardee, *Handbook of Ancient Hebrew Letters* (Chico, CA: Scholars Press, 1982). A general survey of the functions of scribes in the monarchy is given by Nili S. Fox, *In Service of the King* (Cincinnati: Hebrew Union College Press, 2000), 96–105.

37. Christine Schams, *Jewish Scribes in the Second-Temple Period* (Sheffield: Sheffield Academic Press, 1998), surveys occurrences of the term "scribe" in Judean literature, but without exploring wider implications.

38. The standard translation of *šōṭēr* as well as *sōpēr* in the Septuagint is *grammateus*. In her close word-study, Christine Schams finds that the *grammateis* in the various Septuagintal passages function in various ways, some of which are not usually associated with *grammateis* in Greek literature: "leadership positions with unspecified functions; high royal officials with representative, administrative and financial responsibilities, and with reading expertise; professional writing; advisory and public functions as wise and educated men; an association with the law; and... an army official" (*Jewish Scribes in the Second Temple Period*, 83). Whether *sōpĕrîm* or *šōṭĕrîm* were involved, these are the range of functions in which scribes served in Egypt, Mesopotamia, and elsewhere in the ancient Near East.

39. Philip R. Davies, *Scribes and Schools* (Louisville, KY: Westminster John Knox, 1998), 77, 83.

40. Arguments for early existence of schools appear in Bernard Lang, "Schule und Unterricht in alten Israel," in *La Sagesse de l'Ancien Testament*, ed. M. Gilbert (Louvain: Leuven University Press, 1979), 186–201; and André Lemaire, *Les écoles et la formation de la Bible dans l'ancien Israël*, OBO (Fribourg: Éditions Universitaires, 1981), esp. 52–57; and for scribal schools, see E. W. Heaton, *The School Tradition of the Old Testament* (Oxford: Oxford University Press, 1994). Criticism of such arguments is in F. W. Golka, "The Israelite Wisdom School or 'The Emperor's New Clothes,'" in *The Leopard's Spots: Biblical and African Wisdom in Proverbs* (Edinburgh: T&T Clark, 1993); Graham Davies, "Were There Schools in Ancient Israel?" in *Wisdom in Ancient Israel*, ed. John Day et al. (Cambridge: Cambridge University Press, 1995), 199–211; and James L. Crenshaw, *Education in Ancient Israel: Across the Deadening Silence*, ABRL (New York: Doubleday, 1998).

41. Cf. Carr, *Tablet of the Heart*, 122.

42. See further the discussion in ibid., 124–25.

43. See further ibid., 129.

44. In other doublets in Proverbs, mother figures along with father, but not explicitly in an instructional role: 10:1; 15:20; 19:26; 20:20; 29:15; 30:11, 17.

45. So also Carr, *Tablet of the Heart*, 130.

46. See further Glendon E. Bryce, *A Legacy of Wisdom: The Egyptian Contribution to the Wisdom of Israel* (Lewisburg, PA: Bucknell University Press, 1979); Michael V. Fox, "The Social Location of the Book of Proverbs," in *Texts, Temples, and Traditions: A Tribute to Menahem Haran*, ed. Michael Fox et al. (Winona Lake, IN: Eisenbrauns, 1996), 227–39; and Carr, *Tablet of the Heart*, 129–30.

47. Fox, "The Social Location," 227–39, comments caustically that "wisdom literature was indeed extensively taught and copied in the scribal schools, but so were math, geography, administrative correspondence, and many other types of texts relevant to the future occupations of the pupils. We might just as well call the scribal school the 'Magic School' because scribes wrote magical texts and scribal students copied them."

48. Glendon E. Bryce, *A Legacy of Wisdom: The Egyptian Contribution to the Wisdom of Israel* (Lewisburg, PA: Bucknell University Press, 1979).

49. It is tempting to see in Isa. 5:(7-)14–24 another allusion to scribes who are also "the wise/sages." This is a series of woes against the ruling class in Jerusalem, people who live in luxury while foreclosing on the debts of the poor, having rejected the torah/instruction of the LORD. Among them are "the wise" (v. 21), who would presumably be scribes serving the rulers. Isa. 29:13–14 also appears to lash out at sages.

50. Moshe Weinfeld, *Deuteronomy and the Deuteronomic School* (Oxford: Clarendon, 1972), and many others.

Chapter 5. Orality, Writing, and the Cultivation of Texts

1. James L. Crenshaw, "Transmitting Prophecy across Generations," in *Writings and Speech in Israelite and Ancient Near Eastern Prophecy,* ed. Ehud Ben Zvi and Michael H. Floyd, Symposium Series 10 (Atlanta: SBL, 2000), 41.
2. See, for example, Gabriel Barkay, "The Iron Age II-III," in *The Archaeology of Ancient Israel,* ed. Amnon Ben Tor (New Haven, CT: Yale University Press, for the Open University of Israel, 1992), 349; cf. Amihai Mazar, *Archaeology of the Land of Israel* (New York: Doubleday, 1992), 515; Allan R. Millard, "An Assessment of the Evidence for Writing in Ancient Israel," *Biblical Archaeology Today: Proceedings of the International Congress on Biblical Archaeology, Jerusalem, April 1984* (Jerusalem: Israel Exploration Society, 1985), 301–12; idem, "The Question of Israelite Literacy," *Bible Review* 3 (1987): 22–31. Working with a more critical and nuanced sense of ancient Israelite writing, yet still confident that "the use of writing spread throughout society" by the time of Josiah in the seventh century: William M. Schniedewind, *How the Bible Became a Book* (Cambridge: Cambridge University Press, 2004), 91, 111.
3. This is all the more striking when we consider that the wisdom contained in "the words of the wise" in Prov. 22:17–24:22 was heavily influenced by *The Sayings of Amenemope,* one of the principal Egyptian instructional texts. *Amenemope* and other Egyptian instructional literature such as *Merikare, Anii,* and *Ankhsheshanky* refer to learning from written texts, such as the Supi-book, and to fathers teaching their "sons" to write. But emphasis was clearly on the oral-aural, as illustrated in the teaching of Kagemni: after the sage taught his children orally, his words were transcribed. Then he said, "as for *everything that is in writing on this scroll, listen* to it just as I *said* it" (emphasis mine). The teaching is oral, the learning is aural; the written text is a transcript. See further Donald B. Redford, "Scribe and Speaker," in *Writings and Speech in Israelite and Ancient Near Eastern Prophecy,* Ben Zvi and Floyd, 216. Unlike their Egyptian precursors, Judean scribes/sages do not mention written texts or writing as a medium of learning and instruction or, for that matter, as an aspect of their service among the rulers.
4. So also James L. Crenshaw, "The Primacy of Listening in Ben Sira's Pedagogy," in *Wisdom, You Are My Sister: Studies in Honor of Roland E. Murphy,* ed. Michael L. Barre, CBQMS 27 (Washington, DC: Catholic Biblical Association of America, 1997), 277–87; idem, *Education in Ancient Israel: Across the Deadening Silence* (New York: Doubleday, 1998), 177–83; and cf. Michael Fox, "Wisdom and the Self-Presentation of Wisdom Literature," in *Reading from Left to Right: Essays on the Hebrew Bible in Honour of David J. A. Clines,* ed. J. Cheryl Exum and H. G. M. Williamson, JSOTSup 373 (Sheffield: Sheffield Academic Press, 2003), 153–72. Lest we take the emphasis on speaking and listening in such instructional wisdom as mainly a rhetorical device in what is fundamentally written wisdom, comparable Egyptian texts inscribed on stelae and in tombs state that they were intended to be heard and that the audience, though literate, was intended to listen, as explained by Donald B. Redford, "Scribe and Speaker," 161. Redford supplies many references to skill in oral delivery (before assemblies of rulers or other administrators-advisers as an integral part of scribal instruction in Egypt, pp. 200–205).
5. Here I am heavily dependent on David M. Carr, *Writing on the Tablet of the Heart: Origins of Scripture and Literature* (Oxford: Oxford University Press, 2005), esp. chaps. 1–4, who has summarized the results of studies by specialists on

Mesopotamian, Egyptian, and other scribal cultures and drawn out their implications for scribal practice in Judah-Judea.

6. In contrast to anachronistic assumptions of widespread literacy in ancient Greece, recent critical studies, based on extensive research and analysis, have demonstrated that fewer than 10 percent of the people of ancient Greece were literate. In the Roman Empire, as many as 15 percent may have had some degree of literacy, particularly in the cities. See esp. William V. Harris, *Ancient Literacy* (Cambridge, MA: Harvard University Press, 1989); and the responses to Harris, such as the essays in Mary Beard, ed., *Literacy in the Roman World*, JRASup 3 (Ann Arbor, MI: Dept. of Classical Studies, University of Michigan, 1991), which confirmed his basic conclusions, while refining his views of the different kinds and uses of writing.

7. Catherine Hezser, *Jewish Literacy in Roman Palestine* (Tübingen: Mohr-Siebeck, 2001). This study provides full documentation for the earlier arguments of interpreters of the Christian Gospels and the historical Jesus that the extent and uses of literacy were severely limited in Galilean and Judean society, where communication was predominantly oral; e.g., Werner Kelber, *The Oral and Written Gospel* (Philadelphia: Fortress, 1983); Pieter J. J. Botha, "Greco-Roman Literacy as Setting for New Testament Writings," *Neotestamentica* 26 (1992): 195–215; Richard A. Horsley, "The Oral Communication Environment of Q," in Horsley with Jonathan Draper, *Whoever Hears You Hears Me: Prophets, Performance, and Tradition in Q* (Harrisburg, PA: Trinity Press International, 1999).

8. In the ancient Mesopotamia of cuneiform writing and the Egypt of hieroglyphics, literacy was even more narrowly confined, perhaps to 1 percent of the population, mainly those trained as scribes. See Mogens Trolle Larsen, "What They Wrote on Clay," in *Literacy and Society*, ed. Karen Schousboe and Mogens Trolle Larsen (Copenhagen: Akademisk Forlag, 1989), 134; John Baines and C. J. Eyre, "Four Notes on Literacy," *Göttingen Miszellen* 16 (1983): 65–74; literacy is linked to the structure of Egyptian society in John Baines, "Literacy and Ancient Egyptian Society," *Man* 18 (1983): 572–99; and John Baines, "Literacy, Social Organization, and the Archaeological Record," in *State and Society: The Emergence and Development of Social Hierarchy and Political Centralization*, ed. J. Gledhill, B. Bender, and Mogens Trolle Larsen (London: Unwin Hyman, 1988), 192–214.

9. See especially the work of John Miles Foley in books such as *Immanent Art: From Structure to Meaning in Traditional Oral Epic* (Bloomington: Indiana University Press, 1991); *The Singer of Tales in Performance* (Bloomington: Indiana University Press, 1995); and *How to Read an Oral Poem* (Urbana: University of Illinois Press, 2002), which develop theory of verbal art in relation to materials from various cultures and studies in a variety of disciplines.

10. J. Collins, "Literacy and Literacies," *Annual Review of Anthropology* 24 (1995): 75–93.

11. The hundreds of "ostraca," broken pieces of pottery (the ancient equivalent of scratch paper) with formulaic indications of the name, date, and quantity of wine and oil written on them, found in capital cities and outlying fortress towns, were clearly records of tax collection. So were the more than 1,200 storage jars (for wine or oil) from eighth-century BCE Judah, with their handles stamped (before firing) with certain symbols and the message *lmlk* ("belonging to the king"). See Barkay, "Iron Age," 320, 346; Mazar, *Archaeology*, 410, 455–58; Klaas A. D. Smelik, *Writings from Ancient Israel* (Louisville, KY: Westminster/John Knox, 1991), 94; William Schniedewind, *How the Bible Became a Book: Textualization of Ancient Israel* (Cambridge: Cambridge University Press, 2004), 55–57. Mogens Trolle

Larsen, "Introduction: Literacy and Social Complexity," in Gledhill, Bender, and Larsen *State and Society,* 173–91, esp. 184–85, explains how early writing was used mainly for administrative purposes by centralizing states.

12. We might recall two well-known examples: Jeremiah, received a command from YHWH to "take a scroll and write on it all the words I have spoken to you," but then called the scribe Baruch son of Neriah, who did the writing on the scroll at the prophet's dictation (Jer. 36:1–4; cf. Esth. 8:8–9). In the reign of King Josiah, after the scribe Shaphan read (recited) the book of the law found in the Temple to the king, Josiah himself is said to have read it (recited/*qārā*; 2 Kings 22–23). Another example of how attention to the possible meanings of terms makes a huge difference is one of the texts taken as evidence for widespread literacy in ancient Israel, the reference to what is supposedly a typical "young man" of Succoth, in Judg. 8:13–14. Closer attention to the meaning of the Hebrew term *na'ar,* however, suggests that the *na'ar* of Succoth who supplied the list of officials and elders to Gideon (8:13–14) may have been a servant or attendant (or scribe!) of those city officials.

13. Edgar W. Conrad, "Heard But Not Seen: The Representation of 'Books' in the Old Testament," *JSOT* 54 (1992): 45–59, is a suggestive criticism of the rhetorical representation of books in some books of the Hebrew Bible.

14. Menahem Haran, "On the Diffusion of Literacy and Schools in Ancient Israel," in *Congress Volume: Jerusalem 1986,* ed. J. A. Emerton (Leiden: Brill, 1988), 81–95. Ian M. Young, "Israelite Literacy: Interpreting the Evidence," *VT* 48 (1998): 239–53, 408–422. He concludes: "Apart from the functional literacy of craftsmen, we have argued that there is not one reference in the literary sources to an individual from outside these groups [scribes, administrators, and priests] either reading or writing" (409). Insofar as the Temple and priesthood were, in effect, a branch of the monarchy in ancient Judah, the discovery of "the document of the torah/covenant" in the Temple under Josiah did not involve a "radical shift" in social location from the monarchic state to the Temple, pace Schniedewind, *How the Bible Became a Book,* 111–12.

15. Carr, *Tablet of the Heart.*

16. Susan Niditch, *Oral World and Written Word,* Library of Ancient Israel (Louisville, KY: Westminster John Knox, 1996). Donald B. Redford, "Scribe and Speaker," 151 and n. 22, complains that biblical scholars are "the most egregious offenders" in a debilitating failure to define what type of literacy is in question in Judea and other ancient Near Eastern societies.

17. For discussion of the ways that writing is closely related to oral communication, see Ruth Finnegan, *Oral Poetry: Its Nature, Significance, and Social Context* (Cambridge: Cambridge University Press, 1977); idem, *Literacy and Orality* (Oxford: Blackwell, 1988); Brian Street, *Literacy in Theory and Practice* (Cambridge: Cambridge University Press, 1984); in contrast to the sharper polarization seen by Jack Goody, *The Domestication of the Savage Mind* (Cambridge: Cambridge University Press, 1977); idem, *The Logic of Writing and the Organization of Society* (Cambridge: Cambridge University Press, 1986).

18. Barkay, "Iron Age," 350–51; Mazar, *Archaeology,* 518; Niditch, *Oral World,* 49–50, 62. On one of these bullae the name "Baruch, son of Neriah the Scribe" is visible, which is (also) the name of the scribe to whom Jeremiah dictated his prophetic oracles in Jer. 36. Simple records such as those of debts, of course, could be manipulated by those with writing skills. A passage that has been claimed to attest widespread literacy in late monarchic Judah is the indictment of those "who write oppressive writings . . . to rob the poor . . . of their right" in Isa. 10:1–2. Judging from parallel oracles in Isaiah (e.g., 3:13–15; 5:8–10, 18–24) that indict

the wealthy officers of the monarchy for exploiting the poor, however, these "writers of writings of oppression" are also such officials who, through their scribal retainers, manipulate the debt records to take control of the land of desperate peasants. The increase in these brief administrative writings is hardly a solid basis for the claim of an increase in literacy generally by the seventh century that created the context for writing the earliest biblical books; cf. Schniedewind, *How the Bible Became a Book.*

19. See further Niditch, *Oral World,* 62–63.

20. M. T. Clanchy, *From Memory to Written Record: England 1066–1307* (Cambridge, MA: Harvard University Press, 1979), 125.

21. Michael Harbsmeier, "Inventions of Writing," in Gledhill, Bender, and Larsen, *State and Society,* 253–59; Bengt Holbeck, "What the Illiterate Think of Writing," in Schousboe and Larsen, *Literacy and Society,* 183–96; Larsen, "Introduction: Literacy and Social Complexity," in *Literacy and Society,* 188: "for the illiterate, writing is not just a technology of communication, it has a reality in the field of magic."

22. See further Niditch, *Oral World,* 82–83. Rosalind Thomas, *Literacy and Orality in Ancient Greece* (Cambridge: Cambridge University Press, 1992), 80, similarly suggests that Greek curse tablets on lead from the fifth and fourth centuries BCE were used "to intensify the curse, and perhaps make it even more effective."

23. Less disturbing examples are two rolled-up silver plaques found in a burial cave at Ketef Himmon (Jerusalem) from the late monarchy. That they are inscribed with different versions of a blessing resembling the priestly blessing of Num. 6:24–26 suggests written transcriptions of a well-known and orally pronounced blessing. See Barkay, "Iron Age," 371. For further examples of numinous writing, see Mazar, *Archaeology,* 448–49; and Niditch, *Oral World,* 47–48.

24. Niditch, *Oral World,* 70.

25. Both quotations from ibid., 80–81.

26. The elementary level of communication (e.g., concerning supplies of bread and wine) in short letters on ostraca, exchanged among officers stationed in military outposts, also appears to have been dictated to and read by (lower-level) scribes. Texts are in Dennis Pardee, *Handbook of Ancient Hebrew Letters: A Study Edition* (Chico, CA: Scholars Press, 1982); and idem, "Letters," *ABD* 4:202. Discussion in William Schniedewind, "Sociolinguistic Reflections on the Letter of a 'Literate' Soldier (Lachish 3)," *Zeitschrift für Althebraistik* 13 (2000): 157–67. An unusual letter found at a small military fortress that was probably also an agricultural administrative depot near Yavneh (probably on a royal estate) suggests that on occasion simple formulaic writing could be used on behalf of a corvée worker. See further Klaas A. D. Smelik, *Writings from Ancient Israel* (Louisville, KY: Westminster/John Knox, 1991), 94; Schniedewind, *How the Bible Became a Book,* 103.

27. M. T. Clanchy, *From Memory to Written Record* (Cambridge, MA: Harvard University Press, 1979), 125.

28. See further Rosalind Thomas, "Literacy and the City-State in Archaic and Classical Greece," in *Literacy and Power in the Ancient World,* ed. R. Bowman and Greg Woolf (Cambridge: Cambridge University Press, 1994), 33–50, esp. 34–45; Niditch, *Oral World,* 62–63, 65.

29. The references to "the book of Yashar" (apparently a collection of songs, well-known and orally performed; Josh. 10:13; 2 Sam. 1:18) are rhetorical appeals to the written word because it has authority, perhaps of prestige at the royal court.

30. In fifth- and fourth-century Athens the laws produced by the city assembly were written on monuments. This "publication" of the laws at a time when writing was

becoming more widely used In ancient Greece, however, was not primarily a means of informing the Athenian public of the actual content of the laws (only a fraction of the populace was literate), nor was it primarily a way of recording the laws for future reference or administrative purposes. The inscription of public laws was rather basically "a monument or memorial whose public presence and very existence guarantee[d] the continuing force of the decision it record[ed]." Thomas, *Literacy and Orality,* 85; idem, "Literacy and the City-State," 39–43.

31. Niditch, *Oral* World, 55, where she appeals to the example of the Vietnam War Memorial in Washington, DC.

32. The "found book" recited by Josiah included new teaching (*torah*), such as the prescription that the Passover be celebrated in Jerusalem (2 Kings 23:21–25), that would not have been in the book written by Moses on Sinai. Yet it may be beside the point to make much of the different contents of the two "books of teaching," however, since they were understood as symbolic, monumental, iconic documents that functioned in covenant renewal ceremonies. As Niditch remarks (*Oral World,* 103), to ask whether the document was really found or not at the time of Josiah and whether it was some early version of Deuteronomy are moot questions, since comparative materials indicate that the "found book" theme had to do with validation of political actions or theological positions, as explained in Wolfgang Speyer, *Die literarische Fälschung im heidnischen and christlichen Altertum: Ein Versuch ihrer Deutung* (Munich: Beck, 1971). See also Richard A. Horsley, "The Origins of the Hebrew Scriptures in Imperial Relations," in *Orality, Literacy, and Colonialism in Antiquity,* ed. Jonathan A. Draper, Semeia Studies 47 (Atlanta: SBL, 2004), 111–14.

33. Similarly in Egypt some texts claimed authority "by including accounts of how they were found—after long neglect—in a temple deposit," according to Carr, *Tablet of the Heart,* 81.

34. Clanchy, *From Memory to Written Record,* 18.

35. In a predominantly oral society in which actual legal cases would have been handled mostly by local village courts according to orally cultivated (and probably covenantal) customs, there would have been no need—or the requisite literacy—to consult a monumental writing of covenantal statutes and ordinances deposited in the Temple. Thomas, *Literacy and Orality,* 96–97, mentions that even in the fourth century, when many classics scholars look for them to be relying on written records, Greek politicians "still tended to rely on memory and oral communication."

36. See, for example, Olaf Pedersen, *Archives and Libraries in the City of Assur* (Uppsala: Almqvist & Wiksell, 1986), 12–19; and Thomas, *Oral Tradition and Written Record in Classical Athens* (Cambridge: University of Cambridge Press, 1989), 31.

37. The awesome sacred aura evoked by the presentation and opening of "the document of the teaching of Moses" might be compared with Assyrian royal inscriptions, as discussed by Peter Machinist, "Assyrians on Assyria in the First Millennium B.C.," in *Anfänge politischen Denkens in der Antike: Die nahöstlichen Kulturen und die Griechen,* ed. Kurt Raaflaub (Munich: Oldenbourg, 1993), 101. Karel van der Toorn, "The Iconic Book: Analogies between the Babylonian Cult or Images and the Veneration of the Torah," in *Image and the Book* (Leuven: Peeters, 1997), 229–256, compares the Torah, as in the presentation of the book of Mosaic covenant law presented by Ezra, to the images of the Babylonian gods that were worshipped as sacred objects.

38. At two points Yahweh tells Isaiah to write on a tablet. In 8:1–4 the writing of only eleven letters, as the name of a son, becomes a prophetic sign-act (or a numinous writing with power to effect its message). In 30:8 (8–14) the writing of the message appears to be meant rhetorically, suggesting that Isaiah's prophecy is to have

the effective force of writing, serving as a witness against those who fall under divine condemnation.

39. Karel van der Toorn, "Old Babylonian Prophecy between the Oral and the Written," *Journal of Northwest Semitic Languages* 24 (1998): 55–70, offers a parallel account of prophecy as oral performance that is then communicated to the king via being written down.

40. See further Daniel Boyarin, "Placing Reading: Ancient Israel and Medieval Europe," in *The Ethnography of Reading*, ed. Jonathan Boyarin (Berkeley: University of California Press, 1993), 10–17; Richard A. Horsley, "Introduction," in *Oral Performance, Popular Tradition, and Hidden Transcript in Q*, Semeia Studies 60 (Atlanta: SBL, 2006), 15–18. Similarly in Egypt the term often translated as "read" referred rather to oral performance or recitation, as noted by Carr, *Tablet of the Heart*, 72.

41. See, e.g., Botha, "Greco-Roman Literacy"; Niek Veldhuis, "Mesopotamian Canons," in *Homer, the Bible, and Beyond: Literary and Religious Canons in the Ancient World*, ed. Margalit Finkelberg and Guy Stroumsa (Leiden: Brill, 2003), 9; Christopher Eyre and John Baines, "Interactions between Orality and Literacy in Ancient Egypt," in Schousboe and Larsen, *Literacy and Society*, 100–103; and Carr, *Tablet of the Heart*, 5.

42. Stephanie Dalley, *Myths from Mesopotamia* (New York: Oxford University Press, 1989), xvi; Jerrold S. Cooper, "Babbling on Recovery of Mesopotamian Orality," in *Mesopotamian Epic Literature: Oral or Aural?* ed. Marianna E. Vogelsang and Herman L. J. Vanstiphout (Lewiston, NY: Edwin Mellen, 1992), 117.

43. Oxford MS Heb e 30; see Ernst Würthwein, *The Text of the Old Testament: An Introduction to the Biblia Hebraica*, trans. Erroll F. Rhodes (1979; rev. ed., Grand Rapids: Eerdmans, 1995), 170–71.

44. In Mesopotamia "the primary purpose of recording stories in writing was not necessarily to supply individual readers with a coherent and connected account," but to provide authenticity or authority to rituals or institutions. Dalley, *Myths from Mesopotamia*, xvi.

45. Richard Gordon, "From Republic to Principate: Priesthood, Religion, and Ideology," in *Pagan Priests*, ed. Mary Beard and John North (London: Duckworth, 1990), 189.

46. See Helmut Koester, *Synoptische Überlieferung bei den apostolishen Vätern* (Berlin: Akademie Verlag, 1957), for how Jesus sayings were carried in oral tradition after the Gospels were written.

47. Martin S. Jaffee, "Figuring Early Rabbinic Literary Culture," *Semeia* 65 (1994): 67–73.

48. Doyne Dawson, *Cities of the Gods: Communist Utopias in Greek Thought* (New York: Oxford University Press, 1992).

49. Martin Jaffee, *Torah in the Mouth: Writing and Oral Tradition in Palestinian Judaism, 200 CE–400 CE* (New York: Oxford University Press, 2001).

50. So, for scribal-priestly reciters at Qumran, Martin S. Jaffee, *Torah in the Mouth: Writing and Oral Tradition in Palestinian Judaism, 200 BCE–400 CE* (New York: Oxford University Press, 2001); and for earlier Judean and ancient Near Eastern scribes, Carr, *Tablet of the Heart*, 5. For ancient Mesopotamia, see Niek Veldhuis, "Mesopotamian Canons," 28: "The concept of a library does not seem to exist. Knowledge was located in the heads of school masters, not in collections of tablets."

51. Carr, *Tablet of the Heart*, 8. Note the formulation: the texts incised on the heart were known and identified as written texts. William A. Graham, *Beyond the*

Written Word: Oral Aspects of Scripture in the History of Religion (Cambridge: Cambridge University Press, 1987), 68, makes the important point that in an ongoing tradition of oral teaching, even when it is also written, the revered word comes alive only as spoken by teacher to pupil.

52. Ibid., 81.

53. Carr, *Tablet of the Heart*, 4–9, and repeatedly through the book, stresses the central role of memory in the learning and recitation of cultural texts. As Redford, "Scribe and Speaker," 218, comments about the primacy of orality in learning and recitation of texts in Egypt, "all that the writer-scribe can do is to try to keep abreast of a genuinely oral tradition that enjoys its own vibrant life, and record its momentary stages."

54. Thomas, *Literacy and Orality,* 91. For the text and a discussion of how Pliny, a highly educated and trained intellectual, dictated both his letters and other writings, see Jocelyn Penny Small, *Wax Tablets of the Mind: Cognitive Studies of Memory and Literacy in Classical Antiquity* (London: Routledge, 1997).

55. For Mesopotamian parallels, see Veldhuis, "Mesopotamian Canons," 16. The one detailed account we have of such composition is of Shulgi, king of Ur, commissioning his court poets to compose hymns and then teach them to the singer, who is nonliterate. See Jerrold S. Cooper, "Babbling on Recovering Mesopotamian Orality," in Vogelsang and Vanstiphout, *Mesopotamian Epic Literature,* 113–14.

56. Whether the rhetorical question in Jer 8:8 ("How can you say, 'We are wise and the [teaching] law of the LORD is with us,' when in fact the false pen of the scribes has made it into a lie") is read in the context of Josiah's reform or some conflict over torah in the second-temple period, it is a criticism of the role of scribes, perhaps in the development a "document of covenant/teaching (*torah*)" used to authorize a dominant group's position in Jerusalem.

57. See further Carr, *Tablet of the Heart,* 36, 40–41; who in turn is dependent on Niek Veldhuis, *Elementary Education at Nippur: The Lists of Trees and Wooden Objects* (Groningen: Styx, 1997), esp. 129–136. For an illuminating discussion of how Mesopotamian scribes use already well-known texts (hymns, epics, et al.) in new compositions, in a "living literature" that develops "by adaptation and new production," and not "by preparing faithful editions or by writing commentaries," see Veldhuis, "Mesopotamian Canons," 16–18, 28.

58. Small, *Wax Tablets of the Mind.*

59. Carr, *Tablet of the Heart,* 126–128.

60. Quotes, respectively, from ibid., 8 and 9.

61. Ibid., 128.

62. Niek Veldhuis, "Sumerian Proverbs in Their Curricular Context," *JAOS* 120 (2000): 383–89; and more broadly, Niek Veldhuis, *Elementary Education in Nippur: The Lists of Trees and Wooden Objects* (Groningen: Styx, 1997).

63. Carr, *Tablet of the Heart,* 27–28.

64. Adapting Carr's formulation, ibid., 29. See further Victor Hurowitz, "Spanning the Generations: Aspects of Oral and Written Transmission in the Bible and Ancient Mesopotamia," in *Freedom and Responsibility,* ed. R. M. Geffen and M. B. Edelman (New York: Ktav, 1999), 11–30.

65. Carr, *Tablet of the Heart,* 72.

66. See further Jac J. Janssen and Rosalind M. Janssen, *Growing Up in Ancient Egypt* (London: Rubicon, 1990), 67–68.

67. Nili Shupak, *Where Can Wisdom Be Found? The Sage's Language in the Bible and in Ancient Egyptian Literature,* OBO (Freiburg: University Press, 1993), 297–311. Carr, *Tablet of the Heart,* 85–86.

68. Although Sirach 48:10 is translated in the NRSV as if it contained a citation formula ("it is written"), Benjamin G. Wright, "Eschatology without a Messiah in the

Wisdom of Ben Sira," in *The Septuagint and Messianism,* ed. Michael A. Knibb (Leuven: Peeters, 2006), 320, argues that it cannot be so construed; he suggests that the Greek catches the right sense: "the one who was appointed (or enrolled), ready for the times." The implication, moreover is that this passage does not provide evidence that Ben Sira was working with written texts.

69. See further Teresa J. Morgan, "Literate Education in Classical Athens," *Classical Quarterly* 49 (1999): 46–61, on which this paragraph depends.
70. Ibid., 56.
71. Ibid., 57.
72. Ibid., 60.

Chapter 6. The Cultural Repertoire of the Judean Scribes

1. A. A. DiLella, "Wisdom of Ben Sira," *ABD* 6:939–94.
2. 4QMMT C, 9–11, from 4Q379 frgs. 14–21, discussed in Peter Flint, "Scriptures in the Dead Sea Scrolls: The Evidence from Qumran," in *Emanuel: Studies in the Hebrew Bible . . . ,* ed. Shalom M. Paul et al. (Leiden: Brill, 2003), 290; cf. "the law of Moses, the prophets, and the psalms" (Luke 24:44).
3. Eugene Ulrich, *The Dead Sea Scrolls and the Origins of the Bible* (Grand Rapids: Eerdmans, 1999), 91.
4. Ibid., 11, 14, 40–41; and Ulrich, "The Qumran Biblical Scrolls—The Scriptures of Late Second Temple Judaism," in *The Dead Sea Scrolls in Their Historical Context,* ed. Timothy H. Lim (Edinburgh: T & T Clark, 2002), 67–87, esp. 72–77. See also Emanuel Tov, "The History and Significance of a Standard Text of the Hebrew Bible," *Hebrew Bible/Old Testament: The History of Its Interpretation,* vol. 1 (Göttingen: Vandenhoeck & Ruprecht, 1996), 49–66.
5. Ulrich, *Dead Sea Scrolls,* 11, 8, 12, 23–24, 26, 75, 77.
6. Ibid., 11, 91–92, 102. In "The Qumran Biblical Scrolls" Ulrich insists that the manuscripts of the then not yet biblical books found at Qumran reflect the general situation in Judean society (75, 81, 85).
7. Historical and wisdom books were of less importance at Qumran, judging from the small number of manuscripts found. The dissident scribal-priestly community would have had little interest in books such as Chronicles, Ezra, and Nehemiah if their principal function were as "constitutional" documents laid up in the Temple as authorizing monuments (as discussed in chap. 5).
8. Ulrich, *Dead Sea Scrolls,* 89–90. Similarly, "Since the term *canon* belongs to the post-biblical period, it should not be used for collections of sacred books . . . before the second or third centuries C.E." Flint, "Scriptures," 271.
9. Versus what, despite the evidence they are discussing, still seems to be standard among DSS scholars, as evident, for example, in Flint, "Scriptures"; and James Charlesworth, "In the Crucible: The Pseudepigrapha and Early Biblical Interpretation," in James H. Charlesworth and Craig A. Evans, *The Pseudepigrapha and Early Biblical Interpretation* (Sheffield: JSOT Press, 1993), 20–43.
10. The term "scriptural" is preferable to "biblical" because it would apply to texts such as *Jubilees* and sections of *1 Enoch* and the *Temple Scroll* as well as Genesis or Isaiah. It may still be problematic, however, insofar as it carries some of the same later connotations as "biblical." The term "holy" or "sacred" may also be problematic. As noted in the last chapter, in a society dominated by oral communication, many writings were viewed as having a sacred aura. The occurrence of "*ta biblia ta hagia*" in 1 Macc. 12:9 indicates that the concept was developing (cf. *m. Yad.* 4:6; Rom. 1:2; 2 Tim. 3:15; *1 Clem.* 53.1). But Qumran texts still use the simple term "the book" (1QS 6.6–8; 7.2; etc.), along with the less definite "what is written" (e.g., 1QS 5.17; 8.14), and prior to Qumran the focus

might even have been on "what is recited" from the text (Neh. 8:8). We can imagine that in scribal communities a writing might be respected, even revered, but yet not be treated as holy or sacred in the same way as the ceremonial presentation and recitation portrayed in Neh. 8.

11. Flint, "Scriptures," 294.

12. Seventeen scrolls of such interpretation have been found: six on Isaiah; three on Psalms; two each on Hosea, Micah, and Zephaniah; and one each on Nahum and Habakkuk. Among the scholarly discussions of the Qumran *pesharim* are M. P. Horgan, *Pesharim: Qumran Interpretation of Biblical Books*, CBQMS 8 (Washington, DC: Catholic Biblical Association Press, 1979); Devorah Dimant, "Qumran Sectarian Literature," in *Jewish Writings of the Second Temple Period*, ed. Michael E. Stone, CRINT 2.2 (Assen: Van Gorcum, 1984), 504–5; Lawrence H. Schiffman, *Reclaiming the Dead Sea Scrolls* (New York: Doubleday, 1994), chap. 14; and Shani Berrin, "Qumran Pesharim," in *Biblical Interpretation at Qumran*, ed. Matthias Henze (Grand Rapids: Eerdmans, 2005), 110–133.

13. It seems highly unlikely that the Teacher "authored" most or all of the *pesharim* (as suggested by some scholars), since the Habakkuk *pesher* speaks of him in the third person, and some of the *pesharim* apply prophetic statements to events of the early first century BCE, well beyond the Teacher's presumed lifetime.

14. Although at first some scholars associated the *pesharim* with "midrash," the prevailing tendency is to regard them as a distinctive literary form; see Horgan, *Pesharim*, 229–59.

15. Closest in form to the prophetic *pesharim* are short eclectic documents that give brief comments on a few isolated Torah and prophetic passages, where brief citations from the Psalms or Isaiah are followed by "interpreted, this saying concerns . . . " (the *Florilegium*, 4QFlor; 11QMelch 12, 17). Also, at two points in the *Damascus Rule* (CD), the groups or figures mentioned in Ezek. 44:15 and Isa. 24:17 are decoded in the manner of the *pesharim* (CD 3.1–5, 14–19; cf. Isa. 40:3 in 1QS 8.13–15).

16. It seems a bit of a stretch to make such passages the basis for the broad claim that "the community's interpretation of Scripture" generally "was given by revelation," e.g., by David E. Aune, "Charismatic Exegesis in Early Judaism and Early Christianity," in Charlesworth and Evans, *The Pseudepigrapha and Early Biblical Interpretation*, 137.

17. To take one example of what seems standard, see James C. VanderKam, *The Dead Sea Scrolls Today* (Grand Rapids: Eerdmans, 1994), 43–44.

18. Steven D. Fraade, "Interpretive Authority in the Studying Community at Qumran," *JJS* 44 (1993): 51–59. The following discussion is dependent on and closely engaged with Fraade's insightful analysis, while attempting to discern more precisely how the Qumran community was appropriating texts of Torah.

19. Cf. ibid., 52.

20. Cf. ibid., 53–54, where one phrase ("so too we [scholars] may presume") suggests the inferential character of the argument. It is difficult to see how any of the passages of 1QS or CD suggest a "communal curriculum of studies for children" or "study" (55–56).

21. Ibid., 53.

22. A representative example is VanderKam, *The Dead Sea Scrolls Today*, 113: "Through their special techniques of interpretation the expositors of Qumran also derived from the biblical laws other laws and precepts that, they believed, lay hidden in the revealed words of the Torah. . . . The series of legal texts at Qumran proves the importance of the rules derived from their exegesis of the Torah." For a more subtle and nuanced suggestion, that "the laws of the community were

revealed [or "derived by inspired exegesis"] *from* the Torah of Moses," see Fraade, "Interpretive Authority," 57, 66 n. 68.

23. So also Fraade, "Interpretive Authority," 51 n. 14, 48 n. 6. But the passages offered by Fraade, 1QS 5.8–10 and 8.12–16, discussed above, do not attest his more subtle version of the derivation of community laws from the Torah.

24. Adiel Schremer, "'The[y] Did Not Read in the Sealed Book': Qumran Halakhic Revolution and the Emergence of Torah Study in Second Temple Judaism," in *Historical Perspectives . . .*, ed. David Goodblatt, A. Pinnick, and D. R. Schwartz (Leiden: Brill, 2001), 116, 118, 120; Daniel R. Schwartz, "Hillel and Scripture: From Authority to Exegesis," in *Hillel and Jesus: Comparative Studies of Two Major Religious Leaders*, ed. J. H. Charlesworth and L. L. Johns (Minneapolis: Fortress, 1997), 335–62. Armin Lange, "From Literature to Scripture: The Unity and Plurality of the Hebrew Scriptures in Light of the Qumran Library," in *One Scripture or Many?* ed. Christine Helmer and Christof Landmesser (Oxford: Oxford University Press, 2004), 51–107, argues the thesis that only after the "reforms" of the usurping high priest Jason did self-conscious explicit citation of written passages in books begin. The argument could be much stronger if it were recognized that texts from Qumran produced after Jason's reforms still do not quote written texts very often, and that, in a communication environment where texts were known apart from physically consulting a scroll, scribes often quoted from memory.

25. While the explanation of 4QMMT by George W. E. Nickelsburg, *Jewish Literature between the Bible and the Mishnah* (Minneapolis: Fortress, 2005), 147–49, is very helpful, this text does not appear to be concerned with "disputes over the interpretation and practice of the Torah" (149); it seems rather to be calling its addressees to break with their current practice of sacrifices and purity (for which they stand under the covenantal curses in Deuteronomy), and calling them to the observances recommended in this "letter," which it claims is in accordance with the books of Torah (and the Prophets and David). The issue is Temple practice, and the Torah is appealed to as an authority.

26. Fraade, "Interpretive Authority," 56–57, points out the allusion to Josh. 1:8, but finds a contrast insofar as he reads 1QS 6.6–8 as referring to "sectarian legal study." He then suggests that the "communal study" was "a religious performance."

27. Ritual recitation of a book of Torah at Qumran may have had yet another dimension, that of a redemptively efficacious equivalent of or substitute for Temple sacrifices in this "congregation of holiness" and "sanctuary of people" that "sent up, like the smoke of incense, the works of the Torah" (4QFlor 1.6–7). See further Fraade, "Interpretive Authority," 63–64 and the documentation there.

28. Ulrich, *Dead Sea Scrolls*, 26.

29. See further William A. Graham, *Beyond the Written Word: Oral Aspects of Scripture in the History of Religion* (Cambridge: Cambridge University Press, 1987), 114, 161.

30. Geza Vermes, *Scripture and Tradition in Judaism: Haggadic Studies* (Leiden: Brill, 1961); Daniel J. Harrington, "Palestinian Adaptations of Biblical Narratives and Prophecies," in *Early Judaism and Its Modern Interpreters,* ed. Robert A. Kraft and George W. E. Nickelsburg (Atlanta: Scholars Press, 1986), 239–46; Philip S. Alexander, "Retelling the Old Testament," in *It Is Written,* ed. D. A. Carson and H. G. M. Williamson (Cambridge: Cambridge University Press, 1988), 99–121, goes much too far in extending "rewritten Bible" into a genre; on Qumran, see especially George J. Brooke, "Between Authority and Canon: The Significance of Reworking the Bible for Understanding the Canonical Process,"in *Reworking the Bible,* ed. E. G. Chazon, D. Dimant, and R. A. Clements, Studies on the Texts of the Desert of Judah (Leiden: Brill, 2005), 85–104: http://orion.mscc.huji.ac .il/symposiums/7th/BrookeFullPaper.htm.

31. George J. Brooke, "Between Authority and Canon: The Significance of Reworking the Bible for Understanding the Canonical Process," *http://orion.mscc.huji.ac.il/symposiums/7th/BrookeFullPaper.htm*, p 1, recognizes that the concept of "rewritten Bible" "puts too much emphasis on the closed demarcation of one set of writings and the entirely secondary or derivative nature of the other" and suggests the broader category of "authoritative scripture." Most telling perhaps is the great difficulty that scholars have in analyzing texts such as the *Temple Scroll* according to the assumptions of biblical studies that do not fit the complex textual realities of late-second-temple Judea. An illustrative example is the analysis of the fragments of several scrolls (4Q364–367 and 4Q158) called "Reworked Pentateuch," by Emanuel Tov, "Biblical Texts as Reworked in Some Qumran Manuscripts with Special Attention to 4QRP and 4QParaGen-Exod," in *The Community of the Renewed Covenant: The Notre Dame Symposium on the Dead Sea Scrolls*, ed. Eugene Ulrich and James VanderKam (Notre Dame, IN: Notre Dame University Press, 1994), 112–28. Assuming that certain books were already biblical, and were not only ready to hand and eye but also *the* source of knowledge for narratives and laws and prophecies, scholars assume that the "writer" doing the "reworking" was following "a running text of one of more biblical books." Yet the omissions of "biblical" materials and additions of other materials are sometimes lengthy, and materials from several different books of the Pentateuch are brought together topically in a narrative context parallel to incidents in Genesis (Tov, 114, 114, 124, 127, 128; Sidonie White Crawford, "Rewritten Pentateuch," in *Encyclopedia of the Dead Sea Scrolls* [Oxford: Oxford University Press, 2000], 2:775–76). How can the supposedly derivative "rewritten Bible" text be following a "running text" of the Pentateuch if it frequently changes the sequence, rearranges material? When a sufficient degree of similarity appears in the two texts, they find that "the exact wording of the biblical text is usually clearly recognizable," yet this is "sometimes only vaguely" (Tov, 113, 115).

32. Nickelsburg, *Jewish Literature between the Bible and the Mishnah,* 69; James C. VanderKam, *The Book of Jubilees* (Sheffield: Sheffield Academic Press, 2001), 136.

33. VanderKam, *Jubilees,* 138–39.

34. Ibid., 137.

35. The scribes involved in the production of *Jubilees* were thus following a compositional procedure common among ancient Near Eastern scribes for centuries, adapting old materials (hymnic, legal, legendary, sapiential, et al.) for their own circumstances, a key point in Niek Veldhuis, "Mesopotamian Canons," in *Homer, the Bible, and Beyond: Literary and Religious Canons in the Ancient World*, ed. Margalit Finkelberg and Guy Stroumsa (Leiden: Brill, 2003), 9–28, esp. 16–17. He makes the point, applicable to the relation of old and new texts in later Judea, that texts in a traditional cultural repertory wield authority by "defining what literature is and how new literature is to be produced" (18). But to use the term "canonical" for this stretches its meaning and makes it less useful to distinguish "a closed canon that invites interpretation," as in the study of modern literary canons as well as the Jewish and Christian Bible.

36. See further VanderKam, *Jubilees,* 100–109.

37. Baruch A. Levine, "The Mo'adim of the *Temple Scroll*," in *Archaeology and History in the Dead Sea Scrolls,* ed. Lawrence H. Schiffman (Sheffield: JSOT Press, 1990), 62–64.

38. Ben Zion Wacholder, *The Dawn of Qumran: The Sectarian Torah and the Teacher of Righteousness,* Monographs of the Hebrew Union College (Cincinnati: Hebrew Union College Press, 1983); and Michael O. Wise, *A Critical Study of the Temple Scroll from Qumran Cave 11,* SAOC 49 (Chicago: Oriental Institute of the University of Chicago, 1990).

39. VanderKam, *Jubilees,* 11–12, 87–91, 136.
40. Ibid., 136–37.
41. See further Hindy Najman, "Interpretation as Primordial Writing: Jubilees and Its Authority Conferring Strategies," *Journal for the Study of Judaism* 30 (1999): 379–410, esp. 388, 391, 399.
42. This formulation is provisional because only a few biblical scholars have recognized and begun to explore the relationship between the only recently recognized pluriform and unstable text of books and the only recently recognized oral-and-written scribal cultivation of books. Studies in medieval European scribal cultivation of texts can provide comparative material and tips on approach; for example, M. T. Clanchy, *From Memory to Written Record: England 1066–1307* (Cambridge, MA: Harvard University Press, 1979); Katherine O'Brien O'Keefe, *Visible Song: Transitional Literacy in Old English Verse* (Cambridge: Cambridge University Press, 1990); and A. N. Doane, "The Ethnography of Scribal Writing and Anglo-Saxon Poetry: The Scribe as Performer," *Oral Tradition* 9 (1994): 420–39. On the Deuteronomic history and the book of Jeremiah, see Raymond F. Person, "The Ancient Israelite Scribe as Performer," *JBL* 117 (1998): 601–9.
43. Here are representative illustrations of the general scholarly tendency to take any reference to the figures and events of Israelite tradition and especially any reference to a "book" as evidence for the existence of the Hebrew Scriptures: "It is clear that by the writing of Ben Sira about 200 BCE the Pentateuch and the Prophets were more or less in the same shape as the present Hebrew canon," writes Lester L. Grabbe, "The Law of Moses in the Ezra Tradition: More Virtual Than Real?" in *Persia and Torah,* ed. James W. Watts (Atlanta: SBL, 2001), 99. "Sirach was certainly familiar with the Torah in its written form (cf. 38:24)," writes John J. Collins, *Jewish Wisdom in the Hellenistic Age* (Louisville, KY: Westminster John Knox, 1997), 52.
44. Collins, *Jewish Wisdom,* 55.
45. Ibid.
46. Ibid., 45.
47. J. Marböck, *Weisheit im Wandel: Untersuchungen zur Weisheitstheologie bei Ben Sira* (Bonn: Hanstein, 1971), 85.
48. Collins, *Jewish Wisdom,* 47, 57.
49. If the earlier "books of the teaching/covenant (of Moses)" in the Deuteronomic tradition are any indication, along with Ben Sira's general disinterest in ritual laws, it is likely that this "book of the Covenant" was a version of Deuteronomy. In the Greek version, the second and third lines of 24:23 look almost like a paraphrase of Deut. 33:4. But that appearance may be due to the Greek translator's "intertextuality."
50. On the linguistic situation, see now Joachim Schaper, "Hebrew and Its Study in the Persian Period," in *Hebrew Study from Ezra to Ben-Yehuda,* ed. William Horbury (Edinburgh: T&T Clark, 1999), esp. 15–18. Intermarriage with neighboring elites had compounded the linguistic situation, judging from the complaint in Neh. 13:23–24. Of the families who had intermarried, "half of their children spoke the language of Ashdod, and they could not speak the language of Judah."
51. Joseph Blenkinsopp, "Was the Pentateuch the Civic and Religious Constitution of the Jewish Ethnos in the Persian Period?" in *Persia and Torah,* ed. James W. Watts (Atlanta: SBL, 2001), 54. This volume of essays is a critical review of a much-discussed recent hypothesis by Peter Frei and others, on the basis of evidence from elsewhere in the Persian Empire, that the Torah/Pentateuch as definitive law for Yehud resulted from interaction between local and imperial authorities. There is no evidence in Judean sources that Jerusalem authorities presented their laws for imperial approval, and there is no evidence that the Persian

regime monitored the laws and other literature of their subject peoples, as explained by Blenkinsopp (60–61) and others. In the same volume, Lisbeth S. Fried, "'You Shall Appoint Judges': Ezra's Mission and the Rescript of Artaxerxes," 65–67, argues that Ezra's commission was not to teach "the torah of Moses/ Yahweh" to the Yehudites, but to appoint Persian judges in the province Beyond the River (7:25). "The law/justice/order [dātā'] of your God," moreover, refers not to the local law code of Yehud but to the Persian concept of culturally derived justice/equity according to which the judges appointed by Ezra were to render verdicts (81–84). Cf. Jean Louis Ska, "'Persian Imperial Authorization': Some Question Marks," in the same volume; and Lisbeth S. Fried, *The Priest and the Great King* (Winona Lake, IN: Eisenbrauns, 2004), 212–13, 220.

52. On the following, see Blenkinsopp, "Was the Pentateuch the . . . Constitution?" 56–59.

53. We can appreciate both the likely process of composition and the continuing life independent of the new composition from David Carr's summary of how such composition proceeded among Mesopotamian scribes (*Tablet of the Heart*, 36): "He was composing a new work out of a store of older works that constitute[d] the authorizing building blocks of the new. . . . The scribe was trained from the outset to think by means of blocks of tradition." Similarly, Niek Veldhuis, "Mesopotamian Canons," 16–18, 28.

54. On the following see especially Martha Roth, *Law Collections from Mesopotamia and Asia Minor* (Atlanta: Scholars Press, 1997); Raymond Westbrook, "What Is the Covenant Code?" and Bernard M. Levinson, "The Case for Revision and Interpolation within the Biblical Legal Corpora," both in *Theory and Method in Biblical and Cuneiform Law: Revision, Interpolation, and Development*, ed. B. M. Levinson, JSOTSup 181 (Sheffield: Sheffield Academic Press, 1994), 15–26.

55. Jean Bottero, ed., *Mesopotamia: Writing, Reasoning, and the Gods* (Chicago: University of Chicago Press, 1992), 47; Westbrook, "What Is the Covenant Code?" 24, 30; and Fried, "'You Shall Appoint Judges,'" 76.

56. Fried, "'You Shall Appoint Judges,'" 80.

57. Gary Knoppers, "Rethinking the Relationship between Deuteronomy and the Deuteronomistic History: The Case of Kings," *CBQ* 63 (2001): 393–415; Bernard M. Levinson, "The Reconceptualization of Kingship in Deuteronomy and the Deuteronomistic History's Transformation of Torah," *VT* 51 (2001): 511–34.

58. That the Deuteronomistic History still articulates a positive ideology of kingship, in striking contrast with the book of Deuteronomy (esp. Deut. 16:18–18:22), while using Deuteronomic teaching as the critical criterion for particular kings suggests its composition toward the end of the Davidic monarchy, not under Persian rule. See further Gary N. Knoppers, "Rethinking the Relationship"; Levinson, "Reconceptualization."

59. William M. Schniedewind, "The Chronicler as an Interpreter of Scripture," in *The Chronicler as Author: Studies in Text and Texture*, ed. M. Patrick Graham and Steven L. McKenzie, JSOTSup 263 (Sheffield: Sheffield Academic Press, 1999), 163.

60. Recent treatments of orality and literacy in the composition of prophetic materials and books tend to have greater confidence in the level of literacy than do the very recent studies such as Hezser's and to give a greater role to writing in the composition and cultivation of prophetic materials than do scholars of corresponding Egyptian and Mesopotamian materials. See, for example, the essays by biblical scholars in *Writing and Speech in Israelite and Ancient Near Eastern Prophecy*, ed. Ehud Ben Zvi and Michael H. Floyd, Symposium Series 10 (Atlanta: SBL, 2000); and Joachim Schaper, "Exilic and Post-Exilic Prophecy and the Orality/Literacy Problem," *VT* 55 (2005): 324–41.

61. Jon L. Berquist, *Judaism in Persia's Shadow: A Social and Historical Approach* (Minneapolis: Fortress, 1995), 70–80.

62. Adapting the typology (wisdom sayings, theological wisdom, nature wisdom, mantic wisdom, wisdom through revelation) by John J. Collins, "Wisdom, Apocalypticism, and Generic Compatibility," in *In Search of Wisdom: Essays in Memory of John G. Gammie*, ed. Leo Perdue et al. (Louisville, KY: Westminster/John Knox, 1993), 168.

63. See further Benjamin G. Wright III, "'Fear the Lord and Honor the Priest': Ben Sira as Defender of the Jerusalem Priesthood," in *The Book of Ben Sira in Modern Research*, ed. Pancratius C. Beentjes (Berlin: de Gruyter, 1997), 208–14. His discussion suggests that there may well have been some overlap between what Collins has categorized as knowledge of the created order and mantic wisdom.

Chapter 7. The Wisdom of Jesus Ben Sira

1. Cf. the statement of Bildad the Shuhite in Job 8:8–10: "For inquire, I pray you, of bygone ages, and consider what the fathers have found" (RSV).

2. A. A. DiLella, in Patrick W. Skehan and A. A. DiLella, *The Wisdom of Ben Sira*, AB 39 (New York: Doubleday, 1987), 21–27; cf. William McKane, *Proverbs* (Philadelphia: Westminster, 1970), 3, stating that the fundamental form-critical unit of the instruction is the imperative or admonition; James L. Crenshaw, *Old Testament Wisdom: An Introduction* (Atlanta: John Knox 1981), 17–19, similarly focuses on "proverbial sentences," having the older material in Prov. 10–22 primarily in mind.

3. Some significant illustrations are DiLella, in *The Wisdom of Ben Sira*; and John J. Collins, *Jewish Wisdom in the Hellenistic Age* (Louisville, KY: Westminster John Knox, 1997).

4. For example, Collins, *Jewish Wisdom,* 44. Indicative of the orientation of scholarly interpreters to individual sayings is that they often discern certain "blocks of material" in Sirach or that the book is more "organized" than Prov. 10–22 (e.g., Richard J. Coggins, *Sirach* [Sheffield: Sheffield Academic Press, 1998], 27), but they do not look for and analyze the "blocks" for rhetorical patterns.

5. Alan Kirk, *The Composition of the Sayings Source: Genre, Synchrony, and Wisdom Redaction in Q* (Leiden: Brill, 1998), 93–104, 130–51.

6. See further ibid., 101–3.

7. Helpful analysis of the speeches in Sir. 15:11–20; 27:30–28:7; and 39:13–35, appear in ibid., 143–48.

8. The speeches in the book of Sirach are examples of texts described as "oral derived texts" or "voices from the past." See the analysis and discussion in John Miles Foley, *The Singer of Tales in Performance* (Bloomington: Indiana University Press, 1995); and idem, *How to Read an Oral Poem* (Urbana: University of Illinois Press, 2002), esp. 22–53.

9. See further DiLella, *The Wisdom of Ben Sira,* 64–74.

10. See further M. A. K. Halliday, *Language as Social Semiotic: The Social Interpretation of Language and Meaning* (Baltimore: University Park Press, 1978), 31–35, 111, etc.; John Miles Foley, *Immanent Art: From Structure to Meaning in Traditional Oral Epic* (Bloomington: Indiana University Press, 1991); and idem, "Introduction: What's in a Sign," in *Signs of Orality: The Oral Tradition and Its Influence in the Greek and Roman World*, ed. E. Anne Mackay (Leiden: Brill, 1998), 11–15. For application in biblical studies, see Richard A. Horsley and Jonathan A. Draper, *Whoever Hears You Hears Me: Prophets, Performance and Tradition in Q* (Harrisburg, PA: Trinity Press International, 1999), 164–73, 181–82, etc.

11. Walter J. Ong, SJ, *The Presence of the Word: Some Prolegomena for Cultural and Religious History* (New Haven, CT: Yale University Press, 1967), 56–57, 79–87.

12. On who the wealthy/powerful/rulers are, to the *nādîb* of 13:9, cf. Job 21:28; 34:18; Prov. 8:16; etc. An earlier Egyptian form of instruction on the same topic is in Phibis 10.12–11.23, as discussed by J. T. Sanders, *Ben Sira and Demotic Wisdom* (Chico, CA: Scholars Press, 1983), 92–93.

13. E.g., the Instruction of Ptah-hotep, the Instruction of Kagemi, and the Instruction of Amenemope, as discussed by Sanders, *Ben Sira and Demotic Wisdom,* 67.

14. Not afterward, in contrast to the Greek custom (cf. Plato's *Symposium* 176E) of dismissing the flute girl before the discourse begins in earnest, as pointed out by Collins, *Jewish Wisdom,* 32–33.

15. J. Marböck, *Weisheit im Wandel: Untersuchungen zur Weisheitstheologie bei Ben Sira* (Bonn: Hanstein, 1971); C. Kayatz, *Studien zu Proverbien 1–9* (Neukirchen-Vluyn: Neukirchener Verlag, 1966), 76–119.

16. Cf. Burton L. Mack, *Wisdom and Hebrew Epic: Ben Sira's Hymn in Praise of the Fathers* (Chicago: University of Chicago Press, 1985), 136; Collins, *Jewish Wisdom,* 99–100.

17. Cf. Collins, *Jewish Wisdom,* 108.

18. The praise of Simon in Sir. 50, far from being an "appendix" [vs. DiLella, *The Wisdom of Ben Sira,* 499], is the climactic section to which previous sections are leading.

19. Scribes such as Ben Sira probably did not criticize their aristocratic patrons directly to their face. Their criticism was probably more offstage. In this regard the reflections on "the hidden transcript" of subordinates' discussions among themselves out of the hearing of the rulers by James C. Scott, in *Domination and the Arts of Resistance* (New Haven, CT: Yale University Press, 1990), may be pertinent to scribal circles as well as to peasants and slaves. For application in biblical studies, see Richard A. Horsley, *Hidden Transcript and the Arts of Resistance: Applying the Work of James C. Scott to Jesus and Paul,* Semeia Studies 48 (Atlanta: SBL, 2004).

20. If anything, interpreters make more out of that application than may be warranted. It is the only point in the book of Sirach where wisdom is more or less "identified" with the Mosaic torah. And it is the only point where "the book" of the covenant of the Most High is mentioned. But the textual tradition is problematic. The line in 24:23a is intrusive and, as commentators have pointed out, is a "descent" into prose in otherwise consistent speech patterns of bicola with parallel lines. Sirach 24:23bc, which alludes to Deut. 33:4, fits much better in the context without the intrusive 24:23a. In other passages Ben Sira articulates a more indirect association between wisdom and the commandments, teaching that "the fear of the Lord" is "the beginning/root/fullness of wisdom," identifying the fear of the Lord and keeping the commandments, and closely linking the desire or possession of wisdom with observing the covenant/commandments.

21. See further DiLella, *The Wisdom of Ben Sira,* 334–35; A. Fournier-Bidoz, "L'arbre et la demeure: Siracide xxiv 10–17," *VT* 34 (1984): 1–10.

22. So also Collins, *Jewish Wisdom,* 97–108. Although I agree with many aspects of his reading, there are many respects in which we can be more careful or precise, partly by admitting the political dimension.

23. So also Benjamin G. Wright III, "Ben Sira on Kings and Kingship," 18 (unpublished paper, 2003).

24. As argued in Saul M. Olyan, "Ben Sira's Relationship to the Priesthood," *HTR* 80 (1987): 261–86; and Benjamin G. Wright III, "'Fear the Lord and Honor the Priest': Ben Sira as Defender of the Jerusalem Priesthood," in Pancratius C. Beentjes, *The Book of Ben Sira in Modern Research* (Berlin: de Gruyter, 1997), 192–95.

25. Saul Olyan, "Ben Sira's Relation to the Priesthood," *HTR* 80 (1987): esp. 273, 278–81; Wright, "'Fear the Lord and Honor the Priest,'" 200–208; and Robert

A. Kuyler, *From Patriarch to Priest: The Levi-Priestly Tradition from Aramaic Levi to the Testament of Levi* (Atlanta: Scholars Press, 1996).
26. Olyan, "Ben Sira's Relationship to the Priesthood," esp. 275–76.
27. Simon Swain, *Hellenism and Empire: Language, Classicism, and Power in the Greek World* (Oxford: Oxford University Press, 1998).

Chapter 8. *1 Enoch*

1. My understanding and treatment of the texts that constitute *1 Enoch* are heavily dependent on and deeply indebted to my long association and conversations with George W. E. Nickelsburg and Patrick Tiller, and in particular to Nickelsburg's magisterial commentary, *1 Enoch: A Commentary on the Book of 1 Enoch* (Minneapolis: Fortress, 2001), and Tiller's definitive analysis in *A Commentary on the Animal Apocalypse of 1 Enoch*, SBLEJL 4 (Atlanta: Scholars Press, 1993). I am also indebted to Nickelsburg's many important articles over the last thirty years; but since they are updated in the commentary and listed in its bibliography, I have referenced only the most recent ones in the notes below. Unless otherwise indicated, translations are from George W. E. Nickelsburg and James C. VanderKam, *1 Enoch: A New Translation, Based on the Hermeneia Commentary* (Minneapolis: Fortress, 2004).
2. As known now from the discovery of fragments of four of the different sections of the book among the Dead Sea Scrolls. See J. T. Milik, *The Books of Enoch: Aramaic Fragments of Qumran Cave 4* (Oxford: Clarendon, 1976).
3. Lest we in effect make the Ethiopic version canonical for our consideration of Enoch books, the Book of Giants found among the Dead Sea Scrolls was apparently part of the overall "Enoch" corpus, reminding us that all of these "books" were still unstable and developing.
4. That Mosaic torah is missing in Enoch literature is explored suggestively by George W. E. Nickelsburg, "Enochic Wisdom: An Alternative to the Mosaic Torah?" in *Hesed ve-Emet: Studies in Honor of Ernest S. Frerichs*, ed. Jodi Magness and Seymour Gitin (Atlanta: Scholars Press, 1998), 123–32.
5. James C. VanderKam, *Enoch and the Growth of an Apocalyptic Tradition*, CBQMS 16 (Washington, DC: Catholic Biblical Association, 1984), 37–42; W. Lambert, "Enmeduranki and Related Matters," *JCS* 21 (1967): 126–38.
6. See the discussions of genre, including the applicability of "apocalypse" and "testament," in Nickelsburg, *1 Enoch*; the debate between John Collins and George Nickelsburg in *George W. E. Nickelsburg in Perspective: An Ongoing Dialogue of Learning*, ed. Jacob Neusner and Alan J. Avery-Peck (Leiden: Brill, 2003), 2:373–78, 410–11; and my response "Of Enoch, Nickelsburg and Other Scribes of Righteousness," *Review of Rabbinic Judaism* 8 (2005): 250–56.
7. To use the fragments of several different manuscripts of the Book of Luminaries found among the Dead Sea Scrolls as an example of how the text of Enoch books continued to develop: Two of the manuscripts from Qumran attest a lengthy first section of the book listing the synchronized movements of the sun and moon during a 364-day solar year. This list must have preceded the sections in the Ethiopic version. J. T. Milik, *The Books of Enoch: Aramaic Fragments of Qumran Cave 4* (Oxford: Clarendon, 1976); VanderKam, *Enoch*, 80–83.
8. On the knowledge of earlier Enoch texts in later Enoch texts, see especially the close analysis by Nickelsburg, *1 Enoch*. John J. Collins, "The Place of Apocalypticism in the Religion of Israel," in *Ancient Israelite Religion: Essays in Honor of Frank Moore Cross*, ed. Patrick D. Miller et al. (Philadelphia: Fortress, 1987), 541–42, even suggests an "Enoch movement."

9. The following is based on VanderKam, *Enoch,* chaps. 3 and 4, with summary thesis on 101–2.

10. Along with 107 tablets of omens based on the behavior of animals and 11 tablets of dream interpretation, VanderKam, *Enoch,* 54, 59; A. Leo Oppenheim, *Ancient Mesopotamia: Portrait of a Dead Civilization,* rev. ed. (Chicago: University of Chicago Press, 1977), 225.

11. *First Enoch* 81:1–82:4 is apparently misplaced in the Ethiopic version and originally belonged with chaps. 1–36, as explained at length by Nickelsburg, *1 Enoch,* 334–38.

12. David M. Carr, *Writing on the Tablet of the Heart* (Oxford: Oxford University Press, 2005), 26–27.

13. Michael E. Stone, "Lists of Revealed Things in the Apocalyptic Literature," in *Magnalia Dei—The Mighty Acts of God: In Memory of G. E. Wright,* ed. F. M. Cross et al. (Garden City, NY: Doubleday, 1976), 414–52, isolated such lists in many passages of Judean literature in late second-temple times. Stone's discussion illustrates how the different uses of these lists in various texts has been difficult to understand on the basis of the standard scholarly dichotomy between the reified categories of literature and thought called "wisdom" and "apocalyptic."

14. Laid out in detail in Nickelsburg, *1 Enoch,* 138, 347–48; and VanderKam, *Enoch,* 116.

15. VanderKam, *Enoch,* 117. Balaam follows the well-attested practice of performing elaborate sacrifices with the king to appease the Divine before seeking communication from the Divine (Num. 23:1–6, 14–17, 29–30). On the inscriptions of Balaam "the seer" discovered at Tell Deir 'Alla in the east Jordan valley dating to the end of the eighth century BCE, see Joanne A. Hackett, "Some Observations on the Balaam Tradition at Deir 'Alla," *BA* 49 (1986): 216–22.

16. There may be yet another dimension to the analogy. Just as Balaam was hired by a ruler for his own purpose that was harmful to the Israelites, yet received the divine revelation of blessing on Israel that was contrary to the wishes of his patron, so the Enoch scribes who had been in the service of Judean rulers had received divine visions of blessing on the chosen that ran contrary to the situation of the Judean rulers of the day.

17. Nickelsburg recognizes that the language of *1 En.* 1:3–7 "reflects unconscious combination rather than explicit selective citation" of passages such as Deut. 33:1–3; Jer. 25:31; and Mic. 1:3–4. He is thus moving in the direction of what I am suggesting.

18. In earlier interpretation of "apocalyptic" literature this hyperbolic language of theophany was taken in a literal sense as predicting "cosmic catastrophe," the destruction of the created order. But that was a misunderstanding of such "apocalyptic" language, which stands in continuity with the traditional prophetic register of language dedicated to theophany. Far from cosmic dissolution, the Book of Watchers is concerned with the restoration of the heavenly order.

19. The images of sinners being a curse while the righteous are blessed with joy and fullness of days upon the earth are also rooted in prophetic tradition, as can be seen in Isa. 65:15–16, 18, 20 (with curse in second person and blessing in the third person, as in *1 En.* 2–5). The addressees of the curse, the "wicked/sinners," are vague. Since the contrast with the luminaries seems to exclude the Watchers, they would appear to be humans, presumably foreign enemies, as in the prophets. While Nickelsburg, *1 Enoch,* 133, argues that the "sinners" include (some of) the "Enoch" people, he also points out that "it is difficult to imagine the sharp language of the curses in 5:5–7 being directed . . . toward those who are present at a communal reading of the book." It is difficult to discern anything in the text

that points to a "universal judgment" or an indictment of "humanity's" disobedience, pace Nickelsburg, 149, 157.

20. See the illustrations printed out in Nickelsburg, *1 Enoch,* 153–54.

21. The failure to translate the names of the Watchers, the sons of heaven (the ending particle —*el* indicating their semidivine status), in editions of the text of
1 En. 6:7 may partially obscure this for readers who do not command the ancient
languages. Similarly, the failure to translate their names obscures the correlation
between their identity and the problematic divinatory knowledge that they
taught to humans (8:3): Star-god taught the signs of the stars. . . . Sun-god taught
the signs of the sun. And so forth.

22. Biblical scholars tend to take *1 En.* 6–11 as "in some sense" an "interpretation"
of Genesis 6–9, despite the fact that verbal similarities do not by themselves indicate the direction of dependency between two texts. See, for example, Nickelsburg, *1 Enoch,* 166; and James C. VanderKam, "The Interpretation of Genesis in
1 Enoch," in *The Bible at Qumran: Text, Shape, and Interpretation,* ed. Peter Flint
(Grand Rapids: Eerdmans, 2001), 129–48. Contrary to some claims, however,
the verbal parallels, say between *1 En.* 6:1–7:6 and Gen. 6:1–4, 7, 11–12 are not
that close. The recent research on orality and literacy and on the continuing development of Judean texts in the second-temple period surveyed in chaps. 5 and 6
(above) now place such issues in a different light. Even if one of these texts had
been known to those who produced the other, the limited verbal similarities are
more consistent with the kind of basic familiarity that scribal custodians of cultural traditions would have from oral (and written) cultivation of them. More
likely these were two different but parallel transmissions of the same legend, the
very kind of cultural lore that would have been cultivated in multiple versions.
The fragments of copies of The Book of Giants found among the Dead Sea Scrolls
attest yet another version of the story of the rebellion of the Watchers, the birth
of the giants, and their destructive deeds on the earth (see excursus in Nickelsburg, *1 Enoch,* 172–73).

23. Nickelsburg, *1 Enoch,* 170, 396.

24. Nickelsburg, ibid., 256, argues that Enoch's vision is of the heavenly temple, which
also has the "political" dimension as the court of the King of the universe. The
Hebrew words *bêt* (*bayit*) and *hêkal* (house) can be used for both the king's palace
and for the temple (also constructed by the king, for God). The visionary ascent
through heavenly houses, however, appears to have been patterned more after
Ezek. 1–2 than after the vision of the new Temple/Jerusalem in Ezek. 40–44 (see
both the chart comparing *1 En.* 14–16 with the former [255] and that comparing it with the latter [254, 256]). Martha Himmelfarb, *Ascent to Heaven in Jewish
and Christian Apocalypses* (Oxford: Oxford University Press, 1993), 15, points out
that the heavenly houses in *1 En.* 14 do not correspond to Solomon's temple or
any other described in "biblical" texts. The vision of the chariot throne in Ezek.
1–2 in fact marks the beginning of a trend to dissociate God's heavenly dwelling
from the temple in Jerusalem (11–12). The prophet Ezekiel saw the temple so
defiled that it was no longer a suitable place for the glory of God. Enoch literature
evidently stood in a tradition that remained critical of the rebuilt/reestablished
temple (see esp. on the Animal Apocalypse, below).

25. Nickelsburg, *1 Enoch,* 254–55, provides an elaborate chart of the parallels and
sketches the close similarities with Ezek. 1–2.

26. It may be virtually impossible to distinguish whether the Enoch scribes were simply working creatively from the tradition of revelatory prophetic commissioning
and visions or were themselves caught up in visionary experiences that took the
traditional form they knew about and provided the source for such creativity. It

would surely be inappropriate for modern readers either to take the text at face value as a record of a vision or to deny the possibility that the "Enoch" scribes might have had visions. As can be seen in such texts as Micaiah's vision, Isaiah's call-vision, and Ezekiel's vision, visions like that in *1 En.* 14 would have been deeply rooted and shaped according to a long-standing tradition of such visions that was cultivated in scribal circles. This should make us hesitant to make direct connections between imagery or locations in the vision account and particular circumstances in the "Enoch" visionary's life situation, for example, that the reference to "the waters of Dan, etc." (13:7, 9) indicating both visionary activity in that area and the provenance of this section of Enoch literature in northern Galilee. Dan and Mount Hermon were legendary locations of communication between the human and divine world in Israelite-Judean cultural tradition as well as other cultures. See the lengthy Excursus in Nickelsburg, *1 Enoch,* 238–47.

27. These few lines in the indictment, along with the term "sanctuary" for the highest heaven, have led some interpreters to surmise that the Watchers are meant to represent the priests who have defiled the temple. See, for example, the arguments in Nickelsburg, *1 Enoch,* 230–31, 272, and Himmelfarb, *Ascent to Heaven,* 20–22. However, the Watchers and holy ones are clearly represented in the Book of Watchers as officers of the imperial divine government of the universe, who are supposed to maintain the divinely created order. The argument that the Watchers must be priests insofar as they "approach" God is problematic since Enoch's vision also states that "none of those about him approached him" (14:22; cf. 14:23). And comparison with polemics against the Jerusalem priesthood in later texts such as CD 5.6–7 and *Psalms of Solomon* 8:12 [13] illustrate rather the difference between the latter's accusations of ritual uncleanness of priests and the Watchers' violation of the difference in kind between their own eternal divine heavenly beings and the mortal human earthly beings.

28. Cf. Nickelsburg, *1 Enoch,* 278.

29. E.g., that chaps. 21–23 are "primarily eschatological" or that much of chaps. 21–27 is "eschatological material" (John J. Collins, *The Apocalyptic Imagination* [New York: Crossroad, 1989], 42–43), leading to the suggestion that the Book of Watchers is "our earliest extant example of a Jewish text that is governed by a full-blown apocalyptic worldview," characterized by "imminent future judgment" (George W. E. Nickelsburg, *Jewish Literature between the Bible and the Mishnah,* 2nd ed. [Minneapolis: Fortress, 2005], 52).

30. On dream interpretation, see further VanderKam, *Enoch,* 60–61, 64–65, 67, 68, 70.

31. This basic connection is prominent in the anthologies of oracle fragments of Amos, Micah, Isaiah, Jeremiah.

32. See chart in Nickelsburg, *1 Enoch,* 358, and details in his commentary and in Tiller, *Animal Apocalypse.*

33. Different from the concerns of a theologically oriented commentary such as Nickelsburg's. Tiller, *Animal Apocalypse,* stands somewhere in between.

34. Similarly, Tiller, *Animal Apocalypse,* 101. The tendency in Christian theological biblical studies is to interpret the beasts and birds that violently attack the sheep as "Israel's Gentile predators," "Gentile beasts and birds." E.g., Nickelsburg, *1 Enoch,* 354–55, 383, 398.

35. Following Tiller, *Animal Apocalypse*; cf. Nickelsburg, ad loc.

36. Tiller, *Animal Apocalypse,* 49–51, explains appropriately that the meaning of a sign such as the house must be established on the basis of what the overall story is about and how a particular sign and narrative step functions—and not primarily by reference to biblical texts. Moreover, in both historical and prophetic tradition, Jerusalem became the capital and symbolic center of Israel from the time

of David and Solomon, and especially after the fall of the northern kingdom of Israel, Jerusalem/Zion became a symbol for the whole people (e.g., in prophetic oracles such as Isa. 40).

37. Ibid., 43–45, explains why the house cannot refer narrowly to the tabernacle, contrary to standard interpretation by biblical scholars, since the people stand in it (89:36), not the Lord (the temple, 89:50, would correspond to the earlier tabernacle).

38. Ibid., 49, makes a persuasive argument that "the house" represents the covenantal relationship between Israel and God. Obedience is represented by the sheep dwelling in the house; disobedience is represented by the abandonment of the house or the absence of the house.

39. Nickelsburg says this is the northern Israelites' withdrawal from Jerusalem, *1 Enoch,* 355, 384.

40. These shepherds appear to be a combination of two themes in Israelite cultural tradition. "Shepherds" was a standard metaphor for Israel's (own) rulers, particularly in prophetic oracles that condemned disobedient and negligent shepherds who, for example, had fed themselves on the flock (Isa. 56:11; Jer. 23:2; Ezek. 34; Zech. 10:3). One oracle even has God delivering the flock to shepherds for destruction (Zech. 11:15–17). The metaphor of shepherds is combined with the idea that God had assigned particular peoples/nations to the jurisdiction of certain "sons of God" (Deut. 32:8). See further Nickelsburg, *1 Enoch,* 391.

41. Patrick A. Tiller, "'The Eternal Planting' in the Dead Sea Scrolls," *Dead Sea Discoveries* 4 (1997): 315–23, argues that the "Enoch" people were few, but spoke for a larger group of faithful Judeans who may not have been focused specifically on the figure of Enoch.

42. The "high tower" (clearly distinguished from the "house") had been built on the house by a ruler, apparently as a means of communication with the Lord, who stood on top of the high tower (89:50). In the attempt at rebuilding, after it had been burned down, the tower was only "called" high, and the table before it had polluted bread (89:73). The "table" in the tower (89:50, 73) is the one sign in the allegory that appears explicitly to signify cultic activity. In an interpretation rooted in the standard concept of second-temple "Judaism," Nickelsburg (*1 Enoch,* 355–56 and throughout the commentary) emphasizes the cultic aspects of the tower and house. The importance of "the divinely revealed and sanctioned cult. . . is evident in the repeated references to the major cultic structures: the tabernacle (89:36), Solomon's Temple (89:50, 54, 66), the Second Temple (89:73). All specific instances of Israelite sin involve cultic perversion or the abandonment of the Jerusalem sanctuary" (355–56). Throughout the allegory, however, the blindness and straying of the sheep appear to be a more general departure from the path they were taught, as Tiller suggests, *Animal* Apocalypse, 331.

43. The implications of Tiller, *Animal Apocalypse,* 36–38, 48, are that the camp was the historical ideal. While noting Tiller's reading, Nickelsburg nonetheless thinks that the new house has the characteristics of the temple as well as the city of Jerusalem (404–5).

44. Definitive delineation of the six discourses that structure most of the Epistle of Enoch in Nickelsburg, *1 Enoch,* 420–21, etc.

45. See ibid., 415–18, for a discussion and chart of the woes.

46. Those who would like to see specific phrases from the indictments in *1 En.* 94–104 matched with the corresponding phrases in Amos, Isaiah, or Habakkuk can see my earlier article, "Social Relations and Social Conflict in the Epistle of Enoch," in *For a Later Generation,* ed. Randall Argall et al. (Harrisburg, PA: Trinity Press International, 2000), esp. 111–15. Here I am purposely inviting readers to discern the broader political-economic relationship of exploitation

portrayed in the woes of prophetic lawsuits, which are rooted in Mosaic covenantal principles.

47. See also other texts of Mosaic covenant such as Josh. 24; and applications of covenantal principles in the "covenant code" of Exod. 21–23, Deuteronomic legal teachings, and covenantal mechanisms summarized in Lev. 25. These covenantal procedures of ancient Israel are similar to the principles of what James C. Scott calls the "moral economy of the peasant" in other peasant societies in various parts of the world, in *The Moral Economy of the Peasant* (New Haven, CT: Yale University Press, 1976).

48. In the woes and related oracles of Amos, the wealthy rulers in Zion and Samaria leisurely feast and drink and in their lavish houses lounge on exotic beds. But this is all made possible only by their oppression of the poor: expropriating their grain, entrapping them in spiraling debts and debt-slavery by charging interest (forbidden by covenantal law), and manipulating weights and measures, while denying them justice in the courts (4:1–3; 5:11–12, 16–17, 18–20; 6:1–3, 4–7; 8:4–6). In Isaiah, similarly, the wealthy rulers have gained their luxurious life of lavish feasting and drinking by expropriating the land of indebted peasant families, depriving them of their rights. Wise in their own eyes, rejecting the torah of Yahweh/the Lord of hosts, they "call evil good and good evil" (Isa. 5:8–24). And similarly in Habakkuk the wealthy "build a town by bloodshed, and found a city on iniquity" by hoarding what is not theirs, expropriating "goods taken in pledge," and manipulating poor peasants into hopeless indebtedness for their own "evil gain" (2:6–17).

49. See further Nickelsburg, *1 Enoch,* 489, 532, discussing 104:9–10, where "the words of truth" = "words of the Holy One," in comparison with "eternal covenant" = "words of truth" in 99:2.

50. This reading of the Epistle of Enoch, like the reading of the Animal Vision above, would fit with the suggestion that the circle of Enoch scribes was open to and spoke for a larger group of Judeans by Tiller, "Eternal Planting."

Chapter 9. Daniel

1. John J. Collins, *The Apocalyptic Vision of the Book of Daniel,* HSM 16 (Missoula, MT: Scholars Press, 1977), opened discussion of the politics of the book of Daniel and its circumstances. The discussion of Daniel below, especially of the visions, is heavily dependent on Collins's many scholarly investigations over the last three decades, especially his magisterial commentary, *Daniel,* Hermeneia (Minneapolis: Fortress, 1993), which is now the standard critical analysis and interpretation of Daniel. Even at points where, working from a somewhat different perspective and different assumptions, I am pressing the political interpretation and implications of the tales and visions much further than Collins might be comfortable with, I am heavily dependent on and deeply appreciative of his scholarly investigation of text and cultural context.

2. John J. Collins, *Daniel* (1993), 146, suggests that the emphasis on education here reflects the ideal of the Judean sage. He also thinks (138) that the literature of the Chaldeans must be the professional literature of the soothsayers. See also chap. 4, above.

3. Replacing the NRSV's "magicians and enchanters" with the more appropriate translation in Collins, *Daniel* (1993). In other tales as well, the general term of "the wise" seems to include those who possess particular skills, as "dream interpreters, exorcists, Chaldeans, and diviners" (4:6–7, au. trans.; cf. 5:7–8, 11); although "dream interpreters" may also be used as a term that covers other skills, since the widely competent Daniel is called "chief of the dream interpreters" in

4:9. Daniel himself is portrayed in the terms of a Mesopotamian mantic sage, as presented by Jack N. Lawson, "'The God Who Reveals Secrets': The Mesopotamian Background to Daniel 2:47," *JSOT* 74 (1997): 61–76.

4. Lawrence M. Wills, *The Jew in the Court of the Foreign King: Ancient Jewish Court Legends*, HDR 26 (Minneapolis: Fortress, 1990), 55–70. The following discussion of the form of the tales is heavily indebted to Wills's work.

5. Ibid., 68.

6. Ibid., 39–40, 43; Collins, *Daniel* (Grand Rapids: Eerdmans, 1984), 45. Palace friezes represent courtiers with clear ethnic identities, as indicated in Margaret Cool Root, *The King and Kingship in Achaemenid Art: Essays on the Creation of an Iconography of Empire* (Leiden: Brill, 1979), 4–8. As documented in Karel van der Toorn, "Scholars at the Oriental Court: The Figure of Daniel against Its Mesopotamian Background," in *The Book of Daniel: Composition and Reception*, ed. John J. Collins and Peter W. Flint (Leiden: Brill, 2001), 37–54, Judean and other court legends dating from Persian times follow a much older narrative scribal tradition exemplified in a classic of Babylonian court wisdom, *Ludlul bel nemeqi* = "I Shall Praise the Lord of Wisdom [Marduk]." Such tales, moreover, reflected political roles and relationships. Cuneiform correspondence between scholars and Neo-Assyrian kings discloses a world of competing court scribes/sages. The many references to the reversal of fortune of individual scribes/sages points to their dependence on the king's favor for their position, prestige, and very livelihood—the same roles and relationships indicated in the instructional speeches of Ben Sira (chap. 3, above).

7. Collins, *Daniel* (1984), 45; *Daniel* (1993), 36–38.

8. Wills, *Jew in the Court*, 86. Collins, *Daniel* (1984), 46, thinks that, since "the problems the heroes encounter are specifically religious, . . . the traditional tale type is being adapted in Daniel for specifically religious ends."

9. The Old Greek version may take us closer to an early stage in the development of the tales in Dan. 4–6 than the Masoretic text of the later rabbis, as laid out by Wills, *Jew in the Court*, 87–152. Closely related to the continuing development of the text of the legends of Daniel is the oral cultivation of such legends. "They may even have been composed and transmitted orally before entering the [written] literary stage" (ibid., 35, 83–86). Fully aware that these tales were still undergoing development and that in Dan. 4–6 the Masoretic version displays less intense political conflict than does the Old Greek version, we will deal mainly with the (Masoretic) text that is translated in the NRSV, for accessibility for readers.

10. It has been standard, even in recent interpretation, to read the tales in rather vague terms as broadly applicable to Diaspora Judean communities more generally, as a "lifestyle for Diaspora," "the possibility of participating fully in the life of a foreign nation." W. L. Humphreys, "A Life-style for Diaspora: A Study of the Tales of Esther and Daniel," *JBL* 92 (1973): 211–23: "the possibility of a creative and rewarding interaction with the foreign environment [that could work for the good of the Jew]," 213; followed by Collins, *Daniel* (1993), 51, etc.; and *Daniel* (1984), 45, 53. Lawrence Wills, *Jew in the Court*, 35, 197, recognizes that the tales probably did not pertain to the lower class, insofar as they reflect the orientation of the administrative class.

11. These doxologies may well be "redactional" additions when the tales were "collected," as stated by Collins, *Daniel* (1993), 35. But they make explicit what was already at least implicit in the tales, as explained in the following paragraphs.

12. There is no basis in either the dream itself or in Daniel's interpretation for the common eschatological interpretation. The phrase on which that is often based in 2:28 (used again in 10:14; cf. Isa. 2:2/Mic. 4:1; Ezek. 38:16; Hos. 3:5) is best translated "what will be at the end of the era" (not "end of days," as if history were to come to an end), as explained by Collins, *Daniel* (1993), 161.

13. The Roman chronicler Aemilius Sura, as preserved in Velleius Paterculus;
Sibylline Oracles 4:49–101; and the Persian Bahman Yasht. This scheme and other
political oracles in Hellenistic times (e.g., Egyptian Potter's Oracle, Oracle of
Hystaspes, Babylonian Dynastic Prophecy), which were communicated in
dreams and included prophecies after the fact, were concerned with the rise and
fall of kingdoms. Important discussions of this background to the succession of
empires in Dan. 2 and 7 are Joseph Ward Swain, "The Theory of the Four Monarchies: Opposition History under the Roman Empire," *CP* 35 (1940): 1–21;
David Flusser, "The Four Empires in the Fourth Sibyl and in the Book of Daniel,"
Israel Oriental Studies 2 (1972): 148–75; Collins, *Daniel* (1984), 50; Collins,
Daniel (1993), 166–70; and Collins, *Apocalyptic Vision*, 40.
14. As evident in Hesiod, *Works and Days* 106–201, and in the Persian *Zand-i Vohu-
man Yasn*.
15. Collins, *Daniel* (1984), 53.
16. The very combination of "dream interpreters" and "exorcists" (2:2, 10) may point
to the practice of dream interpretation in the Near East, which included a ther-
apeutic removing or dispelling of the evil consequences of the dream, according
to Collins, *Daniel* (1993), 156–57 (and see n. 3 above). The king's own telling
of the dream would thus have been part of the therapy. The legend in Dan. 2 thus
represents Nebuchadnezzar as exacerbating the implication of the dream, about
which he is already troubled, by refusing to divulge what it was about.
17. This test of loyalty is similar to what the Roman emperor Gaius (Caligula) tried
to impose on Judeans in the 40s CE (sacrifice before his statue, which was to be
installed in the Jerusalem Temple; Josephus, *Ant.* 20), and to what the Roman
imperial officials required of early Christians in the second and third centuries
CE (ritual acts of loyalty to the emperor).
18. Thinking that the story encourages the belief that "religious fidelity was compatible with the royal service [and] could ultimately lead to advancement" (Collins,
Daniel [1984], 59) is rooted in the modern Western assumption of the separation
of religion and politics and the narrowing of religion to personal faith. On the latter, see Talal Asad, *Genealogies of Religion: Discipline and Reasons of Power in Christianity and Islam* (Baltimore: Johns Hopkins University Press, 1993). The tale in
Dan. 3 mentions only an imperial decree of toleration for the Judeans' worship of
their god, not a conversion of the king; cf. Collins, *Daniel* (1984), 59.
19. Collins, *Daniel* (1984), 63.
20. Ezekiel is told to hold up to the Egyptian Pharaoh the elaborate allegorical picture of the Assyrian Empire as a great cedar of Lebanon that grew so exalted that
it reached the clouds—so that God gave it into the hand of another empire
because of the arrogance of its power (Ezek. 31:2–14; cf. a different application
of the same metaphor of the great tree cut or broken in Ezek. 17:1–10). That God
struck down rulers for their arrogance and oppression was standard in prophetic
tradition (e.g., Isa. 14:4–11, 12–17). The tower of Babel story (Gen. 11) makes
the same point about the overweening ambition and arrogance of imperial rulers.
21. Matthias Henze, *The Madness of King Nebuchadnezzar: The Ancient Near Eastern
Origins and Early History of Interpretation of Daniel 4* (Leiden: Brill, 1999), esp.
98–99, 204–6. Scholarly consensus sees the exile of Nebuchadnezzar from society and related motifs as derived from tradition about the later Emperor
Nabonidus, which was also known in Judea, as attested by the Prayer of
Nabonidus (4QPrNab), found among the Dead Sea Scrolls at Qumran, as
Collins explains, *Daniel* (1984), 62–63; *Daniel* (1993), 216–19.
22. The tale of "Daniel in the lions' den" in Dan. 6, where the Persian king Darius
is favorably disposed to Daniel, might appear to be an exception. But the story
nevertheless illustrates that the imperial regime (whose high-ranking scribal staff

can manipulate the decrees of the emperor) does not tolerate an alternative or divided loyalty—and the tale provides a model of a prototypical Judean sage who remained unflinchingly faithful to his God despite the threat of death.

23. Philip R. Davies, "Daniel in the Lions' Den," in *Images of Empire*, ed. Loveday Alexander, JSOTSup 122 (Sheffield: Sheffield Academic Press, 1991), 161–63, in contrast with his earlier treatment in *Daniel* (Sheffield: JSOT Press, 1985), 93–96, 112, 120, senses the political conflict in the Daniel tales that many commentaries simply miss. But it goes too far to say that the tales exhibit "qualified approval" of empire. Also, if the tales portray "resistance" to empire, it is at the ideological level, not an active political level, in contrast to the *maskilim* in Dan. 10–12. The conflict, moreover, is not "resolved" at the cultural level by the kings' approval or elevation of Daniel and his friends. That there came to be a whole cycle of tales about Daniel et al. indicates that the conflicts came to a head again and again. Even though Daniel and his friends and the scribes who cultivated the tales about them were an intellectual elite who worked for the ruling elite, under imperial rule they were also members of a subject people. Marvin A. Sweeney, "The End of Eschatology in Daniel: Theological and Socio-political Ramifications of the Changing Contexts of Interpretation," *Biblical Interpretation* 9 (2001): 123–39, senses the political dimension especially of the tales in Daniel, albeit with considerable conceptual unclarity.

24. On the development of the vision form, see Susan Niditch, *The Symbolic Vision in Biblical Tradition*, HSM 30 (Chico, CA: Scholars Press, 1980); Klaus Koch, "Vom profetischen zum apokalyptischen Visionsbericht," in *Apocalypticism in the Mediterranean World and the Near East*, ed. D. Hellholm (Tübingen: Mohr [Siebeck], 1983), 387–411; Collins, *Daniel* (1993), 55; Davies, *Daniel*, 69–70.

25. In Dan. 7:1, 15, 28; 8:1–2, 27; 9:1–2; 10:1–4, 15–17; 12:8, respectively—a framing that the visions in Zechariah lack. For this form in Mesopotamian scribal culture, see A. Leo Oppenheim, *The Interpretation of Dreams in the Ancient Near East* (Philadelphia: American Philosophical Society, 1956), 187.

26. Daniel 7:17, 23, 24; 8:23–25; 11:2, 3, 5, 14, 20, 21; 12:1.

27. A. K. Grayson, *Babylonian Historical-Literary Texts* (Toronto: University of Toronto Press, 1975), 24–37; W. G. Lambert, *The Background of Jewish Apocalyptic* (London: Athlone, 1978), 9–10.

28. The principal developments in the historical crisis are surveyed in chap. 2, above. Cf. the sketches focused on religious history by Collins, *Daniel* (1993), 62–65; and Lester L. Grabbe, *Judaism from Cyrus to Hadrian*, vol. 1, *The Persian and Greek Periods* (Minneapolis: Fortress, 1992), 282–84.

29. Collins, *Daniel* (1993), 280–99; quote from 289.

30. Both quotes are from ibid., 324.

31. The point of the four-beast scheme in Dan. 2 was the succession of empires, which would be destroyed and succeeded by the rule of God. The representation of the beasts in Dan. 7 is their power and rapacious violence, which escalates dramatically with the fourth beast. Davies, *Daniel*, 74–75, also disputes Collins's mythic interpretation of Dan. 7 and sees the beasts as symbolizing kings, but does not discuss the political dimension, which he discerns more clearly in subsequent articles (see n. 56, below).

32. Collins, *Daniel* (1993), 296. Collins appears to recognize that the beasts do not symbolize primordial chaos that is defeated in battle by the divine hero who establishes (cosmic) order in Canaanite and other ancient Near Eastern myth (and in Hebrew enthronement psalms, such as 29; 89:9–10; 96)—in comments such as "The description of the individual beasts . . . cannot be explained from any Canaanite sources now available. . . . The portrayal of the specific beasts is probably determined by biblical tradition" (289). If anything the images of the beasts

(that symbolize the great empires of the ancient Near East) arising out of the sea (that symbolizes chaos) represent a symbolic "turning of the tables" on imperial mythic ideology. In the Canaanite myth of Baal's battle with Yam, or the Babylonian myth of Marduk's battle with Tiamat (*Enuma Elish*), the Storm-Warrior-god of the imperial city/king conquers and kills (establishes cosmic order over) Sea. In Daniel's dream, by contrast, the symbolic beasts of empire derive from the sea (chaos) and exercise gratuitous violence against people ("devouring, . . . stamping"), in effect perpetuating the very chaos that they claim to have conquered in the myths that authorize imperial violence.

33. The most vivid evidence is visual. Reliefs on portals and buildings and other art in Mesopotamia (from Assyrian, Babylonian, and Persian Empires) and elsewhere in the Near East portray hybrid figures such as winged lions. The palace of Darius at Persepolis has doorjambs with reliefs of the royal hero fighting a lion monster. See Collins, *Daniel* (1993), 296; Root, *King and Kingship in Achaemenid Art*, 81; and the older study of Daniel by Moses Stuart, *A Commentary on the Book of* Daniel (Boston: Crocker & Brewster, 1850).

34. Collins, *Daniel* (1993), 299, and see his notes 194–98.

35. Collins, ibid., 319, however, thinks that the images of "teeth of iron" and "claws of bronze" were not in themselves "pejorative."

36. In the account itself there is no reason to divide up the dream into a "throne vision" separate from the vision of the beasts and the vision of judgment, as does Collins, ibid., 299–311.

37. The imagery of the divine chariot was a standard one in Israelite tradition as in ancient Near Eastern culture generally (e.g., Ps. 68:18 [17E]). The fiery wheels were vividly portrayed in Ezekiel (1:15–21). But the register had come to include the river(s) of fire (not of punishment for the wicked, but symbolizing the overwhelming appearance of divine power), clothing as white as snow, and attendants numbering "ten thousand times ten thousand" (cf. 1 Kings 22:19), as well.

38. Cf. the more synthetic presentation in Collins, *Daniel* (1993), 300.

39. That the account of both dream and interpretation are so clearly focused on the divine judgment makes it seem unlikely that what was still a language register for a vision of the throne of God in Dan. 7:9–10 and *1 En.* 14:8–23 had already moved into "speculation about the divine throne" (ibid., 300), as attested in *2 Enoch* and later Merkabah mysticism (see Gerschom Scholem, *Jewish Gnosticism, Merkabah Mysticism and Talmudic Tradition* (New York: Jewish Theological Seminary, 1965).

40. Collins, *Daniel* (1993), 292–94. As Collins explains, such imagery had long been familiar in Israelite-Judean culture, which surely included a great deal more mythic lore than biblical scholars are wont to find in texts of the Hebrew Bible.

41. See references in ibid., 292.

42. Ibid., 313–18.

43. As illustrated in some of the texts produced by the Qumran community, the relationship between the holy ones and (the covenant community of) Israel had become even closer, with both synergism of action on their respective heavenly and earthly levels and interaction across those levels. In the *War Scroll* from Qumran, the desperation of the Daniel visions in the face of western imperial power has been replaced by a bravado of ritual holy war, in which the community of God's holy people has confidence that "the multitude of the holy ones [with God] in heaven" will fight for and with them against the armies of the Kittim (Romans). "For You are [terrible], O God, in the glory of thy kingdom, and the assembly of your holy ones is among us for everlasting succor" (1QM 12.1–7). Community members also sang psalms of thanksgiving that God had "cleansed a perverse spirit . . . that it might stand with the host of the holy ones, and might enter into

community with the assembly of the sons of heaven" (1QH 3 [=11].21–22), and that God had "purified man of sin . . . that he may partake of the lot of Your holy ones" (1QH 11 [19].11–12).

44. There is no indication in the text of Dan. 7 that "one like a human being" was a reference to Michael, identified in Dan. 10:13, 21; and 12:1 as one of the principal celestial agents of God in the governance of history and protector of the Judeans. Collins's argument for taking "the humanlike figure" in Dan. 7 as a reference to Michael appears to be based on the assumption that the same cast of characters in the same pattern of relationships is present in all of the visions, as he states in *The Apocalyptic Vision,* 132–47 (or by working backward from later "apocalyptic" texts, as in *Daniel* [1993], 318–19). But is that an appropriate procedural assumption? This seems doubtful, especially given two of the principal features of the dreams-and-interpretations in Dan. 7–12. If we take seriously the self-representation of this material as (rooted in) visions, we would not expect the dream imagery to be consistent from vision to vision. And since it appears that the vision and interpretation in Dan. 8 originated after that in Dan. 7, and the narrative in Dan. 10–12 after both, the situation and its interpretation may have changed. See also Davies, *Daniel,* 106.

45. Collins, *Daniel* (1993), 322, 324, where he continues: "Political and economic considerations are not acknowledged explicitly. . . . The interests of the visionary appear to be rather mystical, focusing on the heavenly throne and the angelic world."

46. Ibid., 377. On the portrayal of Antiochus Epiphanes, see Paul Niskanen, "Daniel's Portrait of Antiochus IV: Echoes of a Persian King," *CBQ* 66 (2004): 378–86.

47. That it includes the Mosaic aspect, however, seems likely from the inclusion of the lengthy Deuteronomic prayer of covenant renewal in Dan. 9.

48. Collins, *Daniel* (1984), 101–2, says that "Daniel's perspective is that of the world-kingdoms rather than of the internal Jewish tensions." But the fact that he does not "take sides in the struggles between the Seleucids and the Ptolemies" suggests that he rejects imperial rule generally. Daniel's perspective is rather that of God's transcendent rule, and his main concern is coming to grips with the overwhelmingly destructive impact of imperial rule on Judea and the temple-state.

49. That the same combination of terms, *maśkîl* and *rabbîm* (the many), was used for the master and the members of the group/community suggests that "the many" in Dan. 11:33 also would have been a more confined group than "the common people" in general (cf. Collins, *Daniel* [1993], 385).

50. Ibid., 386.

51. Antiochus's measures in Jerusalem are typical of measures taken by imperial or other authoritarian regimes to control protest and resistance to their previous practices of oppression, as explained in Richard Horsley, *Jesus and the Spiral of Violence* (San Francisco: Harper & Row, 1987; Minneapolis: Fortress, 1992), chap. 2.

52. Collins, *Daniel* (1993), 390, summarizing an argument by George W. E. Nickelsburg, *Resurrection, Immortality, and Eternal Life in Intertestamental Judaism* (Cambridge, MA: Harvard University Press, 1972), 12.

53. Collins, *Daniel* (1993), 394–98, quote from 398. His critical examination of texts from Qumran, for example, concludes that they do not refer to a resurrection of individuals after death. Prophetic texts often adduced as evidence for earlier belief in resurrection speak rather of the restoration of the people of Israel. Having been ruled by imperial lords after the conquest and destruction of Jerusalem, the Judean people will be restored after Yahweh takes action to punish their rulers (see esp. Isa. 26:5, 13, 19, 21, reading *yšb-/yōšēb-* as "rulers" rather than "inhabitants," as in NRSV; similarly, the valley of dead bones that come to

life "are the whole house of Israel," Ezek. 37:11; and Hos. 6:2). These are some of the most striking texts in the prophetic tradition on which the scribes who produced Daniel and Enoch texts built in affirming the restoration of the people as a whole (Dan. 7:13–14, 27; 12:1; *1 En.* 90:28–37). But they are not particularly pertinent to resurrection.

54. Just how vague and elusive "resurrection" can be is attested in the multiple qualifications of Collins's discussion. Scholars agree that Dan. 12:2 "is referring to the actual resurrection of individuals from the dead, because of the explicit language of everlasting life (*Daniel* [1993], 392). Yet the Hebrew expression translated "life everlasting" "occurs only here in the Hebrew Bible," and "the precise understanding of 'everlasting' is open to question" (392). The Hebrew Bible passages that he adduces on the language of sleeping and awaking for death and resurrection (Jer. 51:39, 57; Job 14:12) do not attest it. The pseudepigraphic passages (*1 En.* 91:10; 92:3) adduced for awakening as resurrection are read quite differently by Enoch scholars such as Nickelsburg (*1 Enoch* [Minneapolis: Fortress, 2001], ad loc.). The term "awaken" means resurrection (392), yet as used in 12:2 by Daniel "does not require that the sinners are raised from Sheol" to experience their disgrace (Collins, *Daniel* [1993], 392). Daniel "does not address the form of the resurrection," yet somehow gives "information about the resurrected state" in 12:4 (392). If our aim is to appreciate images, motifs, and statements in their textual, cultural, and historical contexts, it would be best not to impose the general concept of "resurrection."

55. Collins, *Daniel* (1993), 393; Davies, *Daniel,* 110, who then also discerns (116–17) that Dan. 12:2–3 is about vindication rather than resurrection.

56. See further the reflection on these and a number of related passages in other texts by Michael E. Stone, "Lists of Revealed Things in the Apocalyptic Literature," *Magnalia Dei—The Mighty Acts of God: In Memory of G. E. Wright,* ed. Frank M. Cross (Garden City, NY: Doubleday, 1976), 430–31.

57. Philip R. Davies, "Reading Daniel Sociologically," in *The Book of Daniel in the Light of New Findings,* ed. A. S. van der Woude (Louvain: Leuven University Press, Peeters, 1993), 357, senses something similar simply from nuances in the text, without more systemic sociological analysis such as in chap. 3, above.

58. Davies, "Reading Daniel Sociologically," 360–61; similarly Collins, *Daniel* (1984), 101: a substitute for cultic purification. Subsequently Collins leans toward a more individualistic salvation: "The primary goals of the *maskilim* are not in the political realm. Rather they concern purity and communion with the angels" (Collins, "Daniel and His Social World," *Interpretation* 39 (1985): 140; similarly *Daniel* [1993], 389).

Conclusion: Understanding Texts in Contexts

1. Typology adapted from John J. Collins, "Wisdom, Apocalypticism, and Generic Compatibility," in *In Search of Wisdom: Essays in Memory of John G. Gammie,* ed. Leo Perdue et al. (Louisville, KY: Westminster/John Knox, 1993), 168.

2. John J. Collins, *Daniel,* Hermeneia (Minneapolis: Fortress, 1993), 54. He also includes "heavenly ascent," but it is not common or prominent in the texts he includes. Collins's discussion of "Genre and Constituent Forms" and so forth (52–60), as is standard in scholarship on apocalyptic literature, focuses almost entirely on Daniel, *1 Enoch,* and other texts standardly recognized as "apocalyptic," without much attention to the historical development from prophetic and other precedents. Nickelsburg, *1 Enoch* (Minneapolis: Fortress, 2001), challenges the standard treatment of the apocalyptic genre by exploring Enoch texts as having an outer form of testament instead of apocalypse. Philip R. Davies, *Daniel*

(Sheffield: JSOT Press, 1985), 66–75, questions whether the concept "apocalyptic" applies to either the tales or the visions in Daniel. Earlier yet, Michael E. Stone, "Lists of Revealed Things in the Apocalyptic Literature," in *Magnalia Dei—The Mighty Acts of God: In Memory of G. E. Wright,* ed. Frank M. Cross (Garden City, NY: Doubleday, 1976), 442, raised serious questions about the applicability of "apocalyptic" to many texts so categorized.

3. Collins, *Daniel* (1993), 56.

4. Ibid., 56. Only in the tenth week of the "ten-week" vision, with the judgment of the Watchers and a "new heaven," can the imagery be called somewhat "cosmic." But is there any reason to take the judgment of the Watchers as anything other than as symbolizing that God is finally bringing history/human affairs back under control by judging the errant heavenly powers? Or to take the "new heaven" as symbolizing anything other than order in the heavenly governance of the world so that people can live in peace, somewhat as in Isaiah 65? Perhaps the images of something cosmic come from Revelation, although even there the seemingly cosmic images are surely not meant to be taken literally as a metaphysics.

5. It is puzzling that interpreters of Daniel and Enoch literature find a "periodization of history" to be such a marker of a supposedly distinctive new worldview. The "periods" in Dan. 7 and 8 are the succession of empires: the actual sequence in ancient Near Eastern history. And the "periods" in Enoch literature, for the "ten weeks," simply follow the major steps in the history of Israel long established in the historical segment of Judean culture (as in Genesis, Exodus, and the Deuteronomic History): pre-Noah/flood; the periods starting with the great heroes Noah, Abraham, Moses, respectively; the period of the monarchy ending with the destruction of Jerusalem; and the second-temple period ending with the scribes/sages who receive wisdom.

6. Collins, *Daniel* (1993), 56.

7. In line with the observations by Collins in "The Place of Apocalypticism in the Religion of Israel," in *Ancient Israelite Religion: Essays in Honor of Frank Moore Cross,* ed. Patrick D. Miller et al. (Philadelphia: Fortress, 1987), 548. As discussed in chaps. 8 and 9 (above), the attendant in the divine council in Dan. 7:16 and the various voices or figures in 8:13–14, 15–17; 9:21; and 10:5–6, 10, 18; and 12:5–7 stand in a long prophetic tradition of heavenly figures who speak to or are overheard by the prophet or visionary, a tradition that runs from Micaiah ben Imlah through Isaiah to Ezekiel and Zechariah (1 Kings 22:19; Isa. 6:1–4; 40:1–11; Ezek. 1:4–28; Zech. 1). Similarly "the holy ones" in Dan. 7:18, 21–22, 25 and the "host of heaven/stars/holy ones" in 8:10, 24 are developments (not departures) from the traditional Israelite understanding of the "children of God" as the heavenly council of Yahweh, the divine sovereign who gives particular attention to Israel/Judea. The heavenly princes of Persia and Greece, along with Michael as the prince/advocate-defender of the Judeans in 10:13, 20–21; and 12:1 are similarly a development of the understanding of divine governance of human affairs in the prophetic and psalmic repertoire, most visible in the Song of Moses (Deut. 32:8–9).

8. Collins, *Daniel* (1993), 60. The suggestive comparative study by Paul Niskanen, *The Human and the Divine in History: Herodotus and the Book of Daniel* (London: T&T Clark, 2004), questions the characterization of Daniel as deterministic and eschatological in ways complementary to my argument.

9. Collins, *Daniel* (1993), 56, 60.

10. As Collins realizes (ibid., 60), the idea of individual salvation via resurrection different from the restoration of the people was "worked out gradually" only "in the following centuries." The scholarly concept of "resurrection" is another synthetic construct badly in need of critical analysis of particular sources, accompanied by critical analysis of modern habits of thought.

11. See esp. John J. Collins, introduction, in *Apocalypse: The Morphology of a Genre,* ed. John J. Collins, Semeia 14 (Missoula, MT: SBL, 1979); and John J. Collins, *The Apocalyptic Imagination* (New York: Crossroad, 1989), 2–8.
12. George W. E. Nickelsburg, *Jewish Literature between the Bible and the Mishnah,* 2nd ed. (Minneapolis: Fortress, 2005), 52, finds in the Book of Watchers the earliest text that displays "a full-blown apocalyptic worldview," consisting in a set of spatial, temporal, and ontological dualisms.
13. Discussion of how unlikely it was that peasants would have been influenced by scribal texts appears in Richard A. Horsley, *Jesus and the Spiral of Violence: Popular Jewish Resistance in Roman Palestine* (San Francisco: Harper & Row, 1987), 129–45.

Index

Main discussions are indicated by boldfaced numerals.